ewed b

18 0

14

12 I

07

05 D

11 NOV 20

Women's Writing in English

Series Editor:
Gary Kelly, Professor of English, University of Alberta, Canada

Published Titles:
Anthea Trodd, *Women's Writing in English: Britain 1900–1945*

Women's Writing in English: Britain 1900–1945

Anthea Trodd

Longman
London and New York

Addison Wesley Longman
Edinburgh Gate
Harlow
Essex CM20 2JE
England
and Associated Companies throughout the world.

*Published in the United States of America
by Addison Wesley Longman Inc., New York.*

First published 1998

ISBN 0 582 28914 9 CSD
ISBN 0 582 28915 7 PPR

British Library Cataloguing-in-Publication Data

A catalogue record of this book is available
from the British Library

Library of Congress Cataloging-in-Publication Data

Trodd, Anthea.
    Women's writing in English : Britain, 1900–1945 / Anthea Trodd.
        p. cm. — (Women's writing in English)
    Includes bibliographical references (p.   ) and index.
    ISBN 0–582–28914–9 (csd). — ISBN 0–582–28915–7 (ppr)
        1. English literature—Women authors—History and criticism.
    2. Women and literature—Great Britain—History—20th century.
    3. English literature—20th century—History and criticism.
    I. Title. II. Series.
    PR116.T76 1998
    820.9'9287'09041—dc21   97–38883
                                                             CIP

Set by 35 in 10/12 pt Bembo
Produced by Longman Singapore Publishers (Pte) Ltd
Printed in Singapore

Contents

General Editor's Foreword

Women's Writing in English provides a comprehensive survey of women's writing in English from the Middle Ages to the present, and from around the globe. Recent feminist scholarship and criticism have pointed out ways in which women's writing has been excluded from or marginalized in the literary canon. Accordingly, the volumes in this series consider not only literary kinds of writing, including fiction, drama, and poetry, but also non-literary kinds, in which women were often pioneers, ranging from religious devotion and conduct books to books for children, from journalism to popularizations of science, theology, history, political economy, and so on.

Each volume in the series is based on original research and opens with a section placing women and women writers in the economic, social, cultural, literary, and publishing conditions of their time. Subsequent chapters examine critically the work of individuals and groups of writers and various kinds of writing in the particular region or country during a specified period. There is discussion of both major and minor figures; of writers now securely placed in the literary canon as well as those writers less well known. Volumes close with substantial sections of reference information, including bibliographies, chronologies, and author biographies. Although the volumes have a broadly similar structure, the authors of individual volumes are free to develop lines of inquiry and critical argument as they see fit. Above all, we want the series to be used by students and teachers on a range of courses, including those concerned with women's writing itself, with established literary periods and genres, and with particular focuses in cultural studies, social history, education and writing for children.

Gary Kelly

vii

Preface

This book is a history of women's writing in Britain between 1900 and 1945. The beginning of a new century can, in this case, be argued as marking a distinct period. Although the formal and thematic concerns of the New Women writers of the 1890s anticipated later modernist developments, most of those writers did not publish significantly after 1900. In the first years of the Edwardian period women writers were most prominent in the genres of children's writing and romantic fiction; in 1902, an *annus mirabilis* for published male writing, the most important and influential work by a woman was *The Tale of Peter Rabbit*. From that specialized beginning to the new century women's writing re-expanded and diversified into prominence in a range of genres, including published autobiography, where they had hitherto been little represented, and the new field of academic discourse.

This is specifically a history of the relations, whether helpful, emulative or dismissive, between women writers. A key moment in this history appears at the beginning of Chapter 6, in the embrace of Woolf and the popular romantic novelist Berta Ruck, a socially enforced collision of high and low, which occasioned Woolf's rueful recognition of the public perception of them both as 'lady writers'. This book replays that embrace; innovative, 'lowbrow' and 'middlebrow' writers in fiction and non-fiction shared themes and concerns, and they had all to contend with the gulf between their perception of themselves as professionals and the public perception of 'lady writers'. That gulf between professionalism and ladyhood, and the context of the women's movement, which informed to some degree the self-consciousness of all women writers as writers, afford a particular coherence to the history of women's writing in this period.

This book draws gratefully on the many studies of individual women writers of the period, and of genres, of the past two decades. I would like to thank the general editor of the series, Gary Kelly, for his support and encouragement in the project. I am also very grateful to my colleagues in the Department of English at Keele University for affording me teaching and administrative relief in the early stages of this project, and for listening to, and arguing with, seminar papers based on this book. I also owe debts to my doctoral students, especially Rowena Gay, Hilary Skelding and Deborah Wynne, who talked to me about popular and magazine writing in the later nineteenth century, and thus greatly helped my understanding of what followed. I am indebted also to the students in my undergraduate course on writing between the wars; their discussions over a number of years have helped to form this book.

Acknowledgements

The Publishers are grateful to the following for permission to reproduce copyright material:

Carcanet Press Ltd for part poems 'She comes over the lawn, the young heiress . . .' by Elizabeth Daryush from *COLLECTED POEMS*. © Carcanet 1976 and 'Benicasim' by Sylvia Townsend Warner in *COLLECTED POEMS* edited C. Harman. © Carcanet 1982; George and Margaret Hepburn for part poems 'Note on Method' and 'In the House of the Soul' by Anna Wickham from *THE WRITINGS OF ANNA WICKHAM: FREEWOMAN AND POET* edited by R.D. Smitti (Virago, 1984).

CHAPTER ONE

Women in Early-Twentieth-Century Culture

In 1911, at the height of the women's suffrage campaign, the South African born writer, Olive Schreiner, published her polemical history of women, *Woman and Labour*. It was, she explained in the introduction, merely the surviving fragment of a great work on women on which she had been working throughout her writing life. The original concept was of 'a general view of the whole vast body of phenomena connected with women's position', tracing the history of women from primitive times to the modern world, but that manuscript had been destroyed during the Boer War. That concept then resolved into a determination to provide 'a bird's-eye view of the whole question of women's relations to labour'.[1] The final published work treated what would have been a minor section of the projected whole, an account of contemporary middle-class 'female parasitism'. Schreiner's failure to realize her ambition for a more comprehensive account is symptomatic of the problems of the many women writers of the period 1900–45 who sought to explain the role of women in culture. This was a period of intensive reassessment of women's situation, reassessments continuously revised in response to the suffrage movement, the two World Wars, and the Depression. Many women sought both to reclaim the history of women by the construction of histories and by historical and sociological research, and to outline new roles and agendas for women. The complexities of the continuous pressures on such writers to redefine their analyses in response to a changing situation can be demonstrated by a brief comparison of three such works from different points in the period. *Woman and Labour*, despite its incomplete state, came to be regarded as the guidebook of the women's movement. Ray Strachey's *The Cause: A Short History of the Women's Movement in Great Britain* (1928) was for many years the major history of the suffrage movement, but appeared at a time when the women's movement she celebrated was deeply riven. Virginia Woolf's controversial essay on the intimate links of patriarchy

1

and fascism, *Three Guineas*, which appeared in 1938, the year of Munich, and proposed the abolition of the word 'feminist', was responding to the shifts and divisions in feminism in the period between the wars. The forms and approaches of these three histories illuminate the problems of women seeking to construct an analysis of women's cultural situation.

Schreiner's book, with its vast projected sweep, and ambitions to understand women's cultural development within an evolutionary framework, was a product of the debates of late Victorianism. The original conception of the book dated back to the 1880s, when Schreiner first came to England, to her participation in debates about the significance of evolution in understanding the role of women, and to her membership of the discussion group, the Men and Women's Club, which offered a rare forum for the sexes to discuss with each other their ideas about their respective social and cultural roles.[2] The suffrage campaign is not central to her discussion; it is adduced rather as evidence of women's instinctive recognition that 'without the reaction of interevolution between the sexes, there can be no real and permanent human advance' (ch. 3). The women battling for the vote have a 'profound if vague consciousness of ends larger than they clearly knew' (ch. 3), but Schreiner is not primarily interested in the vote, but in the exclusion of women from labour. Most of the book is concerned with the analysis of female parasitism, examining the construction of middle-class femininity as Mary Wollstonecraft had done over a century before. The middle-class woman is seen as the ultimate symptom of decadence, cut off from both the labouring women of the past and those of the present. (Ruth Furst and Ann Scott have examined the influence on her analysis of her experience of class segregation in an extreme form in South Africa.[3]) Her account of female parasitism is placed within a historical narrative of the gradual exclusion of women from the workplace and from productive work, a narrative modelled after the accounts of women's disempowerment by Bachofen and Engels,[4] and which in turn inspired the social historian Alice Clark's influential *The Working Life of Women in the Seventeenth Century* (1919).

Schreiner's work outlines several themes in early-twentieth-century feminist debate. Her insistence on the centrality of an active female sexuality to the new relationship to be defined between men and women was very influential in the new century. It was qualified by her desire to see the end of the prostitute and the spinster, whom she presents as two complementary types of deformed womanhood, a qualification which persists throughout the period. Her claim for the intimate and inevitable association of maternity and pacifism, so influential on the next generation of pacifists, is expressive of a central confusion in contemporary feminism which often sought both to claim equality with men and to proclaim the distinctive moral

2

superiority of women. *Woman and Labour* is informed throughout by Schreiner's expressed regret that she has not produced the work she planned. Although she had wished to write a great comprehensive history of women's development to provide perspective for the narrowly focused demand for the vote of Mrs Pankhurst's troops, she has ended by concentrating on the problems of middle-class women. Her failure is symptomatic of the greatest problem of women writers seeking to voice the aspirations of women during this period, that of mediating between middle-class and working-class needs.

Strachey's *The Cause* is a very different kind of writing from Schreiner's suggestive, prophetic fragment, an orderly celebration of the progress of women over the last century and a quarter, beginning with Mary Wollstonecraft, following the lives of the great pioneers in the various feminist causes of the Victorian period, and culminating in a long account of the eventually successful campaign for the suffrage, and of the opportunities now available to women. The illustrations reinforce the narrative, beginning with individual portraits of the isolated pioneers, and moving on to group portraits of suffragettes, Newnham hockey team, war-workers. The last picture celebrates the arrival in the House of Commons in 1920 of Nancy Astor, the first woman MP to take her seat. (Constance Markievicz, the imprisoned Sinn Fein activist, had been the first woman elected in 1918.) Astor stands in a shaft of light, flanked by the male leaders of the Tory and Liberal parties, the epitome of women's triumphant assimilation into the centre of national power. The book's first appendix, however, is something quite different, the fragmentary reverie 'Cassandra', written by Florence Nightingale in the 1850s but published here for the first time. Nightingale's bitter reflections on wasted female potential, on the lack of outlet for female energies, on the discrepancies between the outer decorum and the inner yearnings of dutiful young women, provides a reference point for the distance women have travelled to the achievements Strachey chronicles. It is a familiar narrative of the journey from the Victorian darkness in which Cassandra raged to the light which shines upon Nancy Astor, a narrative deployed in many novels of the period. The inclusion of 'Cassandra' also invites the reader to consider the distance travelled by women's writing, from Nightingale's fragmentary, unpublished, confessional work to Strachey's group biography which demonstrates that it is now possible to record the history of women working together in the public sphere in forms which emulate the official histories of men.

Strachey had been the close ally of Millicent Fawcett, President of NUWSS (National Union of Women's Suffrage Societies), the federation of groups working for the suffrage by constitutional means. The approach of *The Cause* emulates Fawcett's liberal progressive views, constitutionalism,

3

and famous organizational skills. The emphasis is on common purpose; groups and individuals are placed by their contribution to the patient, inexorable accumulation of advantage in the women's cause. Strachey, however, was writing at a time when the women's movement was divided about agendas. The year in which women between twenty-one and thirty finally achieved the vote, 1928, might seem an appropriate time for a celebratory history of the women's movement, but it was also a time of clear division between the 'Old Feminism' which Fawcett had embodied and the 'New Feminism' now adopted by the organization over which she had presided. Strachey's narrative, in insisting on common aims, chooses not to foreground contemporary divisions, or those in the suffrage campaign which had anticipated them.

The account of the suffrage campaign itself subordinates dissension to the general narrative of common effort. The most publicized suffrage group was not NUWSS, but Emmeline Pankhurst's WSPU (Women's Social and Political Union), which substituted militant activism for NUWSS's diplomacy. The two organizations offered rival constructions of womanhood. The NUWSS ideal of the rational, well-educated woman working with, and on an equal footing with, men was opposed by Mrs Pankhurst's troops who combined violent demonstrations with extravagant displays of femininity. Cicely Hamilton, dramatist and popular suffragist speaker, who herself favoured businesslike garb, described the 'costume-coding' which Pankhurst insisted on her troops adopting, the flowing skirts and obligatory large hats which enhanced the ongoing street spectacle of oppressed, defiant femininity which the WSPU and the police staged between 1906 and 1914.[5] Pankhurst was rejecting Fawcett's ideal of woman modelled on the best male examples for a street-theatre which highlighted traditional feminine attributes, clothes sense, emotionalism, irrationality, helpless suffering. Behind this insistence on a traditional performance of femininity lay a claim to the distinctiveness and superiority of female morality much more entrenched that Schreiner's argument for a pacifism grounded in maternal feelings.

Beyond these two rival organizations, and the splinter groups which broke from the WSPU between 1907 and 1914, were the working-class women who had become activists through trade unionism and socialism, and who were often antagonized by the militant activities of the mostly middle-class WSPU, and by the demand by both NUWSS and WSPU for women's suffrage under the same conditions of property qualification which currently enfranchised men. Trade union organizers such as Mary MacArthur and Margaret Bondfield of the Federation of Women Workers were campaigning for adult suffrage, and saw as counter-productive a violent and heavily publicized campaign for women's suffrage, which would enfranchise very few working-class women.[6]

It was this exposure of class divisions by suffrage activity, and the criticisms that the women's movement was concentrating on one issue of largely middle-class interest, at the expense of the more urgent needs of working-class women, which were central to the division in the women's movement after the war. In 1918 the suffrage was awarded to women over thirty. In 1925 Eleanor Rathbone, the new President of NUWSS, now renamed NUSEC (National Union of Societies for Equal Citizenship), announced the adoption of a 'New Feminism', proclaimed by its new campaign plank of family allowances. The 'New Feminism' marked a general shift from emphasis on equal opportunities towards emphasis on the distinctive needs of women, and on campaigning for measures to offer distinctive protection to women. This attempt to develop a new, more domestically oriented feminist ideology was responding to the criticisms that the women's movement hitherto had been too exclusively middle-class, and had concentrated on the suffrage and on professional opportunities. The dangers which Old Feminists perceived in this approach were articulated by the novelist and journalist Winifred Holtby; the New Feminists, Holtby suggested, were reviving a traditional image of women as essentially domestic, and reinforcing ideas that the aspirations of the sexes were fundamentally distinct.[7]

Ten years after *The Cause* Strachey's in-law, Virginia Woolf, published *Three Guineas* (1938). Throughout the 1930s the concerns of feminism were overshadowed by issues of poverty and unemployment at home, and the rise of fascism abroad; Woolf's essay responds to this by exploring the centrality of relations between the sexes to the development of militarism. Fascism is not an exclusively foreign phenomenon, but an extension of the patriarchal organization of British society. She calls for women to combat this by disassociating themselves from the institutions of patriarchal society. Strachey was one of the few readers who responded enthusiastically; she told Woolf it was 'simply perfect'.[8] Her response is indicative of the manner in which feminists at this time were engaged in continual revision of their approaches, for in many ways *Three Guineas* reads as a sustained attack on the kind of history which *The Cause* represents. Even the illustrations, mockingly presented photographs of men in various kinds of ceremonial garb, seem to subvert the kinds of ambition to group membership and public life to which the illustrations of *The Cause* aspired. Woolf's invitation to her women readers to boycott the public and professional world, abjure male institutional models, and recognize the intimate links of patriarchy with fascism, demolishes the successful progress Strachey described, and substitutes for the public memorializing of female achievement a kind of writing much nearer Nightingale's 'Cassandra'. She suggests a ceremonial abolition of the word 'feminist':

5

The word 'feminist' is destroyed: the air is cleared: and in the clearer air what do we see? Men and women working together for the same cause. The cloud has lifted from the past too. What were they working for in the nineteenth century – those queer dead women in their poke bonnets and shawls? The very same cause for which we are working now.[9]

The air will be cleared by the rejection of a particular kind of women's history, which charts the progress of women towards recognition in, and assimilation with, the patriarchal world. Instead women must work with men to create better social forms by emphasizing their distinctive female qualities and drawing on the strengths of their outsider status in patriarchal society.

Three Guineas is responding to the complex shifts in the analysis of women's situation during the interwar period. In calling for the abolition of the word 'feminist', Woolf was echoing Holtby, a proclaimed Old Feminist, who had written in 1926, 'I desire an end of the whole business, the demands for equality, the suggestions of sex warfare, the very name of feminist'.[10] Holtby's abolition, however, was in a utopian future; Woolf was calling for an immediate ban, and, in the spirit of New Feminism rather than Old, was associating it with an emphasis on the distinctive qualities of women. Women had no significant stake in public or professional life, they had no real citizenship. As outsiders they were well-placed to analyse the circumstances which had created Europe's inexorable progress to war throughout the decade. Woolf is thus reviving Schreiner's claim for the distinctive role of women as peacemakers, although the claim is now based on outsider status rather than maternity. *Three Guineas* is addressed to the two most vexed feminist questions of the period: how to mediate between the rival claims of equality and distinctiveness, and how to justify the centrality of feminism to national life.

Schreiner's attempt to write a comprehensive history of women had failed. The women writers who followed her in analysing women's situation all wrote in the consciousness that they were mediating between conflicting claims and rival constructions of the female within the women's movements. Two important analyses, Dora Russell's *Hypatia or Women and Knowledge* (1925) and Holtby's *Women in a Changing Civilization* (1934), acknowledge this by being organized around series of stereotypes. Russell's *Hypatia* examines a series of female archetypes in chapters named after Greek figures of mythology and history. Russell, whose feminism was primarily concerned with campaigning for birth-control and progressive education, calls for the replacement of the virgin huntress, Artemis, as icon of the women's movement, by Demeter, mother-goddess and patron of the harvest. 'The early feminists were what history and tradition made them, and could not at the time of their rebellion have been otherwise',[11] but modern feminists must shift the emphasis from the career ambitions of committed spinsters to the more central needs of mothers. Russell's attack is partly directed to the model of feminism which had developed in close association with the 'purity campaigns', the late Victorian campaigns against sexual exploitation, and which was sometimes in antagonistic relation with the birth-control campaigners.[12] Her polemic, published in the same year that Eleanor Rathbone proclaimed the New Feminism, is expressive of the major shift in the women's movement.

Holtby, an Old Feminist and spinster, organized the central section of her *Women in a Changing Civilization* around a series of cultural stereotypes of women presented as characteristic of a transition period in women's development. These stereotypes include the female blackleg labour resented by male workers for lowering pay and status, the flapper who embodies postwar hedonism and irresponsibility, the frustrated and neurotic spinster, and the obsessive homemaker. Russell and Holtby wrote from very different perspectives; the fact that they both chose to organize their discussions around rival stereotypes of women indicated their awareness both of the difficulties of mediating between the claims of different groups of women, and of the way in which existing stereotypes influenced developments within the women's movement. The rest of this chapter will emulate this recognition by examining the perceptions of women during this period in different social roles, as mothers, wives, working women and spinsters, and begin by looking at the most significant absence from the women's voices analysing their aspirations at this period.

THE WORKING-CLASS WOMAN

The voice of the working-class woman speaking directly to the reader was largely absent from published writing in this period. The opportunities for writing, the leisure, the room of one's own, were absent, as was the idea of publishing what, if written, was seen as a private chronicle. The early 1900s saw increased interest in studying and recording the experience of working-class women. Sociological investigations such as Maud Pember Reeves's *Round About A Pound A Week* (1913), based on her study, sponsored by the Fabian Society, of thirty working-class Lambeth homes, or Florence Bell's *At the Works: A Study Of A Manufacturing Town* (1907), based on thirty years' research into Middlesbrough life, examined in detail the distinctive experience of working-class women, using verbatim quotations from their informants to affirm the authenticity of their reports. Sylvia

Pankhurst's record of domestic life in the East End of London during the Great War, *The Home Front* (1932), also used verbatim quotation and individual case-history to construct her portrait of the forgotten war experienced by working-class women. What is largely missing from the period is the working-class woman's voice outside quotation marks. The perception of the suffrage movement as middle-class was enhanced by the absence of published record by those working-class women who were engaged in the campaign. It was not until the 1940s, for instance, that the working-class suffragette, Hannah Mitchell, began to write her account of her earlier life and political activity, *The Hard Way Up*. It was found among her papers at her death in 1956, and first published in 1968 during the revival of interest in feminist issues, providing a significant expansion of the perspective of suffrage experience.

Much writing of the 1930s focused on working-class experience, but primarily on the male experience of unemployment, with the women presented as suffering extras; this is for instance the focus of the documentary account of unemployment in Jarrow, *The Town That Was Murdered* (1938), by the town's combative MP, Ellen Wilkinson, who had earlier written *The Clash* (1929), one of the few novels to make female working-class political experience central. Wilkinson's shift of focus is exemplary of the 1930s consensus that, in a time of mass male unemployment, feminist issues had to take second place. A counter was provided in 1937 when the Mass Observation movement was founded and enlisted volunteers throughout the country to record their daily experiences. In its emphasis on the value of recording all kinds of everyday activity, Mass Observation encouraged working-class women to write down their experiences; one respondent was Nella Last, a Barrow joiner's wife, whose recorded experiences for 1939–45 were eventually published in 1981 as *Nella Last's War*. However, the only work by a working-class woman published and widely read in the period was, significantly, Flora Thompson's *Lark Rise to Candleford* trilogy (1939–45), a record of a vanished rural world, which, despite its precise and unsentimental approach, fitted within the nostalgic vogue for rural writing.

One collection of autobiographical writings which did reach publication, and anticipated Mass Observation's focus on daily experience, was the Women's Cooperative Guild's *Life As We Have Known It*, published by the Woolfs' Hogarth Press in 1931. The Guild, founded in 1883 to encourage women to participate in the local activities of the growing Cooperative movement, had already published one collection of its members' writing, *L*____ *on Maternity* (1915), and this led the General Secretary, Margaret ___n-Davies, to encourage members to narrate their lives. The short ___aphies collected record memories going back to the 1850s, hard ___nestic service and manufacturing, struggles to feed and clothe families, long histories of political activism. Woolf, who normally refused to write prefaces to the works of other writers, agreed on this occasion, because the work in question, she argued, was not a book; it was 'fragments. These voices are beginning only now to emerge from silence into half articulate speech.'[13] Woolf's introduction is structured around the cultural gulf she perceives between the classes, between her socialist sympathies and the impossibility of communicating with the Guild's members, between her subjectivity and the wholly different kind of subjectivity experienced by the writers.

This combination of guilty reaching out and perception of impassable gulf is characteristic of much of the fiction of the period. The inexplicable, inarticulate, often faintly menacing working-class figures, the landladies and servants, who loom intermittently in the novels of Woolf and of Dorothy Richardson, Jean Rhys, Rosamond Lehmann, exemplify the tendency described by Cora Kaplan for women writers to define their subjectivity by projecting a regressive model of femininity on to women in other cultural groups.[14] Other fictions, such as the documentarist 1930s novels of such writers as Holtby, Storm Jameson, Lettice Cooper, seek to dissipate the mystery and make connections between the situations of middle- and working-class women, but in doing so encounter problems in constructing the subjectivity of their characters. The theme of Cooper's 1935 novel, *We Have Come To A Country*, is the necessity of completely rethinking social relations. Her middle-class heroine is swept up in political activity centred on an unemployment centre in Leeds; in her private hours she arranges flowers. It is difficult to resist the temptation to read this as satire, although it is quite clear in the text that the flower-arranging is intended to place Laura's inner creativity, serving a similar purpose to the fruit arrangement which consolidates Mrs Ramsay's dinner-table in Woolf's *To The Lighthouse* (1927). Precisely because Cooper is so attentive to the relations between the classes, and so aware of the undercurrents of cynicism which the working-class women direct towards their middle-class helpers, she encounters difficulties in finding ways to describe Laura's subjectivity which Woolf does not with Mrs Ramsay.

MOTHERS

The new century saw increased public focus on women as mothers. It was crucial to the public image of both suffrage leaders, Pankhurst and Fawcett, that they were not only the widows of progressive and supportive feminists,

9

but the mothers of gifted young women who exemplified the advances women could make into the public sphere. The main occasion for the focus on motherhood, however, was the increasing panic about the supposed degeneracy of the British race, which was intensified by the discovery that fewer than half of the men who volunteered for the Boer War between 1899 and 1902 met the (low) requisite physical qualifications. This panic was coupled with concern about the much publicized decline in the birth-rate. Anna Davin and Jane Lewis have analysed the ensuing 'politics of motherhood', as politicians and press called for supervision and instruction to educate better mothers of the race, and socialists and feminists pointed to the need to improve environmental conditions and diet.[15] The eugenics movement was at its height in Britain at this period, but political concern about racial degeneracy was tempered by an anxiety not to meddle with the sanctity of the patriarchal home, and resulted in a focus on the ignorance of mothers as the explanation for the problem, and on health visitors and instruction as remedies. The Women's Cooperative Guild's *Letters on Maternity* and Reeves's *Round About A Pound A Week* countered by emphasizing the desperate economic and environmental needs of mothers. The pioneer educationalist, Margaret McMillan, publicized the plight of the inner city child; Carolyn Steedman has described her campaigns for the redemption of the slum child as the key to national revival.[16]

The focus on the mother as potential saviour of the race, but sorely in need of education, continued after the war; worries about racial degeneracy, and the influence of the eugenicists, ensured that the most prominent and publicized motherhood campaign in the postwar decade was for birth-control. The birth-control pioneer, Marie Stopes, in her bestselling manuals of 1918, *Married Love* and *Wise Parenthood*, urged the importance to racial development of planning and spacing pregnancies. Her Society for Constructive Birth Control and Racial Progress, and the clinics she founded to make information accessible to working-class women, achieved acceptability because they advanced an idea of planned motherhood as the key to national revival. Other bodies, such as Dora Russell's Workers' Birth Control Group, flourished in the 1920s within this climate. In the 1930s, however, the emphasis on the national value of birth-control was countered by worries occasioned by the decline of the birth-rate; Enid Charles's *The Twilight of Parenthood* (1934) was influential in spreading fears of underpopulation.

Throughout this period mothers were subjected to a battery of advice and information by health visitors and advice manuals designed to equip them better to perform their national service. It was an age of child-care experts commanding great prestige, exemplified by the bestselling manuals of Sir Frederick Truby King, whose stern advice never to humour crying babies by picking them up dominated a generation of mothers between the wars; the novelist Naomi Mitchison records how it was only with her eighth child that she dared risk the future of the race by resisting King's advice.[17] The New Feminists sought to correct the emphasis on the ignorant mother who required instruction by calling on the state to assume more responsibility. The inclusion of maternity benefits in the 1911 National Health Insurance Act had heralded the beginnings of state assumption of responsibility for maternal and child health. Eleanor Rathbone's *The Disinherited Family* (1924) and her campaign for family allowances, to be paid to the mother, were based on an insistence that the state recognize the national service mothers undertook. However, neither this campaign, nor the attempts of the birth-control campaigners to achieve state-supported family planning, achieved their goals until after the Second World War.

This intensive focus on the national duties of motherhood, and on the failings of individual mothers, is the context for representations of mothers in fiction and autobiographical writing in this period. Nightingale had commented in 'Cassandra' on the relative absence of mothers from Victorian fiction; her particular complaint was that fiction evaded treating the problem of daughters seeking to reject conformist domestic models of femininity offered by their mothers. Woolf took up Nightingale's theme in her 1931 essay, 'Professions for Women', where she described the writer's need to reject the ideal of sacrificial womanhood of the previous generation, personified in the Victorian figure of the Angel in the House. There was, however, a significant variant on this, the narrative of the daughter seeking to define herself in relation to a mother who had already herself rebelled against the domestic role. The autobiographical writings of the suffrage leader, Sylvia Pankhurst, and the traveller, Freya Stark, have strong similarities here. Both Emmeline Pankhurst and Flora Stark vigorously rejected the Angel in the House role for themselves. Mrs Pankhurst ran an unsuccessful gift shop, before finding a more fulfilling outlet in leadership of the militant suffragettes. Mrs Stark dedicated her energies to the management of an unsuccessful carpet factory in Italy; 'my mother's life shot out into its own sunlight, respectable but eccentric, and devastating to most of the lives around her' remembers Stark.[18] Sylvia Pankhurst's account of her developing attempt to define a distinctive role for herself within the suffrage movement her mother dominated, records, though less explicitly, a kindred sense of devastation. Other women writers were aware of a powerful but unacted upon frustration; Storm Jameson records of her mother, a Hull housewife, 'the fits of rage in which she jerked the venetian blinds in her room up and down, up and down, for the relief of hearing the crash'.[19]

Although the ideal of the mother of the race was so dominant in this period, attempts to realize the subjectivity of this ideal are rare. Mrs Ramsay

11

in *To the Lighthouse*, who is attempting to inculcate in her daughters the same feeling of protectiveness for the imperialist male which she practises herself, and who sometimes takes on the appearance of some maternal goddess, has clear relations with the cult of mothers of the race, and with the return of Demeter for which Dora Russell called. The figure of Linda, in Katherine Mansfield's 1918 story 'Prelude', exulting in and alarmed by her fecundity, also responds to the period's focus on maternity. The closest approach in fiction to realizing the Demeter figure is in Mitchison's historical novel, *The Corn King and the Spring Queen* (1931), in the figure of Erif Der, who perceives her fertility as part of her service to the community.

More often fiction depicts the absence of social support or sympathy for mothers. In the early part of the century feminist novelists such as May Sinclair in *The Creators* (1910) and Elizabeth von Arnim in *The Pastor's Wife* (1914) bitterly satirize the cultural superstitions and prejudices to which the new mother is subject. Rebecca West's autobiographical novel, *The Judge* (1922), attacks the stigmatizing of the unmarried mother. In the mid-1930s a group of important novels treated the taboo subject of abortion. Campaigning for abortion at this period was confined to cases where there was a threat to the mother's health; when Mitchison, in her 1935 novel *We Have Been Warned*, depicted an abortion clinic in the Soviet Union, where abortion had been legalized, she encountered demands for revision from her publishers, who had passed the promiscuous but fertile Erif Der.[20] Backstreet abortions were described in Jean Rhys's *Voyage in the Dark* (1934), F. Tennyson Jesse's *A Pin to See the Peepshow* (1935) and Rosamond Lehmann's *The Weather in the Streets* (1936), though Rhys was required to abridge that section of her novel. In all three the abortion episode is used to define the heroine's inability to survive in a world which exploits her.

WIVES

The nineteenth century had seen a series of measures which revised the marital situation of 'coverture', by which the married woman's legal identity was subsumed within that of her husband. The Married Women's Property Acts of 1870 and 1882, around which the major feminist campaign of the nineteenth century was fought, had won married women control of their earnings and of their inherited wealth. A series of acts had advanced the custody and guardianship rights of wives over their children, although it was not until 1925 that they achieved equal guardianship rights with the father. In 1891 a husband's right to confine his wife under his roof had been successfully challenged. The inequality of the Divorce Act of 1858, by which husbands could seek a divorce on the grounds of simple adultery, wives only for aggravated adultery, was overthrown in 1923, and in 1937 the grounds were extended to desertion and insanity.

Coverture, with its understanding that the husband must be the dominant partner, had divided the growing women's suffrage movement in the 1880s, when the main organization had decided for strategic reasons to support a bill to give the suffrage to spinsters and widows only, believing that, as this did not challenge coverture, it had a better chance of success. The bill failed, but the strategy left a legacy of suspicion and distrust between married and single supporters of the suffrage. Coverture assumed that in marrying the wife became a radically different being, quite distinct from her single self. By 1900 the principle was much eroded, but its Victorian ally, the cultural doctrine of separate spheres, whereby the public sphere was reserved for men, and women were responsible for the private sphere, remained powerful as the base for the anti-suffrage campaign. The most prominent woman anti-suffragist, the novelist Mrs Humphrey Ward, whose chosen nomenclature indicated under what terms a woman should appear in the public arena, argued on the basis of separate spheres. Ward was a pioneer of nursery education, and supported higher education for women, but she believed it to be inappropriate that matters of national policy, which might include the use of physical force, be decided by women.[21]

One of the most influential suffragist attacks on the separate spheres was Cicely Hamilton's lively polemic, *Marriage as a Trade* (1909), which sought to demystify marriage and the private sphere by analysing them in the language of the public sphere. Wifehood should be seen, not as an inherent destiny, but as the main line of work to which women had access. Hamilton's principal aim is to restore the distinction between the woman as 'an entity in herself' and her professional characteristics, a distinction easily recognized in men, but lost sight of in women, though 'woman, as we know her, is largely the product of the conditions imposed upon her by her staple industry'.[22] She analyses marriage as an unsatisfactorily managed industry, particularly compromised by its absurd entry qualifications. The requirement of female modesty means that a woman must 'attain to her destined livelihood by appearing to despise it' (p. 30); the apprenticeship in exclusive attention to feminine attractions is inadequate for the work to be undertaken thereafter. Moreover this industry discourages initiative; the woman 'is fitted for her trade by the discouragement of individuality and eccentricity and the persistent moulding of her whole nature into the form which the ordinary husband would desire it to take' (p. 7). Any trade, however, will encourage combination and solidarity, and the women's match-making resented by men is a kind of unofficial trade unionism.

Hamilton is also careful to distinguish between the roles undertaken by the middle-class and working-class wife. In a telling passage she describes how in middle-class homes carving is the husband's role, in working-class homes the wife's (p. 93). The middle-class husband's role as provider and patriarch is emphasized, and the wife is one recipient of the ample to adequate provision he distributes. In the working-class home, where the provision is inadequate, it is the wife who distributes it, meeting the short-fall in her own person. (Reeves's *Round About A Pound A Week* is elo-quently detailed on the requirements of self-denial on working-class wives seeking to keep the breadwinner going.) Hamilton uses the passage to fur-ther demystify marriage by demonstrating how much trade conditions may vary. Women have been divided from each other by such inequities, and from other forms of labour in general. Her argument, like Schreiner's in *Woman and Labour*, is framed by a history of women's gradual exclusion from the workforce, and the growing division between workplace and home.

By the latter part of the nineteenth century the middle-class concept that a man's status and respectability were defined by his ability to keep his wife out of the workplace had spread to the working-class. Between 1901 and 1931 only 10 per cent of married women were recorded as working; although the Great War occasioned the entry of a number of women into the workforce, there was a mass exodus of married women in the imme-diate postwar years to accommodate the re-entry of demobilized men.[23] Although the Victorian doctrine of separate spheres was under extensive attack in this period, married women had never been so heavily absent from the workforce before. Many white-collar jobs refused to employ married women, and required existing women employees who married to retire. Workers involved in this exclusion and enforced exodus included clerical workers in the Civil Service, telephone operators, many secretaries and shop assistants. Local authorities might choose not to employ married women as teachers or medical staff, and most did operate marriage bars, though few enforced them also for cleaning jobs. Married women who participated in the workforce did so, therefore, mainly in the jobs with lowest pay and status, and other women were required to retire to the home on marriage. The understood rationale for this was the employed married woman's inability to care properly for her family. It was a situation which drew firm lines between the perceived roles and duties of middle-class and working-class women, and between those of married and single women. The choice between marriage and work was widely accepted among women; in a 1930 poll, for instance, women Civil Service workers overwhemingly supported the retention of the marriage bar. Holtby, lamenting this, pointed out that the scant opportunities for promotion encouraged women to see marriage as an escape to the refuge of the home.[24]

The period between the wars saw extensive emphasis on wives' home-making abilities. A number of magazines, launched in the immediate post-war period, such as *Homes and Gardens* (1919) and *Good Housekeeping* (1992), undertook to advise the new middle-class phenomenon, the servantless home, to counsel the housewife on organizing her time, preparing meals, beautifying the home. They claimed to offer new standards of practical advice, substituting professional expertise for the more amateur approach of prewar magazines. *Good Housekeeping* publicized its on-site fully equipped kitchen, in which the cookery editor tested all the recipes published. In 1924 it established the Good Housekeeping Institute, in which it tested all the domestic appliances and other products newly on the market, so that the magazine could offer the housewife consumer scientific guidance among the products in its buoyant advertising section.[25] Women's magazines and advertisements worked together to guide the housewife through the consumer revolution, and encourage a self-image of the domestic expert. Towards the end of the interwar period the enormous and enduring popularity of *Woman*, launched in 1937, confirmed the success of the domestic advice model of women's magazine.

This concept of the home as a controlled and beautified space, which dominates the magazines and advertising of this period, is implicitly opposed to a notion of the Victorian home as family mausoleum, in which the housewife's creativity is trammelled by the clutter of past ages. Alison Light has described the celebrations of the home as a space newly available for control and creativity, the luxuriating in space and privacy, of much of the women's writing of the period.[26] Works which made domestic routine their central topic included E.M. Delafield's *Diary of a Provincial Lady* (1930), based on the most popular feature in the feminist weekly, *Time and Tide*, and Jan Struther's 'Mrs Miniver' series in *The Times* in 1937, which chronicled upper-middle-class domestic routine in the same year that *Woman* began addressing domestic routine for a more popular market.

Other writers perceived the new focus on homemaking as confirming a retreat into acceptance of the separate spheres. Rebecca West, writing in *Time and Tide* in 1924, attempted to argue against this conclusion and bridge the perceived gulf between feminists and homemakers by insisting that the women's magazines were simply trade papers like their male professional equivalents, and that they had contributed substantially to the postwar improvement in housekeeping standards.[27] Holtby, another member of *Time and Tide*'s editorial board, found the dominant emphasis on homemaking in the period disturbing; 'women's unacknowledged fear lest, robbed of domestic work, they should find no real function in life, does

15

unceasing damage to standards of domestic architecture and furnishing'.[28] Holtby's description of the new homes beautiful as 'little hells of restlessness' partly echoes the prewar observations of Maud Pember Reeves that the unhappiest Lambeth homes she visited were those where the wife put the highest priority on tidiness. Critics of the concept of the home beautiful frequently focused on the rapidly expanding suburbs, and the negative side of lower-middle-class opportunities to experience a privacy hitherto undreamt of. Elizabeth Bowen's short story, 'Attractive Modern Homes' (1941), summarizes the arguments against the new suburban home with its modern conveniences and its lack of historical experience or neighbourhood qualities.

Perhaps the fiction which responds most strongly to the pressures exerted on the young wife by the emphasis on high standards of housekeeping between the wars is Daphne du Maurier's enduring bestseller, *Rebecca* (1938). In Manderley du Maurier contrives a house which is both family mausoleum, complete with portraits and a prewar complement of servants, and also exemplifies the interwar ideal of home beautiful, created by the heroine's predecessor, Rebecca, a terrifying example of the new ultra-competent homemaker, equally adept at interior decoration schemes, flower arranging or organizing social functions. Overwhelmed by this domestic arrangement which reinforces the terrors of the traditional great house with the large hell of restlessness Rebecca created within it, the young heroine longs to escape to the less exacting milieu of the kind of seaside bungalow which will soon replace Manderley. Eventually she escapes housekeeping altogether to the arid security of life in a hotel, a dubious escape from the perils of homemaking already so described by Bowen in her first novel, *The Hotel* (1927).

The other terror of the heroine of *Rebecca* is her feeling of inadequacy as a sexual partner for her husband in comparison with her glamorous predecessor. A model of wifely fears at this period, she is tormented not only by her homemaking inadequacies, but by the expectations imposed by the increasing emphasis on the centrality of sex relations to marriage and to the individual identity. Stopes's *Married Love* gained its general acceptability from its emphasis on the national need for happy homes to create an improved race; the means to that happiness, Stopes urged, was the recovery 'of the profound primitive knowledge of the needs of both sexes'.[29] The book was dedicated to husbands, who needed to study both the individual sexual identities of their wives, and the general laws of the 'periodicity of the recurrence of desire' (p. 57); instinct was so weakened by civilization it was no longer a guide, and both partners must replace it by working at their relationships. Stopes's injunction to married couples to recognize that 'their bodily union is the solid nucleus of an immense fabric of interwoven strands reaching to the uttermost ends of the earth' (p. 23) endorses an engrossing, sexually active, monogamous relationship as the one ideal for which individuals strive; celibates and other deviants from the model have mistaken the way.

The rhapsodic manner in which Stopes asserts her beliefs has clear literary parallels with other expositions of the centrality and religious importance of sexuality. Furst and Scott have pointed out the similarities to passages on the central sexual relationship in Schreiner's *Woman and Labour*,[30] and, despite D.H. Lawrence's stated rejection of Stopes's scientific approach, his 1928 essay, 'A Propos of *Lady Chatterley's Lover*', echoes much of what Stopes says about the loss of instinctive sexual wisdom, the importance of attuning to lost seasonal rhythms, the modern blind alley of celibacy. Beyond Stopes was the new and growing authority of psychology and psychoanalysis, of the best-known of the 'sexologists', Havelock Ellis, and the growing knowledge of Freud's writings, an authority viewed with apprehension by several writers of the period, including Woolf, Mansfield and Holtby. Endorsing Stopes's attempts to give the monogamous sexual relationship the centrality and reverence once accorded religion were the bestselling romantic novelists, whose own rhapsodies in this period also pioneered in the more explicit description of sex in novels. Elinor Glyn in *Three Weeks* (1907) and E.M. Hull in *The Sheik* (1919) experimented with the exclusive structuring of novels around a series of sexual encounters between two characters. Ethel M. Dell, the largest selling novelist between the wars, detailed the therapeutic sado-masochistic courting rituals of her couples. Even the demurer Berta Ruck encountered criticism from some conservative fans when her young lovers affirmed the naturalness of their relationship by swimming naked together in a Welsh mountain pool in *The Lad Has Wings* (1916). All these emphasized the centrality and exclusiveness of the sexual relationship of their lovers.

These writings assumed a congruence between sexual fulfilment and social stability. Variants on this model within marriage which explored other possibilities for fulfilment included such minority arrangements as the open marriage which Naomi Mitchison describes in her autobiography, or the marriage 'semi-detached' for work purposes which Vera Brittain describes in *Testament of Experience* (1957). Divorces remained costly and relatively inaccessible to poorer couples until the introduction of legal aid for divorce in 1948. The Divorce Law Reform Act of 1923 placed women on an equality with men by allowing them to petition for divorce on the grounds of simple adultery, but divorces remained below four thousand a year. The Divorce Reform Act of 1937 added desertion and insanity as grounds for divorce; the number of divorces rose sharply during the unsettled conditions of the Second World War, but declined thereafter. The most

17

popular play by a woman in the 1920s, Clemence Dane's *A Bill of Divorcement* (1921), considerably anticipated the 1937 Act by depicting the harrowing situation of a husband recovering from a fifteen-year mental breakdown derived from shell-shock, and returning from hospital to his home to discover his war-bride has divorced him and is about to marry another. Dane's play owed its success to the gusto with which it explored both points of view. The wife is allowed to affirm the importance of a modern fulfilling relationship by breaking with an almost forgotten past which suddenly threatens to engulf her, and going off with her lover. It is her teenage daughter (the role in which Katherine Hepburn made her film debut), representative of the independent modern girl, who accepts the need to come to terms with family responsibilities, and resolves to be her father's support. Despite its harrowing portrait of the 'betrayed' husband, the play endorses the strength of voluntary alliances as against outgrown ties.

WORKING WOMEN

The widespread operation of the marriage bar in white-collar jobs, and the expectation that a wife who worked was compromising her care of her family, and her husband's status, meant that the phrase 'working woman' usually described a woman engaged in manual labour or a celibate professional. The phrase 'working girl' had different associations. The 1890s had seen a steep rise in white-collar jobs for women, as typists, clerks, receptionists, elementary school teachers, and a corresponding new lifestyle developed for the young women employees. This was most extensively celebrated in the thirteen volumes of Dorothy Richardson's stream of consciousness fiction, *Pilgrimage* (1915–67), which was based on her experiences as a dental receptionist in London in the 1890s and 1900s. Richardson hymned the new possibilities for women, the room of one's own, the new freedom of the streets, and the bus and bicycle journeys which represented it, the ABC teashops in which women could eat unaccompanied, the theatres and concerts and window-shopping. She provided a vocabulary of images for later writers who described the identity of the woman who had escaped from family life to a life of independence and (very modest) hedonism and consumerism.

Between the wars, as women's jobs in light industries expanded, and more working-class young women could be identified with the image of the independent, consumerist modern girl, that image became more troubling.

Strachey, Holtby and Russell all feel obliged in their histories to make space to defend the modern girl against charges that she is irresponsible, hedonist and promiscuous. Holtby's defence identifies the high visibility of these girls, and their proclaimed preoccupation with fashion, cosmetics and the lifestyle of Hollywood film stars, as the source of tension. Sally Alexander has described the cultural opposition in the 1930s of two figures, the unemployed male, turned off from one of the heavy industries which bore the brunt of the Depression, and the fashionably dressed young woman working in one of the light industries mostly in the south which developed and flourished during this period.[31] The shift of labour away from the old heartlands of heavy industry, and the very unequal experience of the Depression in different parts of the country, were thus represented by an opposition of dispossessed mature male to immature female revelling in the social and economic freedoms of her (brief) working life.

This gendered opposition of labour styles was the perception of socialists. Conservative observers were more likely to contrast the hedonist working girl with their ideal of the controllable young domestic servant of yore. There was a sharp fall in entry into domestic service in this period; in 1901 42 per cent of the female workforce were employed as domestic servants, but by 1931 that had dropped to 30 per cent. Domestic service thus remained a major source of employment for women until the Second World War, but was increasingly perceived as unattractive in comparison with the relative autonomy afforded by other sources of work.[32] One job applicant in the 1930s described how she resisted the Employment Exchange's attempts to persuade her into domestic service; 'my parents had rather brought me up to look upon domestic service as the last resort'.[33] Eventually she succumbed to the blandishments of a family who promised to treat her 'like a daughter', but after three days, each of thirteen hours, escaped, to train eventually as a nurse. The promise of daughterhood was exactly what critics of the decline in applicants for domestic service extolled; young women were seeking to escape the paternal security and control of the middle-class household. The notion of domestic service as the most appropriate work for working-class girls remained powerful throughout this period, supported by occasional eruptions of outrage about female dole claimants who had allegedly refused domestic work. The employer–servant relation was demonstrably in breakdown; the resentment on the employer side is documented in, for instance, Woolf's diaries and in *Rebecca*.

The high profile of the working girl between the wars was prepared by the large entry of women into the workforce in the Great War. Nursing was the obvious choice for women, and provided the first experience of work for many middle-class young women, including the writers Vera Brittain, Agatha Christie, Rose Macaulay and Freya Stark. Brittain pointed

19

out in her *Testament of Youth* (1932) how, apart from the work experience, nursing also relaxed the relations between the sexes, abnormally constrained before the war. Many other women went into male jobs in industry and agriculture; in *The Cause* Strachey presents their demonstrable capability in these jobs as crucial both to the granting of the suffrage and to the enhanced self-esteem with which women emerged from the war. However, the perception that women had had a 'good war' became a source of tension between the sexes. It was also challenged by, for instance, Sylvia Pankhurst who pointed to the contrast between the middle-class women training for work in the munitions factories (as Sylvia Townsend Warner did) and acting as drivers, 'how important, how joyously important, they were, their gait more triumphantly instinct with pleasure than ever it was in the ballroom',[34] and the working-class mothers in the East End bearing the brunt of war privation at home.

The Second World War afforded women opportunities for work on a greatly expanded scale, as Britain became the first country to mobilize its entire population, and also new possibilities for self-esteem and comradeship. Again this experience was followed by an enforced exodus after the war as the men were demobilized. Many women found the expected transformation back to their prewar selves hard to accept. The Barrow housewife Nella Last, who spent the war working at the local centre of the Women's Voluntary Service, confided to her diary as the war ended:

> I love my home dearly, but as a home rather than a house. The latter can make a prison and a penance, if a woman makes too much of a fetish of cleaning and polishing. I will not, *cannot* go back to the narrowness of my husband's 'I don't want anyone else's company but yours – why do you want anyone else?'[35]

In one of the jobs most emphatically designated male, Lettice Curtis, one of the women pilots of the Auxiliary Transport Authority (ATA) which undertook the ferrying of planes between airfields, and the first woman qualified to fly four-engine bombers, also recorded the exhilaration of responding continually to new challenges at work, and the erosion of gender segregation enabled by the war. She also recorded the postwar reversion and the obliteration of the ATA's record, calling the last chapter of her history 'As if they had never been'.[36]

In flying bombers, albeit not on fighting missions, Curtis was entering one of the areas most associated with masculine skill and prestige. Only the war made this acceptable, and the women pilots of the ATA are absent from the many war films of the 1940s and 1950s which celebrated the war in the air. Although this period saw the entry of women into many areas of professional expertise and in 1919 the Sex Disqualification (Removal) Act ruled that no one should be disqualified by sex from entry to public functions or posts, there was continued resistance to this entry and the threat to professional status it contained. In the late nineteenth century the concept of professionalism had become increasingly important; Harold Perkin has described how that concept was defined by attempts to control the supply of expertise by limiting entry to the profession and to the collective bodies which represent it.[37] The coincidence of the emergence of this concept with that of the women's movement ensured many painful struggles; professionalism was often defined in relation to the concept of separate spheres, aligning men with professionalism and women with amateurism.

The professions remained apprehensive about female entry. The medical profession, the body most sensitive to the threat to status during the Victorian assault on the professions, continued to defend its hard-won status; although many women were accepted for medical training during the First World War, in the 1920s all but one of the London teaching hospitals closed their gates to women, arguing the need to rectify a threatened imbalance in the profession.[38] The influx of dedicated but inexperienced recruits into nursing during the war had tended to intensify the perception of nursing as vocational rather than professional, supporting a gender divide between male experts and amateur female 'angels' in the medical profession. One of the major aims of the Six Point Group, the feminist body fighting to implement the Sex Disqualification Act, was to achieve equality of entry to the Civil Service, which continued between the wars to exclude qualified women applicants from its administrative grades. There was much tension in the teaching profession over the threat to the status of male teachers implied by the increased entry of women into secondary school teaching. The academic profession remained resistant; in 1931 there were only sixteen women among the 845 professors in the country's universities.[39] One distinguished scholar who was denied professorial status, the classicist and anthropologist Jane Harrison, called her 1925 autobiography *Reminiscences of a Student's Life*; Jane Marcus has suggested that the title hints at a gender division in her profession, where men are professors but women eternally students.[40] Harrison might also be seen as embracing the fluidity of the student role, a voluntary self-exclusion from professional pomp of the kind Woolf urged in *Three Guineas*.

Such divisions between male professionalism and female amateurism were habitually enforced by the exclusion of women from male bodies conferring pomp and circumstance on their members. In 1902 a strongly sponsored attempt to enrol the physicist Hertha Ayrton as the first woman member of the Royal Society was defeated when the Society received legal advice that a married woman could not function as a member.[41] (Despite the Married Women's Property Act, Ayrton's ownership of her intellectual achievements remained in doubt.) Throughout this period the House of

Lords refused to admit the few hereditary peeresses; Lady Rhondda, editor of *Time and Tide*, records in her autobiography how even the rubric 'Exceptional Woman', which men were often happy to concede as a mode of confirming the mediocrity of other women, failed to gain her admittance.[42] The House of Lords was eventually to open its doors in 1958; one of the first four women life-peers, the economist Barbara Wootton, had an exemplary career between the wars as 'Exceptional Woman' in male fields, as scholar, college principal and magistrate, but titled her 1967 autobiography *In A World I Never Made*. Wootton's sense of distance and alienation from the world in which she was, in career terms, so successful is expressed particularly strongly in reference to life at Cambridge, which did not formally admit women to degrees until after the Second World War. The most famous image characterizing the relation of women with Oxbridge between the wars (though Oxford admitted women to degrees in 1920) is Woolf's description in *A Room Of One's Own* (1928) of her exclusion as a woman from the college grass. That sense of exclusion expressed by Woolf and by Wootton also haunts the novels of university life: Rosamond Lehmann's *Dusty Answer* (1927), Dorothy Sayers's *Gaudy Night* (1935), and Rose Macaulay's *They Were Defeated* (1933). All celebrate the powerful glamour of Oxbridge life, but situate it outside the women characters in the 'real' male Oxbridge, the world of tradition and ceremony from which they are excluded.

SINGLE WOMEN

This phrase covered two groups, both widely perceived as threatening to social stability. One was the young woman in her brief period of independence from domestic responsibility, and (if working, which many middle-class girls still were not) of some economic freedom. Her threat was embodied in her appearance, in the clothes which were no longer a guide to social class, and the make-up which was no longer a signal of sexual availability. The word 'flapper' was in general use to describe the highly visible, pleasure-loving, modern girl, but when, in 1928, the suffrage was awarded to women between twenty-one and thirty, press agitation over the dangers of enfranchising the flapper imported to the word some of its earlier existence as a slang term for a loose woman.[43] Prostitution, like domestic service, was in observed decline between the wars; one explanation frequently offered was the competition from casual amateur labour. In this grey area of supposition the flapper became a threat to public morality, and paradoxically the reduction in prostitution was perceived as socially destabilizing. It was no longer so easy to distinguish the roles of women in public places; many cafés, including those at railway stations, refused to serve women after dark if unaccompanied by men, signalling their nostalgia for an age of clearer social categories when all women in public at that time might be assumed to be potential prostitutes. Holtby satirized this belief as it was applied to the many women returning late from work.[44] The fluidity of definition, the disappearance of clear social representations, is internalized in Rhys's *Voyage in the Dark* (1934), where the exploited heroine, Anna, declines from chorus-girl through masseuse to something understood by others as prostitution. The word is not admitted to Anna's consciousness and does not appear in the novel; Anna rejects the persistent attempts to categorize her by people who understand what girls of her kind are about. The novel endorses these attempts to defend herself, but the defence has a class aspect; Anna's refusal to recognize these definitions is partly endorsed in the narrative by her middle-class origins which distinguish her from her working-class colleagues and their clearer recognitions of who they are.

The other group of single women was the confirmed spinsters, the heirs of the redundant or odd women of the Victorian period. Schreiner linked the spinster with the prostitute as symptoms of a diseased civilization which had reduced and over-specialized women's roles, and looked to the disappearance of both in a Utopian future of sexually fulfilled working wives and mothers. However, unlike prostitutes, spinsters were not a diminishing group between the wars; the imbalance between women and men, which had been a subject of concern since the mid-nineteenth century, was increased by the First World War. Over half the women in their late twenties in 1921, the women whose sweethearts had gone to war in 1914, had not married by the outbreak of the next war in 1939.[45] This circumstance relaxed the objections of middle-class families to working daughters and to the education that would assist them to work, and, in combination with the marriage bar, negated Russell's hope that Demeter would soon replace Artemis as feminist model.

Some writers celebrated the possibilities for women released from the expectation of marriage. Hamilton's *Marriage as a Trade* treats spinsterhood as an exciting new career freed from the over-restrictive working conditions of women's 'staple industry'. Holtby's bestselling novel, *South Riding* (1935), presents a new model of spinster heroine, a working-class, high achieving headmistress, partly modelled on Ellen Wilkinson. Both writers were fighting the existing stereotypes of spinster. The threat seen embodied in the emancipated new woman of the 1890s had developed in the 1900s into the caricature figure of the ugly half-deranged spinster suffragette popular in the press, the stereotype against which Pankhurst directed her costume-coded troops. A further burden was what Christine Bolt has called 'the sexualization of spinsterhood';[46] where the Victorian spinster might be perceived as a social failure or suspected of dangerous intentions on all single men, the profile of the early-twentieth-century spinster was created by the writings of the sexologists. In her critical work, *Virginia Woolf* (1932), Holtby described the way in which this new form of authority replaced the constraints of the doctrine of separate spheres:

> at the very moment when an artist might have climbed out of the traditional limitations of domestic obligation by claiming to be a human being, she was thrust back into them by the authority of the psychologist. A woman, she was told, must enjoy the full cycle of sex-experience, or she would become riddled with complexes like a rotting fruit.[47]

Stopes's *Married Love* warned of such dangers of prolonged celibacy as neuralgia, neurosis, fibroid growths, lack of inspiration or of identification with cosmic forces. Other writers echoed this warning, Russell's *Hypatia*, for instance, suggesting that the neurosis inevitably produced by celibacy might often evolve into insanity. *South Riding* was intended to present a counter-model to such alarming pictures, and F.M. Mayor's 1925 novel of spinsterhood, *The Rector's Daughter*, depicts the misery of a woman continually suspected of neurosis by her acquaintance.

Behind the dangers of celibacy lurked a greater perceived threat to social stability, lesbianism, which in the 1920s assumed a high profile in the public imagination for the first time. It was not subject to legislation; a 1921 project to make it so was abandoned from fears of the dangers involved in publicizing it among women who were unaware of its existence.[48] That publicity was lavishly provided in 1928 when Radclyffe Hall's *The Well of Loneliness* was found an obscene libel. Hall's intention had been to publicize in the popular fictional form of romance the description of lesbianism as congenital in Havelock Ellis's *Sexual Inversion* (1898), a book which had itself been withdrawn from sale in Britain by Ellis after the prosecution of a bookseller.[49] Hall's publishers, Cape, had hoped that the author's sincerity and informative intentions, and the sobriety with which they issued the novel, would protect the work. In the event the book's condemnation, with the magistrate declining to hear the forty literary experts assembled to testify to the book's worthy intentions, furnished a massively publicized profile of lesbianism and a focus for lesbian feeling.

Hall's downfall, apart from the sheer bad luck of attracting the attention of the witch-hunting *Sunday Express*, may have been precisely the informative nature of the work and its insistence on scientific categorization, combined with the use of the accessible form of romance. The literary experts who rallied to the work's defence were less enthusiastic in private; Woolf described it as 'so pure, so sweet, so sentimental, that none of us can read it',[50] while Sylvia Townsend Warner recorded in her diary the comment of another expert, the journalist Naomi Royde Smith, that it should be handed to every schoolgirl as a warning of the kind of book that they might end up writing.[51] The sales of Woolf's *Orlando*, which had been published just before *The Well of Loneliness* was condemned and was by far Woolf's most successful book to date, almost certainly benefited from the publicity and the excitement about the newly defined lesbianism. The fact that neither *Orlando*, nor Lehmann's *Dusty Answer* (1927), nor Warner's *Summer Will Show* (1936), suffered the fate of *The Well of Loneliness* may be attributed to their emphasis on fluidity rather than fixity, the absence of scientific explanation of the lesbian. *Dusty Answer*, which was a scandalous but not criminal success, engendered great excitement, and letters variously offering the author both secure lesbian and heterosexual homes.[52] The main characters in the novel, however, elude categorization; the heroine is passionately, tremulously attracted to two beautiful, sexually ambivalent persons, one of each sex. Only those persons' other objects of attraction, effeminate man and masculine woman respectively, represent fixity, and are in their availability for categorization rendered unattractive to the reader, just as the repulsively mackintoshed Miss Kilman in Woolf's *Mrs Dalloway* (1925) may be contrasted with the ambivalence and fluidity of the figures in *Orlando*. There was a gulf between Hall's construction of lesbianism within the terms of Ellis's scientific explanation of it as a congenital affliction, and other novelists' exploration of a more fluid uncommitted sexuality, which included lesbianism but subjected only minor characters to categorization.

A NOTE ON NATIONAL IDENTITY

Throughout this period and until the great postwar migrations, Britain remained an ethnically homogeneous society; most of the women writers of this period were of British ancestry. In *Three Guineas*, however, Woolf asserted that women, excluded from many privileges of citizenship, and deprived of nationality if they married foreigners, could only say 'As a woman I have no country. As a woman I want no country. As a woman my country is the whole world' (ch. 3). Many women writers felt a strong local patriotism, for instance Holtby and Jameson for Yorkshire, and Mary

25

Webb for Shropshire, but the idea of a semi-detached national identity is central to women's writing of this period.

Modernists embraced a repudiation of nationality; exemplary was the relation to national identity of Kent-born Winifred Ellerman, who renamed herself after one of the Isles of Scilly, Bryher, established herself in the expatriate, Anglo-American modernist community in Paris, lost her nationality legally when she married an American, and regained it through her second, British husband. For other modernists, such as the New Zealander, Katherine Mansfield, and the Dominican, Jean Rhys, deracination was a given; Rhys's exploration of the situation of the colonial woman, coming 'home' to an incomprehensible society, is the most powerfully alienated of the period. Elizabeth Bowen's ambivalence to modernism is qualified by her identity as an Anglo-Irish writer, and the divided loyalties that enforced. Other writers who brought an experience of other cultures into British writing were Schreiner and the Australians Anna Wickham and Henry Handel Richardson. In this period for the first time such experience was prominent in women's writing in Britain.

NOTES

Place of publication is London, unless otherwise stated.

1. Olive Schreiner, *Woman and Labour* (Virago, 1978), p. 21.
2. See Lucy Bland, *Banishing the Beast: English Feminism and Sexual Morality* (Harmondsworth: Penguin, 1995).
3. Ruth Furst and Ann Scott, *Olive Schreiner* (Deutsch, 1980).
4. Friedrich Engels, *The Origin of the Family, Private Property and the State* (1884); J.J. Bachofen, *Das Mutterrecht* (1861).
5. Cicely Hamilton, *Life Errant* (Dent, 1935), pp. 75–6.
6. See Jill Liddington and Jill Norris, *One Hand Tied Behind Them: The Rise of the Women's Suffrage Movement* (Virago, 1978).
7. Winifred Holtby, 'Feminism Divided', in the *Yorkshire Post*, 26 July 1926; reprinted in *Testament of a Generation: The Journalism of Vera Brittain and Winifred Holtby*, ed. Paul Berry and Alan Bishop (Virago, 1985), pp. 47–50.
8. *The Diary of Virginia Woolf*, ed. Anne Olivier Bell (Hogarth Press, 1984), V, p. 149. Subsequent quotations are from this edition.
9. Virginia Woolf, *Three Guineas* (Hogarth Press, 1986), ch. 3.
10. Holtby, 'Feminism Divided', p. 48.
11. Dora Russell, 'Hypatia or Women and Knowledge', in *The Dora Russell Reader: Fifty-Seven Years of Writing and Journalism*, ed. Dale Spender (Pandora, 1983), p. 9.

26

12. See Bland, *Banishing the Beast*; Sheila Jeffreys, *The Spinster and Her Enemies: Feminism and Sexuality 1880–1930* (Pandora, 1985).

13. *Life As We Have Known It by Co-operative Working Women*, ed. Margaret Llewellyn Davies (Virago, 1977), p. xxxxi.

14. Cora Kaplan, 'Pandora's Box: Subjectivity, Class and Sexuality in Socialist Feminist Criticism', in *Sea Changes: Essays on Culture and Feminism* (Verso, 1986).

15. See Anna Davin, 'Imperialism and Motherhood', *History Workshop*, 5 (1978), pp. 9–65; Jane Lewis, *The Politics of Motherhood: Child and Maternal Welfare in England 1900–39* (Croom Helm, 1980).

16. Carolyn Steedman, *Child, Culture and Class in Britain: Margaret McMillan 1860–1931* (Virago, 1990).

17. Naomi Mitchison, *You May Well Ask: A Memoir 1920–40* (Gollancz, 1979), p. 29.

18. Freya Stark, *Traveller's Prelude* (John Murray, 1950), p. 21; Sylvia Pankhurst, *The Suffragette Movement: An Intimate Account of Persons and Ideals* (Longmans, Green, 1931).

19. Storm Jameson, *Journey from the North* (Collins and Harvill, 1969), I, p. 33.

20. Mitchison, *You May Well Ask*, pp. 172–9.

21. Mrs Humphrey Ward reported in *The Times*, 27 February 1909, p. 9.

22. Cicely Hamilton, *Marriage as a Trade* (Chapman and Hall, 1912), p. v.

23. See Jane Lewis, *Women in England 1870–1950: Sexual Divisions and Social Change* (Hemel Hempstead: Harvester Wheatsheaf, 1984), pp. 147–55; Louise A. Tilly and Joan Scott, *Women, Work and Family* (Methuen, 1987), pp. 194–205.

24. Holtby, 'The Wearer and the Shoe', in the *Manchester Guardian*, 31 January 1930, collected in *Testament of a Generation*, pp. 64–7.

25. See Alice Head, *It Could Never Have Happened* (Heinemann, 1939), pp. 59–64.

26. Alison Light, *Forever England: Femininity, Literature and Conservatism Between the Wars* (Routledge, 1991).

27. Rebecca West, 'On a Form of Nagging', in *Time and Tide*, 31 October 1924, reprinted in Dale Spender, ed., *Time and Tide Wait for No Man* (Pandora, 1984), pp. 58–63.

28. Winifred Holtby, *Women in a Changing Civilization* (Bodley Head, 1945), p. 139.

29. Marie Stopes, *Married Love* (Putnam's, 1919), p. 18.

30. Furst and Scott, *Olive Schreiner*, pp. 292–4.

31. Sally Alexander, 'Becoming a Woman in London in the 1920s and '30s', in *Becoming a Woman and Other Essays in 19th and 20th Century Feminist History* (Virago, 1994), pp. 203–24.

32. See Tilly and Scott, *Women, Work and Family*, pp. 151–2; Lewis, *Women in England*, pp. 190–2.

33. A.R. Jephcott, *Girls Growing Up* (Faber and Faber, 1942), p. 19.

34. Sylvia Pankhurst, *The Home Front: A Mirror to Life in England During the World War* (Hutchinson, 1932), p. 38.

35. *Nella Last's War: A Mother's Diary*, ed. Richard Broad and Suzie Fleming (Sphere, 1981), p. 282.

36. Lettice Curtis, *The Forgotten Pilots: A Story of the Air Transport Auxiliary 1939–45* (Olney: Nelson and Saunders, 1971).

37. Harold Perkin, *The Rise of Professional Society: England Since 1880* (Routledge, 1989).

38. See Spender, ed., *Time and Tide Wait for No Man*.

39. Carol Dyhouse, *No Distinction of Sex? Women in British Universities 1870–1939* (UCL Press, 1995), p. 138.

40. Jane Marcus, 'Invincible Mediocrity: The Private Selves of Public Women', in Shari Benstock, ed., *The Private Self: The Theory and Practice of Women's Autobiographical Writing* (Chapel Hill: University of North Carolina Press, 1988), pp. 114–46.

41. Joan Mason, 'Margery Stephenson', in Edward Shils and Carmen Blacker, eds, *Cambridge Women: Twelve Portraits* (Cambridge: Cambridge University Press, 1996), pp. 121–2.

42. Margaret Rhondda, *This Was My World* (Macmillan, 1933), p. 235.

43. See Billie Melman, *Women and the Popular Imagination in the 1920s: Flappers and Nymphs* (Macmillan, 1988).

44. Winifred Holtby, 'Ladies in Restaurants', in the *Manchester Guardian*, 28 March 1930, reprinted in *Testament of a Generation*, pp. 67–70.

45. Lewis, *Women in England*, p. 4.

46. Christine Bolt, *The Women's Movements in the United States and Britain from the 1790s to the 1920s* (Hemel Hempstead: Harvester Wheatsheaf, 1993), p. 231.

47. Winifred Holtby, *Virginia Woolf* (Wishart, 1932), p. 29.

48. See Montgomery Hyde, *The Other Love: A Historical and Contemporary Study of Homosexuality in Britain* (Heinemann, 1970), pp. 176–82.

49. See Michael Howard, *Jonathan Cape, Publisher* (Cape, 1971); Jean Radford, 'An Inverted Romance: *The Well of Loneliness* and Sexual Ideology', in Radford, ed., *The Progress of Romance: The Politics of Popular Fiction* (Routledge and Kegan Paul, 1986), pp. 97–111.

50. *The Letters of Virginia Woolf*, ed. Nigel Nicholson (Hogarth Press, 1980), VI, p. 524. Subsequent quotations are from this edition.

51. *The Diaries of Sylvia Townsend Warner*, ed. Claire Harman (Virago, 1995), p. 26.

52. Rosamond Lehmann, *The Swan in the Evening* (Collins, 1967), pp. 66–7.

CHAPTER TWO

The Conditions of Women's Writing

The literary history of the earlier twentieth century in Britain is usually treated as a succession of periods, Edwardian, modernist, the 1930s, in which, unlike the preceding Victorian age, male writers are perceived to predominate. Despite the new educational and professional opportunities, the emphasis upon women's issues in this period and the advance of women writers into various writing fields, the established literary chronicle is heavily masculine. The one woman writer of undisputed eminence is Virginia Woolf, who is described in the frame of modernism, or of its local setting, Bloomsbury.

At the turn of the century women were most strongly represented in children's writing and romantic fiction. If we take 1902 as a representative year, it saw the publication of Henry James's *The Wings of a Dove*, Joseph Conrad's *Heart of Darkness*, Arnold Bennett's *Anna of the Five Towns* and Conan Doyle's *The Hound of the Baskervilles*. The most notable literary achievements by women that year were Beatrix Potter's *The Tale of Peter Rabbit* and E. Nesbit's *Five Children and It*. This might seem appropriate confirmation of the strong Edwardian reaction against Victorian literature as feminized. Part of the newness of the Edwardian age, coinciding as it did with the new century, was its sense of release from the perceived dominance of the moral seriousness of Victorian writing. That seriousness was exemplified by George Eliot, and thus in a time of intensifying feminist activity, Edwardian literature was perceived as very firmly masculine.[1] Rebecca West, writing in 1912 in the feminist journal *The Freewoman*, pointed to the identification of literary excitement with male writers such as Wells, Conrad and Bennett, and the failure of a serious woman writer such as May Sinclair to generate the same excitement, and asked 'why women have refused to become great writers?'.[2]

As modernism became dominant in high literary culture after the First World War, the Edwardian giants were shaken. Woolf demolished the reputations of Wells, Bennett and Galsworthy in the essay 'Mr Bennett and Mrs Brown' (1923), one of the key texts of modernism. Woolf, however, was the only British woman writer to achieve high status in modernism, which was an aggressive, revolutionary movement, engaged in establishing its own dominant institutions, and, like Edwardian writing, in reaction against the feminized Victorian age; Sandra Gilbert amd Susan Gubar have argued persuasively for the strength of this reaction.[3] It was not, therefore, a movement in which women could easily assume prominence. Political events also discouraged an emphasis on women's issues. In the 1920s the interest in the war poets and in war writing further emphasized male dominance in literature. In 1919 Cicely Hamilton published a war novel, *William: An Englishman*, in which a progressive, suffragist couple, trapped in Belgium at the outset of war, grasp what the really important issues are. This dramatic and well-received *mea culpa* was symptomatic of the doubts about feminism and female demands which characterized the post-war period; the achievement of the suffrage combined with guilt about the unequal burden placed on men in the war to make women's issues appear of secondary importance even to a leading feminist. These doubts were intensified in the 1930s, as unemployment at home and totalitarianism abroad again produced an emphasis on male experience and male writing. Two important recent studies by Valentine Cunningham and Alison Light have described the need to reinsert women's writing in the literary history of this period.[4]

The pressures of external events sidelined women's issues. Parallel to this was the intensive constructing of literary tradition as English became central to the national curriculum. At the turn of the century English, which had begun as a discipline appropriate for the abilities of women and working-class students, was developing a central role in the curriculum as the discipline in which the cultural centrality of Englishness, the essential expression of the national spirit, was enshrined.[5] As English became a subject for study for male students, and chairs of English were established in the universities, many histories of English literature emerged for this new market, designed to establish an authoritative literary tradition. The tradition was established by the new, and mostly male, profession of lecturers in English, and by men increasingly conscious of themselves as literary professionals. It was a tradition in which women writers occupied a small place, and in which Jane Austen, who figures in the histories of this period as the greatest woman writer, defined the limits of female creativity, beyond whom no advance could be expected. The literary and academic professions were anxiously guarding their newly enhanced status, and in the process they established a tradition of literature as male, in which only Jane, the exquisite spinster, occupied an indisputable place.

The tendency of traditions to define themselves as male is interestingly apparent in another kind of construction of tradition, Claud Cockburn's lively *Bestseller: The Books Everyone Read 1900–1939* (1972). In his introduction Cockburn protests at the academic habit of discussing literature with reference only to the literary giants and without acknowledgement of the bestselling books which 'everyone read'. He goes on to discuss fifteen bestsellers, of which only three, Margaret Kennedy's *The Constant Nymph* (1924), E.M. Hull's *The Sheik* (1919) and Mary Webb's *Precious Bane* (1925), are by women. The proportion bears no relation to the actual place of women in the bestseller field in the period. An earlier work, Michael Joseph's manual, *The Commercial Side of Literature* (1925), demonstrates a similar tendency; although the market leader, Ethel M. Dell, is often cited as the example of a bestselling writer, detailed references to the content of bestsellers are invariably to works by male writers. Although it was a truism in the earlier twentieth century that men predominated in literature and women in popular writing, when it came to establishing a tradition of popular writing it seemed that what Gaye Tuchman has called the process of 'edging women out' prevailed.[6]

Complementary to this process of establishing a male tradition was the insistence of the women writers of the period that women's writing was making a fresh start, that for the first time women had the opportunity to create a writing distinctive to themselves. Dorothy Richardson, in her 1938 foreword to *Pilgrimage*, speaks of herself as searching for an alternative mode to 'male realism'. Rebecca West's first book was an iconoclastic study of Henry James. Woolf, in *A Room of One's Own*, presented the great Victorian women writers as shackled by convention. This picture of the centuries of silence and imprisonment endured by female creativity was important to the early twentieth-century woman writer's concept of herself; she could not afford to draw on any idea of a strong female tradition. Where the male modernist's revolutionary target was a heavily feminized Victorian culture, Richardson and Woolf and West measured themselves against the great male writers of the previous generation, behind whom stretched centuries of obscurity and disablement. Male and female constructions of tradition could hardly have been more different.

At the turn of the century the three highest literary profiles among living women writers were probably those of Olive Schreiner, Mrs Humphrey Ward and Marie Corelli. Schreiner was struggling with writer's block and had produced nothing but short fictions for years. Ward, author of the admired and bestselling theological romance, *Robert Elsmere* (1888), was prominent on platform and in committee as a leading opponent of the suffrage campaign. Corelli was the bestselling romantic novelist; reviews rubbished her works which provided the Fowler brothers with a substantial number of their examples of grammatical howlers in their 1906 grammar manual, *The King's English*. Each of these writers might be seen to exemplify certain popular ideas about female creativity which were to be formalized in the interwar period in the attempts to categorize writers by heights of brow. Schreiner was the tormented highbrow struggling with a burden of genius too large for her frail body and nerves; Ward, the busy, instructive, middlebrow lady writer engaged on numerous committees; Corelli, the semi-literate entrepreneur whose success showed how far apart serious and popular fiction now were, and who assisted the definition of serious fiction as male and popular as female. For the next forty years women writers could be accommodated to these categories.

The rest of this chapter will examine the world in which women writers sought to establish themselves, looking first at the conditions of the literary market, and then at how women related to the profession of writing in a time of increased emphasis on the concept of professionalism, and at the disputes over categories of brow which were a major feature of interpretation in the period.

THE LITERARY MARKET

The attempt to categorize writers by heights of brow, discussed below, was one response to an expanding and diversifying market. The twentieth century opened on a boom in fiction and in periodicals, and on an increasingly fragmented market where specialized audiences were targeted. The world of writing and publishing had undergone major upheavals in the late nineteenth century, as advances in printing, paper production and distribution encouraged the rapid rise of the popular press, and in book production also the targeting of particular audiences and increasing specialization intensified. Although the unified market of the Victorian period was largely a myth, a powerful regret for its supposed loss is pervasive in the early twentieth century. That regret centred particularly on two novelties. One was the new journalism, supposedly the creation of the 1870 Education Act with its provision for universal literacy. The proliferation of periodicals, however, offered larger opportunities for writing, in articles and reviewing, and in the flourishing genre of short stories. The other focus of regret was the new breed of entrepreneurial bestselling novelists, exemplified by Corelli, who overrode bad reviews and comments on her poor English, dispensed with the services of an agent, and addressed herself directly to the public she was justifiably convinced was listening. Her biggest seller, *The Sorrows of Satan* (1895), carried a prefatory note announcing that no review copies had been sent out; Corelli relied on her public, not on reviewer approval. She also refused to allow her works to appear in cheap reprint series. These successful publicity ploys confirmed Corelli's status as the pre-eminent example of the writer as entrepreneur, and increased the visible gulf between her popular audience and that for the less popular works of writers still dependent on the intervention of reviewers. This gulf between the traditional elite and the new popular audiences was often perceived in gendered terms, James's audience versus Corelli's.[7]

The 1890s were a period of decisive changes in the production and distribution of books, as the publishing industry attempted to control a changing market. One major change came in 1894. Throughout the Victorian period the three-volume novel, priced at thirty-one shillings and sixpence, had been the mainstay of publishers and of the circulating libraries, the principal customers for novels, but in that year Mudie's Library and W.H. Smith's agreed that they would no longer accept them. This agreement led immediately to the collapse of the three-decker, and for the next fifty years novels were published in a single volume format at a standard price of six shillings, rising between the wars to seven shillings and sixpence. The second change came in 1900 when publishers and booksellers responded to the perceived threat of discounts and cheap reprint series by launching the Net Book Agreement which established net prices for books and a set period before cheaper reprints were allowed, an agreement which lasted until 1995.[8]

In the Edwardian period and thereafter publishers were torn between two particular models for their relations with their writers. One was that of the traditional paternalist, who nurtured his stable of talent, exemplified by John Murray's hopes for Rose Macaulay whose early novels he published; 'she takes criticism in the proper spirit . . . I take a great interest in Miss Macaulay, and believe she will do a really good book some day, but she needs guiding'.[9] (Macaulay later won a novel competition run by Hodder and Stoughton, and switched to them.) The other model was that of the risk-taker backing a hunch on an unknown writer, as Fisher Unwin did when they gambled on the often rejected manuscript of Ethel M. Dell's *The Way of an Eagle* (1912) and found themselves with an author who, despite bad reviews and refusing all personal publicity, sold like bread for the next thirty years.

The book market continued to expand throughout this period; both World Wars imposed restrictions on paper, but revealed an increased wartime appetite for reading. The 1930s were another period of innovation in response to the perceived potential for expansion. Book tokens were

33

successfully launched in a national scheme, sponsored by publishers, to persuade a larger public to think of books as gifts.[10] Some firms moved to specialization, notably Mills and Boon, hitherto publishers of general fiction and educational works, who decided to concentrate on the large audience for romantic fiction. By making their names synonymous with a particular genre they solved the problem, often lamented by publishers, of low imprint recognition by the reading public; Mills and Boon's readers bought the imprint, not the author, effecting a major shift in a field hitherto dominated by the Corelli–Dell line of stars.[11] The big success story of the decade was Allen Lane's launch of the first cheap reprint paperback series, Penguins. This began with the reprint of ten popular novels, which included Webb's *Gone to Earth* (1917), Christie's *The Mysterious Affair at Styles* (1920) and Sayers's *The Unpleasantness at the Bellona Club* (1928). The success of these led to expansion into other series, the green-covered crime series, the Pelican non-fiction series and the topical Penguin Specials in 1937, the Puffin series for children in 1940.[12]

The main customers for books continued to be the libraries; the public libraries gradually through this period took over from the circulating libraries as the major buyers of books. In the early 1900s libraries were funded by a charge on the rates limited to one penny; Woolf in 1919 described the results in Lewes Public Library: 'full of old ghosts; books halfway to decomposition. A general brownness covers them. They are as much alike outwardly as charity children' (*Diary*, I, p. 300). In the same year the Public Libraries Act removed the penny rate limit and extended the power to establish libraries to the counties. Public libraries expanded rapidly throughout the 1920s, and, after a brief retrenchment period in the early 1930s, boomed again in the later part of the decade, with local government spending on libraries and museums increasing by 45 per cent between 1933 and 1939. Children's sections and reading rooms were established, and, responding to public demand, libraries took an increasing amount of fiction and became central in local communities.[13]

Mudie's, the Victorian giant among circulating libraries, became dependent on the carriage trade and declined in this period, finally closing in 1937. In 1900, however, there was the launch of a new library venture which catered innovatively to the rapidly expanding reading public and was to become the major player among circulating libraries in this period. Florence Boot, wife of the founder of Boots the Chemist of Nottingham, had been experimenting for some years with a twopenny lending service for books, run from the chemists' shops and stocked by surplus stock bought mainly from Mudie's. In 1900, under the direction of a recruit from Mudie's, Boots formalized its lending service as Boots Booklovers' Library, a national lending service in which the libraries coexisted with the chemists' stock, and expanded as Boots expanded. A loss leader, designed to draw customers to the shops, the library had selling points which confirmed a new democratic approach to library borrowing. It introduced open access to shelves, allowing direct access to the books without the necessary mediation and advice of an assistant. Open access had been pioneered by Clerkenwell Public Library in 1895 and was gradually adopted by other public libraries as funding for conversion of buildings became possible, but in 1900 it was still a radical concept. Comfortable furniture encouraged customers to linger and browse. Subscribers' membership tokens enabled them to exchange books at any branch of Boots.[14]

These attempts to encourage female customers to regard changing a library book as part of the general shopping day proved very successful. By 1930 Boots had 250,000 subscribers who could change their book at any one of 340 branches, and had become the largest of the subscription libraries. Its main rival, W.H. Smith's Library, once Mudie's major Victorian competitor, could also offer subscribers the opportunity of borrowing in the familiar context of daily shopping. By the 1930s the two libraries, with their largely female clientele and their context of middle-class shopping, had become synonymous with the middlebrow reading public, and are so depicted in the satirical description of 'Smoots Library' in Elizabeth Bowen's 1938 novel, *The Death of the Heart*. Boots, however, would have lent out Bowen's novels, included Jean Rhys and Sylvia Townsend Warner among its subscribers, and was often more willing to order controversial books for subscribers than were public libraries, which were subject to local censorship preferences. In addition in the 1930s twopenny lending libraries were established in newsagents and tobacconists, to cater for working-class readers outside the range of the other libraries; they held stocks of popular fiction (romances, crime novels, school stories) for borrowing, alongside popular periodicals for sale.[15]

The 1930s also saw a proliferation of book clubs, the forerunner of which was the Times Book Club, founded in 1905 as a lending library for all annual subscribers at no extra charge. In 1929 the Book Society was founded on the model of the existing American Book of the Month Club; a panel of well-known writers selected the monthly recommendation, and it was mailed to subscribers on the day of publication, offering immediate access to books combined with guidance from literary experts. The formula proved very successful, increasing the publicity and sales for recommended works, adding to the competitive anxieties of writers (Woolf, whose *Flush* (1933) was a Book of the Month, agonized over the failure of *The Years* (1938) to be nominated), and spawning a number of successors, including the Left Book Club launched by the publisher Victor Gollancz, and the cheap reprint clubs, Readers' Union and World Books, which served a public for whom Penguin were the only existing paperbacks. The book clubs proved extremely effective in generating discussion and publicity about books.

PROFESSIONALISM

In the later nineteenth century writers were increasingly engaged in organizing themselves as professionals. The major institutional expression of this was the Society of Authors, founded in 1883 to campaign for the protection of writers by copyright laws; this campaign led to the international copyright agreement with the United States in 1891, and ultimately to the Copyright Act of 1911, which remained in force to 1995. The concept of the writer as professional in his or her possession of a property of literary expertise was extended in other developments. N.N. Feltes has described the evolution at the turn of the century of ideologies of literary value, expressed particularly through the variations on the formula of 'the best books'.[16] Journals and authors published lists of best books; publishing series, such as Oxford's World's Classics, launched in 1901, and Dent's Everyman's Library, launched in 1906, were established to bring readers a comprehensive library of the best in world literature. The new professors of English established canons in their histories of literature. The *Times Literary Supplement*, launched in 1902, was an exclusive forum for the discussion of the best books, in addition to the literary review columns in general journals. All these activities enhanced the concept of the writer controlling the supply of literary expertise.

Within this climate of intensified consciousness of professional status, the professional claims of women writers were often questioned. The Society of Authors admitted women as members from 1889, and to its council from 1896, but the time-lag was indicative; women were not inevitably regarded as professionals. There was a similar lag in admission to the Academic Committee, founded in 1911.[17] By 1921 when the Society of Bookmen was founded, exclusion of women was inadmissable, but the society's name is expressive of the masculine aura of literary professionalism. Other institutions maintained older attitudes; Woolf was enraged in 1935 to be told by E.M. Forster that a proposal to admit women to the London Library Committee had been rejected because they found 'ladies impossible' (*Diary*, IV, pp. 297–8). The term 'lady writer' was frequently used in this period as a synonym for the amateurism which made the definition of professionalism

36

possible. Confusingly, it was frequently applied to the market leaders, the star romantic novelists whose earnings could hardly be described as amateur.

More attractive to the institutions of literary professionalism were the women writers who remained remote from their world. A memorable vignette of this division was provided by the famous occasion in 1928 when the Prime Minister, Stanley Baldwin, made a speech at a dinner of the Literary Fund in which he praised the neglected novels of Mary Webb, who had died the previous year, and, as her publishers, Cape, had hoped, provided publicity which propelled Webb's novels into the bestseller lists.[18] In the preface to *Precious Bane* in the 1929 de luxe illustrated edition of her works which his speech had made possible, Baldwin valued Webb precisely for her remoteness from London. (Webb herself had bitterly resented her exclusion from the London literary world.) Her strength, for him, lay in her obscurity in an obscure shire, and her female sensitivity to the Shropshire landscape. A similar construction of the woman writer as closer to the natural than to the professional world may have informed the enthusiasm of Sir Humphrey Milford, Chairman of Oxford University Press in the 1930s, for the rural novels of Constance Holme, secure from the literary world in her Westmoreland fastness; Holme was the only contemporary writer all of whose novels appeared in World's Classics. Like Webb and another Milford enthusiasm, Flora Thompson, she exemplified a concept of the woman writer as identified with a world sharply divided from that of the contemporary professional, living in the border countries (literally with Webb and Holme), and mediating between professional men and the natural world.

Women writers' identification with the institutions of literary professionalism, then, was uncertain. They did achieve some institutional respectability, as when Storm Jameson in 1939 became the British President of the international association of writers, PEN. An annual prize, the Femina/Vie Heureuse Prize, established as an award for under-recognized writers and sponsored by two French journals, was usually won by a woman writer. Hamilton's *William* was the first winner in 1919; later winners included Holme, Webb, Woolf, Radclyffe Hall, Stella Benson and Stella Gibbons. Such awards bridged the world of institutional respectability in which women were not natural members, and the world of publicity in which they were much more central. The most widely read and publicized writers of the period, the popular romantic novelists Corelli, Florence Barclay and Elinor Glyn, addressed themselves directly to their publics in their books and through fan clubs and lecture tours, and defined themselves as professional in their earning capacity and dedication to their public.[19]

This alternative professional world of marketing was much more accessible to women than the world of literary committee-rooms, and, as publicity outlets diversified, many women writers relished their emergence from

37

obscurity; Hamilton in her autobiography describes the extraordinary experience in 1909 of seeing her name on the outside of a London bus carrying an advertisement for her successful play, *Diana of Dobson's*. Some of the most popular writers, notably Dell and Christie, could afford to shun personal publicity, but most writers of this period were very aware of the advantages involved in the excitements surrounding book publication at this period, in the form of prizes, Book of the Month selections in Britain and America, book-promotion tours, and the authority accorded the more regarded reviewers. Woolf, who abhorred publicity, nonetheless followed the fortunes of the Femina/Vie Heureuse Prize and other such awards closely in her diary. Other writers took up the opportunities of lecture tours organized by their American publishers; Sinclair, Brittain, Warner and West each toured the United States to promote their first successful book. Success in the American market was especially sought; West relied on American assignments, and Warner was supported in old age by her regular short story contributions to the *New Yorker*, based on contacts made when she toured the States in 1927 to promote her first novel, and Book of the Month choice, *Lolly Willowes*. Brittain's income, on the other hand, suffered badly when her pacifist campaign during the Second World War damaged her in the American market. The British Council, established in 1935 to promote British culture abroad, was another organizer of lecture tours; West's 1935 tour of Yugoslavia for the Council provided the material for her major work, *Black Lamb and Grey Falcon* (1942).

It was journalism, however, in which most women writers of the period developed their writing voice and persona, and on which they relied for their income. Woolf, who continually deplored the distractions journalism offered away from proper writing, formed her voice in her Edwardian journalism, and it was not until the success of *Orlando* in 1929 that her income from her books exceeded that from her journalism.[20] The 'new journalism' of the 1880s and 1890s greatly extended the opportunities for women to enter the profession; in 1903 James, an inveterate observer of the successes of women in the changing literary market, centred his novella, 'The Papers', on the figure of the desexed, scoop-hungry woman journalist. In 1895 the Society of Women Journalists was formed, and by 1901 had 200 members.[21] Advice manuals for these recruits to the fourth estate were published, including in 1898 the young Arnold Bennett's *Journalism for Women*, which the bestselling romantic novelist, Berta Ruck, was still urging in 1935 as the indispensable guide to entry to the profession.[22] Bennett was to become the most influential reviewer of the early twentieth century, and a figure who defined the male literary profession for many women writers. It would be difficult to overemphasize his utility to them, both as a negative model to Richardson, Woolf and West, exemplifying the Edwardian novelist's obsession with materiality, and as positive model to such documentarist novelists of the 1930s as Jameson, Cooper and Phyllis Bentley. Bennett himself revealed in his memoir, *The Truth about an Author* (1903), that during his Potteries childhood the principal agent of his introduction to literary culture had been the *Girl's Own Paper*, the market leader among women's magazines in the 1880s.[23]

Journalism for Women, based on Bennett's experience as editor of the magazine *Woman* (no relation to the mass-circulation weekly launched in 1937), outlined a vast existing gulf between the world of professional journalism and the female amateur hoping to enter it, but saw that amateurism not as innate, but as the product of inappropriate training for an exclusively domestic sphere. The manual sought to remedy this amateurism by offering practical advice about the targeting of specific journals; the principal mistake of women journalists was to fail to understand the need to address themselves to an increasingly specialized market. Their preferred literary form was the 'reverie', often called 'From my Window'; they 'were too prone to write down vaguely their vague fancies about things in general', and to direct these randomly into the market.[24] Instead they could turn the objects in their environment to use, visiting libraries to work up articles on historic furniture or famous beds, and bringing detailed practical advice from their domestic experience to the woefully impressionistic cookery and fashion columns proliferating within the new periodicals. Bennett offered women writers a model of professionalism based on the translation of domestic experience into marketable specialisms. Even at this stage the basis for antagonism with Woolf is evident. Her pioneer exploration of modernist techniques in the short story, 'The Mark on the Wall' (1917), is pointedly unconcerned with material objects, let alone their marketable histories, and formally develops from the female 'amateur' form, the reverie.

In calling for women to abandon the voice of private reverie and adopt a professional stance, Bennett was highlighting one of the major decisions women writers of the period had to make. It was in journalism that many experimented with the kinds of public and professional personae available to them. The nature and range of those voices were formed by the journals within which they wrote. The major divide was between general journals and those catering specifically for women, which might include the choice between a general and a specifically female authorial persona. The famous contradiction in Woolf's *A Room of One's Own* between writing as a woman and writing in conformity to an androgynous ideal, evolved in a world where this was a daily decision for women writing in a range of different journals.

Within the field of journals targeted specifically at women the major division was between the feminist journals and the women's magazines. In the Edwardian period there was a proliferation of journals representing the different strands in the suffrage movement, allowing women the opportunity of exploring the voices of public polemic. Among them were *Votes for Women* for the WSPU, the *Common Cause* for the NUWSS, the *Vote* for the Women's Freedom League, and the *Women's Dreadnought* for Sylvia Pankhurst's breakaway East London working-class branch of the WSPU. Most ambitious of these journals was the *Freewoman: A Weekly Feminist Review*, founded in 1911 by Dora Marsden, another refugee from the WSPU, as a journal which discussed a wider range of women's issues than the suffrage. The title was exhortatory. The topics discussed in the *Freewoman* included working conditions for women, the endowment of motherhood, child abuse, prostitution and homosexuality, and a discussion circle was founded round the journal to discuss the topics aired there. West and Richardson were among the contributors.

The publishing history of the *Freewoman* might seem exemplary of the process of 'edging women out'. The journal established clear links between feminism and modernism, especially in its focus on the centrality of gender politics, but these links were to develop the journal away from its initial stance as directly political. In 1912, in financial difficulties and boycotted by W.H. Smith for its political and sexual radicalism, the journal foundered, and, after an appeal for funds to subscribers, was relaunched as the *New Freewoman*. The revived journal continued the political radicalism of its predecessor, but increasingly was also used as an outlet for modernist poetry and criticism. Ezra Pound, introduced to the journal by West, and looking for an English outlet to complement the American journal, *Poetry*, became increasingly influential in directing the policies of the *New Freewoman*. In December 1913 the journal was relaunched yet again as the *Egoist*, and by 1916, when it published Joyce's *Portrait of the Artist as a Young Man* as a serial, it had become entirely devoted to the promotion of modernist writing. Marsden left in 1914, and West, after a period as literary editor and repeated clashes with Pound over the journal's direction, also resigned.[25]

The metamorphoses of the *Freewoman* revealed the antagonisms of modernism and feminism. Another of the modernist journals with which Pound was associated, the Vorticist *Blast*, had proclaimed in its first issue of 1914 that 'the moment a man realises himself as an artist, he ceases to belong to any space or time'. This emphasis on repudiation of circumstance was inimical to feminism, and, though feminism and modernism briefly co-existed in the *New Freewoman*, and indeed in *Blast*, where West published the feminist short story 'Indissoluble Matrimony', a break was inevitable. The later avatars of the *Freewoman* dropped the discussion of topical political issues which had been its major distinction. Where women contributors survived it was in the modernist exploration of women's consciousness.

Richardson and May Sinclair continued to write for the journal as modernists, and it was in the *Egoist* that Sinclair wrote the famous review of Richardson's *Pilgrimage* which launched the phrase 'stream of consciousness'. The whole history of the *Freewoman* demonstrated the links and antagonisms between women in the feminist movement and in modernism.

The major legatee of the upsurge of feminist journalism at the period of the suffrage campaign was the feminist weekly, *Time and Tide: An Independent Non-Party Weekly Review*, launched in 1920 with an all-woman board of directors, and managed and bankrolled by Lady Rhondda. *Time and Tide* was committed to maintaining a distinct feminist political voice and developing the polemical strengths women had explored during the suffrage campaign; Dale Spender has described its innovatory early years.[26] It was particularly concerned with monitoring the effects of the Sex Disqualification (Removal) Act of 1919 in affording equal opportunities within the professions, campaigned for more women MPs, and regularly assessed the attitudes of male MPs, especially to women's issues. Directors included Hamilton, West and Elizabeth Robins, who had all been prominent polemicists in the suffrage campaign, and Holtby and E.M. Delafield. Although the focus was primarily political, the journal, launched in the first wave of euphoria after the award of the suffrage, aimed to cover the full range of activities in which women might be engaged, maintain an extensive feminist network to replace the redundant suffrage societies, and provide a specific forum for women's writing. Almost every woman writer of any note wrote for it during the 1920s. West wrote a regular theatre column, extracts from Woolf's *A Room of One's Own* appeared in 1929, but the single most popular contribution was Delafield's regular comic column, 'Diary of a Provincial Lady', collected in book form in 1930. In this the narrator is a middle-class woman living in the provinces, trying to keep up with cultural events via her weekly copy of *Time and Tide*, eagerly entering the competitions, and struggling not very successfully with books recommended in its reviews such as Woolf's *Orlando* or West's *Harriet Hume*. The series was a satire on the limits of metropolitan journalism and a reminder of the kind of context in which the journal might be read. The later publishing history of *Time and Tide* repeated that of the *Freewoman*. In the 1930s it responded to the shift away from interest in feminism towards the urgent domestic and international crises, and became less specific in its political focus, while carrying an increasing proportion of literary and cultural items. In subsequent decades it became a literary magazine, staffed largely by men.

The alternative version of the journal addressed specifically to women was the women's magazine; in the late nineteenth century a number of these were among the new publications introduced for the new mass reading public, and the mixture of housekeeping guidance and romantic fiction was established. In 1900 the market leader was the *Girls' Own Paper*, which, unlike its male equivalent, addressed itself to a general public, and specialized in housekeeping advice and domestic fiction. The end of the First World War saw a further proliferation of magazines in this field to supplement it, and such other Victorian survivals as *Home Chat*, the Scottish *People's Friend* and the upmarket *Lady*, and these journals were much more specific in targeting audiences. *Vogue*, the journal for high fashion, was launched in 1916; 1919 saw the launch of *Peg's Paper*, a magazine of romantic fiction and celebrity gossip targeted specifically at the female factory-worker, *Schoolfriend* to cater for the large market for girls' school stories, and *Homes and Gardens* to cater for the middle–class homemaker for whom domestic service was no longer possible, a field in which it was joined by *Good Housekeeping* in 1922. In 1937 *Woman*'s addition of colour printing to the formula of domestic and personal advice and romantic fiction made it the first mass–circulation weekly.[27]

The women's magazines proved a point of entry for many women writers working in the less prestigious areas of writing. The romantic novelist, Berta Ruck, spent years writing articles and short fiction for *Home Chat*, until in 1914 the response of readers to a short serial induced her to expand it into a novel, *His Official Fiancée*, and launched her on a career of two popular romantic novels a year for the next thirty years. Another bestselling romantic novelist, Annie S. Swan, began her career with romantic serials in the *People's Friend*. The children's writer, E. Nesbit, embarked on the first of her children's novels after publishing a twelve-part serial about her own childhood, 'My Schooldays', in the *Girls' Own Paper* in 1897. Her novels, however, were mostly serialized in the much more prestigious general journal, the *Strand Magazine*, alongside the works of Doyle, Wells and Kipling. Another childhood reminiscence, which first appeared in a woman's magazine, was Flora Thompson's *Lark Rise to Candleford*, which originated as a sketch in the *Lady*, the genteel journal of country life. There was much cross-over between the feminist journals and the women's magazines; Mary MacArthur, the trade union leader and editor of the *Woman Worker*, wrote regularly for *Home Chat*, and West, Holtby and Woolf all at some time contributed to *Good Housekeeping*. However, the women's magazines required the construction of a domestic persona, and were seen by many as antithetical to feminist ambitions. West, sensitive to the need to maintain compatible relations between political feminism and the domestic advice journals, complained in *Time and Tide* in 1924 that she was always being congratulated by men for 'being among the women journalists who have lifted from women the reproach of being unable to write anything but Aunt Peg's Recipes in *Home Twitters*'.[28] Such denigration, she argued, was only another sign of the tendency to categorize men's interests as large and women's as small.

West, whose authorial persona was formed from writing for both feminist and domestic journals, was arguing against treating the success of the women's magazines of the 1920s as evidence of a postwar, post-suffrage retreat into homemaking. Many Old Feminists, however, saw the establishment of women in general audience journals, and in fields hitherto considered male, as crucial. Vera Brittain's account of the importance she attached to writing a first leader for the *Yorkshire Post* exemplifies this attitude. The first leader in a newspaper carried the heavyweight political comment and traditionally women did not write it, but in 1927 President Coolidge announced that he would not be contesting the US presidency for a second term at a time when all the top male staff of the *Post* were on holiday. Brittain responded enthusiastically to the importance of the occasion. 'If I could produce a good editorial on President Coolidge, it would be more useful to the woman's cause than a dozen speeches from feminist platforms.'[29] The role of the woman contributor in the mainstream journal remained problematic, however; she might only find a highly vulnerable place as a specialist in women's issues. When Kingsley Martin took over as editor of the *New Statesman*, he dropped Brittain and her woman's column, arguing that there should be no issues which were not of interest to both sexes.[30] This was entirely representative of the general tendency in the 1930s to subsume women's issues within the general political range.

The group of magazines representing the alternative male establishment, modernism, offered another kind of home to women seeking to escape conventional domestic roles. Bryher recorded how, forbidden to go on an archaeological expedition by her wealthy parents, she found the 'way to freedom' from their conventional expectations, not in the feminist movement, but in the little magazines of modernism. If Pound's takeover of the *Freewoman* as an outlet for his own priorities looked like a classic case of 'edging women out', the avant-garde little magazines which proliferated in the 1910s and 1920s had great significance for many women. Gillian Hanscombe and Virginia Smyers have described the activities of the Left Bank group of American and British women writers which Bryher joined in the 1920s as an alternative avant-garde network to Bloomsbury. The group's journalistic output, however, was limited by a defiantly anti-professional stance. Bryher's autobiography describes the production of endless short-lived little magazines, and how any less ephemeral mode of publication was regarded as artistic betrayal. 'If an MS was sold to an established publisher, its author was regarded as a black sheep, and for his own safety moved to the Right Bank.' Later when Bryher bankrolled a little magazine, the film journal *Close Up*, and edited it with her husband, Kenneth MacDonald, she was disconcerted to find it become unusually successful for its genre. *Close Up*, which ran from 1927 to 1933, and carried a regular column by

43

Richardson, as well as contributions on the German cinema by Bryher, had five thousand readers, upsetting to an editor used to 'half the copies unsold and growing dusty in some corner'.[31]

Although many of the women writers of this period entered the profession via a period of intensive journalism and continued to write articles and reviews throughout their careers, the question of how far the woman writer should define herself as journalist remained. The figure of the battered hack, struggling to grasp her opportunities in the expansive but damaging world of journalism, and hoping to write more substantial works in the intervals between assignments, became a recognized type for defining the woman writer as professional. Brittain, the epitome of the woman journalist seeking to extend the range of women's reportage, recorded in her three *Testament* books her worries that she was frittering away her creativity. Woolf, whose literary career began in reviewing for the *Times Literary Supplement*, was lamenting the distraction of journalism as early as 1908, and refusing at least to review fiction; later she valued her ability to refuse to write reviews or prefaces.[32] In 1940, reading in Brittain's biography of Winifred Holtby, *Testament of Friendship*, of the intensive journalistic activity which Holtby maintained till her death, she wrote 'oh Lord how I loathe that scribbling business: 35 novels to be reviewed for *Harper's Bazaar* in one morning in a bungalow' (*Letters*, VI, p. 381). For Woolf Holtby was the type of the woman hack, the dark reverse of the woman artist; the fact that one of Holtby's assignments had been a critical book on Woolf herself only increased her anguish. Holtby's *Virginia Woolf* was presented as a tribute from a writer who had chosen political activism to one who had chosen to 'maintain that equilibrium and concentration which are necessary for an artist', and insisted on the interdependence of the two kinds of women writer.[33] On other occasions Woolf could view the woman forced to maintain herself through journalism with some awe as possessor of an experience largely hidden from herself; in 1933 she said of West, 'she is tenacious and masterful and very good company, having also battered about in the stinking underworld of hack writers' (*Letters*, V, p. 259).

Woolf's reactions to those women writers entirely committed to the professional world defined her own doubts about the possibility and desirability of admission to the male professional world, doubts most extensively discussed in *Three Guineas*. These doubts were widely canvassed in the interwar period, and the multiple significances of the idea of a room of one's own expressed the various attitudes to entry into the professional world. To many women writers it had a talismanic significance as the escape from the constraints of family life. Brittain describes in *Testament of Youth* the importance of the London studio flat she shared with Holtby in the early 1920s; 'it was a supremely uncomfortable existence – and yet I felt I had

44

never known before what comfort was. For the first time, I knew the luxury of privacy, the tranquil happiness of being able to come and go just as I wished without interference or supervision.'[34] For Brittain the flat symbolized not only privacy, but her entry to a world of economic independence and professional status, where she supported herself by journalistic work. For Woolf, in *A Room of One's Own*, the idea of 'room' puns on the question of whether there can be room for women in the professional world, and whether women should attempt to enter it. In the second chapter Woolf describes the situation of her room in a street where 'domesticity prevailed', and where she can watch from her window the incredible self-confidence of the male professionals as they set off for work. Her capacity to write derives from this life distinct from male professionalism; the room represents a privacy which excludes both domestic cares and the necessity of working in the hack underworld.

One of the most successful writers of the period, Agatha Christie, emphasizes in her autobiography the importance of not having a room of her own. Interviewers seeking a photograph of Christie at work in her study were disappointed. 'All I needed was a steady table and a typewriter . . . A marble-topped bedroom washstand made a good place to write; the dining-room table between meals was also suitable.'[35] While the interviewers' expectations suggest an acceptance of the concept of the woman as professional writer, embodied in her possession of a room devoted to professional activity, Christie insists on an older model of the woman writer. She can only write her novels in the interstices of domestic work, or in the vicinity of her archaeologist husband's professional work when she accompanies him on field trips to the Middle East. These work patterns conform to the model exemplified by Jane Austen as Woolf presents her in *A Room of One's Own*, writing her novels in the common living-room, and putting them aside whenever domestic or social demands required. By emphasizing her adherence to these work patterns, Christie constructs an image of the woman writer as essentially contained within the domestic rather than the professional world. It was a construction frequently deployed by women writers at the period; the historical novelist Margaret Irwin, for instance, describes in the preface to her novel, *The Stranger Prince* (1937), how she has derived much of her material from books snatched from the shelves in friends' houses in the brief intervals before dinner, and not in a properly scholarly fashion from the British Museum.

The primacy accorded Austen in the literary histories was seen to reside in the distinctiveness of her femininity; she represented the achievement of literary distinction within an entirely female and domestic sphere. Woolf's Austen in *A Room of One's Own*, rejecting the inappropriate cadences of masculine prose for a style created within an entirely domestic context,

45

while George Eliot accepts male standards and 'commits atrocities' with them, is in accord with the judgement of the literary histories. So is Elizabeth Bowen's short popular literary history, *English Novelists* (1942), when it offers a conventional opposition of Austen, 'the most nearly flawless of English novelists' to the 'opaque and pedestrian' Eliot.[36] Austen, working within an entirely domestic context, represented a view of the woman writer which did not engage with professionalism. Eliot, on the other hand, a journalist fully committed to the professional world and fighting for her status there, represented the embarrassments and uncertainties of women's entry into that world, and the mistake of believing full admission was possible. As women increasingly entered the professions, and the woman writer came to be regarded as a professional, a nostalgia for the privacy of nineteenth-century writers, even of Eliot, seized many. Rosamond Lehmann describes this nostalgia in her autobiography, *The Swan in the Evening* (1967), when she recalls how the publicity attending *Dusty Answer*, and the public assumptions that she exemplified the radical postwar woman writer, made her long for the Victorian habit of writing under a pseudonym; 'I thought with yearning of the androgynous disguises, the masculine masks they had adopted for the sake of moral delicacy; of the unimpeded freedom to immerse in the creative and destructive element which anonymity had bestowed on them'.[37]

THE BATTLE OF THE BROWS

On 25 March 1941 *The Times* ran a fourth leader, 'The Eclipse of the Highbrow', which dismissed the avant-garde experiments of the interwar period as an unfortunate diversion from the continuous tradition of English culture. These 'arts unintelligible outside a Bloomsbury drawing-room' had been essentially 'anti-democratic', the product of a generation which had lost its best hopes in the 1914–18 War; 'that age is past though some of its ghosts still walk'.[38] Now in the context of the national war effort the continuity of the real English tradition had reasserted itself. The leader invoked the rhetoric of cooperation between the classes prevalent in the Second World War, excluding only the highbrow from the picture of national unity presented and provoking an extensive correspondence from readers who proclaimed themselves middlebrow and asserted that middlebrow writing was the true continuity of the English tradition. The debate acquired an unexpected significance on 3 April when Woolf's obituary appeared on the page after the continued correspondence; Sylvia Townsend Warner, following the 'filthy' debate in wartime Dorset, impulsively assumed it had provoked Woolf's suicide.[39]

The categorization of writing by heights of brow between the wars was not simply a media pastime; it was a means by which the literary world attempted to interpret the changes which had taken place in the expanding and fragmenting market. It was an attempt to naturalize this new market within existing constructions of class, and also within a narrative of a continuous literary tradition. It explained the growth of specialized markets and the existence of rival, though overlapping, fields of professionalism, the institutionalized world of bookmen and committees in which women were marginal, and the world of sales and publicity in which they were central. It was an attempt to establish a hierarchy, which enabled various interests within the literary world to control by interpretation and guidance the threatening expansion of the book market. It also offered a means to explain and control the centrality of women writers in this expanded market; much reference to heights of brow is gendered, though not consistently. The terms of this *ad hoc* categorization were necessarily shifting, if not incoherent, and women writers were fully engaged in this process, both as objects of categorization, associated especially with lowbrow and middlebrow, and as exponents, responding to criticisms of the damaging effects of the influx of women into writing by engaging themselves in the restoration of order through hierarchies. One factor which cannot, however, be clearly aligned with heights of brow is education. None of the six innovative writers discussed in Chapter 8 were university-educated. On the other hand Richmal Crompton, creator of the *William* books, began as a classics scholar; other popular writers with good degrees were Dorothy Sayers, and Alison Uttley of the *Little Grey Rabbit* books.

The concepts of highbrow and lowbrow were well established by the 1890s, as the perceived, and often gendered, gulf between the elite and popular audiences for books became a matter for wide discussion. By the First World War the idea of the highbrow had coalesced with modernism. The modernist writers perceived themselves as an avant-garde, engaged in experiments communicable to an elite audience only, and alienated from, and rebelling against, the established culture. This necessitated the creation of the additional category of middlebrow to distinguish the outworn products of this established literary culture from the lowbrow output of mass culture, and to define them as the expression of the bourgeois society within which the avant-garde existed, and against which they were rebelling. By the 1920s the use of the three terms to categorize writings had become commonplace, and the perception of places in the pecking order more acute. Rose Macaulay's 1920 novel, *Potterism*, which presented England as a family

47

presided over by a patriarch who was a magnate of the popular press and a matriarch who was a romantic novelist in the style of Dell, offered a familiar outline of the lowbrow. Macaulay, who dedicated the novel 'to the unsentimental precisians in thought, who have, on this confused, inaccurate and emotional planet, no fit habitation', was clearly speaking from a highbrow position, but others might have denied her right to that location. Woolf in 1928 commented that Macaulay had 'lived with the riffraff of South Kensington culture for 15 years, become a successful lady novelist, and is rather jealous, spiteful and uneasy about Bloomsbury' (*Letters*, III, p. 501). Woolf's reference to rival geographical locations within the metropolis suggests that increasingly the highbrow was located in, and synonymous with, Bloomsbury and the British version of modernism which Bloomsbury represented.

In invoking South Kensington and the damning term 'lady novelist', Woolf is consigning Macaulay to the ranks of the middlebrow, the most contested of the three terms. Robert Graves and Alan Hodge, in their influential cultural history of the interwar period, *The Long Weekend* (1940), defined the 'mezzo-brow' as somebody who sought guidance in their reading by subscribing to the Book of the Month.[40] The big subscription libraries, with their largely middle-class female clientele seeking advice from genteel assistants, were perceived as a major location of the middlebrow, and one which made clear the translation of class terms into literary categories. As the battle developed, those accused of being middlebrow became defensive. In 1932 the editor of *Good Housekeeping*, Alice Head, provided an outline of the middlebrow reader in positive terms. Head, who had been rushed from a secretarial typewriter at *Country Life* to take over as editor of its stable-mate, *Women at Home*, before presiding over the successful launch of *Good Housekeeping*, had considerable experience in targeting audiences. In her preface to the anthology, *Twelve Best Stories from Good Housekeeping*, she described the book's prospective audience in terms which clearly outlined a middlebrow reader. These readers lived in country houses, comfortable suburban homes, farms in the colonies; they liked stories which were beautifully written, but were not (like highbrow writing) obscure, and they did not insist (like lowbrows) on love interests and happy endings.[41] (The contributors to the volume included Cooper, Delafield and Henry Handel Richardson, all exponents of that genre of interwar fiction which emphasized the factual in its exploration of social life, and used the formulae of the Victorian and Edwardian novel to do so.)

The most extensive explanation of categorization by brow was provided by Q.D. Leavis in her influential study *Fiction and the Reading Public* (1932). In Leavis's analysis of the contemporary literary market, the middlebrow reader is the person whose reading habits are determined by reference to the whole intermediary apparatus of reviews, Books of the Month, prizes and subscription libraries. The highbrow reader can rely upon reviews in a distinctive and smaller selection of their own group journals (Leonard Woolf is cited as a typical highbrow reviewer as Arnold Bennett is a middlebrow one), and the lowbrow reader is out of reach of any such apparatus, and borrows from the twopenny libraries. Middlebrow writers, those who are promoted by the middlebrow apparatus, perform a necessary service in transmitting to a wider public 'ideas and modes of feeling which were commonplace among the intelligentsia before the war', but their works display 'a suggestive insensitiveness to the life round them, a lack of discrimination and the functioning of a second-rate mind', distinguishing them both from the precision of the genuine highbrow and from the 'magnificent vitality' of the under-examined, bestselling, lowbrow novelists, whose strength lies in their ability, in a degenerated culture, 'to excite in the ordinary person an emotional activity for which there is no scope in his life'.[42] Leavis's analysis is supported by an elegiac history of the growth and disintegration of the unified reading public, and challenges both the established literary culture and Bloomsbury.

Woolf's essay, 'Middlebrow', written in the same year in response to a radio talk attacking highbrows by the middlebrow novelist, J.B. Priestley, offers a similar definition of the middlebrow writer as engaged in, and promoted by, the intermediary apparatus of bourgeois literary culture, the committees, prizes, reviews, and she adds the newly established BBC ('the Betwixt and Between Company') to the list. For Woolf, however, these writers are not, as for Leavis, fulfilling an inevitable role in a fragmented culture, but are unnecessary intrusions in the relations between writers and readers. The essay proclaims Woolf's willingness to accept the title of highbrow regularly bestowed on her; she bypasses modernism's revolutionary stance by claiming descent in a continuous tradition from the great writers of previous centuries. A lowbrow is defined as a person without education or cultural pretensions 'who rides his body in pursuit of a living at a gallop across life'.[43] Lowbrows are honoured precisely for their complete uninvolvement in literary matters, rather as Woolf, in the preface to *Life as We have Known It*, admires the working-class autobiographies but denies that they bear any relation to literature. (In 1924, however, she had recognized a type of the lowbrow writer in Berta Ruck, whose books, written to fund her sons' education, were 'harmless' in comparison with middlebrow novels like those of Hugh Walpole (*Letters*, III, p. 133).) Between highbrows and lowbrows there could be good relations, but these are confused by the attempts of the middlebrows to promote culture. Woolf is constructing a kind of medieval pastoral in which lowbrows engage in vital activities, while a small cloistered elite watch and record these, and the middlemen of the whole cultural enterprise of promoting reading within a wider public are excluded.

Historically it was the middlebrows who lost out. The works of Woolf are still in print; so are those of Christie, Crompton, Georgette Heyer, but the middlebrows have not survived so well. John Carey has recently described early-twentieth-century attempts to bridge the gulf between an increasingly inaccessible highbrow writing and the expanding popular audience, taking Bennett as the main hero of this attempt.[44] Many of the women writers who wrote documentarist fiction in the interwar period admired Woolf but took Bennett as a model; like him they sought to bridge the gulf. In the following discussion their work, described in Chapter 5, represents the middlebrow. The work of more formally innovative writers is described in Chapter 3, and three major genres of popular writing in Chapter 6. Chapter 4 discusses poetry, and Chapter 7 non-fiction. It seemed important to include genres into which women had moved in numbers for the first time, so autobiography and academic writing are included, but biography, in which there were no innovations by women comparable to those of Gaskell's *Life of Charlotte Brontë* (1857), is not. Similarly, although there was a surge in polemical dramatic writing by women during the suffrage period, discussed in Chapter 5, that energy was not sustained by the handful of dramas by women which were successful later. Chapter 8 looks in more detail at six writers whose work was exceptionally important and diverse.

NOTES

Place of publication is London, unless otherwise stated.

1. See Elaine Showalter, *Sexual Anarchy: Gender and Culture at the Fin de Siècle* (Bloomsbury, 1991), pp. 59–76.
2. *The Young Rebecca: Writings of Rebecca West 1911–17*, ed. Jane Marcus (Macmillan/Virago, 1982), p. 71.
3. Sandra Gilbert and Susan Gubar, *No Man's Land: The Place of the Woman Writer in the Twentieth Century*, 3 vols (New Haven: Yale University Press, 1987–94).
4. Valentine Cunningham, *British Writers of the Thirties* (Oxford: Oxford University Press, 1988); Alison Light, *Forever England: Femininity, Literature and Conservatism Between the Wars* (Routledge, 1991).
5. See Peter Brooker and Peter Widdowson, 'A Literature for England', in Robert Colls and Philip Dodd, eds, *Englishness: Politics and Culture 1880–1920* (Croom Helm, 1986), pp. 116–63; Brian Doyle, *England and Englishness* (Routledge, 1983).

6. See Gaye Tuchman with Nina Fortin, *Edging Women Out: Victorian Novelists, Publishers and Social Change* (New Haven: Yale University Press, 1989); Claud Cockburn, *Bestseller: The Books that Everyone Read 1900–39* (Sidgwick and Jackson, 1972); Michael Joseph, *The Commercial Side of Literature* (Hutchinson, 1925).

7. See Peter Keating, *The Haunted Study: A Social History of the English Novel 1875–1914* (Secker and Warburg, 1989), pp. 369–445.

8. See R.J.L. Kingsford, *The Publishers Association 1896–1946* (Cambridge: Cambridge University Press, 1970); N.N. Feltes, *Literary Capital and the Late Victorian Novel* (Madison: University of Wisconsin Press, 1992).

9. Quoted in Constance Babington Smith, *Rose Macaulay* (Collins, 1972), p. 56.

10. See Kingsford, *The Publishers Association*, pp. 128–44.

11. See Joseph McAleer, *Popular Reading and Publishing in Britain 1914–50* (Oxford: Clarendon Press, 1992), pp. 100–32.

12. See W.E. Williams, *Allen Lane: A Personal Portrait* (Bodley Head, 1973).

13. See Thomas Kelly, *Books for the People: An Illustrated History of the British Public Library* (Deutsch, 1977).

14. See Arthur Waugh, *A Hundred Years of Publishing* (Chapman and Hall, 1930); Nicola Beaumann, *A Very Great Profession: The Woman's Novel 1914–39* (Virago, 1983).

15. See A.R. Jephcott, *Girls Growing Up* (Faber and Faber, 1942), pp. 98–111.

16. See Feltes, *Literary Capital and the Late Victorian Novel*, ch. 2.

17. See Samuel Hynes, *Edwardian Occasions* (Routledge and Kegan Paul, 1972), pp. 196–202.

18. See Michael Howard, *Jonathan Cape Publisher* (Cape, 1971), pp. 98–102.

19. See *The Life of Florence Barclay: A Study in Personality by One of her Daughters* (Putnam, 1921).

20. See Leonard Woolf, *Downhill All the Way: An Autobiography of the Years 1919–1939* (Hogarth Press, 1967), pp. 143–4.

21. Alan J. Lee, *The Origins of the Popular Press 1855–1914* (Croom Helm, 1976), p. 116.

22. Berta Ruck, *A Storyteller Tells the Truth: Reminiscences and Notes* (Hutchinson, 1935), p. 283.

23. Arnold Bennett, *The Truth About an Author* (Constable, 1903), pp. 25–6.

24. Arnold Bennett, *Journalism for Women: A Practical Guide* (Bodley Head, 1898), p. 61.

25. See Gillian Hanscombe and Virginia Smyers, *Writing for their Lives: The Modernist Women 1910–40* (Women's Press, 1987); Rebecca West, 'The "Freewoman"', *Time and Tide*, 16 July 1926, reprinted in Bonnie K. Scott, ed., *The Gender of Modernism: A Critical Anthology* (Bloomington: Indiana University Press, 1990), pp. 573–7.

26. See Dale Spender, ed., *Time and Tide Wait for No Man* (Pandora, 1984).

27. See Cynthia White, *Women's Magazines 1693–1968* (Michael Joseph, 1971); Billie Melman, *Women and the Popular Imagination in the 1920s: Flappers and Nymphs* (Macmillan, 1988); McAleer, *Popular Reading and Publishing*.

28. Spender, *Time and Tide Wait for No Man*, p. 59.

29. Vera Brittain, *Testament of Experience* (Gollancz, 1957), p. 53.

30. *Testament of Experience*, p. 64.

31. Bryher, *The Heart to Artemis: A Writer's Memoirs* (Collins, 1963), pp. 158, 208, 248. See also Hanscombe and Smyers, *Writing for their Lives*.

32. See S.P. Rosenbaum, *Edwardian Bloomsbury: The Early Literary History of the Bloomsbury Group* (Macmillan, 1994), pp. 339–90.
33. Winifred Holtby, *Virginia Woolf* (Wishart, 1932), p. 28.
34. Vera Brittain, *Testament of Youth* (Virago, 1978), p. 548.
35. Agatha Christie, *An Autobiography* (Collins, 1977), p. 446.
36. Elizabeth Bowen, *English Novelists* (Collins, 1942), pp. 21, 36.
37. Rosamond Lehmann, *The Swan in the Evening* (Collins, 1967), p. 69.
38. *The Times*, 25 March 1941, p. 5.
39. *The Diaries of Sylvia Townsend Warner*, ed. Claire Harman (Virago, 1995), p. 110.
40. Robert Graves and Alan Hodge, *The Long Weekend: A Social History of Great Britain 1918–1939* (Cardinal, 1991), p. 52.
41. *Twelve Best Stories from Good Housekeeping*, ed. Alice Head (Nicholson and Watson, 1932), pp. 7–9.
42. Q.D. Leavis, *Fiction and the Reading Public* (Chatto and Windus, 1939), pp. 71–6, 62–4.
43. Virginia Woolf, 'Middlebrow', in *The Death of the Moth and Other Essays* (Hogarth Press, 1942), pp. 113–19.
44. John Carey, *The Intellectuals and the Masses: Pride and Prejudice Among the Literary Intelligentsia 1880–1939* (Faber and Faber, 1992).

CHAPTER THREE

The Forms of Women's Experience

THE EDWARDIAN TRANSITION

In 1900 Olive Schreiner was still working on *From Man to Man*, the novel she had begun in the Kimberley diamond-fields in the 1870s. This novel was Schreiner's equivalent of Wordsworth's *Prelude*; she continued to revise it throughout her life, and it was published posthumously and unfinished in 1926. *From Man to Man* epitomizes the central quest of women writers in the early twentieth century, the search for new forms in the novel which would express women's experience more authentically than the established literary forms. In the 1890s Schreiner's only publications had been some short dream-pieces and allegories, and her novel begins with a prelude in similar style in which a female child, in whom the creative impulse is still strong and uninhibited, imagines a world of ideal relations between human and animal. The story which follows is based on a familiar Victorian opposition between two sisters who become respectively wife and fallen woman, and on the recognition by Rebekah, the wife, of the interdependence and likeness of their lives. Schreiner continually turns from the narrative to the reveries of Rebekah, once the child of the prelude. The long central chapter, 'Raindrops in the Avenue', is Rebekah's meditation on evolution, civilization and the history of women on a rainy evening as she sits pregnant and sewing. The reverie is punctuated by references to the context of domestic tasks from which Rebekah's thoughts emerge, and, when she wonders about 'the possible Shakespeares we might have had, who passed their life from youth upward brewing currant wine and making pastries for fat country squires to eat',[1] we have an early appearance of the figure of the suppressed woman artist who haunts early-twentieth-century writing, and whom Woolf was to formulate as Judith Shakespeare in *A Room of*

53

One's Own. The narrative focuses on Rebekah's inner life, in a long un-delivered letter she writes to her husband, and in the dreams she narrates to her children in which she recovers the creative energy of her own childhood.

From Man to Man is characteristic of much late-nineteenth-century women's writing which seeks new ways of talking about women's experi-ence outside the fiction of domestic realism in which they had been so successful. In the 1890s a number of writers associated with the concept of the New Woman, including George Egerton, Sarah Grand and Mona Caird, experimented with a range of literary forms, reverie, dream and allegory, polemic and confessional writing, short stories. Schreiner's novel uses all these forms; her central theme, and that of the other New Woman writers, was the gulf women experienced between their social personae and their inner selves, and their writing is devoted to finding means to express this gulf. The 1890s were a period of gender role-playing and ambivalence, in which ideas about the fluidity of identity, later associated with modern-ism, emerged in explorations of social life as performance, and of gender construction.[2] In *From Man to Man* there is a further emphasis on the con-text of women's writing, on how it emerges in the interstices of house-keeping and child-care, or, as in the Judith Shakespeare figure, may fail to emerge at all. Schreiner's own long, unsatisfied struggle with her novel was symptomatic of the problems many women writers experienced in finding appropriate literary forms.

By 1900 the preoccupations of the New Women writers were inform-ing writing not associated with the avant-garde and the little magazines. Elizabeth von Arnim's very popular *Elizabeth and her German Garden* (1898), much reprinted in the Edwardian period, also takes as its central focus the gulf between social persona and inner self. The work is a protracted reverie in which the narrator sits dreaming in her garden, ignoring her housekeeping and entertaining duties as a German gentlewoman. The garden represents an escape to a more natural self, a secret self which has eluded the demands of respectability. The book's uncontroversial success depended on its charm and on the popularity of gardening writing of all kinds, from the gardener Gertrude Jekyll's manuals to Frances Hodgson Burnett's children's classic, *The Secret Garden* (1911), but the book is about a woman refusing to enter the house and assume her expected role. Elizabeth's discovery, endorsed by her husband, that women are legally 'nobodies', is treated, in the spirit of New Woman writing, as liberating, opening up possibilities of exploring and redefining the self.[3]

The Edwardian period was dominated by male writers, and there was no distinct group of women associated with innovation in fiction as in the 1890s. There were, however, several writers, among them von Arnim, May Sinclair and Ada Leverson, who continued to explore the gulf between women's desires and their social roles. Jane Eldridge Miller has argued persuasively for the ways in which these writers anticipated the concerns of the women modernists, and has described how their writing emerged from the women's issues which occupied the political high ground at this period.[4] The first pages of von Arnim's *The Pastor's Wife* (1914), which Miller suggests as a major example for her argument, introduce us to the potential for self-discovery of the heroine, Ingeborg, as she is briefly alone in London, relishing the freedom and anonymity of the London streets, and the escape from her customary identity they offer. Ingeborg, however, is between roles; her brief freedom transfers her from being bishop's daughter to pastor's wife, and the rest of the novel returns her to a drawing-room comedy in which she is required to play the role assigned as child-bride to an East Prussian pastor. The narrative develops in a series of comic dialogues in which Ingeborg struggles incompetently and reluctantly with her roles. 'I'm a wife, I'm a mother. I'm everything really now except a mother-in-law and a grandmother. That's all there is still left to be.'[5] Rebelling against her 'wild career of unbridled motherhood' (ch. 22), she elopes to Italy with an artist, only to discover herself trapped in another stereotypical woman's role. The conclusion parodies two male masterpieces, Ibsen's *The Doll's House* and Fontane's *Effi Briest*; this Nora's escape does not succeed, this Effi finds her Prussian husband has barely noted her absence and left her farewell letter unread.

The major formal strategy of *The Pastor's Wife* is its division between Ingeborg's puzzled reveries and the comic dialogues in which she performs automatically in the roles allotted to her. This use of long stretches of dialogue largely unglossed by commentary is characteristic of the period. The established relations between dialogue and commentary in earlier fiction are breaking down; they no longer function in alternation as part of an integrated whole. Instead the dialogue appears in oppositional blocks to the reveries in which Ingeborg explores her identity, a separation indicative of her divided being. There is a similar approach in Ada Leverson's trilogy, *The Little Ottleys* (1908–17), the story of a disintegrating socialite marriage, in which the comic dialogues which occupy most of the trilogy are used to indicate the success with which the characters play roles and suppress their knowledge of the true state of their relationship. The problematization of dialogue in fiction at this period serves two major functions, to indicate the characters' engagement in unthinking performance of their social roles, and as part of the withdrawal from the authorial commentary of much Victorian fiction, now associated with an oppressive tradition and outworn authority. Later developments from this problematization included both the reduction of dialogue by Richardson and Woolf, and the purely dialogue novels of Ivy Compton-Burnett.

55

Edwardian novel which develops scenically through long stretches is May Sinclair's *The Creators* (1910), subtitled 'A Comedy', in central figure, Jane Holland, is a novelist of genius committed to psycnological realism, but in her personal life condemned to perform a series of banal roles. The social performance required of Jane exposes popular assumptions about women as artists; Jane's conventional in-laws assume that female creativity is incompatible with good health, and particularly with motherhood. Much of the novel's black comedy revolves around their attempts to confine the physically robust Jane to the role of invalid, and her own infection by their assumptions. These ideas influence Jane's male comrade in genius; the novel begins with a description of a Royal Academy portrait of Jane as a tragic muse, prophetic, brooding and sombre, and, though he criticizes the banality of the picture, he fails to perceive Jane as a sexual being until they have both married other people. *The Creators* is an ambitious novel, exploring both the need for fiction to develop new forms capable of expressing modern experience, and the relations of gender and creativity. At the end two friends muse on the future of Jane whose career, both as experimental artist and as married woman, remains uncertain and unassimilable to existing models.

THE MODERNIST PERIOD

During the war decade a number of writers who associated themselves with what became known as modernism were engaged in achieving its recognition as the dominant literary movement, in associating it with kindred movements in other art forms, and in disassociating it from other forms of writing, past and current. Modernists perceived themselves as responding to a crisis in literary forms, itself part of a wider social crisis of which the First World War was the most spectacular manifestation. Their work was marked by the use of particular formal practices, which included in fiction a movement away from the authority and coherence of narrative commentary to decentred narrative; a rejection of what D.H. Lawrence called 'the old stable ego'[6] for an emphasis on the fluidity and discontinuity of identity, often expressed through the 'stream of consciousness'; disruptions of chronology; and a vigorous engagement of the reader in the difficulties of interpretation. Modernists emphasized the significance of these practices as a break from existing tradition, and much later criticism has canonized their work as the only noteworthy literary achievement of the period.

56

The relation of women writers to modernism was quite exceptionally complicated. As the writers associated with modernism grouped themselves in the battle formation appropriate to their revolt against established tradition, the process of edging women out became apparent. A classic example of this is the evolution of Dora Marsden's *Freewoman* into Ezra Pound's *Egoist*, described in Chapter 2. Moreover many male modernists saw themselves as in revolt against a specifically feminized Victorian tradition of domestic realism.[7] For women, however, the revolt against existing literary convention emerged through the stimulus of the women's movement, and for women modernists the traditions against which they were rebelling were exemplified by the male Edwardian realists. Dorothy Richardson, in her preface to *Pilgrimage*, speaks of the need to find a female response to the realism practised by Arnold Bennett, and Bennett is also the principal example of an outmoded realism in Woolf's seminal declarations of modernism, 'Modern Fiction' (1919) and 'Mr Bennett and Mrs Brown' (1923). As modernism became more self-conscious and exclusive, however, the writers who distinguished themselves as modernist saw their literary activity as entirely distinct from that of other women writers; two sometimes antagonistic groups emerged from the intensive Edwardian engagement with women's issues: the modernists and those (to be discussed in Chapter 5) who foregrounded content rather than formal innovation. Moreover, women modernists augmented the emphasis on breaking with the past by their specific need to demonstrate that, after centuries of suppression, the woman artist was making a fresh start. Recent feminist criticism has worked to trace the links between gender discourse and modernism, and to expand the modernist canon for women, pointing to a range of writers whose innovative practice was grounded in their struggle to find new forms to express women's experience.[8]

The women writers who have always been indisputably identified as modernist are Richardson, Mansfield and Woolf. Sinclair is a transitional figure, a successful Edwardian novelist highly responsive to modernist developments. Between *The Creators* and her most important postwar novel, *Mary Olivier* (1919), she was active in the suffrage movement, and developed a strong interest in psychoanalysis, helping to found the London Medico-Psychological Clinic. Her later work exemplifies the influence of both these movements on developing ideas about the presentation of identity in fiction. Sinclair became an influential reviewer on the developing modernist scene; in a 1917 review in *The Egoist* she adopted the term 'stream of consciousness' from the psychologist William James to describe the method of the first three volumes of Richardson's *Pilgrimage*. For Sinclair Richardson had solved many of the problems with which she herself had been struggling, and had developed a method which enabled

57

her to present women's experience in a fully modern and authentic manner. The novel's method of total immersion in the consciousness of the central figure enables Richardson above all to abolish 'the wise, all-knowing author', one feature by which the inauthenticity of previous fiction was identified.[9] *Mary Olivier* is Sinclair's own response to her reading of Richardson, and of Joyce's *Portrait of the Artist as a Young Man*, serialized in the *Egoist* in 1916. *The Creators* had eliminated the author as far as possible by its extensive reliance on dialogue. *Mary Olivier* moves from dialogue to reverie, eliminating the author completely, and immersing the reader in the consciousness of Mary as she develops from young child to middle-aged woman.

The objective of *Mary Olivier* is to remove from the heroine all external sources of support, such as family members (removed by drink and heart disease), or prospective suitors (removed by family opposition or bad timing), and leave the heroine with nothing but her inner life as a source of identity. The plot is a reverse of the kind of Victorian plot where, as in *Bleak House* or *Villette*, the initially bereft heroine accumulates personal relations and enhanced status as she proceeds through the story. In Sinclair's critical study *The Three Brontës* (1912), Emily Brontë emerges as 'the supreme instance of the self-sufficing soul, independent and regardless of material event'.[10] The story, which bereaves Mary Olivier of all external sources of happiness and leaves her entirely dependent on her inner life, presents a journey modelled on Emily Brontë's. It also announces clearly that these inner resources are the central study of the modern novel.

Sinclair's especial concern is to find ways of representing two traditionally neglected areas, Mary's developing awareness of her sexuality, and her intellectual life. Music is an important metaphor for her half-realized sexual feelings. At one point she tries to play Chopin's Sonata Apassionata soundlessly. 'Her fingers crept along the keyboard; they flickered over the notes of the Sonata Apassionata: a ghostly, furtive playing, without pressure, without sound. And she was ashamed as if the piano was tempting her to some cruel, abominable sin.'[11] Sinclair's treatment of Mary's sexuality is informed by her study of psychoanalysis, but also by the hystericization of women popularized by such study. For Mary's relatives, as for the in-laws in *The Creators*, artistic creativity in a woman is associated with morbidity, and especially with morbid sexuality. Mary dreads the fate of her Aunt Charlotte, a woman obsessed with the matrimonial intentions of every man she meets. Charlotte is the victim of her society's expectations, and in the choice of her name Sinclair is commenting bitterly on the illegitimate association of sexual obsession and artistic expression. *The Three Brontës* attacks biographers' prurient fascination with Charlotte Brontë as a frustrated spinster.

Much of the novel is concerned with Mary's self-education, and the development of her intellectual beliefs through her reading of Spinoza, Kant, Spencer, Haeckel. Like Schreiner in *From Man to Man*, Sinclair continually reminds us of the domestic context of her heroine's intellectual life; Mary's reading is a matter of chance borrowings and continual interruptions. This is partly a criticism of the way women of the period were likely to acquire learning, but Sinclair also wishes to remind us how ideas exist in a whole context of feeling and mundane activity by which they are shaped. While the disquisitions in *From Man to Man* are polemic punctuated by reminders of the domestic context, Mary Olivier's intellectual musings are more thoroughly integrated with the general flux of Mary's impressions.

By the time *Mary Olivier* was published, four novels by Dorothy Richardson had appeared. Richardson herself disliked Sinclair's phrase 'stream of consciousness', and rejected all attempts to categorize her search for a new literary form which would authentically register women's experience. *Pilgrimage* is difficult to classify even in terms of its published status; it is a series of thirteen novels, or a thirteen-volume novel. The first eleven novels, beginning with *Pointed Roofs*, appeared under their separate titles between 1915 and 1935. The last two appeared only in the collected volumes of *Pilgrimage*, respectively in 1938 and, posthumously, in 1967. *Pilgrimage* is a prolonged and exclusive immersion in the consciousness of Miriam, who is a teacher and governess in the first three volumes, and from volume four, less conventionally, a dental receptionist in London in the 1890s. It was the work which most decisively proclaimed women's inner life to be the new subject of fiction. Mansfield and Woolf were guarded in their responses, discussed below, but others recorded the revolutionary impact of the first volumes; Bryher speaks of Richardson as 'fighting . . . for the elementary rights of an inarticulate body of women' and as 'the Baedeker of all our early experiences'.[12]

Richardson's narrative was intended to record more extensively than any previous novel the context of sensation, impression and reverie in which the protagonist exists. Any reduction of information about the impressions flooding Miriam's consciousness would run the danger of a return to the traditional methods of categorizing women's experience. For Richardson her method was distinctive to female experience. In her foreword to the collected *Pilgrimage* (1938) she admits only limited influence by Henry James's narrative innovations with point of view. Proust and Joyce are praised for their break with tradition in their parallel experiments with stream of consciousness, but the emphasis throughout *Pilgrimage* is on the inadequacy of even the greatest male writing to represent women. A visit to a production of *The Merchant of Venice*, magnificently dominated by

Henry Irving, leads Miriam to the realization that Shakespeare's plays 'show women as men see them'.[13] A reading of *Anna Karenina* disillusions her about the great nineteenth-century realist tradition. Much of the external life of the novels is concerned with Miriam's arguments with a male novelist, Hypo Wilson, based on H.G. Wells. The progressive Hypo is eager to find a role for women writers, urging Miriam to fill in the interstices of existing literature, by 'annotating the male novelists, filling out the vast oblivions in them' (*Dawn's Left Hand*, ch. 9). Hypo is intellectually convinced of the distinctiveness of women's experience and the need to find new forms to record it, but his exhortations to Miriam inevitably propose a gendered hierarchy. Reading *Anna Karenina* with her Russian lover, Michael Shatov, she discovers the difference of men as readers. For Shatov, for whom reading is a process of analysis and classification, Tolstoy's Anna is 'a most masterly study of a certain kind of woman' (*Deadlock*, ch. 2). For Miriam, for whom reading is about immersion and understanding, the reading reveals the limitations of both Shatov and Tolstoy. Reading to a woman friend she reflects that men read 'with voices that were a commentary on the text . . . as if they were the authors of the text . . . they were like showmen' (*The Tunnel*, ch. 30).

Richardson's own writing abolishes the authorial commentary which is one pretext for this male appropriation of experience. Late in the sequence Miriam muses 'being versus becoming. Becoming versus being. Look after the being and the becoming will take care of itself' (*Clear Horizon*, ch. 6). She sees the traditional novel as planned around male strategies of becoming and dominance. 'Bang, Bang, Bang, on they go, these men's books, like an LCC tram, yet unable to make you forget them, the authors, for a minute' (*Dawn's Left Hand*, ch. 9). The title *Pilgrimage* suggests a quest, a becoming, but the novels move away from this, recording a delighted immersion in experience for its own sake, which is seen as distinctively female. They appeared separately, but their status as individual works, striving to conclusion, is undermined by the absence of many of the distinguishing marks of novels. There is no preliminary scene-setting, and the last pages are entirely inconclusive, and could often not even be described as marking the end of an episode. The story between is of the responses of Miriam, who herself rejects the male model of purposeful career-making urged on her by Hypo in favour of immersion in the flow of experience. For the planned dominant authorial persona Richardson substitutes the female consciousness of Miriam, who is, as Stephen Heath points out, a myriad I ams.[14]

The novels/volumes do have some distinctive story characteristics. The first three conduct Miriam through the familiar round of jobs available to genteel Victorian women, teaching in Germany and England, and

60

governessing. The fourth and longest, *The Tunnel*, delivers Miriam to her new white-collar job, and to the new experiences of living alone in London. The sixth, *Deadlock*, revolves around her translation work; the tenth, *Dawn's Left Hand*, centres on Miriam's affair with Hypo. Their separateness, however, is subordinated to their place in the whole, and to the expectation that a sympathetic reader will be sufficiently immersed to pick up distant references. Musical performance, as in Sinclair, is used as a metaphor for authenticity of feeling. Near the end of *Interim* Miriam plays Chopin for herself alone at night; the passage picks up a scene early in *The Tunnel* where Alma Wilson, Hypo's wife, plays Chopin in company, and confidently expects the sympathetic reader to place the reference, and to recall Miriam's dislike in *Pointed Roofs* for the way girls are taught to present themselves as performers in public.

Richardson's distinctions between male becoming and female being were further illuminated in her film criticism; she was the woman writer most enthusiastic about the new art. Between 1927 and 1933 she wrote a regular column in the film monthly *Close Up*, under the title 'Continuous Performance'. Cinema was for Richardson an opportunity to escape from the old modes of role-playing and male dominance of discourse represented by the theatre, the possibility of another kind of perception of the world. Her columns have two major themes, both relating to the idea that cinema is an art of being as opposed to the becoming of the theatre. The earlier columns are a celebration of the new modes of perception encouraged by the cinema. In her foreword to *Pilgrimage* she preferred the term 'slow motion photography' to 'stream of consciousness' to describe her method, and one column subtitled 'Slow Motion' praises the intensification of perception of movement and being which cinema audiences have come to accept through the technique.[15] Later columns are devoted to the implications of the coming of the talkies, for Richardson specifically gendered. Silence, the absence of dialogue constructed around male ideas of women, had allowed woman on the screen 'to shine from its surface just as she was' (4 (March 1928), pp. 51–6). One column, 'The Film Gone Male', argues that with the coming of dialogue film has moved to a state of purposeful becoming, while in silent cinema the reliance on suggestion, on 'the changeless being at the heart of all becoming', had allowed women's experience to emerge into the light (9 (March 1932), pp. 36–8). In 'Dialogue in Dixie', Richardson, reviewing the film *Hearts of Dixie*, describes the similar restrictions placed on the representation of black experience; silent, the black performers communicate directly with the audience, only to lose that ability when speaking the dialogue written for them by white screenwriters. The result is 'pure film alternating with the emergence of one after another of the persons of the drama into annihilating speech' (6 (September 1929), pp. 211–18). Again, in 'Pictures and Films', she complains of the restrictions imposed by dialogue on the imaginations of the audience, the loss of 'unlimited material upon which the imagination of the onlooker could get to work unhampered by the pressure of a controlling mind that is not his own mind' (5 (January 1929), pp. 51–7). Silent cinema had offered subordinated groups such as women and blacks and, indeed, audiences, the opportunity to participate in the representation of their own experiences. Spoken discourse, the medium of the dominant white male group, had entered the medium and destroyed that brief possibility.

Richardson's own continuous performance in fiction worked in parallel with the silent cinema both in the celebration of slow motion as a method and in her descriptions of how dialogue estranges and controls. The famous description in *The Tunnel* of Miriam's first entrance into the lodging-house room she will occupy for the next ten volumes is exemplary of Richardson's slow motion technique, prolonging Miriam's instant perception of the drably furnished room in the late afternoon light over five pages, measuring minute shifts in her response, and celebrating the promise of freedom and space the room offers. The male Edwardian novelists, as Woolf complained in 'Mr Bennett and Mrs Brown', saturated their fictions in the details of material existence to establish the determination of character by environment. Richardson's saturation technique moves to liberate Miriam through the lingering emphasis on material detail, which serves primarily to establish the riches of Miriam's inner life as she assimilates bed, carpet and window into her experience. Such slow motion descriptions of material things, asserting their importance as vehicles for inner radiance, are Richardson's equivalent of Joyce's epiphany, the moment of revelation in the everyday. In *Pilgrimage* they also celebrate the new freedom of the woman working and living alone in London. Miriam's London is the London of the 1890s, the world in *fin de siècle* writing of Jack the Ripper, fog and the demimonde, but already the twentieth-century London of new possibilities. 'The doors and windows of her cool shaded room opened upon a life that spread out before her fanwise towards endless brilliant distances' (*The Tunnel*, ch. 27). Richardson establishes the new geography of London for the newly mobile woman worker, in which the streets, shops and skyline promise new freedoms, and buses and ABC tea-shops have an iconic beauty.

As in earlier women's novels dialogue is problematized. Like the coming of sound to film, the dialogue scenes represent the forces which attempt to control Miriam and assign her to accepted female roles. Miriam early realizes that the performance of dialogue in a hierarchical social context, where roles are clearly defined, privileges men. In *Pointed Roofs* she resents her father 'playing the role of the "English gentleman" ' (ch. 2), and is distressed at a friend's praise of her own abilities in playing a lady; 'you can act so splendidly . . . if I were clever like you I should do it all the time, be simply always gushing and charming' (ch. 12). The theatre becomes a representation of the way that in scenes of spoken discourse men will always dominate, and women play roles written by men. Hypo, with his programme of becoming, will always dominate their discussions. Miriam's relations with Shatov are described through their gendered modes of reading, through Miriam's translation work, and translation as a metaphor for understanding the experiences of others.

The existence of other subordinated groups, however, is only dimly registered in *Pilgrimage*. Outside Miriam's room, which represents personal space and privacy, is the rest of the house, mystified in the figure of the landlady, who evokes 'the large dusty house, the many downstairs rooms, the mysterious dark-roomed vault of the basement, all upright in her upright form; hurried evening cleansings, swift strippings of grey-sheeted beds, the strange unfailing water-system, gurgling cisterns, gushing taps and lavatory flushes, the wonder of gaslight and bedroom candles, the daily meals magically appearing and disappearing' (*Interim*, ch. 9). When Miriam walks around London she is conscious of the presence of old flower-sellers and beggars, 'the last hidden truth of London, spoiling the night' (*Revolving Lights*, ch. 1). These landladies and beggars haunt other modernist novels, figures of mystery and magic excluded from realized experience. The most telling accusation brought against modernists by the documentarist novelists of the 1930s such as Storm Jameson was their exclusion of vast areas of experience. As Richardson evolves a vocabulary for talking about the self's minutest experiences, she also deliberately forgoes the vocabulary for talking about other groups. As the Baedeker of her generation, Richardson was immensely influential in providing a guide to the new territory of women's experience opened up by new working conditions, and in exploring new ways of presenting women's subjectivity, but the construction of that subjectivity depended on the presentation of others as mysterious.

The year *The Tunnel* was published, 1919, was an important year in the development of women's modernism; it also saw the publication of *Mary Olivier*, of Mansfield's short story 'Je Ne Parle Pas Français', and of Woolf's modernist manifesto 'Modern Fiction', her short story 'Kew Gardens', and her second novel *Night and Day*. Both Mansfield and Woolf discussed *The Tunnel* in reviews which suggested Richardson's importance for their own perceptions of themselves as modernist women writers. Mansfield, the more critical, argued that Richardson's distinctive method of composition by 'bits, fragments, flashing glimpses, half scenes and whole scenes, all of them quite distinct and separate, and all of them of equal importance' was fatally lacking in form and selectivity.[16] Richardson's 'passion for registering everything that happens in the clear shadowless country of her mind' was matched two months later by Sinclair; in a review of *Mary Olivier*, Mansfield complained that fiction was drifting too far towards autobiography, and to a total immersion in detail which rejected order and selection. 'Is it not the great abiding satisfaction of a work of art that the writer was master of the situation when he wrote it?'[17] Mansfield's use of 'he', commonplace at the time, nonetheless reveals a fear that women are allowing themselves to claim, and be confined to, a distinctive area of writing based on rambling personal reminiscence, and devoid of the attributes of selection, order and emphasis which characterize great art; that they are accepting, that is, the area of the amateur rather than the professional. Richardson's very specific rejection of order and selectivity as characteristic of the male emphasis on becoming is judged as failing by the standards of high art.

Woolf was altogether more responsive to the suggestiveness of Richardson's methods in *The Tunnel*, but she also questioned the absence of selection and order in 'the flying helter-skelter' of the composition; 'sensations, impressions, ideas and emotions glance off her, unrelated and unquestioned, without shedding quite as much light as we had hoped into the hidden depths'.[18] In 'Modern Fiction', later in the year, she described the project of modernist fiction in terms very close to those she used for Richardson's methods, speaking of the search for forms to catch 'the myriad impressions – trivial, fantastic, evanescent, or engraved with the sharpness of steel' of 'an ordinary mind on an ordinary day'.[19] The essay's antagonist is the same as Richardson's, Edwardian male realism with its order and materiality. Woolf later used her 1923 review of Richardson's eighth volume, *Revolving Lights*, to explore her concept of the 'woman's sentence', suggesting that Richardson had developed a distinctive syntax for her concern 'with states of being and not with states of doing'.[20] The review became the basis for her longer discussion of the woman's sentence in *A Room of One's Own* (1929).

The work of both Mansfield and Woolf will be more fully described in Chapter 8. This chapter will discuss their writing around 1919, when they sought, in competitive emulation, more authentic forms of expression for women's experience, and focused this search especially on the short story. The short story, a form much explored by the New Women writers of the 1890s, had become central to modernist innovation, with Chekhov's stories, which were appearing in a thirteen-volume translation by Constance Garnett between 1916 and 1922, as the major model. The short story experiments of Mansfield and Woolf are suggestive of the way women writers related to modernism, claiming centrally innovative forms, and developing their possibilities for the distinctive representation of women's experience and consciousness. In a 1920 review of Richardson's fifth volume, *Interim*, Mansfield referred to *Pilgrimage* as 'a nest of short stories',[21] a comment which revealed the common ground between its vast sprawl and the genre in which Mansfield worked. Richardson rejected the traditional plot of incident in favour of a sequence of epiphanies, and the 'old stable ego' for a minute attention to the shifting inner life of her protagonist. The short story offered similar possibilities for escaping from 'the wise all-knowing author' towards a shifting, fragmenting, discontinuous consciousness. Short stories rejected the grand plan, the traditional emphases, of the novel, but, unlike Richardson, they discovered new forms of selection and emphasis. In 'Modern Fiction' Woolf praised the way in which Chekhov recomposed his short stories around new principles of significance and order:

> the emphasis is laid upon such unexpected places that at first it seems as if there were no emphasis at all; and then, as the eyes accustom themselves to twilight and discern the shapes of things in a room we see how complete the story is, how profound, and how truly in obedience to his vision Chekhov has chosen this, that, and the other, and placed them together to compose something new. (p. 193)

Between 1917 and 1920 Woolf and Mansfield were exploring the possibilities of the short story as developed by Chekhov for their own ambitions in women's writing, and reinforcing each other's enthusiasm. The key texts here are Mansfield's 'Prelude', developed from a longer story, 'The Aloe', and published by the Hogarth Press in 1918, and Woolf's 'The Mark on the Wall' (1917), the first publication of the Hogarth Press, and 'Kew Gardens', which Mansfield read in manuscript, and was excited by, in 1917.

In 'Prelude' Mansfield moved from her earlier short fiction of incident to a new concept of the short story, centred on an idea of the fusion of feeling and image which she derived from her admiration for the Symbolists. She wrote in 1917:

> when I write about ducks I swear that I am a white duck with a round eye, floating in a pond fringed with yellow blobs and taking an occasional dart at the other duck with the round eye, which floats upside-down underneath me. In fact, the whole process of becoming the duck (what Lawrence would perhaps call the 'consummation with the duck and the apple') is so thrilling that I can hardly breathe, only to think about it. For although that is as far as most people can get, it is really only the 'prelude'. There follows the moment when you are *more* duck, *more* apple or *more* Natasha than any of these objects could ever possibly be, and so you *create* them anew.[22]

This passage interprets Mansfield's criticism of Richardson's method of simple immersion in the objects of her contemplation; for Mansfield this immersion is only a prelude to the artistic recreation of these objects, which revolutionizes the relationship between them and the authorial persona. Mansfield also seeks, however, to distinguish her method from the male grand design, Lawrence's 'consummation'; (Lawrence's version of Mansfield's method was Gudrun and her miniature sculptures in *Women in Love*, 1920). What she has produced is a 'prelude' to the later possibilities of the short story.

The initial concept of 'Prelude' was as a novel envisaged in terms of shape and light; Mansfield compared it in one letter to a Paris barge:

> one of those boats was exactly what I want my novel to be – Not big, almost 'grotesque' in shape I mean perhaps *heavy* – with people rather dark and seen strangely as they move in the sharp light and shadow and I want bright shivering lights in it and the sound of water. (*Letters*, I, pp. 167–8)

Mansfield's determination to apply the lessons of the Symbolists carried her from novel through the longer form of 'The Aloe' (published post-humously in 1930) to the more concentrated 'Prelude'. The story is of the experiences of a New Zealand family's first day in a new house; the material omitted in the process was of the discursive, overtly social kind of her earlier collection of stories, *In a German Pension* (1911). The story's exploration of the experience of maternity, originally duplicated in the figure of Mrs Trout, is now concentrated in Linda and her response to the mysterious, relentless fecundity of the garden, and the central symbol of the aloe:

> Linda looked up at the fat swelling plant with its cruel leaves and fleshy stem. High above them, as though becalmed in the air, and yet holding so fast to the earth it grew from, it might have had claws instead of roots. The curving leaves seemed to be hiding something; the blind stem cut into the air as if no wind could ever shake it.[23]

The aloe is first perceived by Linda's daughter, Kezia, and it mediates between their responses to the complexities of life and being female, and also between Linda's conflicting maternal impulses; later when she sees the aloe bathed in moonlight she identifies exultantly with it.

Mansfield rejects Richardson's practice of a narrative centred in one consciousness, instead shifting between the distinctive modes through which the women characters plot their perceptions – Linda's hallucinatory intima-tions of maternity, the romantic fantasies of Linda's unmarried sister Beryl, the servant Alice's comparable reveries, Kezia's childish perspective – as each interprets the new landscape. Transitions between these perspectives are plotted through minute repetition of detail; in the duck-killing scene Kezia is distracted from her distress by the hired man's ear-rings, and this effects the transition to the kitchen scene and Alice's preoccupation with her dress. Thence we move via the dining-room discussion of drastic alterations to Beryl's dress, overheard by Alice, to the arrival at table of the duck, headless and dressed for dinner. The focus on details which effect the transition between scenes also conducts a grim subtextual discussion of the related situation of the different women, the preoccupation with dressing, with being appropriately prepared for their role in life, which links them to the duck. (Mansfield's exultant identification with her duck in her description of the story's composition here takes on a different significance.) This grimness remains, however, at the level of suggestion; the story resists closure throughout, and ends, significantly, not in the consciousness of one of the 'dressed' adults, Linda, Beryl or Alice, but with Kezia, whose creative impulses, like those of the child in the prelude to Schreiner's *From Man to Man*, are still powerful and uninhibited.

Mansfield's other major story of 1918 was 'Bliss', 'the famous flawless "Bliss" ' as her main heir in the short story, Elizabeth Bowen, called it, before going on to describe it as 'disagreeable'.[24] The 'flawlessness' of this story lay in its precise structuring around a false epiphany; its other major importance was its exploration of the specific problem of representing women's sexuality in fiction. The postwar decade saw an intensive public debate about women's sexuality, and the problem for innovative fiction, in this climate of a new public awareness and explicitness, was to find ways of representing women's sexual imaginings in an area of writing already staked out by two particular groups, the sexologists and the writers of romantic fiction. In 'Bliss' a young wife, Bertha, attempts to comprehend her sudden access of desire, locating it in household appearances, in her social role as wife and mother, and finally, and for the first time, in her husband and in a seductive woman guest. She exults in finding an appropriate symbol for herself in the flowering pear-tree in the garden, only to discover that the two human objects of her desire are secret lovers. Woolf in her 1931 lecture, 'Professions for Women', described the representation of women's sexuality as one of the two major problems confronting the contemporary woman writer; the other and related problem was obliterating the pervasive Victorian image of the Angel in the House. She imagines her woman writer in reverie over a deep lake; she 'had thought of something, something about the body, something about the passions, which it was unfitting for her as a woman to say'.[25] Woolf externalizes the problem here as one of conflict with conservative male notions of decorum, but in 'Bliss' the problem is located in Bertha's consciousness, in her inability to define to herself what is happening.

The term Bertha uses to define her access of desire defines her alienation from her body and inability to interpret her feelings, and also indicates the writer's need for a vocabulary to articulate the sexual feelings newly available for discussion. The failure of 'Bliss' lies in its conformity to the terms

67

of the contemporary debate about female sexuality. Mansfield's intention was to satirize the new expertise of the sexologists, but Bertha is too exemplary of her time. She is caught between the Victorian repression of passions and her naive attempts to appropriate the new wisdom to herself.[26] She is thirty, the age at which, Marie Stopes suggested the same year in her *Married Love*, women in British culture often came belatedly, and thus dangerously, to awareness of their sexuality. Despite its schematic over-representativeness, in defining the distance between a fully possessed sexuality and a woman divided from this possibility by old and new conformities, 'Bliss' was a very influential model for the representation of women's sexuality. Woolf disliked 'Bliss', but Clarissa in *Mrs Dalloway* (1925), reliving a moment of 'rapture' identified with Sally Seton, is a response to that model.

Woolf's admiration for Mansfield's innovations was strictly limited. In 1923 she wrote:

> while she possessed the most amazing *senses* of her generation so that she could actually reproduce this room for instance, with its fly, clock, dog, tortoise, if need be, to the life, she was as weak as water, as insipid, and a great deal more commonplace, when she had to use her mind. That is, she can't put thoughts, or feelings, or subtleties of any kind into her characters, without at once becoming, where she's serious, hard, and where she's sympathetic, sentimental. Her first story which we published, Prelude, was pure observation, and, therefore, exquisite. (*Letters*, III, p. 59)

Mansfield's choice of the short story form was, therefore, for Woolf, as for Lawrence, the inevitable choice of a talent which lacked the ability to plot larger structures. For Woolf the use of the short story lay in the freedom it offered for fictional experiment which could then be reapplied to the novel. In her early reviewing in the Edwardian period she had preferred to review bad biographies rather than bad novels, because non-fiction at least offered escape from fictional conventions and was thus more suggestive for her own fictional experiments. Her early stories include 'The Diary of Joan Martyn' (1906), the short story in the mode of historical research, and 'Memoirs of a Novelist' (1909), the short story as review. In her first major modernist short story, 'The Mark on the Wall', published with a story of Leonard Woolf's in *Two Stories* (1917), Woolf again explored the suggestiveness of other genres for fiction, breaking down the distinction between fictional and non-fictional prose. Her story models itself on the Victorian essay, her specific model her step-grandfather Thackeray's 1861 essay, 'On a Chalk-mark on the Door'. Both essays are reveries which take off from an unexplained mark, but Thackeray was concerned with the mark's provenance, pursuing a train of association within a world of exclusively social significances, using the mark to consider the variety of household tensions it might suggest. The movement of Woolf's reverie is determinedly inwards, rapidly leaving the question of the mark's provenance. She empties her immediate environment of social meanings to follow the imaginative associations, shifts of perspective and genre possibilities that the mark's shape and colour suggest, a historical fiction about a room where Shakespeare sits, a learned discourse on the prehistory of tumuli, a fantasy of an underwater excursion. The importance of this experiment lay in the way the freedom and irresolution of the form enabled Woolf to explore the possibilities of mixing genres to represent the inner life in fiction, and to declare her departure from the Victorian world saturated in social meaning. It also celebrated a distinctively feminine escape from the world of given meanings, the pretensions of order and knowledge; 'what are our learned men save the descendants of witches and hermits who crouched in caves and in woods brewing herbs, interrogating shrew-mice and writing down the language of the stars?'.[27]

'Kew Gardens' was an experiment in the representation of sensation closer to Mansfield's methods. Mansfield responded enthusiastically; 'your Flower Bed is *very* good. There's a still, quivering, changing light over it all and a sense of those couples dissolving in the bright air which fascinates me' (*Letters*, I, p. 327). In her late autobiographical 'A Sketch of the Past', Woolf talked of the difficulties of finding ways to represent the experience of the dynamism of life as she had felt it in childhood:

> one must get the feeling that made her press on, the little creature, driven on as she was by the growth of her legs and arms, driven without her being able to stop it, or to change it, driven as a plant is driven up out of the earth, up until the stalk grows, the leaf grows, buds and swells. That is what is indescribable, that is what makes all images too static, for no sooner has one said this was so, than it was past and altered.[28]

'Kew Gardens', exploring plants and humans as interchangeable parts in a dynamic pattern, is an attempt to catch that movement, the 'myriad impressions' which she was urging as the proper subject of fiction in 'Modern Fiction', published just before the story. The instability and absence of familiar reference which Woolf had explored in 'The Mark on the Wall' is pursued further, in the narrative's rapid unprepared moves between the perspectives of humans, insects and flowers. Conventional ideas of size and proportion disappear when the narrative is localized within the consciousness of a snail. Like Mansfield in 'Prelude', Woolf escapes from the central 'I', but goes much further in the destabilizing of narrative authority as the distinct identity of the human species dissolves; humans are observed, like the flowers, in terms of colour and shape, and their conversations rearrange themselves into 'a pattern of falling words' beside 'the flowers standing cool, firm and upright in the earth'. In its unstable, decentred narrative, its problematization of dialogue as pattern rather than meaning, its exploration of a group identity in terms other than the social, 'Kew Gardens' marked an extreme stage in the development of the modernist techniques Woolf was to transfer to her novels.

The third short story which Woolf saw as crucial to her development of new fictional techniques was 'An Unwritten Novel' (1920), a writer's speculative reverie about a fellow railway passenger. As the writer attempts to construct a coherent identity fron the passenger's appearance, from her imagined home environment, from various existing fictional conventions to which she can be related, she becomes increasingly aware of her subject's elusiveness. The end celebrates the extraordinary mystery of human identity and the immense quest on which the writer is engaged. Woolf reworked the situation in 'Mr Bennett and Mrs Brown' (1923), which speculated on Bennett's imaginative incapacity to record the essence of the old woman opposite him in a railway carriage. Bennett's supposed incapacity rested in his traditional definition of character through circumstance and environment. Both writings demonstrated the need for new modes of interpreting women's experience, the story by showing a woman writer learning the need to change, the essay by showing a male writer failing to interpret a female subject.

It was while writing 'An Unwritten Novel' that Woolf imagined how the novel could be transformed. 'Suppose one thing should open out of another – as in An Unwritten Novel – only not for 10 pages but 200 or so – doesn't that give the looseness & lightness I want; doesn't that get closer & yet keep form & speed, & enclose everything, everything . . . mark on the wall, K[ew] G[ardens] & unwritten novel taking hands & dancing in unity' (*Diary*, II, pp. 13–14). She envisaged a new form of novel emerging to replace *Night and Day*, which Mansfield's review had humiliatingly described as 'a novel in the tradition of the English novel . . . we had never thought to look upon its like again'.[29] Woolf recorded her distress at Mansfield's judgement that her second novel was an agreeable anachronism reminiscent of Jane Austen, and Mansfield's contrasting enthusiasm for 'Kew Gardens' probably encouraged her belief in her short story innovations as the way forward. *Jacob's Room* (1922), her first modernist novel, was the product of her imagined dance of short stories. It was followed by *Mrs Dalloway* (1925), which also evolved from the idea of linked short stories, and by *To the Lighthouse* (1927), written after Woolf had completed a set of eight short stories developed from *Mrs Dalloway*. In the same year she published her third modernist declaration, 'The Narrow Bridge of Art' (1927), which described the need to move away from a fiction of sociological detail towards forms closer to poetry and to drama. It was through the short story, with its freedom from the detail of the traditional novel, that Woolf explored the development of her novels.

ALTERNATIVES AND SUCCESSORS

The experiments of Richardson, Mansfield and Woolf in the war decade marked the main phase of women's experiments within modernism. This section will examine two further groups of innovative writers, looking first at three writers who emerged in that period and whose fictional innovations were perceived as important, and then at the younger writers, first publishing in the 1920s, who made their distinctive accommodations with modernism. The work of the three earlier writers, Rose Macaulay, Ivy Compton-Burnett and Stella Benson, was outside canonical modernism, but all sought to develop forms of fiction appropriate to the new experiences of the twentieth century. Macaulay, who published her first novel in 1906 and was an influential figure on the London literary scene until the 1950s, shared the modernists' impatience with the traditional preoccupations of novels; 'all I am interested in when I write them is the style – the mere English, the cadences etc; and sometimes when I make a joke. As stories, as characterizations, they bore me to death.'[30] Her satirical novels explored ways of escaping this boredom. *Told by an Idiot* (1923) anticipates Woolf's *The Years* (1937) in attempting to describe the relation between public events and the inner lives of the individuals on whom they impinge. As in *The Years*, the narrative follows an upper-middle-class family from the 1880s to the present day, examining the ornate structures and false consciousness of Victorian public and family life as they proceed towards their disintegration. Macaulay also anticipates *Orlando* (1928) in presenting the succession of periods as a series of satirical impressionistic pastiches in which the characters, galvanized by their emergence in yet another epoch, rapidly adopt the costumes, conventions and clichés appropriate to the new age. Macaulay's primary concerns are with the disjunctions between the crude roles constructed by history and public opinion, and the individuals who have to find a way of using these roles to negotiate a place in the external world. These disjunctions are particularly difficult for the women characters who wake to each new age to find yet another role as New Woman awaiting them; as one character wonders 'were girls and women really always newer than boys and men?'.[31] The novel's pathos lies in the difficulties these women encounter in accepting the crude gender roles history constructs for them; as its title suggests, it is entirely pessimistic about the possibilities of constructing a usable public life, and lacks the buoyancy and playfulness with which *Orlando* reconstructs gender.

Ivy Compton-Burnett, who, like Macaulay, became a prestigious figure in the London literary world, developed a distinctive formula, to which she adhered from her second novel, *Pastors and Masters* (1925). Compton-Burnett

71

addressed the familiar problems – the authorial persona, the materiality of Edwardian fiction, the problematization of dialogue – but she abolished the first two problems by writing novels almost entirely in dialogue. Her novels are strongly plotted stories of domestic power struggles, cruelties and revenges, set among country-house families in the period before the First World War, conducted in dialogue which is highly stylized, allusive, epigrammatic, modelled on Wilde's plays and James's novels, and responding with unfailing elegance to the domestic horrors it discloses. The absence of authorial intervention is registered by the omission even of indications of exits and entrances. In her fullest summary of her writing, a 1945 radio talk, Compton-Burnett placed herself as an alternative tradition to modernism, with Mansfield, rather than Woolf, standing in as representative of modernism's failures. 'I think it better for a novel to have a plot. Otherwise it has no shape, and incidents that have no part in a formal whole seem to have less significance. I always wish that Katherine Mansfield's "At the Bay" was cast in a formal mould.'[32] In her insistence on the importance of shaping the narrative through tight plotting, and her invocation of the influences of Jacobean tragedy, Restoration comedy and Jane Austen ascribed to her by favourable reviews, she presented herself as a representative of order, tradition and continuity, solving the problems of contemporary fiction without the break with the past which modernism attempted. At the same time she criticized the elaborate descriptions of environment in earlier fiction, and revealed that she always skipped them as uninformative about character. The talk suggests a skilful targeting of audience by a judicious compromise between concessions to modernity, in the rejection of Victorian prolixities of description and authorial commentary, and a cultivation of the traditional which placed her as continuing the main line of fiction.

Compton-Burnett's novels deliberately eschewed topicality; she claimed to have no 'real or organic knowledge of life later than about 1910', endorsing, from a different viewpoint, Woolf's claim in 'Mr Bennett and Mrs Brown' that human nature changed in that year.[33] Alison Light has described how her dissection of the hidden horrors of Victorian family life was designed to appeal both to the anti-Victorianism of the 1920s and to conservative yearnings for the order represented by the country-house.[34] Her deliberate bypassing of the topical, combined with the absence of reference to the material environment, suggests that the exchanges of her characters represent eternal problems. *More Women than Men* (1935), for instance, appears to promise topicality in its situation in a girls' school; tensions and tyrannies in all-female institutions were popular fictional material between the wars. That promise, however, is ostentatiously unfulfilled; the focus is almost exclusively on domestic power and cruelty, the novel's evil matriarch directs her schemes as mother rather than headmistress, the numerically outnumbered male characters figure more prominently than the other women, and the pupils are silent and marginalized throughout. The narrative's briefly suggested concerns with women and institutional power, female education, working women, are pointedly displaced for a depiction of a matriarch-dominated family in lethal internal struggle; powerfully implicit is the suggestion that contemporary debates have not disturbed the real order of things. It was to this elaborate and coherent assumption that Compton-Burnett owed the fact that reviewers compared her crime plots with Aeschylus and the Jacobeans rather than with Agatha Christie.

The distinctive characteristic of Stella Benson's fiction, admired by Mansfield, Rebecca West and, more guardedly, Woolf, was the very marked disjunction between its highly topical content, based on Benson's varied experience of the suffrage movement, war-work and China, and the distancing she achieved by her treatment of the material. Her first novel, *I Pose* (1916), described by West as 'the only novel of genius about the suffrage',[35] is in the allegorical mode, presenting a series of encounters between a militant suffragette and a male gardener, both nameless, exploring the adoption of new poses in a world where the old stereotypes no longer work. The foreword of her war novel, *Living Alone* (1919), warns 'this is not a real book. It does not deal with real people and should not be read by real people.' It adopts the mode of childish fantasy as the only possible, appropriately inadequate, response to the experiences of the First World War. The heroine, employed in dubious wartime office work investigating benefit claims, 'collecting evidence from charitable spies about the Naughty Poor', is rescued from her unrealized existence by the eruption into her life of a witch, witches being those people sufficiently conscious of their alienation to perceive the world clearly.[36] In the novel's central chapter an air-raid on London is experienced first below ground, where it gradually becomes apparent that most of the people in an increasingly overcrowded shelter have been prematurely roused from graves in the nearby churchyards, and then in an aerial conversation between the English witch and her German counterpart, poised above the bombardment on their broomsticks.

Benson's major achievement, *Tobit Transplanted* (1931, the more attractive American title was *The Faraway Bride*), was written in China where she lived from 1922 to her death in 1933, and also explores the gulf between private experiences and public conventions about how those experiences are registered. The novel is 'about' the experiences of White Russian refugees in Manchuria, and her preface, a lucid informative account of tensions among the various ethnic groups, arouses reader expectations of a documentary novel. The novel which follows uses Benson's usual techniques of fantasy and distancing to disappoint any such expectations, sinking the well-informed, well-intentioned persona of the preface to pursue the separate, unbridgeable reveries of a group of exiles. The heroine Tanya, a version of the enchanted, heartless princess of fairy-tale, when confronted with yet another desperate lovelorn suitor, is unable to divert her attention from a caterpillar drowning in the milk. Tanya, in the secrecy of her fantasy life and her inability to assemble her priorities in conventional order, is the central expression of alienation in the novel. In the consciousness of other figures, the Russian Anna, once a governess in England, and the Chinese Chew, who once studied there, Benson explores the vast, almost unimaginable cultural distances they have traversed, and the private fantasies they use to explain these journeys to themselves. Like Woolf in 'Kew Gardens', Benson dissolves the human consciousnesses into the landscape, exploring the sheer strangeness of participation in a dynamic natural world, and often focusing on the consciousness of the dog, whose failure to find familiar smells is treated on the same level of importance as the alienation of the humans.

Benson's treatment of the great contemporary public experiences as they impinged on the individual was one attempt to bridge the gulf between the documentarist novelists who discussed urgent topical subjects with traditional fictional methods, and the modernists who experimented with new forms of representation of private experience and consciousness. Her success was limited, but her struggles to relate the public world and the alienated self are central to the period, and her recourse to the mode of fantasy was one taken by several writers in the late 1920s. Sylvia Townsend Warner's first novel, *Lolly Willowes* (1926), used a story of initiation into witchcraft to explore the inner life of a surplus woman. West's *Harriet Hume* (1929) employed extravagant fantasy as the only appropriate mode to discuss the relations of public man and private woman. Woolf's fantasy of gender-construction, *Orlando*, was followed by *Flush* (1933), which continued Benson's exploration of the strangeness of existence through location in the consciousness of a dog.

The leading writers who emerged in the decade from 1925, after the main moment of modernism, were Jean Rhys, Elizabeth Bowen, Sylvia Townsend Warner, Rosamond Lehmann and Antonia White. The work of the former three is discussed in Chapter 8. Warner worked with fantasy, allegory and historical fiction in writing which, increasingly informed by her commitment to communism, moved from focus on the individual to the political experience of the group. The novels of the other four were all identified with the traditional preoccupations of women's fiction. They worked with the modes of domestic and romantic fiction, with the figure of the young girl entering adult life, or the woman as victim of man and slave of love. The feminist writings of the first decades of the twentieth century had emphasized independence, an escape from the conformities and role-playing expected of women; this fiction's return to the domestic and sexual paralleled the shift to New Feminism within the women's movement. Bowen's novels achieved a distinctive revision, informed by the techniques of modernism, of the tradition of domestic realism. She also became the major woman exponent of the short story; her discovery, during the Second World War, that the form was more flexible and responsive than the novel to a time of turbulent uncertainty duplicated the earlier experiences of the modernists.[37] Rhys's works were more identifiably within the modernist tradition; like Woolf she developed the technique for her economic, lyric explorations of consciousness in her novels through experiment with the short story. In her writings, as in those of Lehmann, women's lives are shown as determined by their sexuality; they appear as victims and devotees of love, emotionally and economically enslaved by men. They are mistresses, amateur prostitutes, whose Bohemian lifestyles only emphasize the narrow bounds of their lives. Rhys's novels and short stories explore the consciousness of women who live between absorption in an inner world of romantic fantasy, fashion and popular song, and awareness of their economic dependence on their sexuality.

In Lehmann's novels the focus is on emotional, rather than economic, dependence. Her first novel, *Dusty Answer*, drew on the false epiphany model of Mansfield's 'Bliss' to represent its young heroine's sexuality as a powerful but ambivalent force seeking direction and identity. In its emphasis on the uncertainties of the development of sexual identity, and the power, confusion and volatility of sexual feelings, the novel, like 'Bliss', registered fiction's increasing awareness of psychoanalysis. With that awareness went assumptions about neurosis as the specific and inevitable state of being for women. In *The Weather in the Streets* (1936) Lehmann organizes her narrative around the fragmenting identity of Olivia, secret lover of a married man, who is also her social superior. Sections in third person narrative frame the second section, in which the idyllic stage of the affair up to Olivia's pregnancy is reported in the first person, as Olivia excludes all intimations of difficulty from her consciousness. This section breaks down in incoherent fragments, and the third person narrative is restored, as Olivia's perceptions of external contingencies and constraints break in with the onset of pregnancy. Only in dream can Olivia now feel 'in bliss'; as in Mansfield the word defines the distance from any realization of fulfilled sexuality. The succeeding scenes, where Olivia seeks an abortion, replay the locations of the second section, stripping away the glamour from the country cottages and pubs where the affair was conducted, and extending the deglamourizing process to the whole promise of metropolitan freedom

75

for women celebrated by earlier writers. The flats and parks and ease of transport which seemed to offer freedom, the restaurants, despised by Olivia's lover, where women can eat alone, are comprehensively trashed. The conclusion, suggesting that Olivia's divided, dependent and neurotic state will continue indefinitely, confirms women's emotional and economic dependence on men.

With *The Ballad and the Source* (1944) Lehmann turned from the victimization of women by men to women's relations with each other, and the dangerous narratives they construct about them. The novel is a story of a destructive mother–daughter relationship, told through a series of narrators. The development to adulthood of the frame narrator, the child Rebecca, is conducted through the detective process by which she constructs from these stories a complete narrative to explain the mystery which the neighbouring family represent. The first narrator, an old family servant, offers a traditional oral narrative in which the omissions and distortions are easily recognizable, but with the second narrative, by the novel's charismatic matriarch, Sybil, the novel puns ominously on 'plot'. Sybil has written novels which damaged the people they represented, and in private life her plots, her insistence on shaping life in patterns around her, are even more destructive. There are frequent references to the way in which images both transmit emotion and freeze the original source of emotions in the ballad which commemorates them. In the climactic scene Sybil's deranged daughter smashes a statue of her dead child in an attempt to liberate the spirit within. The reliability of the third and least manipulative narrator, Sybil's eldest grand-daughter, is seen to be based on her rejection of her family's artistic pretensions in favour of a medical career; she will tend the source of life rather than seeking to control it through multiplying narratives, which construct further images of victimization.

The success of Antonia White's bestselling *Frost in May* (1933) derived in part from her extension of the public debate about sexuality into a child's perceptions of the rituals and relationships of her convent school. The novel was a revelation of a secret world of intense female friendships and heightened emotions. Nanda's access to being 'blissfully happy' comes during a school play when her powerful and ambivalent response to the performances of two loved friends has to be explained away to the watchful nuns. Later Nanda is expelled for writing a novel based on her reading in the romantic fiction of the period, and her emotional capacity for dealing with the world is irreparably stunted. The strength of *Frost in May* lay in the contrast between the manner, sharply focused, clear, naive, and the helplessness of the heroine. White's later writing history was expressive of the identification of women and neurosis, a subject which she discussed extensively in her diaries. She had a nervous breakdown after the novel's publication, entered psychoanalysis, and between *Frost in May* and its belated sequel, *The Lost Traveller* (1950), recorded in her diaries the progress of her writer's block and her longing to escape from the autobiographical mode to greater objectivity. White is in some ways an emblematic figure as woman writer in the 1930s. The success of *Frost in May* depended on its revelation of an unknown, exclusively female world, exemplary of the retreat of much highly regarded women's writing into topics indisputably within the female domain. This retreat, combined with her lavishly recorded procrastination in writing her second novel, was suggestive of the failure of confidence in the ebullient belief in the possibilities of the woman writer expressed by so many in earlier decades.

NOTES

Place of publication is London, unless otherwise stated.

1. Olive Schreiner, *From Man to Man* (Virago, 1982), p. 219.
2. See Ann Ardis, *New Woman, New Novels: Feminism and Early Modernism* (New Brunswick: Rutgers University Press, 1990); Elaine Showalter, *Sexual Anarchy: Gender and Culture at the Fin de Siècle* (Bloomsbury, 1991).
3. Elizabeth von Arnim, *Elizabeth and her German Garden* (Macmillan, 1906), 'January 1st'.
4. Jane Eldridge Miller, *Rebel Women: Feminism, Modernism and the Edwardian Novel* (Virago, 1994).
5. Elizabeth von Arnim, *The Pastor's Wife* (Smith, Elder, 1914), ch. 21.
6. D.H. Lawrence, *Letters*, ed. James Boulton (Cambridge: Cambridge University Press, 1979), II, p. 183.
7. See Sandra Gilbert and Susan Gubar, *No Man's Land: The Place of the Woman Writer in the Twentieth Century*, 3 vols (New Haven: Yale University Press, 1984).
8. See Lyn Pykett, *Engendering Fictions: The English Novel in the Early Twentieth Century* (Edward Arnold, 1995); Bonnie K. Scott, ed., *The Gender of Modernism: A Critical Anthology* (Bloomington: Indiana University Press, 1990) and *Refiguring Modernism*, 2 vols (Bloomington: University of Indiana Press, 1995).
9. May Sinclair, 'The Novels of Dorothy Richardson', *The Egoist*, 5 (1918), pp. 57–9, reprinted in Scott, *The Gender of Modernism*, pp. 442–8.
10. May Sinclair, *The Three Brontës* (Hutchinson, 1912), p. 170.
11. May Sinclair, *Mary Olivier: A Life* (Virago, 1994), p. 183.
12. Bryher, *The Heart to Artemis: A Writer's Memoirs* (Collins, 1963), pp. 124, 34.
13. Dorothy Richardson, *Pilgrimage* (Dent/Cresset, 1938), II: *The Tunnel*, ch. 14.
14. Stephen Heath, 'Writing for Silence: Dorothy Richardson and the Novel', in Suzanne Kappeler and Norman Bryson, eds, *Teaching the Text* (Routledge and Kegan Paul, 1983), pp. 126–47.

15. *Close Up*, 4 (June 1928), pp. 54–8.
16. Katherine Mansfield, *Notes on Novelists* (Constable, 1930), pp. 3–4.
17. Mansfield, *Notes on Novelists*, p. 42.
18. *Essays of Virginia Woolf*, ed. Andrew McNeillie (Hogarth Press, 1986), III, p. 11.
19. Virginia Woolf, 'Modern Fiction', in *The Common Reader: First Series* (Hogarth Press, 1962), p. 189.
20. *Essays of Virginia Woolf*, III, p. 367.
21. Mansfield, *Notes on Novelists*, p. 140.
22. *The Collected Letters of Katherine Mansfield*, ed. Vincent O'Sullivan and Margaret Scott (Oxford: Clarendon Press, 1984), I, p. 330. Subsequent quotations are from this edition.
23. 'Prelude', in *Collected Stories of Katherine Mansfield* (Constable, 1953), p. 34.
24. Elizabeth Bowen, 'A Living Writer: Katherine Mansfield', in *The Mulberry Tree: Writings of Elizabeth Bowen*, ed. Hermione Lee (Virago, 1986), p. 77.
25. Virginia Woolf, 'Professions for Women', in *The Death of the Moth and Other Essays* (Hogarth Press, 1942), p. 152.
26. Kate Fulbrook, *Katherine Mansfield* (Hemel Hempstead: Harvester Wheatsheaf, 1986).
27. Virginia Woolf, *The Complete Shorter Fiction*, ed. Susan Dick (Triad Grafton, 1989), p. 87.
28. Virginia Woolf, 'A Sketch of the Past', in *Moments of Being*, ed. Jeanne Schulkind (Hogarth Press, 1985), p. 79.
29. Mansfield, *Notes on Novelists*, p. 111.
30. Quoted in Constance Babington Smith, *Rose Macaulay* (Collins, 1972), p. 129.
31. Rose Macaulay, *Told by an Idiot* (Collins, 1923), pt. 1, ch. 2.
32. 'Conversation between Ivy Compton-Burnett and Margaret Jourdain', in Charles Burkhart, ed., *The Art of Ivy Compton-Burnett* (Gollancz, 1972), p. 26.
33. 'Conversation', p. 27.
34. See Alison Light, *Forever England: Femininity, Literature and Conservatism Between the Wars* (Routledge, 1991).
35. Quoted in Joy Grant, *Stella Benson: A Biography* (Macmillan, 1987), p. 83.
36. Stella Benson, *Living Alone* (Macmillan, 1919), ch. 2.
37. Elizabeth Bowen, Preface to American edition of *The Demon Lover*, reprinted in *The Mulberry Tree*, pp. 94–9.

CHAPTER FOUR

The Modest Poets

This was not a period when women poets in Britain commanded much attention. The early twentieth century in English poetry offers a particularly striking example of that control of access to high culture, and especially to that form of high language which is poetry, which Cora Kaplan has described as a central problem for women poets.[1] At a time when possibilities for women seemed to be expanding in many areas, the contest for the central literary form became so intensive that their claim upon it was even more tenuous than usual. The many constructions of English literary tradition in the early 1900s presented literature as a central justification for Britain's national and imperial eminence, and accorded poetry the highest place within that tradition. It was in poetry, and especially in Shakespeare, that English literature was seen to justify that pre-eminence, and the spate of literary histories for the new students of English, and of anthologies for classrooms, enforced the point.[2] This emphasis on the role of poetry in Britain's imperial destiny made the role of the woman poet difficult to define. The succeeding movements of Georgianism and modernism both perceived themselves as revolutionary programmes, the weightiness of whose claims left no place for women. In the second decade there were no female contributors to the series of anthologies published to define the Georgian poets' claim of a renewal in English poetry. As modernism became the ascendant force in poetry no British women modernist poets emerged of the stature of Woolf in prose, or of the American poet H.D. The women poets studied in this section were, with the single exception of Edith Sitwell, routinely described by their admirers by such adjectives as 'modest', 'obscure' and 'neglected'; the responses to their work demonstrate the particular difficulties women poets had in positioning themselves within the poetic culture in this period of intensive struggle for the poetic crown. It is not possible to discuss them in terms of groups and movements,

79

but as a list of individuals modestly cultivating what niches were available within the poetic tradition.

These difficulties are exemplified by Alice Meynell, in 1900 the most respected woman poet. Meynell had been publishing poetry since 1875, and was to publish four more collections before her death in 1922. She was better known, however, for her prose, the many sketches and critical essays she published in various journals; Bennett's *Journalism for Women* cites her as the best available model for women's prose. Many of these essays discuss the marginal position of the woman poet, in studies of forgotten writers of the past, or in comment on her immediate predecessors, on Christina Rossetti's 'thinnest beaten gold', and Elizabeth Barrett Browning's 'uneasy force' and 'futile strife'.[3] Her most anthologized poems, the short lyrics 'Renouncement' (1893), 'The Lady Poverty' (1896), and 'The Rainy Summer' (1913), suggest a deliberate embrace of a limited emotional range. Her most eminent male admirer, George Meredith, wrote a sonnet, 'To A.M.' (1896), which addressed her as 'proud Reluctant', and suggested that she made fear of publicity and fame the condition of her writing, and the basis of her attraction.[4] Meredith's sonnet is sensitive to the situation of the violet by the mossy stone which attempts to answer back; for Woolf in the next generation Meynell is a problematic literary type of the Angel in the House. She is antagonistic to 'the tight airless Meynell style' but 'I was aware of some sweetness and dignity in those lives compared with ours . . . it strikes me that one or two little poems will survive all that my father ever wrote' (*Diary*, III, pp. 250–1). Woolf's expectation that Meynell's short lyrics will survive Leslie Stephen's weighty discursive prose strikes both ways; her comparison invokes the defeat of patriarchal weight by female slightness, but also acknowledges the supremacy of poetry, the masculine art.

Meynell's intense self-consciousness about the place of women in the traditions of a patriarchal society was demonstrated in 1917 by two poems in the collection, *A Father of Women and Other Poems*. The title-poem addresses itself to the massive losses of the war, invoking them to look forward to a world where the relations of fathers and daughters must change radically:

> Our father works in us,
>   The daughters of his manhood. Not undone
> Is he, not wasted, though transmuted thus,
>   And though he left no son. (p. 380)

In a 'crippled world' there is a need to revalue female inheritance, a need which will enable women such as Meynell to 'crush in my nature the ungenerous art/Of the inferior'. The poem's radicalism, with its suggestion that war requires a complete redefinition of family values, is qualified by its epigraph from Dryden's 'Ode to Mrs Anne Killigrew'; the citation of literary authority on the topic of father–daughter relations places the poem firmly in a continuous literary tradition. Meynell's other poem on female descent, the lyric 'The Two Shakespeare Tercentenaries', employs the central conceit that Meynell's dates (1847–) now embrace Shakespeare's (1564–1616). This metaphor of embrace allows Meynell to translate unexceptionable reflections on Shakespeare's unsurpassable achievement into gendered terms; she is not only an unworthy daughter, but by implication a tender but uncomprehending mother, with 'ignorant arms that fold/A poet to a foolish breast', and whose 'waste', a key Meynell word, is the context for his achievement:

> Child, Stripling, Man – the sod.
> Might I talk little language to thee, pore
> On thy last silence? O thou city of God
> My waste lies after thee, and lies before. (p. 384)

The pioneer psychoanalytical critic, Maud Bodkin, analysed this lyric in her 1934 study, *Archetypal Patterns in Poetry*, as an example of the positive creative force which the father's image might have for the woman poet, but, in this pastiche Metaphysical lyric in which Shakespeare becomes God of the poetic universe, Meynell is also questioning the roles through which women may relate to men.[5]

The Poetry Bookshop, founded by Harold Monro in 1913, published much of the new poetry of the second decade, including the *Georgian Poetry* anthologies. These, with their definition of a renewed virile English poetry, excluded women poets, but Monro also published the work of the three most interesting women poets who emerged in this period, Charlotte Mew, Anna Wickham and Frances Cornford. In his 1920 critical survey, *Some Contemporary Poets*, Monro's descriptions of their claims as women poets indicate the kinds of situations available for women within the genre. Mew's poems, which he had unsuccessfully urged for inclusion in the third *Georgian Poetry*, were 'modest' and 'authentic', comparing favourably with the long poems and grandiose ambitions of Elizabeth Barrett Browning in the mid-Victorian period. Wickham should be read by men seeking to understand the woman's point of view in sexual relations, and Cornford was slight and charming.[6] The word 'modest' is so often applied to Mew, whose poems are distinguished by a powerful emotionality and hallucinatory intensity, that it seems to have been evoked by her personality, and her marginal situation as a woman poet (perhaps even by her surname, what else would a poetess do?). Monro's admiration was shared by Hardy, who described her as 'the greatest poetess I have come across lately, in my judgment, though so meagre in her output'.[7] However, until the Poetry

Bookshop published her first collection, *The Farmer's Bride*, in 1916, her published output was mainly in prose, short stories and essays. Despite Hardy's admiration, *The Farmer's Bride* sold poorly. The Civil List pension, for which Hardy successfully sponsored her, proved an additional source of anxiety; she attempted to return it, fearing she was not producing sufficient poetry, and her other collection, *The Rambling Sailor*, published in 1929, the year after her suicide, contained few poems not already written by 1916.

Mew lived half her life in the Victorian period, and in form and subject her poems describe the struggles of transition from Victorianism to modernity, the frustrations with an inheritance with which she can never come to terms. Like her friend, May Sinclair, her main contact with the literary world, she saw Emily Brontë as the Victorian woman writer who spoke most strongly to the modern condition, describing her in an essay of 1904 as 'an appalling personality . . . a great artist and a repulsive woman', who yet 'lived long enough to lift such a cry for liberty as few women have ever lifted'.[8] The qualification of Brontë's status as exemplary woman artist by reflections on her failure to accommodate to any acceptable social role is indicative of Mew's own problems in representing her desires and ambitions. 'The Quiet House', one of the most powerful poems in *The Farmer's Bride*, enacts those difficulties. In this poem, in which a demure and childlike voice reports on the reduction of a large Victorian family, through death and departure, to father and daughter, and on the daughter's barely intimated and aborted romance, the original stanzaic form becomes increasingly irregular as orderly domesticity is disrupted by suggestions of suppressed violence. This is a Victorian tragedy of the buried life of female passion, and the last line, 'I do not care; some day I *shall* not think; I shall not *be*!', echoes Christina Rossetti's lyric, 'Life and Death'. In the central, and most irregular, section of the poem, however, orderliness and decorum break down completely; the traditional rose, which represents the inner flowering of the speaker's passion, takes on a hallucinatory intensity:

> A rose can stab you across the street
> Deeper than any knife:
> And the crimson haunts you everywhere –
> Thin shafts of sunlight, like the ghosts of reddened swords, have struck
> our stair
> As if, coming down, you had spilt your life. (p. 18)

Jan Montefiore has compared these lines to Sylvia Plath's use of traditional images to represent a personal hallucination close to derangement.[9]

Other poems adhere more closely to Victorian models. 'The Changeling', which is in the fantasy tradition of Rossetti's 'Goblin Market' and Arnold's 'The Forsaken Merman', expresses a sense of permanent estrangement from normal domestic humanity through the voice of a changeling child, and uncertainly embraces an affinity with the natural world clearly informed by Brontë. Mew's longest poem, 'Madeline in Church', a dramatic monologue in rhyming free verse, takes its form and situation, a sinner in church, from Robert Browning, to construct a distinctively female experience of religion. The speaker initially feels remote from Christ, able to respond only to the church's sensuous and aesthetic appeal, and to memories of her own voracious explorations of life: it is through this voracity that she works her way to a sense of Christ's approachability. When finally she can focus on His scarred hand, and can see herself like Mary Magdalene as 'something altogether new' for Him, making Him in effect her last and greatest client, she has discovered her female closeness to God.

Mew seems to have found advantage in the distance allowed by the dramatic monologue. Two of her most achieved poems are 'The Farmer's Bride' and the later 'On the Road to the Sea' (1921), in which the forbidden desirability of the female love-object is explained within male narratives. The poem which is nearest to an explicitly lesbian affirmation, the free verse monologue 'The Forest Road', is also the most melodramatic. In this poem Mew draws on her feelings about the antagonistic relations between humans and the natural world; in a 1913 essay, 'Men and Trees', she had lamented that 'the London trees are all prisoners of men', but 'though the great tropical forests are being penetrated, they are not yet ours' (p. 388). Here the forest represents the other world of fulfilled desire for which the speaker longs, the sleeping female lover the inescapable doubts and anxieties of the human world. Her flowing hair, like that of Porphyria in Browning's monologue 'Porphyria's Lover', is the emblem both of desirability and vulnerability. 'I must unloose this hair that sleeps and dreams/About my face, and clings like the brown weed/To drowned delivered things'. Torn between guilt and irritation at the lover's demands, the speaker finally releases both of them violently into that other forest world where human desire is no longer tormented by guilt; 'I hear my soul, singing among the trees!' (pp. 21–2).

'The Farmer's Bride' again draws on Mew's sense of the otherness of the natural world, the traditional remoteness of the female object of desire explained in terms of the familiar alignment of women with nature and men with culture. A young farmer meditates on his inability to communicate with his feral bride, whose closeness to the natural world defines his own estrangement from it, and a delicate pastoral lyric becomes an agonized account of inevitable marital estrangement. The poem is close in feeling to Mary Webb's novel, *Gone to Earth*, which appeared the following year, but Mew's choice of the male standpoint emphasizes further the unbridgeable gulf between the human and natural worlds. In 'On the Road to the Sea' the speaker is again male, a soldier departing for war who seeks some kind of permanence from a chance encounter with a woman. His wish to touch her life in some way, to move her, to become part of her past, which might have remained at the level of the sentimental and charming, is dramatized in a volatile succession of moods, which acknowledges the implicit resentment and envy in the soldier's contemplation of the woman's potential future ('I want your life and you will not give it me' (p. 30)), but also the tenderness with which he contemplates that future. Mew's most anthologized war poem is her most dignified and public, 'The Cenotaph' (1919), but 'On the Road to the Sea' has a dramatic fluidity and emotional range which seems to benefit from the distancing through a male persona.

Where Mew and Meynell sought to situate their poetry within the mainstream tradition, Anna Wickham explicitly presented herself as the voice of womankind in a series of poems which, unlike Mew's 'meagre output', numbered over a thousand published; (many manuscripts were apparently lost when her home was bombed in 1943). Many of these poems were extremely brief, epigrams and short lyrics dramatizing a range of situations illustrative of women's distinctive experience and outlook. The title poem of *The Contemplative Quarry*, published by the Poetry Bookshop in 1915, refers to the anomalous situation of the woman who, as the traditional object of male pursuit and poetry, seeks to rhyme her own situation. Wickham sought to create in her poems a distinctive female tradition which, in its break from the central male tradition, must accept its isolation from established ideas of canonical acceptability. She said of herself, 'I may be a minor poet but I'm a major woman',[10] and wanted all her published work to be prefaced by the following quatrain:

> Here is no sacrificial I,
> Here are more I's than yet were in one human,
> Here I reveal our common mystery,
> I give you *woman*. (p. 1)

In the same year as *The Contemplative Quarry*, Richardson published *Pointed Roofs*, and began Miriam's exploration of her myriad I ams. Wickham's work of this period participates in an exploration and celebration of the distinctiveness of women's experience and creative impulse comparable to Richardson's.

Wickham's poems exploring her myriad I ams are combative, dramatic, engaged in outlining, and often celebrating, an eternal gender war. She was friendly with the Lawrences from 1915, wrote 'Imperatrix' (1916) to Frieda, and argued with D.H. Lawrence; her writings, like Lawrence's, read as immediate reports from a vigorous debate about the relations of the sexes. Her own explorations of this topic emerged from a turbulent marriage in which her husband confined her to a mental hospital after she had her first poems published by a vanity press in 1911; one of her retaliations was the poem, 'The Homecoming' (1921), which described his death in a mountaineering accident, anticipating his actual death thus in 1929. Many of her poems drew on her own translation from childhood in Australia and musical training in Paris to London domesticity. 'Nervous Prostration' (1916) satirizes the conformities of men 'of the Croydon class'; although 'The Tired Man' (1915) professes to speak sympathetically for the husband seeking domestic calm, whose 'wife is walking the whirlwind/Through night as black as ink' (p. 191), the ink aligns the wife's turbulence with a creativity which reproaches his torpor. Other poems dramatize utopian partnerships. The early 'Song of the Low-caste Wife' (1911) celebrates the strength and wisdom with which women may return from the exile of lowliness to help their lofty partners. In 'Song of Ophelia the Survivor' (1936) a strong recovered Ophelia offers refuge to a sick tormented Hamlet. Two of her best poems celebrate fulfilled sexuality; in 'The Fired Pot' a housewife 'passionate about pins and pence and soap' is saved by a chance sexual encounter, while 'The Mill' uses the metaphor of a water-mill at work to celebrate the creativity of the sexual act.

Wickham explored the same contradiction as Woolf in *A Room of One's Own*, calling for a distinctively female poetry, but also in 'In the House of the Soul' (1936), arguing that the true artist must be spiritually bisexual. In the poem marriage is the metaphor for the artist and the 'husband' speaks:

> I, the mime and master of surprises,
> Who have fooled that mob with fifty new disguises –
> You, who sit still in the soul
> Like a quiet wife;
> You, who are Control,
> Weaving the long continuous thread of life. (p. 270)

The traditionalism of the marriage, with the weaving wife providing the continuity and patience on which achievement ultimately depends, might seem surprising, but metaphors of domesticity are central to Wickham's work. She subtitled her 'Fragment of an Autobiography', written in 1935, 'Prelude to a Spring-clean', and describes herself as irreparably torn between two models of womanhood. As mother she has for three decades 'been putting things away in loathsome sets of drawers', and her frustration has 'ruined' her sons in the process. She diagnoses her kindred failure as a poet, 'I feel that women of my kind are a profound mistake', and cites Mew's suicide as evidence for this statement (pp. 52–3). (Wickham hanged herself in 1947.) In her poems suburban and Bohemian lifestyles are often opposed, but the enforced orderliness suggested by the 'loathsome sets of drawers' appears also in her struggles to escape what she saw as her dangerous facility with versification. In 'The Egoist' (1915) she speaks of the need to reject 'ear-perfect rhyme' and 'write my rhythms free (p. 173). Free verse represented to her liberation from the constraints of domestic womanhood, but many of her poems are neat, orderly, epigrammatic, rhymed verse. Despite her defence of a rough argumentative exploratory verse she lamented in 'Self-Analysis' (1915) that she still lacks 'the straight and ordered flame'; 'my work has the incompetence of pain' (p. 192).

Frances Cornford, whose collection *Spring Morning* was published by the Poetry Bookshop in 1915, was, like Meynell, a poet who spoke from within a strong male culture. Her relationships define her situation: Darwin's grand-daughter, wife of the eminent classicist Francis Cornford, confidante of Rupert Brooke, mother of John Cornford, poet of the Spanish Civil War. Her most famous poem, the triolet 'To a Fat Lady Seen From a Train', evokes a child's bafflement at the joyless rituals of adult life. Many of her poems are pastorals of Cambridge life, but the speaking voice is again from outside; 'A Glimpse', which Yeats anthologized along with the triolet in the *Oxford Book of Modern Verse* (1936), evokes river, elm-tree and scholar, a pastoral continuity in which Cornford participates through her sons until 'all my children's children grow old men'. In 'Autumn Morning in Cambridge', which Monro selected as her most representative poem, the speaker is again marginal to the pastoral of learning, watching with childlike wonder as 'the men go to lecture with the wind in their gowns'.[11] In the later 'Grand Ballet' (1932) she again speaks with wonderment at male performance, recalling Nijinsky dance before the First World War. Here the sense of the fragility of human ceremony and achievement, implicit in the earlier pastorals, becomes explicit; Nijinsky's descent into madness shortly after figures the plunge into apocalypse of an entire civilization.[12] Sylvia Townsend Warner praised Cornford's poetry for its 'immediacy', its removal of 'the author's chaperoning presence'; through the voice of childlike wonder which Cornford often adopts, her absence of chaperoning authority, she questions the appearances of the established world.[13]

Modernism, the dominant force in poetry of the interwar period, was an international movement, its headquarters Paris and New York. The London-born Mina Loy, for instance, followed the usual path of modernist poetry when she travelled first to join the Anglo-American community in Paris, and then to settle as a modernist poet in New York. In Britain in the 1920s the modern woman poet was represented by Edith Sitwell who, unlike any other woman poet in this period, exploited considerable gifts for performance and publicity. Sitwell's adroit cultivation of controversy departed from the usual stance of modesty and accepted marginality in the woman poet, but she also declared her belief in the need for women writers to discover their own distinctive form of writing. In a 1925 article

86

in *Vogue*, 'Some Observations on Women's Poetry', her judgements on the women poets of the Victorian period are comparable to Woolf's on the women novelists in *A Room of One's Own*. Rossetti is praised for seeking distinctively female forms of poetry. 'Christina Rossetti in her poetry found only, and made use of, a technique and a manner suitable to female muscles, whereas Mrs Browning used a technique and a manner which is only suitable to a man ... No woman writing in the English language has ever written a great sonnet, no woman has ever written great blank verse.' In place of Barrett Browning's muscular deployment of masculine forms, she urged a particular stance; 'women's poems should, above all things, be eloquent as a peacock, and there should be a fantastic element, a certain strangeness, in their beauty'.[14]

Sitwell's advocacy of peacocking was appropriate for the pages of *Vogue*, but had further significances. If the violet was the implicit model for the woman poet, Sitwell was offering an alternative, more high-profile (and male) model from the natural world. The discrepancy between the peacock's decorative plumage and its discordant shriek was important; Sitwell's high-pitched voice was a distinctive part of her performances, notably in *Façade*, where it offered an estranging counter to the mellifluous pastiches of Victorian poetry. Most importantly the peacock was an emblem of Sitwell's attack on the Georgian poets' representation of the natural world. Their emphasis on the natural endorsed poetry's special relationship with nature, which in turn underpinned the centrality of poetry to English claims to cultural hegemony. Sitwell's poetry reconstructed a natural world of decorative artifice and literary convention. In 1922 one of her more sympathetic critics, Amabel Williams-Ellis, compared her poems to 'Murano glass dolls';[15] Sitwell's appeal to the 'minor' decorative arts was deliberate. She first became a major figure in 1916 when she began publishing her annual anthology, *Wheels*, which ran until 1921, and deliberately challenged the then dominant ideology of Georgian poetry, opposing to its celebrations of the natural world a mock pastoral of emphatic artifice, in which features of the natural world became human artefacts, theatrical backdrops, nursery furniture.

In 1923 *Façade*, her experimental collaboration with the composer William Walton, was performed to great controversy; Sitwell spoke her lyrics from behind a curtain to emphasize the sybilline status and impersonality of the poet. Again there was the appeal to art forms of low status in the lyrics modelled on dances, 'Hornpipe', 'Tarantella', 'Polka', 'Valse', 'Fox-Trot'. Many of the lyrics were modelled on the Victorian nonsense-verse of Edward Lear, and sought to dissolve the boundaries between that and higher poetry; in the most frequently anthologized lyric, 'Sir Beelzebub', a critical child's voice questions the sonorities of its Victorian elders. It was

87

that child's voice and poetry 'as irrational as "Sing a Song of Sixpence" '
which Sitwell's most powerful admirer, Yeats, praised, explaining it as representative of postwar disillusionment:

> Her language is the traditional language of literature, but twisted, torn,
> complicated, jerked here and there by strained resemblances, unnatural
> contacts, forced upon it by some terror beating in her blood, some
> primitive obsession that civilization can no longer exorcise . . . I think I
> like her best when she seems a child, terrified and delighted by the story
> it is inventing.[16]

In the long satirical poem, *Gold Coast Customs* (1929), Sitwell explored
the primitivist analogy for her child perspective. Here, like many poets,
she responded to the increasing social consciousness of the period in a
poem which treated Ashanti cannibal rituals as analogy for Mayfair society,
exploiting and devouring its victims in the back streets. During the 1930s,
however, Sitwell wrote little poetry, turning, for financial reasons, to prose.
Her notoriety as a poet was maintained by the journal *New Verse* (1933–
39), which published many of the young poets of the decade and regularly
targeted Sitwell as representative of all they sought to abolish in poetry. As
performer, publicist and female aristocrat she helped *New Verse* crystallize
its desired image of the poet as male, sympathetic with the proletariat, and
impersonally dedicated to the public utility of poetry. Her *Street Songs* (1942)
temporarily revived her reputation in a period of national consensus; the
most reprinted poem in this collection, 'Still Falls the Rain', was dignified,
compassionate, much more traditional than Sitwell's earlier work, and, like
Mew's war poem 'The Cenotaph', not very characteristic of its author.

Sitwell defined a new kind of persona for the woman poet, based on
performance and difference, in which she distinguished herself from the
dominant schools of male poetry. Most of the other woman poets who
were first published in the 1920s and 1930s were closer to Meynell in
defining themselves within the mainstream tradition. Sylvia Townsend
Warner's work is discussed in Chapter 8; her first published work was a
collection of poems, *The Espalier* (1925), and she continued to publish
poems throughout her life, but it was her first novel, *Lolly Willowes* (1926),
which established her reputation, and she was always better known as a
prose writer. Many of her poems questioned the continuity and significance of English pastoralism by reference to earlier models, Hardy, Anon,
and, in her long satirical narrative of the postwar countryside, *Opus 7* (1931),
Crabbe. Her poetic persona was often constructed around the anonymity
of ballad; 'The Sailor' (1925), the single poem which Yeats selected for
the *Oxford Book of Modern Verse*, is an example of a poem which seems
designed to vanish within the tradition, obliterating all reference to time

88

or gender or personality.[17] The collection on which she collaborated with Valentine Ackland, *Whether a Dove or a Seagull* (1934), in which the attribution of the poems was concealed, offered a different kind of anonymity, the separate identities of the two poets vanishing in a common female construction. The poems inspired by Warner's journeys to Spain during the Civil War, 'Waiting at Cerbere', 'Benicasim' and 'Port Bou', explore a different kind of collective anonymity, no longer that of the English countryside, but of the Spanish people and their supporters.

Elizabeth Daryush, another poet who moved in the 1930s from concealment within the poetic tradition to a more socially conscious verse, had a relation with that tradition which was literally filial; she was the daughter of Robert Bridges, Poet Laureate from 1913 to 1930, and continued his experiments with syllabic metre. Daryush's relations with her published work were continually evolving. She published her first collection of poetry, *Charitessi*, as early as 1911, but in the 1930s she rejected much of her earlier poetry; in her *Collected Poems* (1971), for which she selected and ordered the poems, some of these rejected earlier poems returned, and others of the 1930s were eliminated in their turn. One notable absentee from the *Collected Poems* was the title-poem of *The Last Man and Other Verses* (1936), a dramatic monologue by the earth's last human survivor after a world war representative of Daryush's more explicitly political poetry of the 1930s. The title of the volume was itself a departure from those of her other works, which ran from *Verses* (1930) to *Verses – Seventh Book* (1971), emphasizing metrical experimentation rather than content. Her most famous poem, the sonnet 'Still Life', comes from the 1936 collection; as the title suggests, it is the very inexplicitness which is the poem's strength. It is one of Daryush's experiments with syllabic metre, where, as she wrote, unlike in accented verse 'the fixed element is no longer time but number; the integrity of line and syllable is challenged by the stress demands of sense or syntax'.[18] It is the unexpected tensions thus produced which create the profound unease in this sonnet, as the octave's exquisite evocation of a beautifully laid-out upper-class breakfast is succeeded by the introduction of the human element:

> She comes over the lawn, the young heiress,
> from her early walk in her garden wood
> feeling that life's a table set to bless
> her delicate desires with all that's good. (p. 59)

In the distance measured by the unsettling progression of the syllables, the lawn becomes a minefield through which the uncomprehending heiress walks, in a reference to class relations more powerful than such explicitly threatening poems as 'The Last Man' or 'Children of Wealth' (1937).

Ruth Pitter, who published her *First Verses* in 1920, was another example of a poet who presented herself as half-concealed within the tradition of English poetry. In a radio talk in 1969 Pitter described 'the great genetic difference between poets and poetesses . . . we have a tendency to hide our deepest feelings and men, on the whole, like to advertise them: there is that difference and I like to mark it'.[19] Where Sitwell urged women to cultivate the peacock as their model, Pitter's model of female distinctiveness emphasized reticence and inconspicuousness. She was probably the only woman poet to embrace the term 'poetess', and it was suggestive of her general stance. She cultivated a niche within a continuous tradition of English poetry. It was a niche initially made available by the patronage of the conservative critic Hilaire Belloc, who funded the publication of her earlier works, and her poetry emphasized pastiche of the poetry of earlier centuries and eschewed overt topical reference. Her parallel career, which enabled her to continue writing poetry, was as a craftswoman producing furniture and pottery to traditional models. Her poetry sought to reveal the relations of the spiritual and the mundane, and her two main collections of the 1930s were complementary in this endeavour. *A Mad Lady's Garland* (1934) was a series of comic pastiches of past poetic styles in which creatures questioned the dignity of human endeavour in a context unaware of God. In 'Maternal Love Triumphant', a pastiche eighteenth-century fable, a spider explores the significance of her dedicated and destructive maternity; 'The Cockroach', unsurprisingly, epitomizes modern free verse. *A Trophy of Arms* (1936) countered with the spiritually aware verses, pastiches of seventeenth-century models such as 'The Eternal Image' and 'Weeping Water, Leaping Fire', which described the transcendent visible through material appearances.

Several women poets who produced most of their poetry after 1945 first published in the 1930s. Kathleen Raine, the most frequent woman contributor to *New Verse*, later described her feelings of estrangement from the dominant trends in modern poetry as a student at Cambridge, where Donne was admired and Milton rejected. For Raine this was indicative of the loss of a sense of the mythological informing the natural world, and the urgent need was for a poetry which acknowledged the unavailability of traditional Christian iconography and recreated the mythological sense and the symbols which represented it by drawing on individual dream and vision.[20] Her first collection, *Stone and Flower* (1943), included her most famous 1930s poem, 'Maternal Grief' (1937), which explored the representation of violent primal feeling through images of ritual. In the same year another poet, Anne Ridler, published her first collection, *Nine Bright Shiners*, which included her poems of the 1930s, and in a series of poems, 'Now As Then: September 1939', 'Kirkwall 1942' and 'Ringshall Summer: Remembering

Marvell's "Appleton House" ', evoked the mythological Britain of literature as a context for Britain at war.

Stevie Smith, the most famous British woman poet of the postwar period, was advised by Cape, to whom she sent her poems for publication, to write a novel instead. Smith's distinctive response to the familiar association of women with prose was her first book, *Novel On Yellow Paper* (1936), in which she began to create her public persona, later to become famous through poetry readings, out of the situation of the rejected poet determined to get her poems into print somehow. The 'novel' is a prose monologue into which poems, ideas for poems, and critical discussions of poetry are inserted; it is supposedly written on the office notepaper available to Smith, who was secretary to the publishing magnates Newnes and Pearson, and in the interstices of office work. The secretarial situation is central to Smith's construction of her persona. Her poetry is not a genre apart and superior, but carried on in the context of other kinds of publishing, a secret work-load to be completed. 'That's two off my hands' she comments with relief as she works another poem into her 'novel', and assures the reader 'any poem you may read in these pages you may take it from me has never yet been published: so you get the first look in'.[21] Inserting another poem she urges 'it will break up the page for you, and something fresh to the eye helps the tired brain and aids concentration' (p. 180). These hopeful marketing ploys complement the book's commentary on poetry as a genre co-existing with difficulty with other forms of publication; there are frequent allusions to the vast public for the romantic fiction of the twopenny weeklies, and an exemplary narrative of a male poet who relaunched himself as a 'lady novelist'.

In *Novel On Yellow Paper*, and its sequel, *Over The Frontier* (1938), Smith develops the voice of her poems and discusses the difficulties of representing the speaking voice in print; 'this book is the talking voice that runs on . . . Oh talking voice that is so sweet, how hold you alive in captivity, how point you with commas, semi-colons, dashes, pauses and paragraphs?' (p. 46). The sly, prattling, *faux-naif* voice she creates is located with difficulty, and in rejection of the two dominant female voices she hears in contemporary culture, those of the 'lady novelist' of the twopenny weeklies and of the 'cultured gentlewoman'. Seamus Heaney has described the importance of the speaking voice to Smith's poetry, her cultivation of a persona pitched between 'Gretel and the witch', but has also pointed to the reader's need to be aware of the intonations and understatements, the 'disenchanted gentility', of the English middle class of the period.[22] It is a voice which continually allies itself with genres seen as minor, with fairy-tale, nursery-rhyme and light verse. The frequent quotations and pastiches of past poets, particularly, as with Sitwell, of Tennyson's mellifluities, are part of Smith's critique of Britain's pretensions as an imperial power, which have drawn on the poetic heritage for justification. Smith's cultivation of minor genres as models is in part a rejection of those pretensions; it also indicates her sense that minor genres are the only place a woman poet can go. Near the end of *Novel On Yellow Paper* her persona comments that she is not 'open and receptive to the genius of Shakespeare' (p. 219). Early in this period Meynell had described her inadequacies in relation to Shakespeare; Smith's rejection of Shakespeare defines the modest, precarious but antagonistic role which women poets must adopt to the cultural traditions of imperial Britain.

NOTES

Place of publication is London, unless otherwise stated.

1. Cora Kaplan, 'Language and Poetry', in *Sea Changes: Essays on Culture and Feminism* (Verso, 1986), pp. 69–93.
2. See Peter Brooker and Peter Widdowson, 'A Literature for England', in Robert Colls and Philip Dodd, eds, *Englishness: Politics and Culture 1880–1920* (Croom Helm, 1986); Brian Doyle, *English and Englishness* (Routledge, 1983).
3. Alice Meynell, 'Christina Rossetti', in *Prose and Poetry*, ed. Viola Meynell et al. (Cape, 1947), p. 145; 'Elizabeth Barrett Browning', in *Prose and Poetry*, p. 353. Subsequent quotations are from this volume.
4. *Prose and Poetry*, p. 32.
5. Maud Bodkin, *Archetypal Patterns in Poetry: Psychological Studies of the Imagination* (Oxford: Oxford University Press, 1934), pp. 300–2.
6. Harold Monro, *Some Contemporary Poets* (Parsons, 1920), pp. 75, 199, 203.
7. *Collected Letters of Thomas Hardy*, ed. Richard Purdy and Michael Millgate (Oxford: Clarendon Press, 1988), VII, p. 113.
8. 'The Poems of Emily Brontë', in *Collected Poems and Prose of Charlotte Mew*, ed. Val Warner (Carcanet/Virago, 1981), pp. 356, 368. Subsequent quotations are from this volume.
9. Jan Montefiore, *Feminism and Poetry: Language, Experience, Identity, in Women's Writing* (Pandora, 1987), p. 17.
10. Quoted in *The Writings of Anna Wickham: Free Woman and Poet*, ed. R.D. Smith (Virago, 1984), p. 27. Subsequent quotations are from this volume.
11. Monro, *Some Contemporary Poets*, p. 204.
12. Reprinted in *Women's Poetry of the 1930s: A Critical Anthology*, ed. Jane Dowson (Routledge, 1996), pp. 46–7.
13. 'Women as Writers', in *Collected Poems of Sylvia Townsend Warner*, ed. Claire Harman (Manchester: Carcanet, 1982), p. 269.
14. 'Some Observations on Women's Poetry', in *Edith Sitwell: Fire of the Mind*, ed. Elizabeth Salter and Allannah Harper (Michael Joseph, 1976), pp. 189–90.

15. Amabel Williams-Ellis, *An Anatomy of Poetry* (Oxford: Blackwell, 1922), p. 240.
16. W.B. Yeats, 'Modern Poetry', in *Essays and Introductions* (Macmillan, 1961), p. 501.
17. See Donald Davie, 'Sylvia Townsend Warner', in *Under Brigg Flats: A History of Poetry in Great Britain 1960–88* (Manchester: Carcanet, 1989), pp. 58–60.
18. Elizabeth Daryush, 'Note on Syllabic Metres', in her *Collected Poems* (Manchester: Carcanet, 1976), p. 24. Subsequent quotations are from this volume.
19. Reported in the *Listener*, 29 May 1969, pp. 756–7.
20. Kathleen Raine, *Defending Ancient Springs* (Oxford: Oxford University Press, 1967), pp. 104–5.
21. Stevie Smith, *Novel on Yellow Paper* (New York: Pinnacle, 1982), pp. 26, 28.
22. Seamus Heaney, 'A Memorable Voice', in *Preoccupations: Selected Prose 1968–78* (Faber and Faber, 1980), p. 199.

CHAPTER FIVE

The Fiction of Fact

For the writers discussed in this chapter content was of primary importance; there were urgent issues to be communicated, and an emphasis on
formal innovation was often seen as distracting from the primacy of fact.
Marion Shaw has described the shared concerns of the innovative and
documentarist novelists about the representation of women's lives.[1] However, the latter group's uninterest in the search for new forms to express
women's experience, and ready acceptance of existing forms, marked a gulf
between the two groups. The writers discussed here are the middlebrow
writers, often winning prizes and selling in large numbers, seeing the provision of factual evidence about the lives they describe as their prime task.
The chapter will describe first the novelists who saw their role as communicating urgent topical issues, and then the rural writers who pointed to
loss of contact with the countryside, and the historical novelists who sought
to recover the actualities of life in the past.

THE TOPICAL FICTION OF FACT

In a 1937 article, 'New Documents', in the socialist journal *Fact*, Storm
Jameson called for a new kind of fiction, which would be the equivalent
of the documentary film, the most distinctive British contribution to cinema
in the 1930s. For Jameson fiction had so far failed to respond significantly
to the issues of Depression Britain and fascist Europe. She called for novelists to research the great issues more thoroughly, to innovate in creating
fiction through group-work, above all to eliminate themselves. 'As the

94

photographer does, so must the writer keep himself out of the picture, while working ceaselessly to present the fact from a striking (poignant, ironic, penetrating, significant) angle'.[2] Her named target was George Orwell's *The Road to Wigan Pier* (1937), a documentary which foregrounded the writer's subjectivity, but she also attacked modernist fiction, and its use of the stream of consciousness, 'the static analysis of feeling and thought'. In a lecture the same year, 'The Novel in Contemporary Life', she attacked Woolf as 'an artist whose success has depended on her being able to find in the outer world an image, a symbol, to which she can attach her remarkable capacity for feeling'.[3] 'New Documents' was the counter to Woolf's call in 'Mr Bennett and Mrs Brown' for the examination of individual experience to be freed from the deadening constraints of the descriptions of materiality exemplified by Bennett's work. For Jameson fiction had declined since Bennett's masterpiece, *The Old Wives' Tale* (1908); the modernists Woolf and Joyce had destroyed the links between materiality and individual feeling, and redefined fiction in solipsist terms.

Jameson's perception of a division between modernists and socially committed novelists became a recurrent critical theme. Raymond Williams in *The Long Revolution* (1961) identified the major division in twentieth-century fiction as between the documentary social novel and the innovative personal novel; social and personal relations were no longer presented as part of the same process.[4] Fredric Jameson in his 1975 article, 'Beyond the Cave: Demystifying the Ideology of Modernism', described a situation where 'the truth of our social life as a whole . . . is increasingly irreconcilable with the aesthetic quality of language or of individual experience', and pointed to the bestselling writers whose success in discussing the engrossing major issues of existence in their fiction depended on their continued use of the narrative modes of nineteenth-century realist fiction.[5] Storm Jameson's fictions groped for some way of redefining the traditional social novel in contemporary terms to replace the modernist fiction she despised. Winifred Holtby, a more conciliatory exponent of the fiction of fact, attempted to put the writing of women modernists and women documentarists in the same frame. Her *Virginia Woolf* is devoted to building bridges between Woolf and the women writers who put political content before form, emphasizing the similarity of their concerns, and tracing the split to the suffrage years, when 'writers, painters, musicians and actresses were torn between their obligations to art and their obligations to society', and irrevocable choices had to be made.[6] Holtby's admiration for the work Woolf produced by resisting the call to political action is, however, qualified by what she sees as the faults produced by that resistance, the elimination of materiality, the ignorance of what needs to be done to oppose an entrenched Philistinism, and an exaggerated estimate of the height and impermeability of class barriers. Nonetheless, *To the Lighthouse* is presented as a truer response to the social problems of the age than the genial panoramic populism of J.B. Priestley, a writer who frequently served both Holtby and Jameson as an example of the failings of the commercial exploitation of traditional realism.

During the suffrage years, with their intensive reassessment of the roles and expectations of women, a gulf began to develop between the writers seeking new forms to express women's experience and writers ready to use any available vehicle to direct their political comment to as wide an audience as possible. Polemic and drama were the dominant forms of suffragist writing; dramatic writing by women proliferated. Much of it was intended for amateur production at suffrage rallies, but there were also professional ventures, such as the Co-operative Theatre, managed by Lena Ashwell, which explored the possibility of drama written, performed and managed by women.[7] Appropriately the two writers most actively involved with the suffrage campaign, Elizabeth Robins and Cicely Hamilton, were both actresses. Robins founded the Actresses' Suffrage League, Hamilton the Women Writers' Suffrage League, and both used established forms of fiction, drama and polemic to advance their views. Robins, an expatriate American actress identified with Ibsen roles, wrote the suffrage drama, *Votes for Women* (1907), and immediately recycled it as *The Convert* (1907), the major Edwardian novel to take the suffrage movement as its theme. Her previous major success was her Klondyke romance, *The Magnetic North* (1904), which drew on her own experiences there in 1900. Decisively located within the male tradition of adventure romance, it exemplified Robins's own escape from the constraints of the domestic novel, before feminism provided her with alternative possibilities.

The Convert celebrates the escape of its upper-class heroine, Vida, from the country-house world of set rituals to suffrage activity and the freedom and danger of the streets. There she encounters sexual and police harassment, the ordinary experience of working women, but recovers a sense of identity and power as a woman; the novel rebuts the frequent charge of sexlessness made against the suffrage activists. The scenes of upper-class life, however, read as inferior pastiche Henry James; the novel's vitality lies in the street scenes. Robins's professional descriptions of the suffrage rallies and the performing skills of the speakers are precise and acute. These scenes outline the range of roles available to women: soubrette, vamp, heroine of melodrama, working-class pathos, music-hall comedy; the successful performers are shown to be those who work within available roles and subvert them to their own purposes. Robins significantly fails, however, to find a persuasive new role and rhetorical mode for Vida; she can work subversively within established forms, but cannot envisage new modes of representation.

Hamilton, a character actress in Shakespeare and Shaw, and a popular speaker at rallies, wrote the most successful women's play of the period, *Diana of Dobson's* (1908), a West End hit for the Co-operative Theatre. Hamilton's comedy anticipates Shaw's *Pygmalion* (1914) in its story of a drapery assistant who successfully imposes herself on high society. In the first act Diana is moping in a workers' dormitory; in the middle acts she spends an unexpected legacy on a holiday in a fashionable Swiss resort and attracts an upper-class loafer who finds living on £600 a year impossible. In the last act the pair meet again among the derelicts on the Embankment, but his apparent poverty is simply an experiment to which Diana's satirical comments have goaded him, and they settle down together to live moderately. *Diana* is an engaging example of the well-made play of the period, distinguished by the heroine's scathing feminist rhetoric on working conditions, and by the framing dormitory and Embankment scenes, which emphasize the wide disparities between the lives of working and upper-class women. Unlike Shaw's Eliza, Diana negotiates her social transition without a mentor; her mobility celebrates the ease with which women can adapt to different roles. The play's confidence in the possibilities opening up for women is characteristic of the suffrage period; in contrast the most successful postwar play by a woman, Clemence Dane's *A Bill of Divorcement*, discussed in Chapter 1, emphasizes the burden that the past and inescapable family roles impose on women.

Between the wars, as modernist works became perceived as the dominant innovative fictions, the fiction of such writers as F.M. Mayor and E.H. Young, seriously committed to the representation of women's experience but still using traditional forms, became increasingly self-conscious. Modernism comes to be seen, not as liberating, but as excluding. In Mayor's major novel, *The Rector's Daughter* (1924), justification of traditional fiction becomes an important part of the content; the novel is about the redundancy, not only of the heroine, but of the fictional forms which had once made it possible to treat such people. The inability of the heroine, Mary Jocelyn, to find a place for herself is placed also as a problem of literary representation. There is no longer an acceptable way of talking about Mary's, in fact useful, parish work, her long passion for the married neighbouring vicar, the poetry she writes. To the representatives of the London literary world, which controls literary discourse, hers is 'a life so shrivelled it became absurd', something which is not available for consideration or representation.[8] The Victorian fictions which provided a space for people like Mary are perceived as being as anachronistic as the Church; the reading habits which supported them have disappeared, and with them the possibilities for representing the 'shrivelled' lives within the community. There are several references to the disappearance of the practice of reading books aloud within the family circle, and with that the disappearance both of whole sets of relationships and of kinds of fiction. The Victorian writer most powerfully evoked is Trollope, within whose spacious works there had been room for Mary's kind of unregarded life. The novel's plot reprises that of *The Small House at Allington* (1864), suggesting that Trollope's genial, sympathetic version of the jilted spinster, and her place in the community, is a representation unimaginable in the literary world of the 1920s.

What the novel also describes is a kind of unperceived triumph in which Mary creates an inner space for herself in her writing, a success dimly recognized by the London literati who agree, however, that it would be pointless to publish her poems, 'just the Anglican spinster warbling' (ch. 28). Like Lily's painting in *To the Lighthouse*, Mary's poems exist in self-fulfilment, and not in view of any audience. *The Rector's Daughter* laments the loss of the Victorian novel's capacity for dealing with the external world, but at the same time explores ways of defining the inner life through attention to the mundane externalities within which it contrives to survive. The popular success of this lament for the lost stabilities of Victorian fiction, published, ironically, by the Woolfs' Hogarth Press, suggested an audience responsive to Mayor's outline of the dilemmas of the post-Victorian novel.

Young's much reprinted *William* (1925) also invoked a nineteenth-century model for its story of a middle-class family of the 1920s divided by their responses to the elopement of one of the married daughters, Lydia. Young examines how far *Pride and Prejudice* still offers a recognizable model of family relations, as some family members, led by the energetic mother, perceive Lydia's behaviour as a family shame which must be remedied, and others, including the father, William, argue for the primacy of individual choice in a postwar world where the rules which governed the behaviour of Austen's characters no longer apply. The novel is traditional in form, and relies for much of its effect on its disruption of the expectations roused by the Austen model. Woolf, reading it after its re-emergence as one of the ten reprinted novels which launched Penguin, was surprised to find herself admiring a work so traditional in form, 'so minute and yet so alive. And it's the kind of book I generally dislike' (*Letters*, VI, p. 216). She was responding to the novel's detailed reconstruction of everyday household routine, its celebration of the pleasures of family rituals and town walks, and recording of the minute shifts in the relations of family members.

With the 1930s the demand for writers to place topical content and comment before formal innovation became more insistent. As Jameson records, 'writers found themselves being summoned on to platforms and into committee-rooms to defend society', and 'intellectuals who refused to

protest were in effect blacklegs'.[9] Jameson herself later regretted much of
the time spent in committees, the pressures on writers to engage in direct
political debate rather than creative work, the specific labour of organizing
and editing the anti-war symposium, *Challenge to Death* (1935), in which
Brittain, Holtby, Macaulay and West were also involved, and her failure
under all these pressures to focus sufficiently on her concept of the documentary novel. An emphasis on fact was widely seen as the writer's only
appropriate response to the issues of the 1930s; the silence which greeted
Sylvia Townsend Warner's brilliant allegory of the Spanish Civil War, *After
the Death of Don Juan* (1938), is partly attributable to this contemporary
insistence on the factual as the mode for socialist, or social, commitment.
This merging of fiction and fact could sometimes be comic; the socialist
novelist, Ethel Mannin, provided her much reprinted novel, *Ragged Banners*
(1931), with an index, so that readers, reading the novel as if it were
biography, could properly assess the effects on her perplexed characters of
the indexed influences, socialism and Victorianism, Freud and the Russian
Ballet, D.H. Lawrence and Ethel M. Dell. Woolf had anticipated this trend
in 1928 in her pseudo-biographical *Orlando*, where the provision of an
index spoofs the claims of biographers to scientific certitude.

The kind of success which might be enjoyed by a novel combining
topical urgency with a traditional fictional form was demonstrated by Phyllis
Bottome's bestselling novel of 1937 about a German family divided by
Hitler's accession to power, *The Mortal Storm*. It was rapidly reprinted as
a Penguin Special in 1938; its inclusion in a list otherwise devoted to non-
fiction was described as justified by the urgency of its political theme.
Bottome's romance capably combined the aspects expected of the fiction
of fact, an urgent topical subject in the rise of Nazism, detailed observation
drawn from her own residence in Germany and Austria in the 1930s, a
traditional family narrative, and a strong feminist heroine, who finally skis
to safety over the frontier carrying the record of her murdered Nobel
scientist father's priceless last work which she will continue. The success of
Bottome's combination of topical comment and traditional romance was
reconfirmed in 1940, when the film adaptation, directed by Frank Borzage,
was among the first Hollywood productions directly addressed to the
European situation.

Bottome's attempt to place women's issues, and her heroine's feminist
ambitions (eliminated in the film), at the centre of the European situation
highlighted a central problem for the woman political novelist of the 1930s.
The major exponents were Jameson, Holtby, Bottome and Lettice Cooper.
They were all middle-class, left-wing, had studied at British universities,
or in Bottome's case in Austria, and all came from the distinctive, non-
metropolitan cultures of the north of England. All were strongly conscious

99

of themselves as emancipated women, seeking to advance women's cause, but they were also responsive to demands that individuals should subordinate themselves to the more urgent demands of the community. Their factual fiction emphasizes a move away from the individual; women's issues are presented as part of the general social situation, rather than being foregrounded as they had been in the previous decades. The material of autobiographical experience is subsumed to the life of the community. In this the novelists were responding to the general relegation of women's issues as secondary in relation to the crises of unemployment at home and fascism abroad. In turning back to the representation of the group, they also turned explicitly to nineteenth-century models. Jameson's major fictional work of the 1930s, her 'Mirror in Darkness' trilogy, was intended 'to uncover the social web of the 30s, and the men and women caught in it and struggling', to recover a form of fiction which could explain the contemporary world as *Middlemarch* had explained the Victorian.[10] *Middlemarch* was also the model for Winifred Holtby's analysis of her fictitious shire, *South Riding* (1936). The title of Jameson's trilogy, however, admits a certain desperation, suggesting that the problems of the realist novelist have intensified since Stendhal described the novel as a mirror walking down the road.

Jameson's first volume, *Company Parade* (1934), submerges her self-portrait, Hervey Russell, an aspiring writer in London in the 1920s, in a panoramic narrative of political and literary life. Her ideal in 'New Documents' was the writer who could break through to the reality of experience, who could know what the working-class 'woman's forefinger knows when it scrapes the black out of a crack in the table or the corner of a shelf' (p. 264), and the novel emphasizes the failures of existing writing to establish communication between classes. The rapid transitions that the narrative effects between social groups are unprepared and unexplained, developing a cumulative impression of paranoia on both sides. This is especially evident in the moves between the newspaper magnate and his working-class readers, both incapacitated for useful action by fantasies about 'Them'. Hervey's ambitions for the social novel are grotesquely parodied by her fellow Yorkshire writer, Ridley, apparently based on J.B. Priestley, who plans to write about 'crowds, a fight, a football match, a popular cafe, the fish market, a fair . . . in a broad, jovial, straightforward style'.[11] His unscrupulous management of popular themes to create images of a unified England fouls them for use by more committed novelists.

The 'Mirror in Darkness' series was originally intended to be six novels, but Jameson's narrative never reached the 1930s, and she abandoned the project after the third volume, *None Turn Back* (1937). In this the narrative moves between the activities of both sides during the General Strike, while Hervey undergoes a hysterectomy; at the end both Hervey and the strikers are left to come to terms somehow with the traumatic destruction of their hopes. No new life will grow from what has gone before; renewal must be sought elsewhere. In Jameson's writing this was in commitment to the wider scene of Europe; her most complete example of the group narrative is her wartime novel, *Cloudless May* (1943), which uses the microcosm of a small French town in 1940 to describe France's responses to German invasion. There is no central figure in a group intended to represent as many shades of opinion as possible, and the emphasis is entirely on the details of the German advance and of the multiplicity of French response.

Holtby's most successful novel was her last, the posthumously published *South Riding*, a panoramic reconstruction of the life of a fictitious shire. The workings of local government, 'the first-line defence thrown up by the community' (prefatory letter), provide the novel's framework; each section is named after a particular council committee, with an epigraph provided from the minutes of that committee, and the novel attempts to trace the effects of the council's political decisions in the lives of individuals. The novel works through saturation in detail, and a continued emphasis on the importance of the mundane, factual, and apparently trivial. The reconstructions of council meetings, the quotations from minutes, are in the spirit of Jameson's call for documentary fiction; the insistence that only hard attention to fact can reveal the truth of lives in the 1930s also anticipates Mass Observation later in the decade. The novel also, however, carries the subtitle 'An English Landscape' and an epigraph from Vita Sackville-West's *The Land*, setting the activities of the council within an older frame of reference to the continuity of English rural life. *South Riding* is a regional novel, existing on the boundaries between the topical novel and the rural writing popular in this period. Woolf's reaction, 'I do not like regional novels' (*Letters*, III, p. 380), exposes the gulf between the metropolitan modernist and the writer seeking to evoke a distinctive provincial culture by drawing on Victorian and Edwardian models.

In Holtby's portrait of local government, 'the first-line defence', the role of women is central. In her heroine, the defiantly provincial and celibate headmistress, Sarah Burton, she celebrates the new breed of career professional, the working-class girl enabled by educational advances to create a new role for women in the community. Sarah is tailored for her role by being given the physical appearance of the Jarrow MP Ellen Wilkinson, by her energy in fighting for the wasted female lives around her, and by a comradely relation with the woman alderman who represents women's fight in the preceding generation, and is modelled on Holtby's mother, to whom the book is dedicated. She is also, however, enmeshed in a reprise of *Jane Eyre*, a romance with a Tory squire, who is appropriately equipped with a decaying manor-house and a mad wife, and eventually rides off a cliff in token of the irreversible decay of Toryism. The presence of this Gothic romance at the centre of a documentary celebration of local government is used to suggest the yearnings for personal life which the professional woman must at present sacrifice, but the discrepancy between the Gothic and documentary sections, and the conflicting female aspirations they reveal, fractures the novel. (Like *The Mortal Storm*, *South Riding* became a successful film; the Korda film production of 1938 responded to the regional pride and documentary detail of Holtby's novel, but resolved its contradictions by eliminating the feminist and Gothic elements, and making the squire a Tory progressive, who survives to lead the community.)

Another socialist and feminist narrative of local government, Cooper's *We Have Come To a Country* (1935), is one of the most thoughtful attempts by the fiction of fact to reformulate social relations and find new fictional ways to describe them. Gaskell's *North and South* (1855) is the obvious model for this story of an unemployment centre in Leeds managed by a Ladies Committee, and the misunderstandings and conflicts between these middle-class women seeking to intervene in an industrial dispute and the working-class men who use the Centre. In Cooper's version, however, the importance of the middle-class hero is significantly reduced. The two most sympathetic 'ladies', Laura and Jessica, both initially focus the frustrations which have led them into voluntary work in erotic obsession with the centre's attractive but incompetent middle-class supervisor, but he is gradually displaced, as the real romance is revealed to be between middle-class women and working-class men. The focus of attraction is the rebellious young socialist craftsman, Ephraim, and the working-class needs and dynamism he represents. When his conflict with the supervisor nearly destroys the centre, it is the women who decide to continue the struggle to find a way of relating across the class divide.

Cooper's narrative is self-conscious about the problems of redefining class relations, the potentially risible associations of genteel philanthropy, and of ladies turned from flower-arranging to industrial relations, and the scorn displayed by the working-class women, who resent the centre as a source of interference and resist attempts to involve them in plans for a leisure which they do not have. The demonstrated marginality of working-class women in Cooper's novel is exemplary of the period's emphasis on the unemployed working-class male, and Cooper is clearly worried by her inability to integrate her working-class women characters. Her next, and best-known, novel, *The New House* (1936), provides a different solution to the problems of talking about middle-class women in relation to working-class needs. Ostensibly a domestic novel, tracing the events of one day in which the spinster heroine moves from the family mansion with her mother, and decides to seek work in London, it also functions as a microcosm of the changes in English society. Much-needed working-class housing will be built where the mansion stood; England will learn to function without mansions or dependent daughters. Nonetheless there is a sense in *The New House* of retreat from intractable problems, from public to domestic life; the representation of family relations replaces that of class relations in the earlier novel, and the shift is suggestive of the problems that the fiction of fact failed to solve.

RURAL WRITING

The writing which recorded life in rural England enjoyed a special kind of prestige in this period. The episode which most strikingly demonstrated this was the 1928 Literary Fund speech in which Stanley Baldwin revived Mary Webb's sales; the link established between the nation's leader and an obscure, recently deceased, Shropshire writer suggested a national unity founded in common love of the countryside. There were many other examples of the prestige attracted by writing about the countryside. Constance Holme's Westmoreland novels were accorded classic status by being published in the World's Classics series; many shared the belief of Sir Humphrey Milford, the series publisher, that it was in country life that the true values were found. Another instant classic was *Lark Rise* (1939), in which the ex-postmistress Flora Thompson recorded her rural Oxfordshire childhood. Holme and Webb both won the Femina/Vie Heureuse Prize, for *The Splendid Fairing* (1919) and *Precious Bane* (1924) respectively; so, ironically, did Stella Gibbons's *Cold Comfort Farm* (1932), the satire which still determines the reputation of the rural writers, but shared in the classic status accorded rural writing. Vita Sackville-West's long rural poem, *The Land* (1926), won the prestigious Hawthornden Prize.

The classic status enjoyed by rural writing in this period derived from the insistently diffused belief that the real England was rural England. Early-twentieth-century writers responded to a changing, industrial, imperial England by constructing a concept of the real England, a rural England in which continuity with the past was still clearly visible, and in which the true values of England still flourished. Forster, Lawrence, Kipling, the Georgian poets, all discovered deep England. Advertising and the propaganda imagery of two World Wars promoted this concept of the true rural

England.[12] Rural writing was perceived to have a crucial role in keeping metropolitan, imperial Britain in touch with her roots; Baldwin wrote in his preface to the 1929 edition of Mary Webb's *Precious Bane*, which he dated from Downing Street, that 'one who reads some passages in Whitehall has almost the physical sense of being in Shropshire cornfields'.[13] The preface capably summarizes the political significance of rural writing, the interdependence of Whitehall and Shropshire, the nation's essential continuity with its rural past, woman's especial affinity with nature playing its role in reminding us of these things. The illustrations by Rowland Hilder for this edition of a novel set in 1800 erase differences between past and present, showing dehistoricized landscapes in which tiny figures in classic smocks give no clue to the date, and the heroine is shown in 1920s style in kneelength dress and plait. Both preface and illustrations work to create a timeless rural England.[14]

The women rural writers, however, did not share these metropolitan certainties about continuity. They wrote about discontinuities and violent change, humanity's increasing estrangement from the natural environment, and the 'lost and forgotten lives', in Webb's phrase, of those who still lived in close proximity to it. Like the documentarist novelists, they were seeking ways of recording the actualities of living, and they struggled with the problems of communicating what they saw as the unjustly marginalized experience of rural life. Their notorious failings of melodrama and 'fine writing', analysed by Gibbons, were symptoms of these difficulties. *Cold Comfort Farm* presents rural fiction as the last home of Victorian melodrama, of plots revolving around family hatreds, ancient houses and violent elemental interventions. The melodrama of these plots, their obvious dependence on Victorian models, was easily parodied, but pointed to an attempt to talk about the gulf between past and present, and the violence of change which created the urban present and estranged it from the past and from the countryside associated with that past.

Gibbons asterisked the passages of fine writing in *Cold Comfort Farm*, satirizing their isolation from the surrounding text. Her point had already been made insistently by Katherine Mansfield. In a review of Sheila Kaye-Smith's *Green Apple Harvest* (1920) she had described 'a novel divided against itself, written with two hands, one is the country hand, scoring the dialect, and the other is the town hand ... pointing out the moon like the "blown petal" of a cherry tree'. She had made the same point about the lyric passages in Holme's *The Splendid Fairing*, commenting that 'this is a little pit dug at the feet of all who write about peasants'.[15] Mansfield identifies interpolated fine writing as a central problem of the rural novelist attempting to find ways of describing modern humanity's relations with the natural environment, but is massively indifferent to those problems, an indifference marked by her lumping together of all Holme's laboriously precise understandings of working identities and relationships under the inaccurate term 'peasant'.

The three women novelists most associated with rural fiction, Kaye-Smith, Holme and Webb, each lived in the country about which they wrote, and presented it as border-country. Kaye-Smith produced a series of novels which came to be known as the 'Sussex novels', among them *Sussex Gorse* (1916), *Green Apple Harvest* (1920) and *Joanna Godden* (1921). They were appearing at the same time as Kipling's Sussex stories, but where Kipling's Sussex is the deep root of a continuously developing Britain, Kaye-Smith's Sussex is 'lost and forgotten'. Her most achieved novel, *Joanna Godden*, is set in the Sussex marshlands, and her heroine is presented as a figure of marginalized, barbaric vitality. The plot, of a woman farmer who sacks her bailiff and farms for herself, and of her relations with three suitors, is taken straight from Hardy's *Far from the Madding Crowd* (1874), but the problem around which the novel revolves is specific to its period. It questions how the modern world can relate to Joanna, who is presented throughout as problematic, an archaic figure to urban dwellers in her direct contact with the land and her freedom from artifice, and in her insistence on flamboyant, highly coloured clothes and furnishings, but also unaccepted as a dominant woman within the traditional rural hierarchy.

The interpolated nature of the fine writing passages in this novel is explained by Joanna's working relationship with the land; 'all she saw was the flooded pastures which meant poor grazing for her tegs due to come down from the coast'.[16] Appreciation of the landscape is assumed to be a characteristic of people not working the land, which leaves the passages of lyric landscape description estranged from Joanna's consciousness, and unlocated except as directed to an urban reader. The problem of how to bridge the gulf between Joanna and this urban reader is solved only in the episode in which Joanna and her second, genteel suitor tour the marshes. His response to the marshes is historical and literary; 'he was astonished to find how little she knew of her own country, and of that dim, flat land which was once under the sea' (pt. 2). There is an unbridgeable gulf between Martin's response to the countryside and Joanna's. Kaye-Smith's divided language – Sussex dialect and emphasis on practicalities on one hand, passages of lyrical guidebook description on the other – expresses this gulf. For the mostly urban reader for whom she is writing, Sussex is picturesque, historical, literary, but she is constantly pointing out that this view is entirely alien to Joanna. Far from confirming the continuities of national life Kaye-Smith's novels, with their frequent moves between different modes of writing, suggest a complete disjunction between rural and urban life.

Holme, who came from a family established as land-agents in Westmoreland for centuries, was the writer who most emphasized the details of working life. She encountered the same problem as Kaye-Smith: how to find a language to mediate between the rural communities she describes and the urban reader estranged from rural realities. A more ambitious novelist, and more responsive to modern developments in fiction than Kaye-Smith, her approach changed decisively. Her first three novels are panoramic Victorian narratives of whole communities; her postwar novels are located in one or two consciousnesses, and, as Glen Cavaliero has argued, clearly influenced by modernist techniques.[17] All Holme's novels are set in coastal Westmoreland, which, in the consciousness of its rural working people, has only one significant external reference point, Canada. Canada is the place to which the tenant farmers emigrate, and from which news of previous family emigrants comes. Holme's habitual early narrative voice is terse, elliptical, knowing, detailed on practicalities, and clearly modelled on Kipling's prose style. These stylistic echoes of the writer most associated with empire enhance the reader's sense of Westmoreland as frontier country, remote from deep England. In *The Lonely Plough* (1914), her most important early novel, the tenant farmers are faced with a choice between living on reclaimed land and emigration to Canada. The whole community lives under a threat created by the expansionist ambitions of the estate's previous land-agent, whose sea-wall, built to protect the reclaimed land, seems increasingly unsafe. Filial and community loyalty prevents his land-agent son, or the tenant-farmers, taking steps to acknowledge and remedy the situation, and a climactic flood sweeps away the reclaimed land and the lives on it. This might seem all too grimly appropriate in 1914 as Britain entered the war, but the narrative endorses the characters' choice, mediating between an insistence that the catastrophe is the bad case which establishes the importance of loyalty even in a dubious cause, and lament for the expendability of those who were sacrificed to make this point.

Holme's Westmoreland is, however, a world invaded by modernity; cars and telephones are widely used, and incomers tango down the lanes. A substantial subplot revolves around the ordinary activities of the community, with set-piece descriptions of choir-practices, hockey-matches and local elections, and the novel is strongest in its recreation of the ordinary busyness of the local community, as it evolves into the modern world. It anticipates Holtby's *South Riding* in its emphasis on local government, and in a subplot about a young woman farmer who breaks with precedent by getting herself elected to the district council, after a campaign targeted at local women. Holme's principal concern is with the practicalities of the working community, but she interpolates a series of lyrical passages under the running title 'The Green Gates of Vision' to suggest her land-agent's unspoken inwardness with the Westmoreland landscape, creating a tension, as Raymond Williams has described, between the documentarist passages and this 'authentic but specialized survival of the green language of Clare'.[18]

In her postwar novels, like another established prewar novelist, May Sinclair, Holme substantially revised her approach to respond to the advances of modernism. Where the prewar novels are panoramic and multiplotted with genteel central figures, the later novels are each set within the consciousness of elderly working persons during one day. *The Things which Belong* (1925), the fourth and last of these, is the story of a Westmoreland couple during a day when they decide whether to join their children in Canada. The rhetoric of loyalty and community has disappeared along with the genteel protagonists. The decision processes of the two are consecutively presented in entirely personal and gender-distinctive terms, with the landscape descriptions used to distinguish their specific modes of being in the world, and even how they position themselves in space. He is at home in his landscape, enjoying his awareness of the hedges, walls and hills which define the limits of his work as the head-gardener of a large estate, and slipping adaptably between them. She is a big woman, impinging decisively on her surroundings, yearning beyond the imprisoning boundaries, and longing for the imagined big sky of Canada. At the beginning of their respective inner monologues they are far apart; the developing action lies in Mattie's changing perception of the familiar landscape, as she gradually decides to stay. In this novel the lyrical passages have almost disappeared; only Mattie's cherished jam-cupboard, the focus of her decision to stay, evokes a distinctive lyricism. *The Things which Belong*, despite its rural setting, has developed in response to the new fiction.

With Mary Webb it was her self-conscious archaism which was cause for congratulation or controversy. Her novels record the remoteness of the countryside, their distinctive attribute the intensity with which they register the violence with which people have estranged themselves from the natural world, and the suffering inflicted on the victims of this process. In *Gone to Earth* (1917) the heroine, Hazel Woodus, is identified on the first page with her pet vixen, Foxy, a creature who offers a glimpse of what women might ideally be, 'a tawny silent form, wearing with the calm dignity of woodland creatures a beauty of eye and limb, a brilliance of tint, that few women could have worn without self-consciousness'.[19] In Webb's novels women share the victim status of animals; the narrative sometimes moves indifferently between the consciousnesses of Hazel and of Foxy, and at the novel's shocking conclusion Hazel dies in flight from the hounds of the squire who has earlier seduced her, preferring to identify with the hunted Foxy than with the human world represented by the hunt. Hazel rages, like the heroines of Sinclair and Richardson, at the subjection of women, but the novel also rages at the domination of species by species, and at man's estrangement from the natural world. The squire is 'the kind of man that supplies the most rabid reactionaries, materialists, imperialists' (ch. 33). Foxy, like a female version of D.H. Lawrence's stallion in *St Mawr* (1925), represents a natural vitality catastrophically suppressed in modern woman.

Precious Bane, Webb's last novel, is presented as the first-person narrative of the heroine, Prue Sarn, living in Shropshire in the early 1800s. Webb creates in Prue's mingling of dialect, archaisms, snatches of folksong, and confessional writing, a voice which emerges from the Shropshire community, as the Scottish writer, Lewis Grassic Gibbon, created in *Sunset Song* (1932) a voice for the Mearns community. Webb's emphasis, however, is specifically on 'us women, living such lost and forgotten lives' (pt. 2, ch. 5), and Prue is increasingly estranged from the community who come together mainly for scenes of violence. A bull-baiting, averted only when the one humane male offers himself as an alternative target for the dogs, foreshadows the final scene when the hare-lipped Prue is nearly drowned as a witch. The almost unrelieved violence of the narrative is opposed only by Prue's growing awareness of her compensatory relation with the natural world. 'It was a queer thing too that a woman who spent her days in sacking, cleaning sties and beasthouses, living hard, considering over fardens, should come of a sudden into such a marvel as this' (pt. 1, ch. 7). In the archaic narrative, as in Holme's postwar novels, sounds an insistence on the countryside as a secret treasurable resource for working people.

Despite their reception as affirmations of the continuity of rural life, it was their insistence on the gulf between countryside and urban modernity which characterized the rural novels. Even Vita Sackville-West's long rural poem, *The Land* (1926), which calls itself 'a mild continuous epic of the soil', and is committed to endorsing continuities, is formally divided. Long passages of agricultural advice are interspersed with pastiche Victorian Romantic verse about the affinity of women to trees, or to fritillaries. It was these discontinuities on which *Cold Comfort Farm* fastened. The cult of rural writing reached its height in the late 1920s; in the 1930s the two most enduringly successful pieces of rural writing of the period, Gibbons's satire and Thompson's *Lark Rise*, each in their separate ways demolished the prestige of the rural novelists. Both works originated in the genteel journal of country life, *The Lady*. Gibbons, a regular reviewer of rural fiction for the journal, used her acquired expertise to satirize the vogue for the genre, and invoke the spirit of Jane Austen to counter it. The story drew specifically on Kaye-Smith's *Sussex Gorse* and Webb's *The House in Dormer Forest* (1920), but included the whole tradition of rural fiction, notably *Wuthering Heights*. Flora, Gibbons's urban modern stranded in darkest Sussex, is an

Austen heroine unchecked by any sense of limitations. Like Emma she seeks to manage and direct the lives of those around her, but unlike Emma she is allowed to be entirely successful, persuading her archaic relatives, the Starkadders of Cold Comfort, to share her interest in the uses and functions of things, and reject their previous obsession with custom and tradition. She fails only with the oldest inhabitant, who, presented with a washing-up mop to replace the usual thorn twig he uses for clettering the dishes, ignores its use value and cherishes it in his bosom. The asterisked passages which announce the arrival of fine writing are pastiche Webb, and point to the disjunction of modernity and the natural world which is Webb's main theme. Gibbons's satire rebuts Webb by insisting on the possibility of making the transition to modernity painlessly, and without the futile anguish with which the rural novelists record the transition.

Thompson's *Lark Rise* (1939) also originated in *The Lady* with the 1937 sketch, 'Old Queenie', the first of several sketches from which the memoir emerged, along with its sequels, *Over to Candleford* (1941) and *Candleford Green* (1943), collected in 1945 as the trilogy, *Lark Rise to Candleford*. Thompson also experienced a rapid rise to classic status, but her memoir was in many ways a tacit rebuke to the rural novels. In place of their violent and disrupted fictions, it substitutes an engrossingly detailed record of a particular hamlet in a particular period, with an emphasis on the facts of everyday life kindred to the contemporary records of Mass Observation. For their fine writing it substitutes a precise and delicate lyricism, justified by its mediation through a child's perception. Moreover, it is authentically a working-class record, the only work by a working-class woman published in this period to achieve classic status, rather than a middle-class writer's attempt to mediate between the urban middle-class reader and the rural poor.

Lark Rise is presented in quasi-fictional form as the story of a child, Laura, rather than as direct memoir, a device already used by the children's writer, Alison Uttley, in her popular 1931 memoir of her Derbyshire childhood, *The Country Child*. It is Thompson's use of a child's perspective, as well as her insistence on practicalities, which enables her to trace the passing of the rural community in which she grew up without the recourse to melodrama which characterized much of the writing of the period. The memories of a lost world become the memories of a lost childhood, and the plot of the trilogy is provided by journeys and departures. *Lark Rise*, the longest of the three, gives a thorough portrait of the hamlet as it existed in the 1880s, its work and leisure practices. The most marked mobility at this stage is that of the daughters who go into domestic service. The book ends with the Golden Jubilee celebrations, and then fast forwards to the death of Laura's brother in the First World War. *Over to Candleford* expands the world described, tracing the visits of Laura's family to relatives in the nearby market town, and noting how 'her freedom of the fields grew less every year'.[20] The book ends with her journey from the hamlet to the village post-office where she works in *Candleford Green*; the last book contrasts Laura's brief glimpses of the 'freedom of the fields', when she delivers the post, with the developing life of the encroaching suburbs. In the process of Laura's transition from childhood, and her journeys within a small area, a whole world is described as having been lost. It was this use of the child's perspective, along with the detailed reconstruction of a way of life, which made Thompson's trilogy the most enduringly successful fiction of fact of the period. It realized the ambitions of the genre by becoming an indispensable source for later histories of rural life, and placing its interpretation of the loss of rural continuities as the accepted truth.[21]

HISTORICAL FICTION

The early twentieth century saw the emergence of women academic historians, most of them working in the areas of social and economic history, and concerned with recovering the under-recorded lives of women and working people. The women's movement created a demand for information about the lives of women in history, and a need to understand how they had lived; history became one of the most popular subjects with women students. By the 1920s historical fiction, unpopular in the Edwardian period, had re-established its popularity and become a genre particularly associated with women readers and writers. The historical fiction of the interwar years reiterated the emphasis on detail and research of the topical fiction of fact. It was one form of fiction, therefore, which tended to rival the Victorian novel in length, often requiring massive documentation to uphold its reconstruction of an under-recorded past way of life; in a time of shorter novels its length was acceptable as one of the guarantees of the authenticity of its reconstruction.

The exception to the unpopularity of historical fiction in the Edwardian period was the fiction of Marjorie Bowen, whose bestselling *The Viper of Milan* (1906) explored, not unrecorded female lives, but a Renaissance despot. Graham Greene claimed that it was her exhilarating relish in her hero's talent for evil which inspired his childhood ambition to be a writer.[22] What the historical setting allowed Bowen was a certain kind of imaginative freedom not available in contemporary fiction; between the wars Naomi Mitchison also took advantage of this freedom which in her case allowed a sexual explicitness not permissible in fiction with a contemporary setting. Historical fiction enabled Bowen to escape the confines of the domestic; in 1938 she described how in childhood she had retreated from the demands that she conform to an accepted model of femininity by imagining herself as one of the dominant, self-controlled heroes of her reading in history, Cardinal Richelieu or William of Orange.[23] She continued to explore this escape successfully for the next forty years, also using the male pseudonyms of George Preedy and Joseph Shearing to cover her prolific concentration on the possibilities for action and control offered by the past.

Bowen's work was about the excitement of exploring a male realm of total power, but there was one other influential Edwardian historical fiction, presented with heavy documentation and an emphasis on research, which emphasized women's history and the urgent need to recover it. It was called tersely *An Adventure*, appeared in 1911 over the names Elizabeth Morison and Frances Lamont, pseudonyms for the Oxford academics, Charlotte Moberley and Margaret Jourdain, and recorded the authors' belief that in 1901, on a visit to Versailles, they had experienced some form of time travel back to the Versailles gardens of 1789, and had seen Marie Antoinette. There were four subsequent editions of this work, each advancing yet more documentary evidence, and the Trianon Adventure became one of the century's most widely discussed psychic events. Its importance for historical fiction, as distinct from the history of psychic phenomena, lay in its exploration of different kinds of recovery of the past. First the authors recount in detail their own direct experience of a lost world, then the research they have undertaken in French archives in the intervening decade. As conscientious academics they have set out to test their hypothesis, and have not published their results until everything they have found convinces them that the Trianon gardens in which they walked were authentically those of 1789, and they have established historical identities for everybody they met there.

In the last section, 'A Reverie', they move entirely into fiction, reconstructing the thoughts of the imprisoned Marie Antoinette in 1792 as she blames herself for her failure to influence the king, and yearns back to her Trianon gardens, and especially to a summer day in 1789 when she had been briefly conscious of sympathetic passers by. These, of course, are Moberley and Jourdain, who are setting up a two-way current of sympathy with their doomed queen. Her yearnings for her situation to be understood have occasioned their travel; their response justifies their excursion into historical investigation. In this section Moberley and Jourdain are moving beyond their emphasis on detailed research to a more emotional involvement with their subject, expressing an urgent desire to import into the past a specifically female sympathy they feel to be lacking in most historical reconstruction. Their bypassing of academic methods to create through psychic experience their own field of research, and then investigate it, was, to put it mildly, unprofessional, but in their emphasis on the need to recover the past for a specifically female viewpoint, and in their combination of fact and empathy, their narrative is very suggestive of the methods of much subsequent historical fiction.[24]

In seeking to recover the history of Marie Antoinette, Moberley and Jourdain are representative of a major trend in historical fiction, the focus on the female royal. A tradition of queen-oriented history had been established in the Victorian period by the popular historian, Agnes Strickland, and her imitators, a tradition offering an alternative history of graceful suffering femininity in tacit victimized opposition to the onward course of male power.[25] The entrapment of these queens in their roles, and often in literal prisons, provided a kind of genteel continuation of the Gothic tradition in fiction. It was this tradition on which Moberley and Jourdain drew, and at a time when women were effecting their emancipation, and academic historians such as Eileen Power and Alice Clark were reconstructing the lives of ordinary working women, the suffering queen remained a potent model. Rebecca West, in her 1922 novel, *The Judge*, suggests that Mrs Pankhurst's public persona drew on this model, linking her suffragette heroine's childhood fantasies about Mary, Queen of Scots to her hero-worship of the character representing Pankhurst. Both idols embody a concept of graceful femininity permanently victimized by men.

The fictions which best promoted this enduring model between the wars were Margaret Irwin's series of novels about royal persons, which began with *Royal Flush* (1932). This novel, like its successors, is presented as existing on the frontier between fiction and biography; the prefatory note tells us 'none of the characters in this book are imaginary'. Despite the romantic pessimism of Irwin's novels, their emphasis on the documentary is in the spirit of the fiction of fact. The frontispiece portraits and prefatory references to sources reassure the reader that the novel is a carefully researched product, but also seek to define the distinctions between Irwin's kind of fiction and history proper; in the preface to *The Stranger Prince* (1937), for instance, she tells us that she has not read all of Clarendon's *History of the Rebellion* as a professional historian would. In *Royal Flush* Irwin places an obscure female victim, Charles II's youngest sister, Minette, at the centre of her elaborate reconstruction of the court of Louis XIV. Minette, trapped, and eventually murdered, within a history seen entirely in terms of male dynastic politics, appears to us throughout the novel as a damaged child; she has strong affinities with the young heroines of Bowen, Lehmann and White. One scene where she swims naked at night, watching the dangerous world unobserved, is clearly modelled on a scene in

Lehmann's *Dusty Answer*; both versions emphasize the vulnerability of their heroine as she attempts to interpret the mysterious adult world, but Irwin's revision also figures the helplessness of the woman historian, watching the inexorable entrapment of her heroine.

In later Irwin novels we have Louise of Bohemia in *The Bride* (1939), a royal variant of the Judith Shakespeare concept, painting pictures to support her family in exile, which are then signed by the male artist, Gerard Honthorst, and in *The Gay Galliard* (1940) the inevitable suffering queen, Mary Stuart. Her most popular novel, however, was *Young Bess* (1944); it is entirely appropriate to Irwin's methods that her Elizabeth I appears not as Gloriana, a figure belonging to the male world of politics and adventure, but, like the obscure Minette, as a traumatized child. *Young Bess* moves away from fictionalized biography towards a family story, in which the teenage Bess lives permanently in the shadow of her executed mother, suffers neglect, is infatuated with her kindly stepmother's glamorous fourth husband, and becomes the humiliated subject of an investigation into child sexual abuse. Although Irwin wrote two sequels which brought Bess nearer, but never to, the throne, and the accession of another Elizabeth in 1952 prolonged the trilogy's popularity, Irwin effectively recovers Elizabeth for women's history by stripping her of her political skills and power, and domesticating her as a vulnerable and damaged child.

There have been several critical analyses of historical fiction's habitual provision of role-models for its female readers from among female royalty. Lilian Robinson has summarized the negative conclusions; historical fiction, in its preoccupation with choosing heroines from among the spouses, relatives and mistresses of royal males, endorses a view of history as essentially male property, and eschews the opportunities which the genre offers to trace the connections between public and private life. Instead its narratives prolong class division, and an archaic recognition of separate spheres, casting female characters in domestic and sexual roles only.[26] Other critics have argued for another role for such fiction. Carolyn Steedman has outlined the positive aspects which working-class girl readers may find in the conservative romance, with its preoccupation with suffering queens; such readers, turning to history for role-models and finding mostly undifferentiated drudges, may recover dignity and status for their own worries in identifying them with the suffering, the glamour, even the costumes, of bygone royals.[27] Alison Light has focused specifically on Irwin and the ambivalent significance of her fictions for working-class readers, with the promise of status in the focus on female destiny and on the transformation of female possibilities, countering the generally reactionary class politics.[28]

A victim figure existing in less anomalous relation with the period of women's emancipation was the suppressed artist, introduced by Olive

113

Schreiner in *From Man to Man*, and elaborated by Woolf in *A Room Of One's Own* as 'Judith Shakespeare'. Rose Macaulay's favourite, and only historical, novel, *They Were Defeated* (1933), is structured around such a figure. This novel was based on Macaulay's researches for her critical study, *Some Religious Elements in English Literature* (1931), and attempts a detailed reconstruction of the final flowering of Caroline culture before the Civil War. The title refers to the destruction of this culture by the war, but its central concern is with the young woman poet and scholar, Julian Conybeare, who accompanies the poet Robert Herrick to Cambridge. Caroline Cambridge and its famous personages are reconstructed in elaborate and loving detail, mainly in order to define its glamour and inaccessibility for Julian, whose hero-worshipping of this alluring world is succeeded by a realization of her own inability ever to become part of it. Her lover, the poet John Cleveland, not only ignores her poetry in her life, but after her death passes off her best poem as his. The lament for the passing of this golden age of Cambridge culture is framed by an awareness of its inaccessibility to outsiders, whether women or provincials.

The reader's sense of this gulf is enhanced by Macaulay's decision, in extreme compliance to the documentarist demand for authenticity, to model her dialogue as exactly as possible on the vocabulary, spelling and speech modes of the time; the people she resurrects must be allowed to speak in their own voices. The dialogue of the literary figures pastiches their surviving prose, and is therefore familiar and accessible to the reader. That of the genteel women, with its greater dependence on archaic colloquialism, is less accessible, and that of the dialect-speaking, lower-class characters is practically opaque. At the furthest remove from the reader is an old woman on trial for witchcraft whose dense Devonshire dialect is difficult for her contemporaries to understand, let alone posterity. Macaulay's insistence on the authenticity of her characters' speech serves to demonstrate the ways in which the cultural elite perpetuate their point of view, and the inaccessibility to reconstruction of those who left no written record. It might be read as an oblique plea for Mass Observation.

The other major writers of historical fictions of the period, existing in tacit opposition to the conservative romance, were the left-wing novelists and the writers of family sagas; both focused their fiction on groups rather than individuals. The two most important left-wing novelists, Sylvia Townsend Warner and Naomi Mitchison, explored the roles available to women in history. Warner's major works, written during her most active communist period and discussed in Chapter 8, all have historical settings and were extensively researched, though she refused to call them historical novels, regarding them primarily as comments on contemporary events. The socialist novelist, Naomi Mitchison, claimed as her field the unrecorded lives of the barbarians of the ancient world. Holtby's book on Woolf cites Mitchison's reconstruction of her barbarians' consciousnesses as an example of the kind of awareness outside Woolf's scope, setting up an opposition between the elitism of Bloomsbury and the vast area outside.[29] Mitchison's growing involvement with socialism, her interest in documentary, and her readings in anthropology, especially James Frazer's *The Golden Bough*, all informed her work. Her first novel, *The Conquered* (1923), is presented as the alternative barbarian version of the conquest of Gaul, the version which has been almost obliterated by the written record of imperialism, Caesar's *Commentaries*. Mitchison's counter-record is written in the manner of a boy's adventure story, with chapter epigraphs from Yeats and from Irish revolutionary songs, which enforce a contemporary reference. The story records a series of Gallic defeats by superior Roman technology, and the gradual erosion of a sense of identity in the enslaved hero. It is an almost entirely male narrative; the only significant female character, the hero's sister, ceremonially commits suicide in the third chapter after reminding her brother of their happy childhood together roaming the moors in an unconquered Gaul. Her removal, therefore, figures not only the elimination of women from the historical record, but also, with its deliberate echoes of *Wuthering Heights*, the suppression of feeling in adult life.

The importance of the barbarians for Mitchison lay in their representation of what modern civilization had lost. Through the rest of the 1920s she wrote a series of stories and unperformed plays based in the imagined culture of Marob, a barbarian community north of the Danube delta in the second century BC. The uses of Marob for Mitchison were finally realized in her major novel, *The Corn King and the Spring Queen* (1931), where she explores the complex relations between the barbarians of Marob and the Greek civilizations of Sparta, Athens and Alexandria. A relationship perceived by the civilized Greeks as entirely one of patronage and instruction is gradually revealed to have many other possibilities. In her autobiography Mitchison writes of her concern in the 1930s with the need to recover the feelings for community of primitive societies, and this novel was her most sustained attempt to reconstruct the modes of barbarian consciousness.[30] It needs its enormous length and detail to contrast them with the civilized, decadent individualism of Athens, and with Sparta's failed attempt to create a populist, militarist group-consciousness in a civilized state. It is, Mitchison argues, the lessons unlearnt from Marob which are important to modern civilizations attempting, like Sparta, to raise their people above individualism.

Mitchison says in her preface that she began with an image of a small girl on a beach, and in this book she explores the possibility for a new kind of heroine. In the figure of Erif Der, the Spring Queen of Marob, her growing questioning of her magic powers, and of her sense of identity with

115

the community, Mitchison represents the potential for a different kind of transition from group-consciousness to individualism, which still incorporates the barbarian sense of community, and of leadership as responsibility rather than power. Erif also represents the comparative freedom which the historical novel offered in the exploration of female sexuality. W.H. Auden wrote admiringly, 'some of the scenes in the Prawn King and the String Queen were hotter than anything I've read. My dear, how do you get away with it?'[31] The answer, as Mitchison discovered when her publishers demanded cuts in her contemporary novel, *We Have Been Warned* (1935), was that the promiscuity of Danubian barbarians was not an issue. Under the protection of the genre of historical fiction Mitchison could explore her ideas of the importance to society of a freely expressed and experimental female sexuality, which advances both Erif's sense of individuality and her responsibility to the community as their icon of fertility. Throughout she is contrasted with the conservative ideal of womanhood embodied by the Spartan Phillyla, whose reward for her adherence to this ideal is to be praised by the enemy for her impeccable behaviour when she and her family are massacred. Phillyla is the heroine of conservative romance, the graceful victimized queen; with Erif Mitchison is attempting to construct a more active and positive model for women.

Erif's political and sexual activity is unusual even among the heroines of historical fiction of the period. The historical family saga, enormously popular between the wars, also rejected the pessimism of the conservative romance in emphasizing potential for change in the future, and in resisting closure, but tended to present women as domestic figures within stories driven by the male family members. Like the contemporary fiction of fact, it offered heavily documented studies, often based on the writer's own family history, of the lives of ordinary people and the contributions they had made to the history of the country. Storm Jameson wrote a trilogy, *The Triumph of Time* (1927–30), based on her shipbuilding family in Whitby in the nineteenth century, before turning to her contemporary documentary novels. The Liverpool novelist, Marguerite Steen, reconstructed an eighteenth-century slave-trading family in the bestselling *The Sun Is My Undoing* (1941). The dramatist Clemence Dane followed a family of strolling players through to their modern incarnation as film stars and matinee idols in *Broome Stages* (1931). All these novels were popular, very long, lavishly detailed in their reconstruction of past worlds, and dependent on Victorian narrative models. *Inheritance* (1932), by the Yorkshire novelist Phyllis Bentley, might be taken as a paradigm for the form, and has strong affinities with Holtby's *South Riding* and other topical fictions of fact. It chronicles the progress of an extended family of self-made mill-owners from the Luddites to the Depression, presenting itself as a history of the

Yorkshire textile industry and its contribution to national history. Its assertion of a strong local pride and a belief in a history which takes place outside the court and the metropolis, its detailed documentation of nineteenth-century working-class and middle-class lives, are made in the context of the Depression, and insist on the need to reconsider the history and future of the industrial north. The story ends with the youngest member of the family refusing to follow his family south, and staying to redefine a future for the mill in the industrial wasteland Yorkshire has become. This final (literal) refusal of closure, the emphasis on continuity, is supported by the novel's reassuring reassembly of past narrative models, Charlotte Brontë's *Shirley* for the Luddite section, Gaskell's *North and South* for the 1840s, Bennett's *The Old Wives' Tale* for the later sections. The continuity of English fiction assures the continuity of local and family life.

The most adventurous of these sagas, Henry Handel Richardson's trilogy, *The Fortunes of Richard Mahoney* (1917–30), undertakes the nineteenth-century history of Australia. Richardson (who was christened Ethel) drew on family letters and diaries to reconstruct the life of a man who represents the agonizing nostalgia of the Victorian Australian. Richard, in his deracination, his variability, his lack of fixed identity, has strong affinities with modernist protagonists. When he visits England in the central volume, the narrative is dragged irresistibly back to Victorian narrative models, especially to *Middlemarch*, but the Australian sections, insisting on the need to find ways of talking about unimagined landscapes, ways of life and forms of identity, bring the usually traditional family saga into some of the same areas of enquiry as the modernist novel. Richardson's fiction, like Warner's, escapes from the insistence on period detail and the traditional models of the genre towards something more adventurous and concerned with the past's impact on the present.

NOTES

Place of publication is London, unless otherwise stated.

1. Marion Shaw, 'Feminism and Fiction Between the Wars: Winifred Holtby and Virginia Woolf', in Moira Monteith, ed., *Women's Writing: A Challenge to Theory* (Hemel Hempstead: Harvester Wheatsheaf, 1986), pp. 175–91.
2. Storm Jameson, 'New Documents', collected in her *A Civil Journey* (Cassell, 1939), pp. 262–74.
3. Jameson, *A Civil Journey*, p. 281.

4. Raymond Williams, *The Long Revolution* (Chatto and Windus, 1961), pp. 274–92.

5. Fredric Jameson, 'Beyond the Cave: Demystifying the Ideology of Modernism', in his *Ideologies of Theory: Vol. 2, The Syntax of History: Essays 1971–86* (Routledge, 1988), p. 131.

6. Winifred Holtby, *Virginia Woolf* (Wishart, 1932), p. 28.

7. See Julie Holledge, *Innocent Flowers: Women in the Edwardian Theatre* (Virago, 1981).

8. F.M. Mayor, *The Rector's Daughter* (Harmondsworth: Penguin, 1992), ch. 28.

9. Storm Jameson, *Journey from the North* (Collins and Harvill, 1969), I, pp. 292–3.

10. Jameson, *Journey from the North*, I, p. 343.

11. Jameson, *Company Parade* (Virago, 1985), ch. 35.

12. See Alun Howkins, 'The Discovery of Rural England', in Robert Colls and Philip Dodd, eds, *Englishness: Politics and Culture 1880–1920* (Croom Helm, 1986), pp. 62–88; Martin J. Wiener, *English Culture and the Decline of the Industrial Spirit 1850–1980* (Cambridge: Cambridge University Press, 1981); Patrick Wright, *On Living in an Old Country: The National Past in Contemporary Britain* (Verso, 1985).

13. Stanley Baldwin, 'Introduction', in Mary Webb, *Precious Bane* (Cape, 1929), p. 11.

14. See Stuart Sillars, *Visualization in Popular Fiction 1860–1960: Graphic Narratives, Fictional Images* (Routledge, 1995), pp. 93–112.

15. Katherine Mansfield, *Notes on Novelists* (Constable, 1930), pp. 252, 102.

16. Sheila Kaye-Smith, *Joanna Godden* (Cassell, 1921), pt. 3.

17. Glen Cavaliero, *The Rural Tradition in the English Novel 1900–39* (Macmillan, 1977).

18. Raymond Williams, *The Country and the City* (Hogarth Press, 1993), p. 254.

19. Mary Webb, *Gone to Earth* (Virago, 1992), ch. 1.

20. Flora Thompson, *Lark Rise to Candleford* (Harmondsworth: Penguin, 1973), ch. 28.

21. See Barbara English, '*Lark Rise* and Juniper Hill: A Victorian Community in Literature and in History', *Victorian Studies*, 29 (1985), pp. 7–34.

22. Grahame Greene, *The Lost Childhood and Other Essays* (Harmondsworth: Penguin, 1966), pp. 14–15.

23. Marjorie Bowen, 'Margaret Campbell', in *Myself When Young by Famous Women of Today*, ed. Margot Oxford and Asquith (Muller, 1938).

24. See Terry Castle, *The Apparitional Lesbian: Female Homosexuality and Modern Culture* (New York: Columbia University Press, 1993), pp. 107–49.

25. Bonnie G. Smith, 'The Contribution of Women to Modern Historiography in Great Britain, France and the United States 1750–1940', *American Historical Review*, 89 (1984), pp. 709–32.

26. See Lilian Robinson, *Sex, Class and Culture* (Methuen, 1978), pp. 200–22.

27. Carolyn Steedman, 'True Romances', in Raphael Samuel, ed., *Patriotism* (Routledge, 1989), I, pp. 26–38.

28. Alison Light, '*Young Bess*: Historical Novels and Growing Up', *Feminist Review*, 33 (1989), pp. 57–71.

29. Holtby, *Virginia Woolf*, p. 116.

30. Naomi Mitchison, *You May Well Ask: A Memoir 1920–40* (Gollancz, 1979), pp. 112–13.

31. Quoted in *You May Well Ask*, p. 121.

CHAPTER SIX

Popular Writing

In 1900 the largest number of women writers were working in children's fiction,[1] and the most widely known woman writer was the romantic novelist, Marie Corelli. Women writers were primarily identified, therefore, with those fields, which continued to expand and develop throughout this period. Corelli's successors were inheriting a tradition established in the 1860s by the queens of the Victorian sensation novel, Mary Braddon and Mrs Henry Wood, both in their domination of the market and in the scandal sometimes attracted by their pioneering of a more explicit sexuality in fiction. The other legatee of the sensation novel was detective fiction, which achieved enormous popularity between the wars and was also dominated by women writers. This genre, appealing to both sexes, and a frequent topic of intellectual discussion, enjoyed a much more upmarket image than romantic fiction, usually classified as 'tosh', or than the respectable, but under-regarded, children's writing.

ROMANTIC FICTION

In 1924 Virginia Woolf recorded a meeting at a party with the popular romantic novelist, Berta Ruck:

a whole room full stood agaze to see the lady novelists embrace. She said Oh if I were Virginia Woolf! I said Oh Berta, if I were you! And for Gods sake, I said, tell me how you do it, and what you get for it, whereupon Berta, rolling her fine eyes about, replied, 'Would you believe me Mrs Woolf I abominate my own books more than I can say, and they only bring me in £400 a piece, and I have to write two every year so

119

long as I and my husband and our boys do live, and its almost impossible to find another plot. I took Romeo and Juliet last time; and its going to be Don Quixote next; for there are only ten plots in the world; and Ethel Dell is my only rival ... you have written in Jacobs room such a description of the beauty of young manhood' (here we embraced once more) and with tears in my eyes I swore to come down to a rosy bower on the river, where they live 'like anybody else' she said; but I doubt it. (*Letters*, III, pp. 119–20)

Woolf's comic account of her meeting with Ruck (whose name she had inadvertently placed on a gravestone in *Jacob's Room*, 1922) summarizes much of the relationship between the respectable woman writer of the period and the writers of romantic fiction. The romantic novelists of the early twentieth century were the great success stories in the marketplace; in 1924 Woolf earned £37 from her books, and Ruck's steady popularity since 1914 seemed unimaginable.[2] Later in the year she wrote 'I doubt any book selling if it isn't by Berta Ruck' (*Letters*, III, p. 133). It was a source of embarrassment to many women writers that to much of the public the high-profile romantic novelist represented women's writing, and Woolf's account of 'the lady novelists' meeting is informed by this awareness. In her version Ruck becomes a composite figure of the romantic writer of the period, embarrassingly identified as a sister in writing, effusive on the beauties of life, commercially acute, intensely vital.

Many women writers expressed their alarm at the anomalous popularity of the romantic novelists in a period of political and educational advance for women. The feminist Lady Rhondda, in her 1933 autobiography, *This Was My World*, confessed with shame that at school in the 1890s she had enjoyed Florence Barclay's *The Rosary* and Ethel M. Dell's novels. It was a false memory; *The Rosary* was published in 1909, and Dell's first novel in 1912, but the strategy was clear. Romantic fiction belonged to childhood, and to the Victorian past; Dell's popularity in the age of emancipation was impossible to contemplate. The romantic lady novelist, perpetuating gender stereotypes, dissolving the boundary between fiction and pornography, exerting a mysterious control over her vast audience, looms in the comment of other women writers as a mystery. Katherine Mansfield's first short story, 'The Tiredness of Rosabel' (1908), analyses the dangerous appeal of romantic fiction for an overworked shop assistant. Rebecca West's article, 'The Tosh Horse' (1928), took Dell as the leading example of the bestselling romantic novelist's affinities with pornography, but admitted the 'demoniac vitality' of her work.[3] Q.D. Leavis's *Fiction and the Reading Public* (1932), tracing the decline of literature in the days of a mass reading public, also attributed the success of the romantic bestsellers to 'the magnificent vitality of the author' (p. 62). (Ruck, recommended to Leavis by Boots Library as a necessary object of study, demonstrated her vitality by swooping down

120

on Leavis in Cambridge to explain what was wrong with her questionnaire.[4]) The product of a new mass reading public and new conditions of production, the bestselling romantic novelists seemed a terrifying phenomenon to other women writers, but the devotion they commanded in the new readership to whom they had responded was undoubted; Ruck records in her autobiography a fan's story of how she read her novels by slowly lowering a piece of paper down the page, line by line, not because she had reading difficulties, but in order to prolong the pleasure of reading as long as possible (p. 104).

What the romantic novelists shared was the success of their response to an expanding readership, and the size and devotion of their followings. The forms of their response were various; despite Woolf's linking of them, Dell and Ruck were operating in different areas. Dell's first novel, *The Way of An Eagle* (1912), was a massive bestseller, and her extravagant compound of sex, violence and religiosity in a Raj setting proved popular through successive novels. Six years later Fisher Unwin, who had accepted it after rejections by other publishers, pressed a copy on the aspiring novelist, Storm Jameson, as a model of how to write a bestseller. (Jameson, who had had Balzac more in mind as a model, later threw it out of the window.[5]) Ruck, on the other hand, embarked on writing novels after years of writing fiction for *Home Chat* and other women's magazines, and her demurer domestic stories were very precisely targeted at her primary audience of young working women with domestic aspirations. Romantic novelists were responding to different audiences and demands, and there was considerable development and variation through the period. The work of Corelli, Barclay and Dell made claims to the promoting of moral and spiritual wisdom; the two novelists whose work is still solidly in print, Georgette Heyer and Daphne du Maurier, have more modern aspirations to historical authenticity and literary elegance.

Corelli's big successes were all published before the turn of the century, but she established the new profile of the bestselling lady novelist, appealing to her vast public over the heads of the reviewers, publicizing her close relations with her fans, adopting the stance of a sage expounding a body of spiritual teaching. The bestselling romantic novelist of the post-1945 period, Barbara Cartland, is recognizably working within the same outline. In the Edwardian period the closest successor to Corelli was Florence Barclay, a vicar's wife whose biggest bestseller, *The Rosary* (1909), combined eroticism and religion in a manner comparable to Corelli's, but within a more domestic format. The twelve-stone heroine cannot credit the hero's assurances that her moving rendition of the popular song, 'The Rosary', has enabled him to see through her materiality to the soul within; his blinding in a sporting accident and her incognito nursing of him reunite them. The

121

novel's adroit blend of modernity (globetrotting heroine, non-sizeist hero) and religiosity won it massive popularity; Barclay, like Corelli, promoted her image of the novelist as moral sage assiduously in lecture tours, book-signing sessions and attention to fan clubs.

Ethel M. Dell's long multiplotted novels, engaging a wide range of characters from the professional and service classes against a background of empire, had the reassuring appearance and solidity of Victorian novels, and the stories are founded on an insistence on the essential difference between the sexes and the importance of maintaining the separate spheres. The role of the naive young heroine is to learn to accept that separateness, a process which begins in her attempts to distinguish the hero among the forbidding appearances of the men around her. Dell's trademark was her ugly hero, whose ugliness both provided an initial exercise in judgement for the heroine and served as confirmation of his difference from her. Central to the novel is some estrangement between hero and heroine derived from their different perceptions of values. In *The Way of an Eagle* the couple's difficulties stem from their first meeting on the North-West Frontier, where the teenage heroine is terrified by the soldier-hero's relish in killing; the novel traces her gradual acceptance of his male aggression.

In *The Keeper of the Door* (1915) the heroine, Olga, helps her best friend, Violet, to escape 'beyond the door', after the doctor-hero, Max, has detected signs of the onset of hereditary insanity in her. Shocked by Max's professional anger at her act of euthanasia, she becomes amnesiac, until finally a visit to the scene of Violet's death restores her memory. In a visionary experience she recognizes that it was Max's male and professional duty to keep the door of life, but that as a woman and friend she was right to respond to Violet's need as she did. Olga and Max can then be reunited in the acknowledgement of perfect difference, recognizing their separate spheres of action and their opposing values. The novel combines two difficult subjects, euthanasia and the heroine's sexual fears. Early in the book Olga longs to escape to India with her favourite uncle; in a dream she rides loftily through the jungle until she is thrown and pursued by wild animals who resemble Max. When she goes to India, bomb-throwing terrorists are more in evidence than wild beasts, her kindly uncle turns out to be a ruthless counter-insurgency expert, and she realizes that she must overcome her dreams of freedom, and fears of male sexuality and alien values, to accept the protection the keepers of the door offer. Dell's novels, with their ugly heroes forcing passionate embraces on terrified teenage heroines against a background of Empire, undertake to explain the realities of women's lives to their female readers. Although the lesson is softened by the religiosity of the language, and the frequent recourse to dream and vision sequences, the novels offer instruction on how to live in an ugly world.

Commenting in 'The Tosh Horse' on the sado-masochistic relations of the lovers in a later Dell novel, *Charles Rex* (1922), Rebecca West expressed surprise that Dell had experienced no censorship problems. In the genre's pioneering of a more explicit discussion of sexuality in fiction the dominant place was taken by Glyn's *Three Weeks* (1907), which describes a series of sexual encounters between a young Englishman and a doomed Slav queen staying incognito at a Swiss hotel, and which sold two million copies in its first decade. The upper-class but impecunious Glyn embarked on her writing career with *The Visits of Elizabeth* (1900), a lightly fictionalized account of several country-house parties she had attended. From the mild scandal of milking her hosts, she proceeded to the major scandal of *Three Weeks*, inspired by the murder in 1903 of Queen Draga of Serbia, whose assassins claimed to be avenging the humiliations her alleged sexual excesses had inflicted on Serbia. (The ten-year-old West was also fascinated by the news coverage of Draga's murder, and later treated it extensively in her *Black Lamb and Grey Falcon*.) Glyn draws on the combination of royalty and murder, on Draga as a focus of excitement about the sexuality of women in public places, and, like many of the historical novelists of the period, on the fascination of queenhood as a glamorous example of the imprisonment of women within oppressive roles and responsibilities. In her version her heroine seeks brief respite in holiday passion from the troubled politics and degenerate husband of her home country before returning there to be murdered.

Glyn's novel abolishes traditional expansive plotting for a story which consists almost entirely of a series of sexual encounters, in which the woman takes the dominant role. Her technical problems were how to organize her narrative around these encounters, and how to develop a vocabulary for discussing the sexuality of her lovers and promoting a heroine who rejects conventional morality. Her most arresting solution was the lovers' first meeting in the hotel restaurant, where the scarlet-lipped, black-hatted queen eats her way through six courses of sophisticated French cuisine, while the mesmerized Paul munches his cold, overdone mutton chop. Later she deploys a vocabulary of tiger-skins, beds of rose-petals, storms, fires, mountain-tops and Venetian canals to differentiate and intensify her lovers' series of passionate encounters. The novel assiduously promotes its pioneering frankness; the queen attacks George Eliot as a scarlet woman who 'did not preach what she practised', and the narrative repeatedly declares the queen's behaviour to be 'beyond our puny reasonings'.[6] In the story's conclusion, however, we learn that her behaviour was dictated by another set of progressive attitudes. Paul learns that before her murder she gave birth to their son, who has ascended the throne of that distant Slav state. Appalled at the prospect of transmitting her husband's diseased genes to the next king, she has sought a genetically favourable liaison and saved the dynasty at the price of her own death. The queen's behaviour thus conforms with the eugenicist policies much favoured in the Edwardian period; like H.G. Wells's New Woman heroine in *Ann Veronica* (1909), the queen's sexual adventurism is in the interests of racial improvement.

This revelation of planned parenthood completes Glyn's presentation of her heroine as a new, sexually aware woman for the new century. Glyn built a career of public appearances on the exceptional success of *Three Weeks*, which extended to Hollywood in the 1920s, where she became a high-profile presence advising on courtship techniques and sex appeal. Her concept of heroine informed many of the screenplays of the period, notably in the high-minded adulteress roles constructed for Greta Garbo. She was thus around to advise when Hollywood came to film the most scandalous bestseller since *Three Weeks*, E.M. Hull's *The Sheik* (1919). Appearing in the year of the Sex Disqualification (Removal) Act, this novel, which confused the boundaries between romantic fiction and pornography, was another major embarrassment to progressive women writers. The tomboy heroine, Diana, is a modern woman, who rejects marriage as 'the end of independence', but, visiting Algeria, is abducted and repeatedly raped by a desert sheik. 'For the first time she had been made to feel aware of the inferiority of her sex . . . every moment she was made to feel acutely that she was a woman, forced to submit to everything to which her womanhood exposed her, forced to endure everything that he might put upon her – a chattel, a slave to do his bidding.'[7] Like Connie Chatterley, Diana comes to accept this slavery as her true destiny, helped by the discovery that the Sheik is the son of a sadistic Scottish Earl, whose battered bride fled into the desert to give birth. At the end the violence of the narrative is justified as necessary to this story of two damaged people, each deprived of a mother in infancy, who reach a stable relationship through the judicious use of sado-masochistic practices. *The Sheik* was the biggest seller of the 1920s, but Hull did not become a public figure like her predecessors. There was no clear public role for a novelist in a debatable land between romantic fiction and pornography, at a time when much magazine fiction was well behind the front lines established by Dell and Glyn.

Berta Ruck represented those writers who established their careers in romantic fiction for the magazines before embarking on novels. She began with stories for *Home Chat* and *Forget-me-not: The Paper for the Engaged Girl*, until a serial in the former attracted such enthusiastic response from the readers that she expanded it from sixty to eighty thousand words to become her first novel, *His Official Fiancée* (1914), the story of a worker marrying her boss. Ruck proceeded to establish herself as a novelist in the war, with stories addressed to the war conditions her readers were experiencing, *The*

Lad with Wings (1915), *The Girls at his Billet* (1916), *The Bridge of Kisses* (1917) and *The Land Girl's Love Story* (1918). She made research trips to aircraft factories and lumber camps, and her characters were young working people, whose lives were disrupted by war. Her autobiography records that another success of 1918, *Sweethearts Unmet*, drew 'countless letters girls and men wrote to me about deprived lives and yearning to get in contact, somehow, with the potential sweetheart that they felt was somewhere in the world, waiting for them' (p. 146). Ruck's success in targeting her wartime audience continued after the war, indeed until the 1960s, with romances about young working people who initially despair of finding a partner. She regarded her main audience as young women, but her autobiography cites letters from male fans, the young engineers and airmen who provided her heroes. The eminent zoologist, Sir Ray Lankester, liked her books because they explained the modern young woman to him, and Ruck saw part of her role as reassuring readers that the modern working girl, despite appearances, was not essentially different from her predecessors.

Ruck had fan clubs, gave interviews, published the *Berta Ruck Birthday Book* (1920), wrote articles of advice, went on lecture tours in the United States. Comparable figures were Annie S. Swan, whose novels emerged from a career writing fiction for the Scottish Thomson press, and Ruby M. Ayres. They represented a concept of the romantic novelist more domestic than that established by Corelli, and they employed the mundane milieux and settings favoured by the fiction in the magazines from which they emerged. Much magazine fiction between the wars eschewed the extravagance of Dell or Glyn, and, when Mills and Boon decided in the 1930s to transform themselves from a general publishing house to one associated with romantic fiction, they launched a line of fictions much closer to Ruck than to Dell.

Another romantic novelist, who devised a distinctive formula which, very unusually for the genre, attracted male as well as female readers, was the Hungarian expatriate, Baroness Orczy. Before she discovered her successful formula Orczy had already published translations, children's stories, and detective fiction, a genre in which she continued to publish. When her French Revolutionary romance, *The Scarlet Pimpernel*, first written in 1902, failed to find a publisher, she adapted it as a play, and its success in that form enabled the publication of the novel in 1905, and its string of sequels, which continued until 1940. *The Scarlet Pimpernel* is a hybrid based on the two major contesting definitions of romance of the period. In the 1880s and 1890s there was an intensive campaign to win back the word 'romance' for male adventure fiction; true romance was set in the more dangerous past or on the frontiers of empire, and was seen to represent a vigorous escape from the feminized domestic realism of Victorian fiction. The writers to whom the word was applied included Rider Haggard, Robert Louis Stevenson and Rudyard Kipling, and their principal advocate in the press was the influential reviewer Andrew Lang.[8] *The Scarlet Pimpernel* is in many respects an addition to this genre, which was principally targeted at a male juvenile audience. A band of daring young upper-class Englishmen, bored by their traditional sporting activities, engage in dangerous exploits rescuing French aristocrats from the guillotine during the Revolution; there is an emphasis on practical jokes and impersonation skills, which gives the novel affinities with the developing genre of spy fiction. However, the novel increasingly focuses on the Pimpernel's French wife, Marguerite, who, bored with the placidity and Philistinism of English life, and humiliated by the public buffoonery of the husband whose identity with the Pimpernel she does not suspect, dreams of the Pimpernel as her ideal man. The constant movement between the Pimpernel's escapades and Marguerite's developing suspicions of her husband's true identity enables Orczy to address herself to two usually distinct audiences for romance.

The novel's double life occasions some discontinuities; in the adventure romance the Pimpernel is an extrovert prankster, in the love romance a psychologically disabled figure, akin to Charlotte Brontë's Rochester, whose distrust of his wife springs from his memories of his mother's insanity. In the sequels Orczy's main problem was to find ways of repeating her dual formula of daring heroics and of a woman's education in love. In the first sequel, *I Will Repay* (1906), a woman realizes she loves the man whom she has denounced to the revolutionary authorities, and the Pimpernel is called in to rescue the unhappy couple. Again as in the original story the final sighting of the white cliffs of Dover serves to represent a stable relationship achieved after great misunderstanding and suffering. Orczy's public persona was comparable to other romantic lady novelists, though when she wrote a work of moral and social guidance, *Sir Percy Looks at the World* (1933), she presented her advice in the persona of her perfect Englishman. The Pimpernel series, however, was a very successful crossing of genres; the Pimpernel has strong affinities with Sherlock Holmes, and was a model for the later detectives of Dorothy Sayers and Margery Allingham, but, in their parallel emphasis on heroines trapped in dangerous situations with men they fail to comprehend, the books belong to the romantic fiction of the day.

The two romantic novelists of the period whose works are still readily available, Georgette Heyer and Daphne du Maurier, have certain characteristics in common. Both presented themselves as professionals rather than sages, substituting for their predecessors' claims to moral and spiritual authority an emphasis on diligent researching of subjects and settings. Both, in their historical fiction, prized authenticity of detail, and would not have passed the solecism of Orczy in giving her heroine the name of the Revolution's leading ideologue, St Just. Both marked their aspirations to professional respectability by aligning themselves with a great nineteenth-century woman novelist. In their works sexuality was much less foregrounded than in those of their immediate predecessors, and there was a compensating emphasis on the home and domestic interiors, and, in du Maurier, landscape. Both developed formulae which served as models to a later generation of romantic fiction writers.

Georgette Heyer had a strong commitment to historical research, evidenced by her novels about William the Conqueror, *The Conqueror* (1930), and about the Peninsular campaign, *An Infamous Army* (1937). Her career, however, was mainly concerned with the development of the formula of the Regency romance, in which she presented her novels as a perpetuation of the Jane Austen tradition. In this she offered the reader a reassurance which proved more durable than that provided by Dell's novels; where they identified with imperial romance and the solidity of the Victorian multiplot novel, both declining in appeal by the 1930s, Heyer went back beyond the Victorians to the supposed stabilities of an earlier England. Her novels avoid the period of the French Revolution, situating themselves either in the mid-eighteenth century or in the Regency, offering that secure reified England to which Orczy's characters continuously aspire. The formula proved successful, and Heyer's claim to be perpetuating Austen was itself sustained by the Regency romances which emerged in the 1960s and modelled themselves on Heyer.

Heyer's discovery of Austen as her model was gradual. In her first major success, *These Old Shades* (1925), she insured herself by recycling the plot of Dell's 1922 bestseller, *Charles Rex*. This was a version of the cross-dressing plot popular in the 1920s, what Ruck called 'the wear-well plot of the girl disguised as a boy' (p. 200), and used herself in *Sir or Madam?* (1923). The plot had the double advantage of deferring the romantic conclusion and allowing the heroine opportunities for individual adventure. In Heyer's version, as in Dell's, the hero uses his unacknowledged recognition that his supposed page is a girl for prolonged power play with her emotions, though Heyer considerably mutes Dell's sado-masochism which had so shocked West in 'The Tosh Horse'. The menacing sexuality of *These Old Shades* is characteristic of the period of *The Sheik*, and eliminated from later Heyer. *The Masqueraders* (1928) has another innocent but streetwise heroine disguised as a boy, this time supported by her brother disguised as a girl. The emphasis is on the possibilities for play which the disguises offer the siblings, who maintain extravagant gender stereotypes in drag, while occasionally escaping surreptitiously to their real roles in manliness and femininity. Published in the same year as *Orlando*, this novel also plays with

127

ideas of the fluidity of gender, and the construction of identity by costume, only to conclude by dismissing the siblings to their fixed roles.

The attempts to establish period in *The Masqueraders* depend almost entirely on lavish descriptions of costume, but by the time Heyer wrote *Regency Buck* in 1935 she had developed a much more comprehensive attention to the creation of period atmosphere; in this novel the Regency romance formula is fully established, with a meticulous reconstruction of fashions and pastimes designed to reassure the reader of the authenticity of the world described. The identification with Austen is made in a scene where the heroine reads aloud from *Sense and Sensibility*; this, we are being told, is Austen's England authentically recreated. The progress towards a Regency identified with Austen moves Heyer's novels away from the emphasis on dangerous or ambivalent sexuality in her earlier novels. The obligatory rich masterful hero whom the heroine eventually marries is increasingly obscured by the furniture and a relish in domestic interiors characteristic of the interwar period. There is a third main character in most of Heyer's novels, a younger man in a relaxed, undemanding sibling relation to the heroine; in *The Convenient Marriage* (1934), for instance, this relationship is foregrounded at the expense of the obscurely perceived hero. Heyer's development of the Regency romance into the 1930s depicts a life where furniture and companionable non-sexual relations are more important than the sexuality which preoccupied novelists in the heyday of Marie Stopes.

Du Maurier's first successful romance, *Jamaica Inn* (1936), drew on several genres; like Orczy she allies herself with male romance in a story of smuggling, her evocation of the hard life of forgotten women in a wild landscape has strong affinities with Webb's rural fiction, and her resolution (the vicar dunit) is in keeping with the detective stories of the period. The main emphasis, however, is on the heroine's growing identification with the wild moorland landscape, and her decision to forgo her dreams of return to the soft southern country of her childhood for marriage to a horse thief. One of du Maurier's major contributions to romantic fiction was the restoration of setting, which in the work of her predecessors had become a perfunctory theatrical backdrop. Du Maurier's identification with the Cornish landscape, in which most of her fiction is set, is part of her presentation of herself as heir to the Brontës; where Heyer claimed to be reviving the domestic and comic tradition of Austen, du Maurier's romances established themselves in the other main nineteenth-century tradition, Gothic romance.

The success of *Rebecca* (1938), the most enduringly successful romantic novel from this period, depended on du Maurier's revival of the traditional Gothic romance, largely dormant earlier in the century, in a contemporary variant. For the old dark house and its terrors, du Maurier substitutes a modern home beautiful, still dominated by the exquisite fashionable taste of its murdered châtelaine, and by the professionalism of the housekeeper. As discussed in Chapter 1, much of the appeal of *Rebecca* lies in its realization of the anxieties of women confronted with the demands for perfection in homemaking of the interwar period. Significant alterations are made in the basic plot model supplied by *Jane Eyre*, just as Heyer introduced an interest in furnishings and costume not visible in Austen. The unnamed heroine-narrator shares Jane's response to the natural world, but lacks her independence and resourcefulness. Where Jane and her predecessor remain polarized types of woman, du Maurier's heroine is ambivalently attracted to the possibilities for passion and wilfulness which Rebecca represents. The sterile deracinated life of the de Winters in their foreign retreat after the exorcism of Rebecca and the burning of Manderley departs from the way Rochester and Jane reconstruct their lives; passion in du Maurier is associated with the past, and does not survive in the tame modernity her characters adopt.[9]

Du Maurier did not regard herself as a romantic novelist, but the steady success of *Rebecca* through the general slump in romantic fiction of the period following the Second World War inspired the boom in Gothic romances which began in the late 1950s and has continued ever since. By 1971 *Time* was pointing out that *Rebecca* had provided the model for the mass romance market which burgeoned in the 1960s.[10] Heyer's Regency romances were comparably influential; the two novelists who returned to canonical nineteenth-century influences established models more enduring than their predecessors who were responding to the sexual turmoil of the earlier twentieth century.

CRIME FICTION

The much-remarked boom in crime fiction of the interwar period was dominated by women writers, who might be seen as reclaiming a genre whose ancestor was the sensation novel of the 1860s. The sensation novel, a genre associated specifically with women writers and readers, had shifted the focus of crime from the highways and the underworld to the home, and especially to the hidden resentments and revenges of female members of the household.[11] Mary Braddon, the woman novelist most closely associated with the sensation boom, was still publishing up to her death in 1916, but from the 1880s to 1914 crime fiction was dominated by Arthur Conan

Doyle's Sherlock Holmes stories, with their emphasis on heroic male ratiocination. Within this period there were women writers who adapted crime fiction to a female perspective. Marie Belloc Lowndes's *The Lodger* (1913), which was much admired by Hemingway and Gertrude Stein and in 1925 became the source for Alfred Hitchcock's first major film, focused on the viewpoint of Jack the Ripper's landlady. Orczy developed two detectives to supplement her major success, the Pimpernel romances, an elderly armchair detective, 'the Old Man in the Corner', and a more active woman detective, Lady Molly. It was, however, the publication of Agatha Christie's first novel, *The Mysterious Affair at Styles* (1920), which announced the reclamation of the crime novel by women writers, who inherited the tradition of the heroic male detective but adapted it to women's interests.

The enormous popularity of crime fiction between the wars, a period which became known as the 'Golden Age' of the genre, was often attributed to readers' desires to escape from the monotony of modern urban life. Christie invoked that explanation in the dedication to her second novel, *The Secret Adversary* (1922), 'to all those who lead monotonous lives in the hope that they may experience at second hand the delights and dangers of adventure'. Q.D. Leavis, in *Fiction and the Reading Public*, described a further widely publicized feature of the interwar detective novel, their popularity with men of the professional classes (pp. 50–1). Thus for women writers crime fiction offered distinctive possibilities. Unlike romantic fiction, it was addressed to a mixed audience with a strong upmarket segment, conferring an unusual kind of status and authority on those who practised it. It offered the opportunity to break away from domestic and romantic fiction into the area of male adventure romance, but it was a flexible form which could be revised to accommodate women's perspectives and interests. An advantage not visible at the time was the longevity of the formulae devised in this period; the four women writers who dominated the field, Christie, Dorothy Sayers, Margery Allingham and Ngaio Marsh, are all still in print.

The dominance of women writers was anomalous in a genre distinguished by features usually associated with a male-dominated field: an emphasis on rationality and on the skilled deployment of a set of rigid formulae, displays of technical expertise in specific areas of knowledge, a large male professional audience, frequent reference in prestigious discourses, even the formation in 1930 of a kind of professional union, the Detection Club, to explore and protect the formulae and practices of the detective writer. Women writers made use of the professional and scholarly reference associated with the genre. The philosopher, R.G. Collingwood, in *The Idea of History* (1946), offered a prestigious analogy for crime fiction, when he compared developments in historiography and in fictional detection. Just as

130

the 'scissors and paste historian', who accumulated material until it became suggestive, had given way to the 'scientific historian', who explored material in the light of a distinct intellectual concept, so earlier fictional descriptions of detection had yielded to the methods of Christie's Hercule Poirot, who early in the detection process formulated a theory with which to investigate the crime.[12] Comparison of the puzzle plot of interwar detection with loftier intellectual endeavours had already been utilized by both Christie and Sayers. In Christie's *Murder in Mesopotamia* (1936), set at an archaeological dig, the detected murderer congratulates Poirot from a professional standpoint on his gifts for reconstruction of the past. Sayers's later stories increasingly emphasize that her detective, Lord Peter Wimsey, has an Oxford First in History, and could have been a leading professional historian if the First World War had not diverted his career.

The anomalous dominance of women writers in the British crime genre was picked up by Raymond Chandler in his famous 1944 essay, 'The Simple Art of Murder', when he called on American crime writers to break free from the British model and return crime to the mean streets where it belonged.[13] Chandler's objection to the English model focused especially on one of its most discussed formulaic features, the restricted milieu such as the vicarage garden; his strong implication was that this feature derived from the feminization of the British crime novel. The classic response was W.H. Auden's essay, 'The Guilty Vicarage' (1948), which argued for the detective story as a pastoral form, in which a restricted and idealized milieu permitted concentration on the resolution of a puzzle, a resolution which performed the function of purifying the community. Auden, however, evaded the subtext of Chandler's argument by taking his examples from pre-Golden Age male writers such as Doyle and Chesterton.[14]

The detective novel as practised by the major women writers in the genre was not as hermetically sealed from external experience as Auden's essay, or the Detection Club's insistence on the need to comply with specific formulae, might suggest. Christie's practice in this period exemplifies the use of the genre to allow experiment within the security of a winning formula. One of the generation of women brought out of the domestic sphere by war-work, she developed the outline for *The Mysterious Affair at Styles* while working in a dispensary; the work not only encouraged her movement into the public arena, but provided her with the training to display technical expertise in her novels in the appropriate area of pharmaceuticals. The war also influenced her first novel; the murder takes place in a country-house in which traditional stability has been disrupted by war, and the detective is a Belgian refugee. Her avowed model for Hercule Poirot and his obtuse British sidekick, Captain Hastings, was the Holmes and Watson pairing, but Poirot shares only the heroic intellectualism of

131

Holmes. Christie created him as an anti-heroic detective, elderly, eccentric, sympathetic with the female point of view, and in later books often turning to female helpers rather than his male sidekicks.

The novel was a modest beginning; the £25 Christie made was from its serialization in the *Weekly Times*, and in her early career serialization was to be her major source of income. At this point she had not adopted the crime novel as her specific genre. Her second novel, *The Secret Adversary* (1922), was a spy thriller; in the early 1920s she was also writing poetry, admiring the innovative fiction of May Sinclair, and writing a historical drama about the heretic pharaoh, Akenaton. It was *The Murder of Roger Ackroyd* (1926) which established her reputation and career as a major crime writer specializing in ingenious puzzle plots. The novel offered the most extensive example of a feature much used thereafter by Christie, the unreliable interior monologue; in later novels such as *Death in the Clouds* (1935) and *Sparkling Cyanide* (1944) she offers her readers access to the consciousnesses of all the murder suspects, without identifying the murderer. The repetition of this device, and her admiration for Sinclair, may suggest that Christie was covertly engaging in her own experiments with the representation of consciousness, and she draws on popular psychology in the facility with which a succession of murderers repress their knowledge of their guilt. The most striking variant on this device was provided by *The ABC Murders* (1936), where Hastings's narrative is interpolated by the fragmentary and distressed interior monologue of a supposed serial killer.

The ABC Murders is set, not in the vicarage garden, but in the British version of the mean streets, the newsagents' shops and race-courses, the downmarket tea-shops and cinemas, usually identified in fiction as (Graham) Greeneland. It was Christie's most obvious departure from the 'guilty vicarage' formula. The story is told in alternation by two deluded male narrators, while Poirot seeks help from several observant women. In *Death in the Clouds* the point of view is that of a young hairdresser; *Murder in Mesopotamia* is narrated by a nurse. Both women, excluded by class and gender from the mostly male professional society they are observing, exemplify an intuitive wisdom and decency not available to those within the group observed. The association with their viewpoints demonstrates Christie's determination to appeal to a popular audience beyond the professional audience with which the genre was credited. Her favourite novels were *Absent in the Spring* (1944), a novel about a middle-aged woman's crisis of identity, one of a series of non-detective novels written under the pseudonym Mary Westmacott, and the hybrid historical detective novel, *Death Comes As the End* (1945), set in Eleventh Dynasty Egypt, and drawing on her unproduced play, *Akenaton*. This story of a young widow's return to the security of a childhood home which suddenly becomes threatening, and of her assumption that danger is located in the squabbling women's quarters and not in the apparent calm of the male world of work, exemplifies Christie's interest in associating the enclosed world of the detective novel more closely with women's interests.

Her most famous use of the female viewpoint, the elderly spinster detective, Miss Marple, was a product of the 1920s interest in the social functions of the surplus woman, although most of the Marple books were published after the Second World War. Miss Marple, introduced in *Murder at the Vicarage* (1930), exemplified a shift from the professional detective, Poirot, to the amateur, to female intuitive wisdom and the community's ability to police itself.[15] Miss Marple's intuitive wisdom is largely a matter of exact class knowledge; in the second Marple novel, *The Body in the Library* (1942), it is her observation of the anomalies in dress and manicure of the corpse which enables her to solve the murder. The increasing conservatism of Christie's postwar novels is expressed in a retreat into a more enclosed and hierarchical society where Miss Marple's exact understanding of class relations can be plausible.

Where Christie in her autobiography cultivated the stance of the woman amateur who wrote books in the interstices of domestic life, and distinguished herself from innovative novelists such as Sinclair and Elizabeth Bowen, her closest rival, Dorothy Sayers, identified herself strongly with professionalism, and with raising the status of the genre. An Oxford First, who worked for an advertising agency, she was a prominent member of both the Society of Authors and of the Detection Club. To the Detection Club's emphasis on the skilled deployment of formulae, she added an insistence on the genre's centrality and distinguished lineage. In a 1935 Oxford lecture, 'Aristotle on Detective Fiction', she argued for detective fiction as the true modern heir of the tragedies described in the *Poetics*.[16] She worked intermittently on a critical biography of Wilkie Collins, the leading male practitioner of the 1860s sensation novel. This never-finished study insisted on the importance of Collins's fictional innovations to mainstream fiction; by conflating his influence on later Dickens with that on crime fiction, Sayers was able to present the latter as the true successor of the great Victorians. In her fourth novel, *The Unpleasantness at the Bellona Club* (1928), literary criticism becomes part of the detective process. The presence on a woman suspect's bookshelves of the work of the leading women innovators, Sinclair, Richardson, Mansfield and Woolf, enables Lord Peter Wimsey to place her as naive and confused, but not homicidal. Wimsey has read and dismissed these writers; his own reading preference for the academically fashionable Metaphysical poets coexists significantly with his knowledge of detective fiction. His policeman sidekick, correct but always one step behind, favours Hardy and James, the masters of the prewar generation.

Sayers's ambitions for the genre are not immediately apparent in her first novel, *Whose Body?* (1922), which begins as a light comedy modelled after P.G. Wodehouse, with a dandified Mayfair detective, his shrewd valet, a dizzy duchess, flatfooted policemen, and an undertaker who has found an example of his professional material displaced in his bath.[17] Later in the book Sayers begins to develop a more serious justification for the genre with which she is experimenting. Christie had early invoked the idea of the detective novel as escape from the monotony of modern life; Sayers employs another current justification for the genre, that its puzzles and solutions were important postwar therapy, exemplified in the revelation that the dandified Wimsey became a detective to cope with the trauma of his war experiences. Like Poirot, Wimsey is distinguished from heroic detectives by eccentricity and effeminacy, and by a reliance on female helpers. In earlier books he employs an elderly spinster, Miss Climpson, who anticipates Miss Marple in embodying the insufficiently tapped wisdom of the redundant woman, and assists Wimsey in tracing the lesbian killer of *Unnatural Death* (1927) and exploring the occult subworld of *Strong Poison* (1930). In later books she is replaced by the more modern figure of Harriet Vane, the Oxford educated professional who has found a niche within crime writing, and whom Wimsey eventually marries.

In the 1930s Sayers, like Christie, attempted to expand the possibilities of the genre; her most formulaic novel, *Five Red Herrings* (1931), was among her least successful. Her distinctive works of the decade were hybrid in nature. *Murder Must Advertise* (1933) draws on her experience of advertising and has strong relations with the documentary fiction of the period. *The Nine Tailors* (1934) conforms to the features of the genre in its use of a vicarage setting and reliance on the technical expertise of campanology, but also associates itself with the rural novel, especially in a climactic flood reminiscent of Holme's *The Lonely Plough*. It shared the high prestige accorded rural writing at the period, winning, unusually for a crime novel, a Book Club recommendation, and being awarded instant classic status. *Gaudy Night* (1935) is a university novel, comparable to Lehmann's *Dusty Answer*, or Brittain's *Dark Tide* (1923); the study of tensions and prejudices among academic women almost displaces the detection element. Sayers, the most ambitious for the status of the genre, was the only one of the four major women crime writers who ceased practising it after the 1930s; she diversified into religious and academic writing, a series of religious dramas and translations of Dante.

Margery Allingham and Ngaio Marsh established themselves as major crime writers in the 1930s. Both introduced their detectives in the self-consciously formulaic situation of a murder during a country-house party, and the early works of both demonstrate their difficulties in establishing

134

a distinctive niche within the genre. Allingham's Albert Campion first appeared in *The Crime at Black Dudley* (1929), which combines its formulaic country-house whodunit with a spy thriller, and is uneasily poised between the two genres. Allingham was clearly testing the market, but by *Police at the Funeral* (1931) she had settled to a puzzle plot (the first victim dunit). The novel's extensive emphasis on tracing the roots of its series of murders to Victorian family life, 'a breeding ground of those dark offshoots of the civilized mind which the scientists tell us are the natural outcome of repressions and inhibitions',[18] relates it to the concerns of fiction at the period. *The Fashion in Shrouds* (1938) is, like Sayers's *Gaudy Night*, a self-consciously ambitious attempt to raise the status of the genre, and similarly addressed to the problems of the woman trying to reconcile a career with her emotional life. The central focus is on Campion's fashion-designer sister Val, whose problems of identity and self-presentation are emphasized by her daily professional concern with dressing to look like a woman, and by the comparison between her and two less troubled women, an actress who specializes in sentimental roles on and off stage, and a spontaneous and unreflecting tomboy aircraft designer. Allingham's difficulties in establishing a niche within crime fiction are highlighted in the protean figure of Campion, and the problem of distinguishing yet another eccentric and effeminate detective with female helpers in an increasingly overcrowded field. In her most successful postwar novel, *A Tiger in the Smoke* (1952), which moves the detective novel into the mean streets, and to a duel between fugitive psychopath and police, Campion is a conspicuously superannuated relic of the amateur detection of the 1930s.

The New Zealander Ngaio Marsh, the last major entrant into interwar crime fiction, distinguished her detective, Inspector Alleyn, by making him a policeman, although his other features, Oxford education, discriminating literary tastes, marriage to a professional artist, derive from Sayers. Marsh's works are otherwise marked within the genre by being the most self-consciously self-referential of the period. Her first novel, *A Man Lay Dead* (1934), where the murder takes place during a game of Murder at a country-house party, invites attention to its deployment of the formulas of the genre. *Death in Ecstasy* (1936) again calls attention to its formal development, when Alleyn speculates on the solutions Christie or Sayers would provide to the mystery he is studying before providing his own different and correct solution. In *Artists in Crime* (1938) he responds to the scene of a murder by comparing it with a scene in a contemporary gangster movie. Marsh's invitations to the reader to reflect on the formulae she is deploying are enhanced in those novels situated in artistic worlds. In *Enter a Murderer* (1935) the murder takes place on stage and Alleyn encounters the problem of interpreting the behaviour of suspects who are all front-rank actors; in *Artists in Crime*, where a model is murdered during a life class, the visual depiction of murder is foregrounded.

Crime was a popular topic between the wars, and, while the crime novelists experimented variously with the genre in attempts to demonstrate its flexibility, the works of other writers who foregrounded crime suggested that the genre trivialized its subject. The title stories of two of Elizabeth Bowen's short story collections, *The Cat Jumps* (1934) and *Look At All Those Roses* (1941), foreground the 1930s fascination with the home as the site of crime; 'The Cat Jumps' takes the formula of a country-house party to suggest the neuroses and instabilities suggested by the interwar fascination with crime. Bowen's story is comic; the case for crime fiction's trivialization of crime is most powerfully put in the novel, *A Pin to See the Peep Show* (1934), by the novelist and criminologist, F. Tennyson Jesse, which, like Sayers's one non-Wimsey novel, *The Documents in the Case* (1928), derives from the Bywaters and Thompson murder trial of 1922. Edith Thompson, convicted with her younger lover for his unpremeditated murder of her husband, on the assumption that as her lover's senior she must have exerted influence on him, raised difficult questions about relations between the sexes which made her a central figure in the interwar mythology of women. The first literary treatment was E.M. Delafield's *A Messalina of the Suburbs* (1924). Sayers, in a book primarily interested in experimental pastiche of Wilkie Collins's methods of multiple narrative, accepts the thesis of Thompson's influence and responsibility, and presents the affair as a squalid suburban intrigue. Jesse's novel, a detailed feminist reconstruction of a suburban woman attempting to reconcile her personal and professional lives, is one of the best examples of the interwar fiction of fact; it is also an impassioned attack on the vicious pomp of capital punishment. In the long final section in the condemned cell Jesse implicitly rebukes the crime novel's emphasis on the puzzle plot, and tendency to end the story at the solution of the puzzle, and criticizes beyond that the false notions of crime the genre instils.

CHILDREN'S BOOKS

In Christie's *The ABC Murders* (1936) Poirot's attention to an adult male suspect is initially alerted when the character admits to enjoying rereading E. Nesbit's *The Railway Children*. The detail is revealing of opposing attitudes to children's literature; the suspect justifies his reading under a 'boys

from eighteen to eighty' rubric, while Poirot is employing a reductive interpretation of Freudian psychology where any attempt to relive childhood
experience is a sign of regression and serious emotional disturbance. The
episode also displays the changing availability of *The Railway Children*; to
Christie in 1936 it is a book classified as children's literature and appropriately located only on the nursery shelves, but its original appearance in
1905 was as a serial in the *London Magazine*. Earlier Nesbit children's stories
had appeared in the *Illustrated London News*, and from 1902 to 1913 her
fantasy narratives ran almost continuously in the *Strand Magazine*. All these
magazines had a general audience; any adult male wishing to read a Nesbit
serial could have done so in perfect security from detective attention.

By 1900 children's literature was well established as a separate category,
and as a growth area within publishing; several publishers had separate
children's lists, and a number of magazines specifically for juveniles existed.
The category of children's books was, however, less clearly defined than
it became in the interwar period. The assumption that the reading interests
of adults and children overlapped extensively was found both in the male
adventure romance, with its emphasis on the therapeutic effects of recap-
itulating the experiences of boyhood, and in the *Girl's Own Paper* which
addressed itself to domestic topics for a general audience, featured serials
with adult protagonists, and assumed that its primary audience was eager
to take on the domestic responsibilities of womanhood.

Women writers had been especially prominent in children's writing
throughout the nineteenth century, and the rapid development of the
market after the Education Act of 1870 extended the opportunities. The
corollary was that by 1900 women writers had become increasingly and
primarily associated with children's writing. The great innovators of the
Edwardian period, Nesbit, Beatrix Potter, Frances Hodgson Burnett, had
all attempted to establish themselves somewhere in the adult market before
finding a secure niche within children's books; in the interwar period
Richmal Crompton was a major example of a very successful children's
writer who repeatedly failed in her attempts to establish herself in adult
fiction. Within that niche writers developed ways of describing the issues
which preoccupied them; Nesbit's stories have clear affinities with the
Edwardian condition of England novels of Wells and Forster, Potter's with
the increasingly popular genre of rural writing. Angela Brazil's rhapsodic
accounts of school life are best understood in the context of the romantic
fiction of Barclay and Dell.

The Edwardian decade saw the establishment in particular of three models
of children's writing popular in the twentieth century: the family adventure
story, the animal story for very young children, and the girls' school story.
E. Nesbit established the twentieth-century model for the first genre; Julia

137

Briggs has argued that her innovations in the model make her 'the first modern writer for children'.[19] Nesbit adapted her interests to the children's adventure story after years of exploration of the possibilities for a literary career; she had attempted adult verse and fiction, and pamphlets for the Fabian Society of which she was a founder member, as well as children's verse and fiction. It was 'My Schooldays', an autobiographical series in the *Girls Own Paper* in 1896–97, which proved the basis for the fictions which established her as a leading children's writer. Despite the title, the series was largely concerned with memories of holiday adventures in which Nesbit had attempted to keep up with her brothers, and of 'the dead silences, the frozen terrors of the long, dark nights when I was little, and lonely, and very much afraid'.[20] The emphasis was on a separate child's world in which pleasures and terrors were alike undisclosed and unknown to adults, and it was this emphasis Nesbit retained in *The Treasure Seekers* (1899). This novel launched her series of family adventures, in which first in domestic settings, and later in fantasy settings, her child protagonists explored worlds of heroic struggle unsuspected by their elders.

A major issue in children's writing is the location of the narrative voice, which must establish some workable relation between writing adult and reading child. In solving this problem women writers might be perceived as having an advantage; Mother Goose is a long-established narrative voice. Barbara Wall has suggested that women writers tend to make less use than men of dual focus narrative techniques, which address a real primary adult audience beyond the presumed primary child audience.[21] In later books Nesbit used a Mother Goose variant, an indulgent Bohemian aunt voice, complicit with the children against adult conformity. Her need to develop a viable narrative voice for her children's fictions was complicated by the fact that, as they all appeared in general audience magazines, she was writing also for a presumed adult secondary audience. Julia Briggs has suggested that this uncertainty about her targeted audience led to her distinctive solution to the problem in her *Treasure Seekers* trilogy. The narrator is the eldest boy, Oswald, who writes of himself in the third person, claiming thus to speak impartially for his siblings, but presenting himself as first among equals. Oswald is the product of a comfortable, bookish, leftish-leaning, middle-class family, self-conscious about the demands of manliness, often exasperated by his sisters, ladylike Dora and tomboy Alice, whose frequent rebellions are used as a counter-commentary to Oswald. Nesbit's method enabled her to speak through a child narrator who yet spoke not as idealized child, but from within his gender and class.

In the later fantasies, and especially the time-travel stories, the girls become more important than their brothers; *The Story of the Amulet* (1906) inaugurates this phase. The later sections of *The Amulet*, serialized in the

138

Strand Magazine, ran there in parallel to Kipling's time-travel children's fantasy, *Puck of Pook's Hill*, and the contrast in their treatment of similar material reveals very different ideas about the introduction of children to history. Kipling's historical personages come forward into the present to recount their contributions to the nation's history to the children, who are later magically induced to forget their experience. The amnesia device emphasizes the inescapability of the interpretation of the past the story is offering; the children's role is to receive this interpretation and internalize it below conscious memory. Nesbit's children have a far more interactive relation with the past; they travel back to it, retain full memory and frequently seek to intervene in history. In one episode of *The Amulet* they transport a neglected slum child from the present to the more congenial and humane society of Britain in 55 BC, and argue with Julius Caesar about the merits of invading Britain. In *The House of Arden* (1908) the past is reached through a chest of old clothes in which the children dress up; history becomes a reserve of alternative possibilities. It is Elfrida, not her brother, who is active and resourceful in exploring the alternative roles history offers, and in the sequel, *Harding's Luck* (1909), she is joined by Nesbit's only working-class protagonist, the crippled slum child, Dickie Harding. Dickie is the true heir to the estate of Arden which, like the house in Forster's *Howards End* published in the following year, represents the continuing inheritance of England, but he eventually resolves to stay in a more congenial Jacobean past. For him, as for the differently dispossessed Elfrida, the opportunity to return to the past involves confronting alternative possibilities, lost ways of living, more attractive social models. For Nesbit fantasy becomes a means of making the social debates of the time available to children.

In *Harding's Luck* Dickie's rehabilitation begins when he grows some plants in his Deptford back-yard. The location was significant. In these years the educationalist Margaret McMillan, as Carolyn Steedman describes, was pioneering her Froebel-based experiments in garden-schools among the children of Deptford.[22] McMillan's vigorous campaigning for gardens as the most nurturing environment for child development was widely echoed in the writing of the period. The gardener, Gertrude Jekyll, devoted a book, *Children and Gardens* (1908), to the subject. Nesbit's 1911 fantasy, *The Wonderful Garden*, centred on a garden whose natural magic affected the lives of city children introduced to it, but her book was eclipsed by another children's story in the same year about the therapeutic effects of gardening for disturbed children, Frances Hodgson Burnett's *The Secret Garden*. The Manchester-born Burnett had established her literary career in the United States in the 1870s, and her biggest success, *Little Lord Fauntleroy* (1886), was a book about children addressed to a primary adult market,

139

tailored to please both American and English readers. *The Secret Garden*, like Nesbit's stories, was first serialized in a general audience magazine, the *American Magazine*, and unlike Nesbit's stories, explicitly addresses both adult and child readers.

In the story addressed to adults *The Secret Garden* is a condition of England novel, which concludes with the restoration of father and son to their roles as responsible Yorkshire landowners; in this public story the garden is the land of England which offers itself as the means of social rehabilitation for those estranged from their natural health. The book's enduring success, however, lay in its private story where Mary, merely an agent of male recovery in the adult story, finds in the garden a private autonomous space. The power with which Burnett explored, like Nesbit, a private children's world secluded from adults established the book's particular significance for girl readers, despite the near exclusion of Mary from the final chapters.

Beatrix Potter's stories also invoked the appeal to childhood of private spaces, rabbit holes, mouse holes, hedgehog holes. The career of the most successful and innovative writer for very young children in the earlier twentieth century was based on thwarted ambitions to be an illustrator of naturalist books, and on private experience of writing for an exclusive child audience. The first work Potter planned was an illustrated book on fungi, but her success began in an illustrated letter she wrote in 1893 to a small child. In 1900 she arranged for the private publication of that letter with black and white illustrations as *The Tale of Peter Rabbit*, and its success among her acquaintance encouraged her to approach the publishers Frederick Warne. The success of *Peter Rabbit*, issued in shilling copies in 1902 with colour illustrations, and selling 50,000 copies within the year, was repeated in the decade 1903–13 by its eighteen successors.

Potter's next publications for Warne were *The Tale of Squirrel Nutkin* and *The Tailor of Gloucester* in 1903; the latter, which had already been privately published, was atypical of the Potter series in having an adult human protagonist, a strong historical nostalgic element, much interpolated verse, and an implicit appeal to adult readers. *Nutkin* returned to the *Peter Rabbit* model with its story of rebellion against adult authority. The prudent young squirrels carry out their rituals of obeisance to Old Brown, while Nutkin performs his aggressive counter-rituals, taunting the owl with riddling songs. The story invites the child reader to participate in the repetitive rituals of a game and in Nutkin's innovative exhilaration in using language, just as *The Tale of Two Bad Mice* (1904) invites enjoyment of the systematic destruction of the dolls' house by the mice, or *The Tale of Mrs Tiggywinkle* (1905) invites the specific enjoyment of girl readers of the hedgehog's domestic routines. Nutkin's final punishment might be seen as providing a moral, but Potter's terse deadpan account presents it as evidence of the distribution of power as it exists in the world.

Graham Greene praised *Two Bad Mice* particularly for its precision of style. Greene's essay, 'Beatrix Potter', is comic in its use of Shakespearean periodization to describe her works, but discriminating in its treatment of individual works. *Two Bad Mice*, classified among the 'great comedies' by Greene, is exact and controlled in matching its terse descriptions of the destruction wrought by the mice to the accompanying illustrations. Each picture and paragraph describes a stage in the destruction; the vigour and energy anticipates the effects of later cartoon films. The same matching precision is found in the extended fight scene in *The Tale of Mr Tod* (1912), for Greene the best example of 'the great near-tragedies'.[23] He quotes the rabbits' approach to the fox's house as an example of Potter's verbal precision and economy in dealing with evil:

> The sun had set; an owl had begun to hoot in the wood. There were many unpleasant things lying about, that had much better have been buried; rabbit bones and skulls, and chicken legs and other horrors. It was a shocking place and very dark.[24]

Potter's success was based on severe control; she enjoyed the nostalgia of *The Tailor of Gloucester*, but eliminated it as inappropriate for a child audience in subsequent books. When in 1929 she agreed to let her American publishers have a collection of whimsical stories, *The Fairy Caravan*, uncharacteristic of her main work, she refused to have it published in Britain. She took a keen pioneering interest in tie-in merchandise, such as dolls and nursery wallpaper, and campaigned vigorously against unauthorized products.[25] It was part of her attempt to maintain the highest professional standards in an area of publication where they had not always been considered necessary.

Although Potter and Nesbit were the major innovators among women writers for children in the Edwardian decade, Angela Brazil was also associated with establishing a genre. In her idylls of school-life Chloe had been liking Olivia for over two decades before Woolf complained in *A Room of One's Own* of the absence of this theme from fiction. Brazil did not invent the girls' school-story genre in Britain; L.T. Meade, the most prolific writer for girls in the 1880s and 1890s, made school experience prominent in her fiction. Brazil's fictions, however, came to concentrate exclusively on school experience, making her name synonymous with the genre. In H.G. Wells's 1909 novel, *Tono-Bungay*, one of the male characters remarks 'Any woman who's been to a good eventful girls' school lives on the memory of it for the rest of her life. It's one of the pathetic things about women, – the superiority of school and college to anything they get

141

afterwards.'[26] Brazil's fictions endorsed these ideas; in her autobiography, *My Own School-Days* (1925), she describes the inadequacy of the various day-schools she attended in Liverpool and Manchester in the 1880s with their lack of a prefect system and their sparse opportunities for games and for 'white-hot' friendships.[27] Her fictional schools were mainly boarding-schools, and designed to supply the commodities which Brazil's day-schools had lacked.

In Brazil's first school story, *The Fortunes of Philippa* (1906), she is still discovering the formula which she established for the genre. Based on Brazil's mother's childhood and, like *The Secret Garden*, the story of a colonial returnee adjusting to English life, the story, like Meade's, is concerned with the heroine's general experience, in which school is a part. Philippa acclimatizes successfully to Englishness, assisted by inheritance of a Tudor manor-house situated on downland running down to the sea. In this book the building which was to become the archetypal setting of the fictional girls' school is still a family residence; its relocation as school in Brazil's later books is an emblem of her redirection of interest to the overwhelming importance of school experience. Philippa's school is wildly eclectic in approach, suggesting that Brazil was uncertain where to situate it in the debates about girls' education then current. Near the beginning the adult characters debate the rival advantages of the athletic outdoors English girl and the French convent-bred girl, and the school seems designed to accommodate both preferences; Brazil also throws in a genuflection to the opponents of academic education for girls when Philippa succumbs to brain fever through overwork induced by a misguided teacher.

Brazil is clearly attempting to keep her school in line with as many educational programmes as possible, but her real interest lies in the friend-ships which school encourages, and Philippa's attempts to engage the exclusive affection of the prettiest and most popular girl in the school. For her the school locale represents a kind of idyllic retreat, allowing almost unlimited possibilities for the development of female friendships. By the time of *A Fourth Form Friendship* (1912) Brazil's formula has stabilized; the action is almost entirely situated in the school, which has now appropriated the manor-house and coastal downland, and is focused on new girl Aldred's attempt to engross popular Mabel by misrepresenting her past experiences. The extensive moralizing accompanying these attempts, and the school's emphasis on household management, link this novel to Victorian juvenile fiction, and the rhapsodic descriptions of the friendship are in the manner of Barclay and Dell. Brazil had, however, devised a formula of situation (the downland school) and theme (the development and vicissitudes of female friendship) on which the school story was to depend in its boom interwar years.

142

In the years immediately following the First World War a number of schoolgirl comics supplied the large market for schoolgirl fiction, which extended well beyond the middle-class reader for whom attendance at boarding-school was a possibility; a 1940 survey by A.J. Jenkinson found that school fiction was the most popular reading among girls of twelve to fifteen; after that it was succeeded by romantic fiction and 'bloods'.[28] The popularity of the genre is attested by the fact that the comics, such as *Schoolfriend* and *Schoolgirl's Own*, were largely staffed and written by men. In the schoolgirl novel Brazil's continuing dominance was challenged by several other women writers, including Elsie J. Oxenham and Elinor Brent-Dyer, who established the formula of the long-running series based on one particular school. Oxenham's *The Abbey Girls* (1920) began a series inspired by the ideals of the British folk-music movement and of the American Camp Fire movement. The girls not only lived in the requisite abbey, but sought to recreate the communal ideals which had once dominated it; in this series country-dance performed in competition took the place usually taken by games. In Brent-Dyer's *The School at the Chalet* (1925) the 25-year-old heroine, tired of her status in Britain as surplus woman, gathers up a clutch of unwanted, sickly or misfit adolescents, themselves potential surplus women, and sets off to make a career for herself by establishing a school in the Austrian Tyrol. By this time the genre has developed self-consciousness; the Austrian girls who flock to the school have all read English school stories, and are anxious to experience the prefect system and a games-dominated curriculum for themselves. A French girl who, in obvious reference to Brazil, yearns for an utterly exclusive friendship, is comically treated throughout. Brent-Dyer and Oxenham, unlike Brazil, are concerned with school not simply as idyll but as process, providing opportunities for later life; in Oxenham's case these are for leisure activities (the cultivation of folk-dance) suitable for gentry life in the local community, in Brent-Dyer's for careers abroad for surplus women.

The adolescent girl was a major focus of attention in the interwar period in the popular press, in the innovative fiction of Bowen, Lehmann and White, in the increasing diversification of writing addressed to her. Several genres which were to flourish after the Second World War were established in the 1930s. Noel Streatfield's *Ballet Shoes* (1936) was the most popular of the career novels which emphasized childhood as process, as training for later life. Enid Bagnold's *National Velvet* (1935) was a forerunner of the pony novels of the postwar period. In Alison Uttley's Nesbit-influenced *A Traveller in Time* (1939) the heroine's adolescent worries and confusions are figured in her repeated time-travel between present day and Elizabethan England, where she works in the kitchens of a great house, and the descriptions of servant life anticipate the emphasis on detail and the everyday in postwar historical novels for children.[29]

143

Jenkinson's 1940 survey found the school story the most popular genre with girls of twelve to fifteen. The most popular genre overall was the story of home life, in which the North American classic writers, Louisa Alcott, Susan Coolidge and L.M. Montgomery, dominated. Interestingly the one British writer who challenged this dominance wrote about a boy, Richmal Crompton of the 'William' series. The survey found that the younger girls responded to it as 'adventure' and the older as 'humour'; 'William' also scored high in the boys' section of the survey. The 'William' books are a classic example of stories which address themselves successfully to several audiences. The first story, 'The Outlaws', was published in 1919 in the women's monthly, the *Home Magazine*; other stories followed in this journal and then in the *Happy Mag*, before the first collection of stories, *Just-William*, was published in 1922. The runaway success in children's writing of the interwar period thus emerged in stories addressed to a primary audience of adult females. Crompton's authorial stance in the earlier William stories owes much to the formula Nesbit established with Oswald in the 'Treasure-Seeker' trilogy, and includes comic exasperation with William's grandiose ambitions combined with a thorough partisanship with him against the adult respectable world. In the story 'Jumble', in *Just-William*, a painting of William representing 'the unconscious, eager wistfulness which is the mark of youth' is exhibited at the Royal Academy.[30] The attribution of this quality to William is not entirely ironic, but frequent targets in these stories are the posturing and exploitative adults who speak of children in these terms.

Many of the early stories turn on William's sudden infatuations with young women, his teachers, his elder brother's girlfriends, the glamorous young American tourist for whom he pretends to be a descendant of Shakespeare in *William the Conqueror* (1926). There are even tomboys of his own age; the dominance of the programmatically hysterical Violet Elizabeth as representative of girlhood occurs only after the formula has stabilized. The stories' focus on these infatuations gives them an obvious resemblance to the other great comic success of the decade, P.G. Wodehouse's Bertie Wooster stories, the first of which was also published in 1919; they also remind the reader that William will one day be like his elder brother. The early stories invite the complicity of female readers not only in William's rebellions against adult life, but in his mother's resignation and his sister's exasperation, both demonstrating a commonsense attitude to the varieties of male behaviour distinct from the many female believers in childhood wistfulness who appear in the stories. At the same time Crompton continues to emphasize William's secret outlaw world; her success with audiences of different ages and genders suggests an exceptional sensitivity to the problem of balancing their claims.

144

Crompton addressed a multiple audience; the great emerging success of the late 1930s was a writer who addressed herself exclusively to the children's market. The main period of Enid Blyton's success, and her dominance of a mass children's market, was a postwar phenomenon, but she was building her reputation within the growing market for children's writing throughout the interwar period. Like the romantic novelists, Berta Ruck and Annie S. Swan, she toiled for years in appropriate periodicals before achieving the status of popular author. Her means of entry was the educational journal, *Teacher's World*, for which from 1922 she provided nature notes and other items suggestive for teachers engaged in interesting small children. Her first full-length story, *The Adventures of a Wishing Chair*, was published in 1937, after serialization in the children's weekly, *Sunny Stories*, for which she had worked since 1922. The next few years saw the publication of several works which inaugurated the series which became the basis of her postwar reputation. These included *Five on a Treasure Island* (1942), the first of the 'Famous Five' series which became the most successful of her family adventure stories derived from the Nesbit model, and *The Naughtiest Girl in the School* (1940), an early example of her several schoolgirl series, and clearly reflecting changing expectations in its title's echo of one of Brazil's most popular books, *The Nicest Girl in the School* (1909). Blyton worked with the formulae established by previous writers to address herself to an exclusively child audience, and her overwhelming success marks the establishment of an entirely distinct child market of the kind Christie had anticipated.

NOTES

Place of publication is London, unless otherwise stated.

1. See *New Cambridge Bibliography of English Literature*, ed. George Watson (Cambridge: Cambridge University Press, 1969), III, pp. 1085–109.
2. See Leonard Woolf, *Downhill All the Way: An Autobiography of the Years 1919–1939* (Hogarth Press, 1967), p. 63.
3. Rebecca West, 'The Tosh Horse', in *The Strange Necessity* (Cape, 1928), pp. 319–26.
4. Berta Ruck, *A Storyteller Tells the Truth: Reminiscences and Notes* (Hutchinson, 1935), pp. 268–70.
5. Storm Jameson, *Journey from the North* (Collins and Harvill, 1969), I, pp. 110–11.
6. Elinor Glyn, *Three Weeks* (Duckworth, 1974), chs 18, 30.

7. E.M. Hull, *The Sheik* (Eveleigh, Nash and Grayson, 1920), chs 1, 4.
8. See Andrew Lang, 'Realism and Romance', *Contemporary Review*, 52 (1887), pp. 683–93.
9. See Alison Light, *Forever England: Femininity, Literature and Conservatism Between the Wars* (Routledge, 1991), pp. 156–207.
10. Martha Duffy, 'On the Road to Manderley', *Time*, 12 April 1977, pp. 65–6.
11. See Anthea Trodd, *Domestic Crime in the Victorian Novel* (Macmillan, 1989).
12. R.G. Collingwood, *The Idea of History* (Oxford: Clarendon Press, 1946), pp. 281–2.
13. Raymond Chandler, 'The Simple Art of Murder', in *The Second Chandler Omnibus* (Hamish Hamilton, 1962), pp. 3–15.
14. W.H. Auden, 'The Guilty Vicarage', in *The Dyer's Hand and Other Essays* (Faber and Faber, 1963), pp. 146–58.
15. See Stephen Knight, *Form and Ideology in Crime Fiction* (Macmillan, 1980), pp. 107–34; Marion Shaw and Sabine Vanacker, *Reflecting on Miss Marple* (Routledge, 1991).
16. Dorothy Sayers, 'Aristotle on Detective Fiction', in *Unpopular Opinions* (Gollancz, 1946), pp. 178–90.
17. See David Trotter, *The English Novel in History 1895–1920* (Routledge, 1993), pp. 225–6.
18. Margery Allingham, *Police at the Funeral* (Harmondsworth: Penguin, 1939), ch. 5.
19. Julia Briggs, *A Woman of Passion: The Life of E. Nesbit 1858–1924* (Hutchinson, 1987), p. xi.
20. E. Nesbit, 'My School-Days', *The Girl's Own Paper*, XIX (1897), p. 264.
21. Barbara Wall, *The Narrator's Voice: The Dilemma of Children's Fiction* (Macmillan, 1991).
22. Carolyn Steedman, *Children, Culture and Class in Britain: Margaret McMillan 1860–1931* (Virago, 1991), pp. 81–97.
23. Grahame Greene, 'Beatrix Potter', in *The Lost Childhood and Other Essays* (Harmondsworth: Penguin, 1966), pp. 122–8.
24. Beatrix Potter, *The Tale of Mr Tod* (Warne/Penguin, 1995).
25. See Margaret Lane, *The Tale of Beatrix Potter: A Biography* (Warne, 1946), pp. 104–9.
26. H.G. Wells, *Tono-Bungay* (Macmillan, 1911), bk. 2, ch. 4.
27. Angela Brazil, *My Own School-Days* (Blackie, 1925), p. 116.
28. See A.J. Jenkinson, *What Do Boys and Girls Read?* (Methuen, 1940), p. 175.
29. See Anna Davin, 'Historical Novels for Children', *History Workshop Journal*, 1 (1976), pp. 154–65.
30. Richmal Crompton, 'Jumble', in *Just-William* (Macmillan, 1990).

CHAPTER SEVEN
Non-fiction

Women wrote in many non-fiction genres in this period: this section will focus on three only. One, academic writing, was a completely new field. In life writing autobiography, rather than biography, is the significant genre, as the publication of women's autobiographical writing became commonplace for the first time. Women were already well established in travel writing, but, as a genre which demands exploration of gender identity, it is central to the concerns of this period.

AUTOBIOGRAPHY

The publishing event of 1907 was the appearance, in three volumes, of Queen Victoria's letters. The editors, A.C. Benson and Lord Esher, justified the publication in their preface by arguing that the letters exemplified the simplicity of, and absorption in, domestic life, which had enabled the late monarch to be an inspiration to her subjects. It was the completeness with which she embodied domestic values which had led her son, Edward VII (who famously did not), to sanction the publication. The editors were addressing the question of whether the private life should be made public; paradoxically it was precisely the cultivation of privacy by this most public of female personages which made publication appropriate. The whole preface emphasizes that the paradigm for women's autobiographical writing was private and domestic. They wrote diaries and letters, rather than memoirs; they exemplified the everyday, obscure life of the home.[1]

The year before Victoria's letters appeared, Virginia Woolf wrote one of her earliest stories, 'The Journal of Mistress Joan Martyn' (1906), in which she imagines a woman historian finding in a Norfolk farm-house the journal of a fifteenth-century woman unknown to history. Joan's journal conforms to the paradigm for women's autobiographical writing, the private reflections of an ordinary woman in her obscure domestic niche, not intended for publication and long neglected. A much later essay, her 1931 preface for the Women's Cooperative Guild's *Life as We Have Known It*, returned to this kind of writing. These short narratives of experience over the previous sixty years by working women, the modern equivalents of the narrative of Woolf's fictitious Joan, confirmed the continuance of the paradigm. Although later in the decade Mass Observation fostered the writing of life-stories among ordinary people, and the last three decades have seen the publication of a number of autobiographical writings from this period, it was unusual at this date that writing such as *Life as We Have Known It* should reach publication.

In the early twentieth century, however, for the first time the expectation that public figures would write their memoirs extended to women. The women who responded to this expectation confronted complex problems of self-presentation. The dominant paradigm was private and domestic, and the traditional antithesis between public life and women meant there were few narrative models for the public woman. In the Victorian period the reception of the economist Harriet Martineau's *An Autobiographical Memoir*, published posthumously in 1877, emphasized the difficulties; Martineau was widely accused of egotism. Many of the autobiographies published during this period suggest the writer's acute consciousness of the antithesis between women and public life, coupled with a sense that women who rejected the paradigm of obscurity and privacy were breaking ranks with their fellows. The classic example is Jane Harrison's slim memoir, *Reminiscences of a Student's Life* (1925), which seems anxious to rebut any claims to public eminence. The feminists Cicely Hamilton and Lady Rhondda occupied many public platforms, but their autobiographies, Hamilton's *Life Errant* (1935) and Rhondda's *This Was My World* (1933), present them as chance eyewitnesses of great events.

This section will focus on three writers, all prominent political activists, who did respond to the challenge of representing the relations of women with public life: Beatrice Webb, Sylvia Pankhurst and Vera Brittain. Their political involvement, and their approach to the narratives which reconstructed them, were different, but shared one striking similarity. Each presented her story as a move away from individualism to incorporation within a group, and each wrote a second volume of autobiography which foregrounds other people.

Woolf admired Webb's *My Apprenticeship* (1926) as a thoroughly planned and rationalized narrative; 'she is trying to relate all her experiences to

148

history. She is very rational and coherent . . . and makes herself fit in very persuasively and to my mind very interestingly' (*Diary*, III, p. 74). She saw the story Webb constructed as a triumphant exercise in relating a woman's life to history, but a method far removed from her own explorations of the way in which the public impinged on the private. *My Apprenticeship* was to Woolf the achievement to be expected from the doyenne of public debate and sociological investigation. Webb's diaries for the period, first published in 1982, were the basis for the 1925 work, and the comparison of the two reveals Webb's struggle to find an appropriate model with which to discuss her long and eminent career in public life, and translate the confessional material of her diaries into a form appropriate for publication.[2] Both works are engrossing narratives; in youth Webb had hesitated between the careers of sociologist and novelist:

> This last month or so I have been haunted by a longing to create
> characters and to move them to and fro among fictitious circumstances.
> To put the matter plainly, by the vulgar wish to write a novel . . .
> Compare it with work in which movements of commodities, percentages,
> depreciations, averages, and all the ugly horrors of commercial facts are in
> the dominant place, and must remain so if the work is to be worthful.[3]

The great Victorian women writers influenced her ambitions. Her early diaries sometimes read like pastiche Charlotte Brontë, and in 1874 the future author of the Minority Report on the Poor Law was worrying that she might grow up like the frivolous Rosamond Vincy in George Eliot's *Middlemarch*. The partially suppressed literary ambitions, so far expressed most fully in her diaries, were extended in *My Apprenticeship*.

Webb had read Martineau's autobiography, and the hostile reviews, in 1877, and felt then that Martineau's focus on herself was justified because it described a progress towards 'the ignoring of self in the wider interests of humanity'.[4] She makes clear on the first page of her own memoir that it is not about herself, but about the processes which instructed her in 'the craft of a social investigator'. Much of the book consists of extensive quotation from those diaries of forty years before. The justification given for these extracts is that they provide hard evidence of the various stages in the evolution of her craft, but they are also a calling up of past selves, a questioning of earlier identities. The dialogue implicit between the italicized diary extracts and the main narrative of 1926 is a powerful commentary on the uncertain evolution of identity. Webb was uneasy about this method, partly because she sensed her husband's criticism:

> In his heart he fears I am overvaluing it, especially the extracts from the
> diaries; the whole thing is far too subjective, and all that part which deals
> with 'my creed' as distinguished from 'my craft' seems to him the
> sentimental scribblings of a woman, only interesting just because they are

feminine. However, I have enjoyed writing it and the book as a whole will have some *value* as a description of Victorianism. (*Diary*, IV, p. 49)

Webb's emphasis on the book's public value as useful, eyewitness material of a past age is representative of the lingering doubts about the propriety of making the female subjective public expressed by many women writers in the genre.

In *My Apprenticeship* Webb gives her public history, tracing the development of her craft, the early friendship with Herbert Spencer, the incognito visits to her working-class relatives in Lancashire, her life as a London rent-collector, another incognito period working in the London sweatshops, her launch as a sociologist collecting material for Charles Booth's *Life and Labour of the People of London* (1891–1902). The evidence for the integration of her life in the evolving craft of sociology is lucidly marshalled in the way which Woolf admired. At the same time part of the book's power derives from the reader's sense of evidence suppressed, an effect intensified by the movement between diary extracts and public narrative. Webb's attitude to her diaries was ambivalent; sometimes they were immensely important to her as a communication with 'some mysterious personification of one's own identity . . . the Unknown, which lies below the constant change of matter and ideas' (*Diary*, I, p. 120). At other times she saw them as a repository for waste and disorder; 'there is much that goes on within one, which one, as a prudent mistress, winks at and overlooks . . . It is not wise to stop the ruffianly-looking vagrant and enquire from him whence he comes and whither he goeth' (*Diary*, I, p. 63). The residual presence of this other self of the diaries, whether mysterious unknown or suspicious vagrant, is most evident in the section of *My Apprenticeship* subtitled 'The Dead Point', where Webb refers tersely to the 'black thread of personal unhappiness' (p. 284) in her life in the 1880s, reminding us we are hearing only of her intellectual and public life. The central theme of her diary in the 1880s is her obsessive passion for the politician Joseph Chamberlain, which in *My Apprenticeship* appears only in terse and inexplicit reference. Chamberlain makes one personal appearance within a long diary extract in which Webb uses his speech to a political rally in Birmingham as a coded discussion of their relationship. She observes his 'intense desire to dominate, to impress his own personality and his own aim on that pliable material beneath him', how 'into the tones of his voice he threw that warmth of feeling which was lacking in his words', and how the crowd 'might have been a woman listening to the words of her lover' (p. 143). The whole scene becomes a highly charged account of how Chamberlain woos both Webb and the electorate.

This one scene condenses the long narrative in the diary in which Webb detailed her passion and her humiliated resentment. In 'The Dead Point'

150

she explains that 'in those days . . . it would not have been practicable to unite the life of love and the life of reason' (p. 284). The diaries replay a conflict of reason and feeling familiar in Victorian fiction, and especially in the novel which seems the closest model for this presentation of unarticulated passion within the exchanges of public life, Charlotte Brontë's *Villette*. At one point Webb tears out sheets from her diary, which treat her feelings for Chamberlain, and seals them in an envelope. At another she sits at a window at night reading the biography of George Eliot, thinking of Eliot's unrequited love for her own friend Spencer, and how they are thus 'curiously linked'. 'A warm moonlight night with soft southwest wind, thinking of a crowded hall, deafening shouts, dead silence except for one voice – the voice of the People's Tribune' (*Diary*, I, p. 129); she is remembering Chamberlain at the rally. It is not, however, only the Chamberlain relationship which is eliminated from the autobiography; Webb regularly restricts information to what is necessary to clarify her intellectual position. In a description of a discussion in 1889 about women's suffrage, which she then opposed, with some male feminists and the very anti-feminist economist, Alfred Marshall, she describes in detail the intellectual positions adopted, but not the embarrassment she records in her diary at the humiliated presence of Marshall's wife, the pioneer academic Mary Paley.

My Apprenticeship has a double conclusion, the completion of training, and the marriage to Sidney Webb, referred to as 'the Other One', whose last-minute appearance is the one awkward narrative moment. Vera Brittain's *Testament of Youth* (1933) encounters the same problem; both writers adopt the traditional romance model of women's fiction to end their narrative, but find it impossible to integrate persuasively with their new stories of women in public life. Webb's second volume of autobiography, *Our Partnership*, published posthumously in 1948, is not organized chronologically, but thematically around various public issues. The residual narrative of self in the earlier volume has been obliterated, completing the move towards 'ignoring of self' by which she had justified Martineau.

A similar movement is traced in the autobiographical writings of another very public woman, Sylvia Pankhurst. *The Suffragette Movement: An Intimate Account of Persons and Ideals* (1931), is both autobiography and group history, with the narrative of Pankhurst's life gradually converging, and becoming merged with, that of the group. At the centre of the book is her decision to forgo her ambitions as an artist and become absorbed in the public life. 'As a speaker, a pamphlet-seller, a chalker of pavements, a canvasser on doorsteps, you are wanted; as an artist the world has no real use for you; in that capacity you must fight a purely egotistical struggle'.[5] Parallel to this rejection is another; the frontispiece is of Sylvia's mother, Emmeline Pankhurst, promising a portrait of family solidarity, but the narrative follows a movement away from family. The young art student first reluctantly sacrifices her ambitions in painting to her mother's political activities, and then becomes involved in a political movement which absorbs her entirely, and necessarily estranges her from her family. The convergence between the individual subject and political activity is mediated through Sylvia's continuing conflicts with her mother, her resentment of her mother's early attempt at independence in establishing a giftshop, and at the later demands to set aside her studies for the suffrage movement, the political estrangement as Sylvia moves closer to socialism.

In the second autobiographical volume, *The Home Front: A Mirror to Life in England during the World War* (1932), Pankhurst, like Webb in her sequel, presents herself as entirely absorbed in the public life, but, unlike Webb, entirely estranged from her family and class. The book is an account of her activities campaigning for working-class women in the East End during the war, and her insistence on public recognition of the exploitation at home encouraged by the war. While in *The Suffragette Movement* she presented herself as representative of the middle-class women struggling for the vote, and the sacrifices of personal ambition and private feeling they were required to make, here she appears in the role of intermediary between the East End and political power. The narrative follows her fights for separation allowances, minimum wages, and for the toy factory and day nursery she ran, but moves to obliterate her within the stories she tells of the individual lives of the women of the East End. There is no attention, as in the previous volume, to her individual aspirations; it is a record of her comprehensive adoption of working-class life, an exploration of the possibilities of full identification with her working-class community comparable to George Orwell's documentaries of the 1930s. This identity is partly expressed through her submersion in the 'little tragedies' of her constituents, and partly through the descriptions of the inadequacies of other politically active middle-class women: her mother and sister as Tory feminists, the trade union leader Mary MacArthur, Beatrice Webb, 'black-gowned and circumscribed, a carefully reared indoor nineteenth-century product who had missed the enlargement of motherhood'.[6] These vignettes emphasize both Pankhurst's general point about the different wars which were experienced by middle-class and by working-class women, and the narrative of her own crossing of the divide.

Vera Brittain, whose *Testament of Youth* (1933) was the most popular woman's autobiography of the period, was a fairly well known journalist, and the author of some not very successful novels, when she wrote her life as a representative woman of the war generation. As early as 1922, she had submitted a selection of her 1913–17 diaries under the title 'Chronicle of Youth' to a publishers' competition. She was unsuccessful then, but the war book boom of the late 1920s suggested that a memoir based on these diaries might succeed. Unlike Webb and Pankhurst she was not a well-known public figure, indeed that was the theme of her book. Rebecca West defended Brittain against critics who commented on her obscurity, saying 'You mean she's not a field-marshal? But it's the psychological sort of autobiography that succeeds nowadays – not the old dull kind.'[7] As West predicted, Brittain's version of autobiography addressed itself successfully to this reaction towards the experience of the unknown and away from the memoirs of great figures. Like Webb she drew extensively on her diaries for the period, using quotations from them to establish a dialogue between her different selves.

As a record of eyewitness experience, *Testament of Youth* is characteristic of the 1930s demand for fact; it is saturated in detail, using an accumulation of information to persuade. It was this which overcame Woolf's reservations:

> I am reading with extreme greed a book by Vera Britain [sic] called The Testament of Youth ... her story, told in detail, without reserve, of the war, & how she lost lover and brother, & dabbled her hands in entrails, & was forever seeing the dead, & eating scraps, & sitting five on one WC, runs rapidly, vividly across my eyes ... Nor has anyone written that kind of book before. Why now? What urgency is there on them to stand bare in public? She feels that these facts must be made known, in order to help – what? herself partly I suppose. (*Diary*, IV, p. 177)

To Woolf it was the surplus of information to form which impressed. To Brittain's American publisher the book appeared too good to be true, and Brittain 'a clever if unscrupulous artist who had produced what one American critic subsequently described as "a novel masquerading as an autobiography" '.[8] The success of *Testament of Youth* depended both on its massive accumulation of detail, in the spirit of the 1930s fiction of fact, and on the way it confirmed many of the established features of the existing legend of the Great War.

There are two major narrative lines in *Testament of Youth*, which both derive from Brittain's response to the boom in male war memoirs. 'Why should these young men have the war to themselves? Didn't women have their war as well? ... Who will write the epic of the women who went to war?'[9] The central section of the book is a female narrative complementary to the existing male memoirs, the story of the sacrifice of a generation told through four doomed young soldiers and the nurse who works and waits and endures their successive deaths. Brittain's prewar engagement to Roland Leighton, their wartime meetings, the partings on railway platforms, the interpolated poems of both, the exchanged roses, his death, her devotion to her brother and his two friends until their deaths, all confirm the existing male tradition of the sacrifice of an idealistic generation. Across this cuts another, feminist, narrative, of Brittain's prewar discontent with provincial gentility, of feminist ambitions recognized through reading Schreiner and Eliot, her interrupted university life resumed after the war, the freedom of the room of their own in postwar London where she and Winifred Holtby begin their careers as journalists. These two narratives, the sacrificed generation and the feminist advance, are in uneasy relation through the book. Brittain uses her self-presentation to mediate between them with continual reference to the deceptive impression she produced. 'I was too much the pretty-pretty type ever to seem aggressively up to date.'[10] The 'pretty-pretty type', with her roses and poems, can figure appropriately in a classical war narrative; her feminism lies in wait for a more appropriate context. Brittain, like Webb, falls back on the romance ending to conclude her narrative with her meeting with 'G' (George Catlin), who has much the same shadowy role as 'the Other One' in the last pages of *My Apprenticeship*. While Catlin's last-minute objection to figuring as a character in the book may partly explain the awkwardness of the end, the parallel with Webb suggests a more fundamental problem. Both women, writing the story of women and public life without much helpful precedent, conclude a candid examination of their lives with a perfunctory and diffident romantic ending, which is not integrated with the rest of the work.

Brittain's second autobiographical volume, *Testament of Friendship* (1940), continues the second volume pattern of removing the author from the foreground, and absorbing her life in another concern. The title of this biography of Winifred Holtby presents it as a sequel to Brittain's previous volume. It is specifically an attempt to describe and dignify the neglected subject of female friendship. The story in outline is very similar to the previous Testament, golden youth, comradeship and early death, with Brittain again in the role of survivor. This time the sacrifice is distinctively female as Holtby's writing career suffers from the demands of family and friends; she is 'the perpetual go between', the victim of 'a noble deplorable exploitability'.[11] Holtby is seen as representative of her generation of women, not only forced to juggle her literary and domestic responsibilities, but torn also between the feminist commitments of journalism and public engagements which will advance the cause of women, and the privacy she needs to write her novels. She enacts the conflicts which Brittain herself experienced; like its predecessor *Testament of Friendship* is the autobiography of a generation. This time, confronting the problem of closure, Brittain offers the reader three endings. There is the sacrifice of the most dedicated literary Martha of her generation; there is the story of the great writer who completed her masterpiece, *South Riding*, and immediately died; and there is the romance ending with 'Bill', Holtby's lost love, turning up at the deathbed. The multiplicity of conclusions lavishly demonstrate the problems, so intense at this period, of shaping a woman's life for the form of public memoir.

TRAVEL WRITING

The relations and distinctions between travel writing and autobiography were illuminated in 1951 when Freya Stark published *Beyond Euphrates*, the volume of her autobiography which covered the period of her most famous travel book of the interwar period, *The Valleys of the Assassins* (1934). For Stark the autobiography is an opportunity to offer an account of her travels in Iraq and Iran closer to her memories of the experience than was the travel book, which had engaged primarily to inform and to entertain. To ensure that closeness, *Beyond Euphrates* follows a method close to that of Webb's *My Apprenticeship*, with contemporary narrative alternating with letters from the period. Stark justifies her use of this method as truer to the reality of experience than the traditional narrative of adventure it reprises in terms somewhat reminiscent of Woolf's 'Modern Fiction':

> no medium has yet been devised for the translation of life into language, nor can any words recall the dazzling fluidity of days. Simple yet fixed in sequence, they fall like the shaft of a cataract into time and through it. Letters give the most faithful picture, because they are fragmentary and concerned merely with the moments as they pass.[12]

Travel books had, in some degree, to promote the public significance of the journey undertaken, to make an addition to public knowledge. Stark's series of autobiographies, recovering the same ground as her travel writing, attempt to find a way of recreating more exactly the personal significance of her experiences.

Travel writing in the Edwardian period was dominated by Gertrude Bell, and *Beyond Euphrates* is haunted by references to that most celebrated woman traveller of the previous generation, who plays a role for Stark comparable to that which Bennett played for Woolf. The great Edwardian, with her political and intelligence connections, her promotion of the public significance of her journeys, her representation of the national interest in the Middle East, had established a model for women's travel writing which Stark rejects. She complains of Bell's *The Desert and the Sown* (1907) that 'she did not have enough adventures, perhaps because she went with her own tents', and turns instead for inspiration to the narratives of the *Arabian Nights* with their 'total want of any ethical aim' (p. 42). It was a significant shift of models from a narrative in which the interest is dependent on the reader's awareness of the political significance of the incidents described, to a narrative which is founded in sympathetic emulation of a classic text of the culture studied, and gives priority to narrative excitement.

Gertrude Bell is treated by Edward Said in *Orientalism* as the major female example of the orientalist, defining the history, archaeology and politics of Syria and Mesopotamia as her field of expertise, immersing herself in the culture as a means of learning to control it, and figuring also in that subgroup of orientalists who were direct imperialist agents.[13] During the First World War she was a founding member of the Arab Bureau, with the job of coordinating military intelligence, and after the war she was involved in the establishment, under British patronage, of the state of Iraq. The plaque marking her birthplace, which commemorates her as 'scholar, historian, archaeologist, explorer, poet, mountaineer, gardener, distinguished servant of the state', defines her success in the largely male fields of ruling class politics and orientalist expertise. Her reputation as a travel writer, however, rests largely on *The Desert and the Sown*, which preceded her political career, and is an account of her journey through Syria in the spring of 1905.

Although *The Desert and the Sown* is structured as a narrative of adventure and exploration, with hardships and unexpected mishaps to be overcome and goals to be reached, it is, as Stark pointed out, short on 'adventures'. The preface indicates Bell's consciousness of the need to justify the importance of her journey, and specifically her female incursion into the orientalist field. 'Those who venture to add a new volume to the vast literature of travel, unless they be men of learning or politicians, must be prepared with an excuse.' Bell's excuse was her representation of a series of encounters with Syrians, in which they were allowed 'to tell their own tale. I have strung their words upon the thread of the road.'[14] By implication Bell's female receptiveness, her lack of male expertise, has enabled her to allow the people of Syria to speak for themselves. The narrative traces Bell's developing inwardness with Arab culture; through her encounters she learns to read the landscape of the desert. 'I looked out beyond him into the night and saw the desert with his eyes, no longer empty but set thicker with human associations than any city' (p. 60). Her records of conversations are, however, given another, more specific importance; they report the Syrians' changing evaluations of the Western powers occasioned by news of the humiliating defeat of Russia by Japan in the Russo-Japanese War. This offers a particularly clear demonstration of how travel writing might figure both as sympathetic immersion in an alien culture and as intelligence gathering.

Despite the preface's justification of the value of female exploration, the narrative recreates the emphasis on comradeship and escape into a purely masculine world found in the male adventure romances of the period. 'So the tale ran on through the familiar stages of blood feud and camel lifting, the gossip of the desert – I could have wept for joy at listening to it again' (p. 15). The desert Syrians represent the pure masculinity which was to become a theme in interwar romantic fiction. Where Bell encounters women, however, as in the meeting with the sheikh's wives who lament that 'you

156

go forth to travel through the whole world, and we have never been to Hamah' (p. 237), the scene registers the pathos of confined oriental women compared with the free Westerner. Unlike such writers as Stark or West in the interwar period, Bell feels no need to mediate between these contradictions, or to register consciousness of the anomalies of female participation in the exhilarations of escape into a world defined by the absence of women. What she does emphasize is how travel offers opportunities for escape from conventional adult roles, as in her account of a stop enforced by the weather: 'I explored the castle from end to end, with immense satisfaction to the eternal child that lives in the soul of all of us and takes more delight in the dungeons and battlements of a fortress than in any other relic of antiquity' (p. 204). Travel allowed Bell to be orientalist scholar and intelligence agent, and to recreate childhood dreams of exploring dream castles and cities, as E. Nesbit's child protagonists were doing at the same period in such works as *The Enchanted Castle* (1907) and *The Magic City* (1910). Even Bell's orientalist conclusion that 'the living world lies westward' (p. 325) emphasizes the East's availability for Westerners at play, exploring roles with a freedom not possible in their own societies.

The emphasis on play was reduced in Bell's later writing, in which she assumes the role of orientalist expert she had disclaimed for *The Desert and the Sown*. Her next travel book, *Amurath to Amurath* (1911), states dual aims, as record of an archaeological expedition, and as a political study of Mesopotamian public opinion during the last crisis of the Ottoman Empire. The list of acknowledgements to heavyweight establishment journals (*The Times*, the *Quarterly Review*, *Blackwood's Magazine*) and to the Royal Geographical Society, indicates Bell's success in establishing herself as professional orientalist. *The Desert and the Sown* was reissued in 1919 as *Syria*, a new title which sought to redefine its identity as political treatise rather than a narrative of travel into the wilderness.

The interwar years saw a boom in travel and travel writing. Elizabeth Bowen's 1932 novel, *To the North*, presents the travel craze as the key to modern experience; her heroine, Emmeline, manages a travel agency with the motto 'Move dangerously', which offers to restore 'the element of uncertainty' to life. Emmeline herself is increasingly mesmerized by 'an immense idea of departure – expresses getting steam up and crashing from termini, liners clearing the docks, the shadows of planes rising, caravans winding out into the first dip of the desert'.[15] For her the substitution of the idea of travel for the home and lover she loses is ultimately tragic, but for most of the travel writing of the period the 'immense idea of departure' emphasized the liberating and self-exploratory possibilities of travel. Travel offered release from the confines of home and family, and specifically from a Britain isolated for several years by the war. The frontier became a metaphor for personal change and redirection.[16] England was increasingly seen as a backwater which failed to supply the sense of dynamic participation in reality offered by other countries. The trips to the Soviet Union undertaken by many left-wing writers, including Beatrice Webb and Naomi Mitchison, were one manifestation of this.

For women writers specifically travel offered, as it had to Bell and to earlier women travellers, escape from the domestic sphere and traditional female roles, and an arena in which to test women's new independence. Many women novelists of the period also wrote travel books. In the early 1930s Cicely Hamilton wrote a series of books on travel in the countries of Western Europe. Vita Sackville-West wrote *Twelve Days* (1928) about her travels in Persia, which provided material for Woolf's *Orlando*. Rose Macaulay interwove her own experience of Portugal with that of previous British visitors in *They Went to Portugal* (1946). Kate O'Brien's *Farewell Spain* (1937), appearing during the Spanish Civil War, emphasized the idea of travel towards countries where life was more intensely experienced than in Britain. Most notably Rebecca West found the travel book more amenable to her preoccupations than the novel, and in *Black Lamb and Grey Falcon* (1942), discussed in Chapter 8, plots her travels in Yugoslavia as a journey of mythic status into the dark heart of European history, where the links between gender wars and the growing European crisis are revealed.

The leading professional women travellers of the interwar period, Stark, Rosita Forbes and Mildred Cable, organized their narratives around the journey from the domestic sphere into wilderness. Forbes travelled in Africa and the Middle East, won medals for her contributions to exploration, and also wrote novels with exotic colonial settings. In her well-received *From Red Sea to Blue Nile: Abyssinian Journeys* (1925) she pursues an irritable journey as the people of Abyssinia fail to supply her with evidence of the distinction between Abyssinia, with its 'romance of an age-old history', and 'raw, native Africa'. Only in occasional ruins, and in the eyes of the Empress Zanditi, 'with the wisdom of a three thousand year old descent', does she find the distinctive Abyssinia she was seeking.[17] The book exemplifies much travel writing of the period in its journey into a wilderness already closely mapped by the traveller's reading in history and romance.

Stark, in her preface to *The Valleys of the Assassins*, justifies her travels in purely hedonist terms. Although she later saw the narrative as more highly structured than the reprise in *Beyond Euphrates*, it is important that the treasure hunt which provides the pretext for the journey is unsuccessful, just as it is important in her other major work of the 1930s, *The Southern Gates of Arabia: A Journey in the Hadramaut* (1936), that she fails to reach her planned destination, the fabled land of Sheba. She is seeking to distinguish her travel writing both from Bell's politically purposeful works

158

and from the observations of tourists. In *Beyond Euphrates* she draws a distinction between the tourism of the domestic majority who 'like to see the world' and the condition of the 'genuinely wild'. 'The genuinely wild is not interested in "seeing the world"; it is exclusively interested in *being*; it digests the world as a cow chews its cud, not for what the grass looks like but for what it does inside' (p. 62). It is, paradoxically, the tourists who are purposeful; they seek to observe and to carry back their observations to the base they have never spiritually left; the real traveller immerses herself in alien experience from hedonist motives.

With this rejection of goals and purposes, Stark's books are organized around a continuous movement between the domestic and the wilderness; she is forever setting out from the shelter and enclosure of temporary homes into the alien and uncertain. Like West in *Black Lamb and Grey Falcon*, she makes much of the comic possibilities in the situation of the woman traveller. There are endless opportunities for slipping back and forth over the frontiers of gender, alternately confronting officials with the anomaly of a woman in charge, and versed in the formulas and ceremonies appropriate to official encounters, and then taking refuge in a dumb and negligible femininity. These encounters on the road are comic, but in the domestic scenes she explores more seriously the range of possibilities for the housebound; sometimes she luxuriates, as in much homebased writing of the period, in the space and comfort of home and 'the pleasant sense of leisure which envelops harems when their masters are absent'.[18] At others she recoils from the isolation; 'beyond these ramparts all the world is the same, dim, vast and unknown, to the ladies of Do'an, a place into whose recesses their husbands vanish, and whence, now and then, Indian pedlars come'.[19] A country squire's estate in *The Valleys of the Assassins* is cosy and idyllic but the traveller must leave before it is too late; 'when the winter closes down, they retire to the windowless refuge of the interior, bring out the "kursi" over the central sunken fireplace, and continue to talk till the snow melts again' (p. 336). The happiest woman she meets is a vivaciously pedantic, bluestocking widow in *The Southern Gates of Arabia*; 'she did what she liked doing, and was virtuous and important as well, and people told her that she was so all the time' (p. 202).

In each book these series of domestic vignettes define the inportance of the wilderness for Stark, the opportunities it affords her to escape the fixed roles played by the women she leaves behind at each stop, and the precariousness of her tenure of this freedom. She may be able to insist on dining on a ridge where she can see the countryside far on each side, a perplexing ambition to her escort, but she is continually reminded of the frailty of women. A chance encounter with two itinerant women, the 'driftwood' of the wilderness, alarms her. In both *The Valleys of the Assassins* and *The*

159

Southern Gates of Arabia her journey is aborted by serious illness, and in the latter book the arrival of the RAF to rescue her emphasizes both her privilege and her frailty as an Englishwoman. Stark's books won medals for their contributions to exploration, but she also uses the journeys she describes to meditate on the precarious situation of women, and the unlikely privilege recently won by Western women.

While Stark and West explored the frontiers of gender through travel, the other great women's travel book of the period, *The Gobi Desert* by Mildred Cable and Francesca French (1942), reverted to the traditional form of the journey as spiritual allegory. Cable and the sisters Francesca and Evangeline French travelled as missionaries in China and Central Asia throughout the interwar period, and Cable and Francesca French produced a series of books recording their experiences. Earlier books such as *Through the Jade Gate and Central Asia* (1927) record in detail the circumstances and the progress of their mission, but *The Gobi Desert*, written after they had left Asia for good, presents their decades of travel as a single unified experience. The decades become a single year, the three travellers are represented as one, and each stage of the journey figures also as a stage in spiritual development. The book won the Royal Central Asian Society Medal, but the abundant geographical and cultural detail serves also to illuminate the allegory. The traveller passes through the single gate which gives access from China to the Gobi, announcing her intention to seek 'the lost', which the frontier guard understand in their own terms as one of the many searches for lost relatives in the desert, and enters a region of illusion and 'psychic perils'.[20] Oases offer a release from the ordinary experience of time, but also a distraction from the journey; the frescoed caves of the Gobi chart the spiritual struggles of earlier travellers, and the temptations of solitude for the artist.

As in Stark's books there is an emphasis on the continual movement away from a succession of homes in which the traveller's situation is contrasted with that of domestic women. There is considerable attention to the conditions of women in these passages; the openness and gender equality in the Mongol homes is compared favourably with the ceremonious, patriarchal Chinese home and the respectable privacy of the Russian home. The primary emphasis, however, is on the kind of spiritual possibility these conditions suggest. As the traveller retraces her steps, the Gobi changes around her; 'the Communists are on the march' (p. 217), and the Japanese invasion of China is threatening the existence of the desert communities. The gate and fort which gave access to the journey are now crumbling ruins. In the book's epilogue the Gobi is described as having ceased to exist, except in the memories of those who travelled there. It takes on the purely allegorical significance suggested throughout; the traveller's circular journey through a dissolving landscape questions the very purpose of travel and travel writing.

ACADEMIC DISCOURSE

The publication of scholarly works by women associated with the universities, a novelty at the beginning of this period, played an immensely important part in enlarging the concept of the woman writer's area of competence. Earlier women scholars had not been able to issue their work within the context of academic discourse, and with the authority of their professional status as academics. During this period the nature of their professional status remained controversial for many, but the notion of the woman academic gradually ceased to be eccentric. The period is bounded by two significant dates within the most resistant field, that of the natural sciences. In 1902 the physicist Hertha Ayrton, whose book that year, *The Electric Arc*, became the standard work on the subject for many years, was rejected for membership of the Royal Society; in 1945 the Society elected its first women members, the physicist Kathleen Lonsdale, and the biochemist Marjory Stephenson, whose *Bacterial Metabolism* (1930) established its subject as a new field.[21]

Women produced major works of scholarship in most disciplines, often, notably, in areas where male scholarship was not entrenched. They were more prominent in new institutions, such as the London School of Economics (LSE), founded by the Webbs in 1895, and in developing disciplines, such as psychology, especially child psychology.[22] Within established disciplines, they were notable in new areas such as social and economic history, which still lacked the prestige of political history, or in new developments, such as the theory of 'imperfect competition' developed by Joan Robinson, the only prominent woman economist. Their work was often concerned with areas and groups hitherto neglected by research. Some of the most influential works were produced by women whose official relation with academe was short-lived, such as Alice Clark's *Working Life of Women in the Seventeenth Century* (1919), written during her research fellowship at LSE, or Q.D. Leavis's *Fiction and the Reading Public* (1932), written during a research fellowship at Girton. Another recurrent feature in their careers is a research trip abroad, a culture shock which proves crucial in redirecting research. Examples are the journey to Greece which turned Jane Harrison towards ritual, the journey to China which redefined Eileen Power's research field, and the years in France during which Helen Waddell discovered her area of study. This discussion will focus on some examples of work within the humanities, one eminent scholar whose career demonstrated the difficulties and possibilities encountered by the first generation of women academics, a group of women historians working within the developing area of social and economic history, and some academic approaches between the wars to the study of literature.

161

The classicist, anthropologist and member of the Cambridge Ritualists, Jane Harrison, was one of the most influential and discussed women of the first academic generation. Her career was bounded at one end by Darwin, whose work persuaded her to reject Christianity, and by her idol, George Eliot, whom she met while a student at Newnham. In the last stages of her career she rethought her work in the light of reading in Freud and Jung, and developed a new research enthusiasm for Russian language and culture. Her autobiography, *Reminiscences of a Student's Life* (1925), relishes the perpetual studenthood she had enjoyed, and the spacious academic life which had replaced the oppressions of Victorian family life:

> I have a natural gift for community life. It seems to me sane and civilized and economically right. I like to live spaciously but rather plainly, in large halls with great spaces and quiet libraries. I like to wake in the morning with the sense of a great silent garden round me.[23]

(It is appropriately Harrison's ghost which haunts Newnham gardens in *A Room of One's Own*.) Harrison also, however, often suffered from the feelings of inadequate training, of isolation and marginality, endemic in her generation. Robert Ackerman has argued persuasively for the positive aspects of precisely this lack of acclimatization in the pomp and decorum of academic life, as enabling her to overcome the restraints of hierarchy and discipline, and sustain and enthuse a lively interdisciplinary group.[24]

Harrison's early shift from the study of classical texts to a preoccupation with archaic art and ritual was confirmed by her first visit to Greece in 1888, a powerfully formative event. Her succeeding work was as a member of the Cambridge Ritualists, a group which also included Francis Cornford and Gilbert Murray, and which worked in loose alliance with James Frazer, whose *The Golden Bough* (1890–1915) was the most famous anthropological work of the period. Her first major book, *Prolegomena to the Study of Greek Religion* (1903), argues for the distinctive and neglected importance of ritual in understanding the development of religion and of art. Harrison's interest in religion was as the embodiment of group emotion; the study of ritual was the key to understanding this social impulse, and a more primitive and more emotionally authentic world. Chapter 6, 'The Making of a Goddess', explores the degeneration of the figures of goddesses; the early figures are powerful patrons of human heroes, but 'with the coming of patriarchal conditions this high companionship ends. The women gods are sequestered to a servile domesticity, they become abject and amorous.'[25]

Harrison's later books continued to respond to contemporary scholarly influences. *Themis: A Study of the Social Origins of Greek Religion* (1912) was influenced by Durkheim's ideas about religion as the expression of society's collective consciousness. *Ancient Art and Ritual* (1913) drew on Roger Fry's

162

writings on contemporary art to discuss the value of the study of ritual as a means to understanding the communal role of art. For Harrison ritual is not only the transitional stage to art, but supplies the 'need for *first-hand* emotion and expression', which the sophisticated art of gifted individuals does not supply.[26] *Epilogomena to Greek Religion* (1921), in response to the work of Freud and Jung, explores the 'unfulfilled desires' expressed in primitive mythology, and the move from group to individual consciousness. One later work which attests Harrison's powerful influence is Maud Bodkin's interdisciplinary study, *Archetypal Patterns in Poetry* (1934), part of which was first published in the *British Journal of Psychology*. Bodkin's Jung-influenced attempt to explain the emotional power of some archetypal literary motifs draws generally on Harrison's work on ritual, and in particular on *Prolegomena* for her study of archetypes of women; the book's interdisciplinary nature is very much in the spirit of Harrison's approach to scholarship.

As the academic study of history increased among women, women historians were associated mainly with the developing area of social and economic history. This area lacked the high prestige of political and diplomatic history, and embraced the domestic and private concerns with which women were associated. In the first three decades of the century one lively group of women historians was associated with the newly established London School of Economics; Maxine Berg has argued that, as a new institution which had not yet acquired hierarchical forms, LSE encouraged interdisciplinary work and the development of particular feminist interests.[27] The group had strong links with the women's suffrage and trade union movements, and with the research activities of the Fabian Women's Group; much of their work was responding to the need imposed by the women's movement for a distinct history of women. They explored this new field of women's history in the wider context of the history of all those who had hitherto been invisible in historical writing; their work was extensively informed by the concerns of the Victorian novel of social commitment, and the attention to the under-recorded already developed there.

One of the major topics which developed from the work of this group was the history of women's work. Bessie Hutchins's *Women in Modern Industry* (1915) and Alice Clark's *Working Life of Women* (1919) exemplified the context and network of connections from which this new women's history sprung. One of the first batch of LSE students, Hutchins lectured intermittently at LSE, while working for the Women's Industrial Council which investigated women's working conditions; *Women in Modern Industry* places women's industrial work in the context of its history over the two previous centuries. Hutchins's concern was to direct attention to the specific history of women in industry, and to the need for distinctive legislation for women, at a time when middle-class feminists were emphasizing equal opportunities. The argument that women's lives and status had deteriorated since the Industrial Revolution was most forcefully put in Clark's seminal study. Clark researched the book as a mature student holding a research studentship at LSE in 1913–14; for most of her life she worked in her family's shoe factory, entering at the bottom and ascending to the board of directors. In *Working Life of Women* she pays tribute to the influence on her work of Schreiner's *Woman and Labour*, and its arguments about women's decline into social parasitism. The book celebrates the wide range of women's activities within domestic industry in the seventeenth century, and points to a decline in activity and status after the Industrial Revolution as home and workplace became gender-segregated. Like Schreiner she laments a deterioration in the relations of the sexes as an inevitable result of this segregation. Clark's book became the classic statement of a lost world of respected women's activity. The classic counter-argument also emerged from an LSE student, Ivy Pinchbeck, who remained in academe to become Reader in Social Studies in London University. Pinchbeck's seminal *Women Workers and the Industrial Revolution 1750–1850* (1930), which traces the entry of women into industry in the earlier years of industrialization, argues that the effects were, on balance, beneficial to women, offering the potential to improve their status, releasing them from isolation and from much manual labour, and allowing some time for leisure activity.

Pinchbeck's tutor at LSE was Eileen Power, whose work within the field of medieval history also focused on the lives of the under-recorded. Power's career, divided between LSE and Cambridge, had some features similar to Harrison's; as with Harrison, a journey abroad was crucial in clarifying her research commitments. In Power's case it was a journey to China in 1920 which she saw as determinant in her interest in the economic development of societies. Like Harrison she was strongly committed to interdisciplinary and collaborative work, leading and inspiring the Economic History Seminar in the 1920s and 1930s, and working closely with the historian R.H. Tawney. Unlike Harrison, however, she was not entirely sympathetic to the communal academic ideal. Although she prefaced her most popular work, *Medieval People* (1924), with an epigraph from *Piers Plowman* praising the cloister, she left Cambridge for LSE in 1921 to escape communal life, and turned down a professorship in Cambridge in 1939 to stay in London. Power's rejection of the communal ideal which Harrison and other earlier women academics had embraced was part of her complex awareness of herself as woman historian. Natalie Zemon Davis has described Power's difficulties in defining the role of the 'motherless' historian in the post-suffrage interwar world, of mediating between her interests in women's history and her fears of the way in which that history could allow itself to be marginalized.[28] She was especially scathing about her influential 1926 article, 'The Position of Women', which appeared as the token woman's piece in the collection *The Legacy of the Middle Ages*, and which she described in terms which drew on feminine imagery as 'one of those "gossips" about social life which ought to be bought by the yard at the department store'.[29]

Power's first book, *Medieval English Nunneries c.1275–1535* (1922), was attacked for its emphasis on the material conditions and social organization of the nunneries to the exclusion of discussion of spiritual ideals. The book, drawing on Power's own experience of community, ranges widely over the arrangements and experiences of women living together, taking in hierarchy, finance, education and housewifery; she describes the routines and also the varied reactions to those routines, the interest in clothes, the keeping of pets, the spiritual disease of accidie. Power's dissatisfaction with the book, a work on community produced within a community, informed her later emphasis on women's history within the context of a wider history of the under-recorded. In her influential 1932 article, 'Peasant Life and Rural Conditions c.1100–1500' in the *Cambridge History of the Middle Ages*, she celebrates the history of the 'inarticulate and despised masses' who 'fed and colonized Europe'.[30] Her *Medieval People: A Study of Communal Psychology* was addressed to the general reader; Power, whose sister Rhoda wrote history works for children, was strongly committed to keeping history accessible to a popular audience. *Medieval People* draws on a range of documentary material to evoke some unheard voices from the great mass of medieval humanity. Power uses manor rolls, deportment books and wills, as well as Marco Polo's chronicles, to evoke a medieval life which ranges across class, gender and race. Like the documentary fiction of the period, it draws on the narrative methods of the Victorian social novelists, and especially on George Eliot.

The emphasis on the under-recorded, on evoking the detail of forgotten lives, was marked among women historians outside the LSE network. Helen Cam was the historian who established herself most successfully within a traditional male field, working on constitutional history at Cambridge and, after the Second World War, at Harvard; her books, *The Hundred and the Hundred Rolls: An Outline of Local Government in Medieval England* (1930) and *Liberties and Communities in Medieval England: Collected Studies in Local Administration and Topography* (1944), emphasize the need to understand how government worked at local level, and the detail of how it affected ordinary lives. Barbara Hammond collaborated with her husband John in the influential trilogy, *The Village Labourer* (1911), *The Town Labourer* (1917) and *The Skilled Labourer* (1919), which reconstructs the forgotten lives of those who had paid the price for the successes of nineteenth-century Britain.

The Hammonds conducted their research outside the academic world, though they won a joint honorary doctorate at Oxford in 1933.

In the field of cultural history Helen Waddell's *The Wandering Scholars* (1927) seeks to recover a lost world, that of the vagrant medieval scholars who produced the poems collected in the *Carmina Burana*. Waddell was an English graduate who moved towards the study of medieval Latin, and, on a funded research trip to Paris, discovered her field in the scholarship and poetry of the later middle ages. In *The Wandering Scholars* she reconstructed the historical context for the poems she later published in free translation in *Medieval Latin Lyrics* (1929). Her purpose in the earlier book is not only to extend the canon by reviving this lyric poetry, but to reveal the forgotten world which had produced it, 'the leaf-drift of centuries of forgotten scholarship'.[31] Beyond that she seeks to revive in the reader an awareness of cultural continuities, of the obscured connections of street-song and scholarship. *The Wandering Scholars* was, like Power's *Medieval People*, addressed to a general audience; in 1933 Waddell published a historical novel, *Peter Abelard*, which extended her attempts to popularize awareness of these forgotten cultural continuities. The success of *The Wandering Scholars* and *Peter Abelard* made Waddell one of the best-known women scholars of her time; her academic life, as a popular lecturer constantly on tour between universities and learned societies, working on the borders of several disciplines, came slightly to resemble that of the vagrants she studied, and determinedly exemplified the continuity of learned and popular which was her subject.

Waddell's evocation of a forgotten, but infinitely desirable Latin world, in which scholarship and creative writing at all levels were in intimate and dynamic relation, was one formulation of the issue central to literary studies at the period: the relation of scholarship and creative writing. Woolf, the woman writer whose work was to attract the largest amount of critical attention, launched a vigorous attack in *Three Guineas* on the academic study of English literature. For Woolf, lectures on literature are 'an obsolete practice', evolved for an era before printing, and now testifying only to the triumph of the literary middleman, and to a dangerous growing reliance on that middleman's dubious expertise, in preference to direct contact with the book (ch. 1, n. 30). Writing about literature could only be desirable as a by-product of creative writing itself; Woolf's own essays on other writers in *The Common Reader*, and in her other collections, were in this tradition, exemplified in the previous generation by Alice Meynell and by the cultural historian, Vernon Lee (Violet Paget), who in her own collection of literary essays, *The Handling of Words* (1923), comments on the impossibility of using lectures as a substitute for reading.[32] Woolf, Lee and Meynell all evoke a world of the cultivated reader, in which understanding of literature could only be absorbed by private reading.

166

Academe's most vigorous response to *Three Guineas* came, ironically, from a woman whose formal association with the academic world ceased at student level; Queenie Leavis was never appointed to any post in the university. Her relations with the academic world were at second hand through her husband, F.R. Leavis. Her response came in the journal *Scrutiny* (again, although she was her husband's major collaborator on the journal and its most vigorous polemicist, her position was never formalized as a member of the editorial board). Nonetheless in her 1938 *Scrutiny* article, 'Caterpillars of the Commonwealth Unite', Leavis speaks for the professional rigours of academe in attacking the 'boudoir scholarship' of *Three Guineas*. The article outlines the professionalism demanded in literary studies, in opposition to the obsolete world of *belles-lettres* which 'the non-specialist like Mrs Woolf' is seen to represent.[33] The essay is the most violent expression of the project of *Scrutiny*, the attempt to construct a professional intelligentsia which reflected seriously and with academic rigour on the place of literature in the modern world.[34] The defined antagonist to this project was the system of values of the London literary world which had emerged from the late Victorian gentleman amateur tradition of *belles-lettres*. For *Scrutiny* those values were currently represented by the Bloomsbury avant-garde, the middlebrow world of prizes and reviews, and most of academe. Leavis's own tenuous and largely antagonistic relation with existing academe only strengthened her belief in the ideal academe she was defending.

Leavis's *Fiction and the Reading Public* (1932), expanded from her graduate dissertation, distances itself from the world of *belles-lettres* by paying serious attention to the mass reading public. Her model was a sociological work, the study of a community's culture by Robert and Helen Lynd in *Middletown* (1929), and her detailed observation of the reading habits of different social groups anticipated Mass Observation. The study was based on the analysis of questionnaires Leavis had distributed among writers of various brows, and the sociological method was designed to import some scholarly rigour into the discipline of literary studies. The book also evokes another lost world, the lost homogeneous reading public of the seventeenth century; Leavis's analysis traces the process of gradual fragmentation of that public, as circulating libraries, the growth of a mass reading public and contemporary media such as the cinema and radio destroyed that method of transmission through a cultured elite which had once maintained the links between street-song and scholarship. The first issue of *Scrutiny*, launched to supply the place of that lost elite, appeared shortly afterwards.

One thread within Leavis's defence of professional rigour was the threat to professionalism posed by many women writers. In 'Caterpillars of the Commonwealth Unite' she writes, 'the position with regard to further

167

female emancipation is that the onus is on women to prove that they are going to be able to justify it, and that it will not vitally dislocate (what it has already seriously disturbed – and no responsible person can regard that without uneasiness) the framework of our culture' (p. 212). This female threat to the rehabilitation of serious cultural standards operated at all levels. Woolf's 'boudoir scholarship' exemplifies the highbrow who had lost contact with the rest of society. In a 1935 article, 'Lady Novelists and the Lower Orders', a title which establishes continuity with a more serious past by echoing George Eliot's 1855 essay, 'Silly Novels by Lady Novelists', Leavis attacks the decline from the Victorian social problem novel, seen in the patronizing ignorance of the fiction of fact as practised by Naomi Mitchison. She cites, as counter-examples to Mitchison's uninformed treatment of the working-class, Victorian working-class autobiography, and the Women's Cooperative Guild's *Life as We Have Known It*. Storm Jameson's 'Mirror in Darkness' trilogy is admitted to be an exception among the flood of socially committed novels which betrayed the lack of an organic community, a work seriously engaged in reconstructing links between the classes.[35] The fiction of Dorothy Sayers, on the other hand, popular fiction laced with Oxford snobbery, was described as exemplifying the degenerate alliance of academe and commercialism in a 1937 article, 'The Case of Miss Dorothy Sayers'.[36]

In a 1941 *Scrutiny* series, 'A Critical Theory of Jane Austen's Writings', Leavis outlines her ideal of the serious professional woman writer. Her intention is to save Austen from the Janeites and their construction of her as divine amateur. The Janeites include academics; Leavis's first target is a lecture on Austen by Caroline Spurgeon, one of the few women professors in existence, and her intention is to establish that, in the general decline of cultural standards which have taken place since Austen's time, it is the professor who is the amateur and Austen who is the professional. Leavis's articles trace in detail the laborious processes of revision which demonstrate Austen's professional rigour. The most important academic work on Austen of the interwar period, Mary Lascelles's *Jane Austen and Her Art* (1939), is dismissed by Leavis in a footnote as a typical Janeite product. Lascelles's work, the first critical study produced after the publication of Austen's letters in 1932, mediates between academic rigour and a concept of the cultural standards embodied in Austen's work quite distinct from Leavis's. In one passage she uses a metaphor of Austen as hostess to suggest the civilized assumptions her work enforces; 'in the part that is warm and well-lit we entertain our friends; the rest is no place for hospitality. And I am convinced that Jane Austen regarded her writing as an act of hospitality. That is the sense in which her novels remained to the last a kind of family entertainment.'[37] Where Leavis offers Austen as the exemplary professional,

168

for Lascelles she represents the need for women to find their own distinctive methods. Hence she emphasizes the emergence of Austen's work from family entertainment, and the practice of hospitality, and compares the use of *trompe l'oeil* effects by Austen and Woolf. Woolf's achievement of 'multiplicity by reflection from innumerable admirably arranged mirrors' is compared to the way Austen 'by presenting her people in perspective . . . indicates recession, and so gives the impression of a limitless human world beyond her visible scene' (pp. 196–7). In this academic opposition of Austen as professional and as woman writer, one of the major issues of women's writing of the period is rehearsed.

NOTES

Place of publication is London, unless otherwise stated.

1. *The Letters of Queen Victoria*, ed. A.C. Benson and Viscount Esher (Murray, 1907), I, pp. v–ix.
2. See Deborah Nord, *The Apprenticeship of Beatrice Webb* (Macmillan, 1985).
3. Beatrice Webb, *My Apprenticeship* (Harmondsworth: Penguin, 1971), p. 395. Subsequent quotations are from this volume.
4. *The Diary of Beatrice Webb*, ed. Norman and Jeanne Mackenzie (Virago/LSE, 1982), I, p. 25. Subsequent quotations are from this edition.
5. Sylvia Pankhurst, *The Suffragette Movement: An Intimate Account of Persons and Ideals* (Longmans, Green, 1931), p. 218.
6. Sylvia Pankhurst, *The Home Front: A Mirror to Life in England During the World War* (Hutchinson, 1932), p. 380.
7. Vera Brittain, *Testament of Experience* (Gollancz, 1957), p. 79.
8. Brittain, *Testament of Experience*, p. 89.
9. Brittain, *Testament of Experience*, p. 77.
10. Vera Brittain, *Testament of Youth* (Virago, 1993), p. 116.
11. Vera Brittain, *Testament of Friendship* (Virago, 1994), pp. 270, 440.
12. Freya Stark, *Beyond Euphrates: An Autobiography 1928–33* (Murray, 1951), p. 83.
13. Edward Said, *Orientalism* (New York: Pantheon, 1978).
14. Gertrude Bell, *The Desert and the Sown* (Heinemann, 1907), p. ix.
15. Elizabeth Bowen, *To the North* (Harmondsworth: Penguin, 1945), ch. 28.
16. On the significance of frontiers see Valentine Cunningham, *British Writers of the Thirties* (Oxford: Oxford University Press, 1988); Samuel Hynes, *The Auden Generation: Literature and Politics in England in the 1930s* (Faber, 1976).
17. Rosita Forbes, *From Red Sea to Blue Nile: Abyssinian Adventures* (Cassell, 1925), pp. 101, 131.
18. Freya Stark, *The Valleys of the Assassins* (Murray, 1934), p. 101.
19. Freya Stark, *The Southern Gates of Arabia: A Journey in the Hadramaut* (Murray, 1938), p. 142.

20. Mildred Cable and Francesca French, *The Gobi Desert* (Hodder and Stoughton, 1942), p. 14.

21. See Joan Mason, 'Marjory Stephenson', in Edward Shils and Carmen Blacker, eds, *Cambridge Women: Twelve Portraits* (Cambridge: Cambridge University Press, 1996), pp. 113–35.

22. See L.S. Hearnshaw, *A Short History of British Psychology: 1840–1940* (Methuen, 1962).

23. Jane Harrison, *Reminiscences of a Student's Life* (Hogarth Press, 1925), p. 88. See Martha Vicinus, *Independent Women: Work and Community for Single Women 1850–1920* (Virago, 1985), pp. 148–57.

24. Robert Ackerman, 'Jane Ellen Harrison: The Early Work', *Greek, Roman and Byzantine Studies* 13 (1972), pp. 209–30.

25. Jane Harrison, *Prolegomena to the Study of the Greek Religion* (Merlin, 1961), p. 273.

26. Jane Harrison, *Ancient Art and Ritual* (Bradford on Avon: Moonraker, 1978), p. 113.

27. Maxine Berg, 'The First Women Economic Historians', *Economic History Review*, 45 (1992), pp. 308–29.

28. Natalie Zemon Davis, 'History's Two Bodies', *American Historical Review*, 93 (1988), pp. 1–30.

29. Quoted in Maxine Berg, 'Eileen Power, 1889–1940', in Shils and Blacker, eds, *Cambridge Women: Twelve Portraits*, p. 166.

30. Eileen Power, 'Peasant Life and Rural Conditions $c.1100$–1500', *Cambridge History of the Middle Ages* (Cambridge: Cambridge University Press, 1932), VII, p. 750.

31. Helen Waddell, *The Wandering Scholars* (Harmondsworth: Pelican, 1954), p. 11.

32. Vernon Lee, *The Handling of Words and Other Studies in Literary Psychology* (Bodley Head, 1923).

33. Q.D. Leavis, 'Caterpillars of the Commonwealth Unite', *Scrutiny*, 7 (1938), pp. 203–14.

34. See Francis Mulhern, *The Moment of Scrutiny* (New Left Books, 1979).

35. Q.D. Leavis, 'Lady Novelists and the Lower Orders', *Scrutiny*, 4 (1935), pp. 112–32.

36. Q.D. Leavis, 'The Case of Miss Dorothy Sayers: *Gaudy Night* and *Busman's Honeymoon*', *Scrutiny*, 6 (1937), pp. 334–40.

37. Mary Lascelles, *Jane Austen and Her Art* (Oxford University Press, 1939), p. 146.

CHAPTER EIGHT

Some Individual Writers

KATHERINE MANSFIELD

In 1908, the year in which she wrote her first short story, 'The Tiredness of Rosabel', the young Katherine Mansfield, newly arrived in London from New Zealand, read Elizabeth Robins's *Come and Find Me* (1908) and hoped that Robins was 'only the first of a great never ending procession of splendid strong women writers' (*Letters*, I, p. 47). Like other writers of that period she imagined the establishment of a fresh tradition of women's writing, no longer deformed by the conditions which had constricted women hitherto, and fully committed to the aesthetic and professional rigours of the artist's life. The 'amateur' approach to writing characteristic of many women was outlined in Mansfield's 1919 review of Constance Holme's novel, *The Splendid Fairing*, which comments on:

> the curious naive pleasure that many women take in writing for writing's sake. The mind pictures them half wonder, half joy, to find that they can put these lovely tender-coloured words together – can string these exquisite sentences out of a morning's ramble in the garden or the meadow or gathering cold seashells ... But it is a dangerous delight, for what so often happens is that they are quite carried away, forgetting all about the pattern they intended to follow or embroidering it so thickly that none but themselves can discover its original outline.[1]

In this passage Holme is used to represent the writing model which women must reject, that of the amateur with no consciousness of audience and no sense of aesthetic responsibility. Autobiography was the most dangerous form for women; in the same year Mansfield criticized Sinclair and Richardson for their failure to impose order on the autobiographical material of their fiction (see Chapter 3). The writer must find a way of translating that

171

'curious naive pleasure', which was the initial strength of women writers, into compelling and intelligible forms.

One advantage of the short story, the form in which Mansfield explored the possibilities of representing women's experience, was the protection its brevity afforded against the autobiographical impulse. Mansfield's fictions shared the openness of the autobiographical fictions she criticized, but in refusing conclusions the short story imposed on the writer the need to seek other kinds of pattern and order, and it was in Chekhov's stories, and in the methods of the Symbolists, that Mansfield studied the possibilities for concentrating her meanings in image and incident.

In her early stories Mansfield explored the conditions within which the female imagination develops. 'The Tiredness of Rosabel', which Elizabeth Bowen describes as 'a daring break with accepted pattern', is structured round a daydream, a kind of exploration of inner life which Mansfield popularized for the short story.[2] Rosabel, an overworked and underfed shop assistant, has ceased to respond imaginatively to her hostile environment; her dreams of wealthy, attentive suitors and high society are described in the terms of the romantic fiction which provides her with her only imaginative stimulus. In other early stories Mansfield adopts the point of view of children, whose lively responses to their environment contrast with Rosabel's exhausted dependence on second-hand fantasy. 'How Pearl Button Was Kidnapped' (1910) narrates in the form of a children's story Pearl's brief escape from her urban home, 'the House of Boxes', to the freedom of a gipsy life. 'The Little Girl' (1912) invokes 'Little Red Riding-Hood' to describe a child's recognition of her father as a source both of fear and of security.[3]

Mansfield later disowned the stories in *In a German Pension* (1911), her first published collection, and based on her stay in Germany in 1909, as too explicit, discursive and overtly autobiographical. The best stories are again situated within the point of view of a child. In 'At Lehmann's' the child is an exploited teenage waitress whose exploration of her new work environment indicates to the reader the conditions which will soon deprive her of her still childish wonder. 'The-Child-Who-Was-Tired' is closely modelled on Chekhov's 'Sleepy', but departs from its model in its treatment of Chekhov's recurrent image of the great muddy Russian highway along which the peasants toil and fall down. In the Mansfield version this becomes a framing device, the child-skivvy's daydream of a stylized monochrome highway, 'a little white road with tall black trees on either side, a little road that led to nowhere, and where nobody walked at all' (p. 757). A general image characterizing the life of the Russian peasant has become a private fantasy which encloses the story as it dominates the child's life, demonstrating Mansfield's search for controlling images in which to focus the meaning of the lives she describes.

172

Between 1912 and 1915 Mansfield experienced writer's block, and it was in her desire, following her brother's death in the war, to recreate her own country and her childhood experiences there, that she rediscovered the power of the short story and began work on what was to become 'Prelude' (see Chapter 3). Bowen, another writer who understood from within the pains and advantages of deracination, thought that Mansfield was 'saved . . . by two things, her inveterate watchfulness as an artist, and a certain sturdiness in her nature which the English at their least friendly might call "colonial" '.[4] Mansfield was an outsider seeking to define her art within the metropolitan literary world. The defensive uses of the child's perspective in this context are obvious; it was both as woman and colonial that she expected critics of 'Prelude' to find it 'a New Primer for Infant Readers' (*Letters*, II, p. 169). Like other colonial writers such as Rhys and Bowen, Mansfield found the short story with its comparative lack of tradition, its availability for redevelopment, a form with which she could explore women's own 'colonial' situation. Reassessing her relations with New Zealand enabled her to think about the development of her art. She was conscious of the dangers of exoticism, criticizing a compatriot's dense descriptions of landscape. 'What picture can that possibly convey to an English reader? What emotion can it produce?'[5] Like her criticism of Holme's redundant landscape description, Mansfield's assumption that she is writing for an English audience for whom New Zealand landscapes must be translated, illustrates her insistence on ensuring that every descriptive detail contributes significantly to the whole. A remembered appearance of the New Zealand landscape suggested her development of 'Prelude', as she recalls 'those mornings white milky mists rise and uncover some beauty, then smother it again and then again disclose it. I tried to lift that mist from my people and let them be seen and then hide them again' (*Letters*, I, p. 331). This use of the landscape as a metaphor for method suggests much about Mansfield's technique, the movement through appearance to the inner life, the discontinuities and transformations of perspective, and the regroupings of the various people and objects revealed by these transformations. She praised Woolf's 'Kew Gardens' for its method of 'dissolving' the humans into the other life of the garden, admiring both the orchestration of the different elements of the story, and the post-Darwinian acceptance of humanity as one species living in the context of others.[6] Her own memories of the shifting forms of New Zealand's landscapes helped her to develop a similar method.

Her major New Zealand stories are the three centred on the Burnell family, 'Prelude', 'At the Bay' (1922) and 'The Doll's House' (1924), along with 'The Garden Party' and 'The Voyage' (1924). In them she developed new ways of describing the relations of the human and natural worlds.[7] At the beginning of 'At the Bay' the New Zealand mists appear again, gradually disclosing the human world within the natural. Later in the story a rock-pool recalls us to the world outside human perception, as the appearances and disappearances of the creatures inhabiting it duplicate those of the humans within the story. The scene anticipates Woolf's marine landscapes in *To the Lighthouse* and *The Waves*. In Mansfield's New Zealand, however, the tiny scattered houses, the people on the beach, exist in a more unstable relation with the non-human world. 'The Doll's House' mimics this sense of the miniature scale of human life by reducing it further, first to the toy house, and then to the little lamp inside on which the children, Kezia and Else, confer a poignant symbolic status. The whole story, with its emphasis on the significance of minute domestic detail, reads as if it were a response to Lawrence's critical portrayal of Mansfield's work in the miniaturist art of Gudrun in *Women in Love* (1920). The story travels inwards, through the miniature house to the tiny lamp within, to reveal the intense emotional power with which the children invest it.

In this story Kezia breaks through the rigid class barriers enforced by her family and school to show the doll's house to the outcast Else. The child's perspective is central to the New Zealand stories, carrying its freight of Romantic assumptions about uncontaminated experience, but more specifically representing the 'curious naive pleasure' in the natural world which could with difficulty be transmitted to adulthood. Mansfield's stories seek ways of representing Kezia's vision, while showing how social roles entirely determine the imaginative lives of the adults. Linda's absorption in her maternity registers everything in her surroundings in terms of that experience, as she wonders at the fecundity and the waste. Beryl's fantasies, derived from romantic fiction and the product of her suppressed panic about her unmarried status, continue the theme of 'The Tiredness of Rosabel', the conditioning of the adult female imagination by second-hand formulas, the loss of ability to respond directly to the world. The freshness of the child's view is explored in 'The Voyage', in which the emotional significance of an orphan's journey across the Cook Straits to a new unfamiliar home is described entirely through details of the journey and landscapes. 'The Garden Party' traces a teenager's still undiminished response to the eruption of death into a social event.

Mansfield's other main groups of stories were those treating the contemporary metropolitan life which she had entered from New Zealand, and these focused on the plight of those who are excluded or estranged from it. Two of the most famous stories are structured round false epiphanies, and a comprehensive destruction of the protagonist's illusions which proved very suggestive for later writers. 'Bliss', and its portrait of a young woman groping for an awareness of her sexuality in a society she finds difficulty in interpreting, is discussed in Chapter 3. In 'Miss Brill' (1922) an impoverished English spinster living in Paris, performing the habitual Sunday rituals which help to maintain her identity, feels a sense of community with the crowd at an outdoor concert which is destroyed by the jeers of a courting couple. The story describes Miss Brill's precarious sense of identity and sexuality as centred in her prized but mangy fox fur, the object of the couple's derision, and in the notoriously harrowing ending her grief is displaced to the fur. Rhys's 1927 short story, 'Illusion', is a more restrained variant of 'Miss Brill', and her novel, *Good Morning, Midnight*, an expansion of the story, as Lehmann's *Dusty Answer* is of 'Bliss'.

In two other stories Mansfield demonstrates the gulf between the literary world and that of ordinary people and genuine feeling. 'Je ne Parle Pas Français' (1919) is a prose variant of Browning's dramatic monologues, an unconsciously self-revealing narrative by a sexually ambivalent Parisian artist and hanger-on, author of books such as *False Coins* and *Left Umbrellas*, which opposes to his cosmopolitan perspective the monolingual sincerity of a stranded English girl. Mouse, like Woolf's 'mouse-coloured persons' in 'The Mark on the Wall', is the ordinary person outside the reach of the artistic discourse of cosmopolitan society. She is the subject which got away, barely perceived as such by the narrator, who persistently foregrounds himself and leaves the story's real subject fitfully glimpsed in the background. Through its deracinated narrator's false emphases the story insists that the artist must engage with authentic feeling, though the story's association of false artistry with bisexuality and bilingualism distorts the point. 'The Life of Ma Parker' also opposes a literary male representing metropolitan culture to a grief-stricken woman inhabiting the world beyond the comprehension of that culture. To the charwoman Ma Parker, who significantly comes from Stratford-upon-Avon, the products of the London literary gentleman for whom she cleans are nothing but dirt and waste. Her displacement from the world he inhabits is represented by her recognition that his house is not a place where she can weep openly for her grandson's death.[8] Where Mansfield's New Zealand stories celebrate a world of primal discovery, her European stories focus on exclusion and division.

VIRGINIA WOOLF

Woolf's letters and diaries for 1938–39 record many complaints about her difficulties in working on the biography, *Roger Fry* (1940). 'I'm fairly distracted with Fry papers. How can one deal with facts – so many and so

175

many and so many? Or ought I, as I incline, to be purely fictitious? And what is a life? And what was Roger?' (*Letters*, VI, p. 226). From the beginning of her writing career in 1904, reviewing books for the *Times Literary Supplement* and the *Cornhill Magazine*, Woolf had regarded biography both with deep suspicion and with fascination as a mode highly suggestive for fiction. By 1908 she was pleading to receive biographies for review rather than novels, finding that the defects of existing biographical method were more suggestive for her fictional experiments than the novels of von Arnim or Marjorie Bowen.[9] Later *Orlando* was presented as a spoof biography, complete with index and acknowledgements. The failure to catch the essence of a human life was the main criticism she brought against Bennett and the other Edwardians in 'Mr Bennett and Mrs Brown'. She was dismissive of Holtby's 1932 study of her, but responded strongly to what she saw as the failures of perception in Brittain's *Testament of Friendship*; 'she [Holtby] had a great deal more to her than Vera Brittain saw' (*Letters*, VI, p. 319). Writing a biography of Fry, a close friend and a representative of Bloomsbury, was a disturbing experience, given her lifelong doubts about the genre. It also, like Brittain's book, raised questions about the relations of biography and autobiography. She described the early pages of *Roger Fry* as 'largely autobiography' (*Diary*, V, p. 214), and in early 1939 began writing her fragmentary autobiography, 'A Sketch of the Past', in parallel to the biography.

Roger Fry raised urgent questions for Woolf about the achievement of Bloomsbury, and the narrative into which she shaped his life was a justification of that grouping of artists and thinkers. 'Such a nice comforting story' was Warner's response to the book, directing her satire at her own relish in reading a narrative of how art could transform someone from the most hidebound bourgeois background into a Bohemian rebel.[10] Fry's story, which, as Warner perceived, was Woolf's simplest, most optimistic narrative, describes the victory of modernism over Victorianism, and is used to justify everything that Bloomsbury represented as a rebel group within the ruling class, a group which espoused anti-imperialist and anti-war politics, and was responsive to international art movements. Fry's organization of the Post-Impressionist Exhibition of 1910 had challenged the ruling class's idea of culture as a 'social asset'.[11] For Woolf in 'Mr Bennett and Mrs Brown' 1910 was the crucial date at which human consciousness forsook the old Victorian certainties. Fry's artistic problems were Woolf's. As an art critic he had through great drudgery 'forged for himself a language that wound into the heart of sensation' (p. 106). He responded with caution to the challenges with which the advent of psychoanalysis confronted the artist. Woolf quotes his response to the suggestion that he should let his subconscious direct his painting: 'the damned thing would only produce a

176

pastiche' (p. 119). (In 1939 Woolf was reading Freud for the first time, although the Hogarth Press had been publishing the English translations of his work for nearly two decades. This belated reading, and her disturbed response to *Civilization and Its Discontents* (*Diary*, V, p. 250), indicate that she shared Fry's reservations about the influence of this powerful new perception.) Above all Fry, in his *Vision and Design* (1920), had insisted on the need to order and analyse sensations; 'if we allow sensations to accumulate unchecked they lose their sharpness' (p. 228). For Woolf in 1920, beginning work on her third novel, *Jacob's Room*, this insistence had offered a useful corrective to the kind of accumulation of sensation practised by Richardson, and even by Mansfield, whose capacity to order her sensations she doubted.

In Woolf's account Fry's moment of victory is the Post-Impressionist Exhibition, related to his fostering of young talent, including Vanessa Bell, and the Omega Workshop, in which he promoted his ideal of a community of artists. She presents, however, a second, quieter victory in the postwar survival of the closed Workshop's still life paintings, 'those symbols of detachment, those tokens of a spiritual reality immune from destruction, the immortal apples, the eternal eggs' (p. 215). The still lifes represent to Woolf art's capacity to organize even the most chaotic experience. 'It is the bringing together from chaos and disorder of the parts that are necessary to the whole. When at last the apple, the kitchen-table and the bread-knife have come together, it is felt to be a victory for the human spirit' (p. 285). In her short stories she experimented with ways of rendering the instability and flux of being for which all images were too static; still lifes suggested a complementary order to this dynamism. The methods of *Jacob's Room*, the novel which announced her evolution to modernism from the more traditional storytelling of her first two novels, developed from this dual emphasis, from the idea of short stories 'dancing in unity', and from the order represented by the still lifes. In this novel she explores how to represent a life through a fluid series of episodes, registered through the sensations and impressions of a wide range of characters; the apparent discontinuities of character and situation are ordered by the new relations the composition reveals.

Jacob's Room was Woolf's war novel; Holtby, who gave the title 'Cinematograph' to her chapter on that novel in *Virginia Woolf*, pointed to the fluent, pictorial method Woolf had evolved for commenting on the experience of the war, a method which 'deals mainly with the external evidence of emotions, even thoughts and memories assuming pictorial quality' (p. 117). As Fry's 'eternal eggs' registered human survival, so Woolf's fluent succession of still lifes represent the absence of Jacob, and the great event of which that absence is an emblem. While the novel's compositions are saturated with the pathos of what is not directly represented, they also indicate the kind of fictional method Woolf is rejecting. The central joke in *Jacob's Room* is that a description of the room is not an adequate way of telling us about Jacob; as well as exploring what still life can represent, Woolf is satirizing Bennett's method of describing character through minute attention to environment.

Jacob's Room is not directly an elegy for golden youth, and it is not an Edwardian novel of character and environment. There is one other kind of novel it pointedly is not, a novel of woman's consciousness in the Richardson manner. Despite Woolf's public praise of the suggestiveness of the method Richardson had evolved, she privately criticized Richardson's dependence on 'the damned egotistical self' (*Diary*, II, p. 14). Her first modernist novel is significantly not about a woman's consciousness, but about a man's room and the resistances it offers to female interpretation. The feminist interests which inform it focus on the special difficulties for a woman in writing, not just a life, which is problematic enough, but a man's life. One further purpose of the descriptions of Jacob's room is to indicate these difficulties of interpretation; 'he had grown to be a man, and was about to be immersed in things'.[12] The still lifes of Jacob's room denote not just his eventual absence in death, but his absence in life from accessibility to interpretation by the various women who desire him. His mother's inability in the final chapter to find any order in his room represents the difficulties all the women in the book have experienced in interpreting Jacob, and perhaps also refers obliquely to the widespread contemporary sense that the war was a male experience not available for female interpretation.

Woolf excised from the novel the episode nearest to the kind of experience central to Richardson's fiction, the description of a Cambridge woman student meditating in her room, published separately in 1926 as 'A Woman's College from the Outside'. The excision of the episode perhaps suggested a reluctance on Woolf's part to place herself in a clearly identifiable, developing tradition of women's writing. Woolf perceived herself in several contexts, of which she found Bloomsbury the most comfortable. Her perception of herself as a woman writer in the mainstream British literary tradition was comically expressed in her 1936 talk, 'Am I a Snob?', where she said 'I have dined with H.G. Wells to meet Bernard Shaw, Arnold Bennett and Granville Barker, and have only felt like an old washerwoman toiling step by step up a steep and endless staircase'.[13] Most complex was her perception of herself in relation to other women writers. In her letters her contemporaries appear fixed in animal images in a kind of literary bestiary. Sitwell is 'a seabird crying so dismally' (*Letters*, III, p. 352), Benson 'a most curious wizened monkeylike woman' (III, p. 489), Macaulay 'a mummified cat' (V, p. 272), Robins 'a hummingbird stuffed' (V, p. 418), and, most arrestingly, West is 'like an arboreal animal grasping a tree, and showing all her teeth, as if another animal were about to seize her young' (V, p. 259). The West description, in particular, suggests Woolf's need to define her contemporaries and their specific qualities as competitors in the particular corner of the literary jungle which was the woman's tradition. It also suggests that what Woolf most admired and envied in them was experience unavailable to her. West 'has battered around in the stinking underworld of hack writers' (V, p. 259), and survived with a special kind of knowledge of the abyss, just as Mansfield had 'knocked about with prostitutes' (IV, p. 366). She admired Brittain's direct, eyewitness assault on the war in *Testament of Youth*, and the fact that Benson had 'seen rivers in Manchuria freeze from side to side in ten minutes' (III, p. 489). Despite such admiration there is through all her descriptions of her woman contemporaries a determination not to be subdued by the alternative possibilities they represent.

A determination to resist invitations to align with the mainstream feminist tradition is registered in her early reviewing days. When, in 1908, the *Cornhill Magazine* offered her a biography of the pioneer Victorian educationalist, Dorothea Beale, Woolf refused, and chose instead to review a biography of Louis XIV's mistress, Louise de la Vallière. Throughout her career Woolf regarded reviewing, financially necessary at this period, as a threat to her creativity. By this time she was struggling with the novel *Melymbrosia*, which was to become *The Voyage Out*, uncertain if she would ever make anything of it, and anxious to avoid reviewing any books which might exert a negative influence. As she explained to no fewer than five correspondents, Beale's life of committees and curricula, and promoting 'awe in the hearts of tremulous, half-educated, earnest women' (*Letters*, I, p. 333), the life of a woman with an established place in the history of women's progress in the public sphere, represented a world alien and potentially destructive to her, while the opportunity to catch the essence of the graceful, shadowy La Vallière, who retreated early from public life into a nunnery, was suggestive for her exploration of fiction:

> I shall reform the novel and capture multitudes of things at present fugitive, enclose the whole and shape infinite strange shapes. I take a good look at woods at sunset, and fix men who are breaking stones with an intense gaze, meant to sever them from the past and the future. All these excitements last out my walk, but tomorrow I know, I shall be sitting down to the inanimate old phrases. As a matter of fact Mlle de la Vallière ought to make something graceful at least. (*Letters*, I, p. 356)

The following year 'Memoirs of a Novelist', Woolf's spoof review of the authorized biography of a fictitious Victorian woman of letters, outlined both the kind of biography she felt most failed its subject and the kind of

179

woman writer Woolf was planning not to be. The writer she imagines, a kind of talentless George Eliot, inhabits the same world of earnestness, progress and sibylline moral influence exerted over female fans, from which Woolf had recoiled in the Beale biography. For Woolf it was important to resist the lure of the increasingly prominent feminist emphasis on entry into public life.

Woolf's first two novels, *The Voyage Out* (1915) and *Night and Day* (1919), both focus on the familiar nineteenth-century figure of the young girl choosing her role and partner in life, a figure to which Woolf was not to return in any of her later novels. Both heroines struggle against the heavy weight of tradition, but are unattracted to the kinds of political involvement to which subsidiary female characters are drawn. Both novels, written before her full engagement with modernism, are organized around a courtship plot, in which a group of characters meet and develop their relationships through a series of encounters and dialogues, with an omniscient narrator in attendance to effect transitions between their various consciousnesses. The distinctiveness of *The Voyage Out* lies in the disjunction between the reader expectations generated by this familiar structure, and by a journey plot promising adventure and romance, and the narrative's insistence that the real life of the novel is elsewhere, embodied in the resistance of the heroine, Rachel, to all the possibilities of life she is offered. It was the Woolf novel longest in development, going through several drafts between 1907 and 1913. Rachel's discovery of the difficulties of placing herself within a male-dominated society is expressive of Woolf's problems in developing a form for her experience within the oppressively rich British literary tradition. Rachel's alienation is often expressed in terms of her relation to books. In her search for identity she looks through the overwhelmingly male *Who's Who*, studies Gibbon's history, but is attracted only by the passages describing the forests and barbarians outside the Roman Empire, and is told by a politician who likes to doze over Jane Austen's books that Austen is the only acceptable woman writer because she writes as a woman. Her lover is eager to write a novel about 'the curious silent unrepresented life of women',[14] but the novel he outlines is in the contemporary Edwardian tradition, and emphasizes how the dense materiality of the environment forms the characters. Literature seems to offer no opening for Rachel who, like Richardson's Miriam, turns to music as a more accessible art.

The story of Rachel's resistance lies also in her fears of her sexuality, and unwillingness to accept the sexual identity presented her; her death from a tropical fever follows on, and seems determined by, her agreement to marry her lover, as well as by the novel's demonstration that there is no viable role for her in society. In Rachel's relations with the older Helen, who, attractive and confident in her own social role, cannot help Rachel find an identity, the novel introduces a recurrent Woolf theme: the ways in which older women seek to introduce younger women to their adult lives. Louise de Salvo has described how successive drafts of the novel eliminated both the figure of Rachel's mother and a homosexual attraction between Rachel and Helen; while Rachel's resistance to male tradition is clearly outlined, Woolf's presentation of her relations with women, and with the traditions they represent, is much more obscure and perplexed.

Night and Day was Woolf's longest, and in some respects most conventional novel, with a courtship plot happily resolved in marriage. This heroine, Katherine, escapes from the weight of tradition into adventure fantasies and mathematics. In her case tradition is specifically literary and Victorian; she is the grand-daughter of a great writer, and helping her mother, Mrs Hilbery, who is failing to write her famous father's biography. Mrs Hilbery was based on Woolf's aunt, Anny Thackeray Ritchie, Thackeray's daughter, who had written some successful novels in the 1860s, but by the 1900s was primarily regarded as a walking memorial of the Victorian literary world, a purveyor of literary reminiscence. In her obituary for her aunt, who died in 1919, Woolf described her as 'the transparent medium through which we behold the dead',[15] but *Night and Day* is alive to the dangers represented by this pervasive influence of the past. Mrs Hilbery lives within her memories of her father's life, the record of which she will never complete. In her habit of writing fragments of the biography between bouts of dusting, she also represents the female amateur tradition of writing carried on in the interstices of domestic work, which Woolf, like many of her contemporaries, was anxious to banish. Katherine, attempting to understand the fictions which people construct for themselves, associates her lover's amorous protestations with her mother's tendencies to traditional storytelling. ' "You go home and invent a story about me, and now you can't separate me from the person you've imagined me to be. You call that, I suppose, being in love ... My mother spends her life in making stories about the people she's fond of." '[16] Storytelling, the fictions which govern conventional relationships, is perceived as a threat by the unliterary Katherine, who demands authenticity, though in this novel romance is allowed to proceed to its conclusion.

Woolf told Beatrice Webb that *Night and Day* was intended 'to discover what aims drive people on & whether these are illusory or not' (*Diary*, I, p. 196). The explanation was carefully adjusted to Webb's sociological interests, but when Woolf attempted in the 1930s to write her own version of the fiction of fact in *The Years*, she saw the new novel as resuming the interests of *Night and Day*. In the interim, particularly wounded by Mansfield's classification of the novel as an anachronistic rewriting of an

Austen novel, she denigrated the work as her last pre-modernist attempt.[17] As described in Chapter 3, she turned to the short stories she had been writing to develop her new approach to the novel in *Jacob's Room*, and throughout the 1920s continued to cling to the short story as necessary protection against the prolixity threatened by the novel form. Her second modernist novel, *Mrs Dalloway* (1925), was planned as a series of short stories, beginning with 'Mrs Dalloway in Bond Street', published in 1923, which were intended to become the novel's chapters. The novel which eventually emerged was unsectioned, the absence of conventional divisions emphasizing the fluidity of its movement between the consciousnesses of several people abroad in postwar London one summer day. In exemplifying the ambition of 'Modern Fiction' to show ordinary minds on an ordinary day, *Mrs Dalloway* rejects the concessions to storytelling of Woolf's first two novels, reduces the use of dialogue even more than in *Jacob's Room*, and eliminates the omniscient narrator. Transitions between the characters' consciousnesses are effected through their physical juxtapositions. Their relationships are explored, not through dialogue, but in memory and through psychic correspondences.

In this novel Woolf turned from the young heroines of her first two novels to a mature upper-class socialite, who posed obvious problems of sympathy for the reader. A character called Mrs Dalloway had appeared in *The Voyage Out*, where her close identification with the role of politician's wife provides a particularly unhelpful example to Rachel. In *Mrs Dalloway* it is Clarissa's separation from her husband's world which is emphasized; her enjoyment of the cool spaces of her home, of buying flowers and organizing a party, relishes the domestic as in much interwar women's writing. With this goes a pleasure in the freedom offered by London's streets, parks and shops which recalls Richardson's celebrations of the city newly available to women; when Clarissa's teenage daughter boards a bus, the vehicle takes on the kind of iconic significance it has in *Pilgrimage*. In her relish in her home and leisure, in her perplexed sexuality as she recalls her one momentary experience of bliss with her friend Sally, in the defining retreat from intimacy which caused her, like a Benson heroine, to marry the man who would impinge least, Clarissa is very much a heroine of the 1920s.

She is also a version of the heroine as redundant woman. She is a social parasite, her sexual life concluded, and, in the mythology of the war just ended, that least sympathetic figure, an upper-class woman without sons. *Mrs Dalloway* is a novel of war guilt, in which Mrs Dalloway represents the group who has apparently suffered least in the war, while the other main character, the shell-shocked lower-middle-class Septimus, represents the most prominent group of victims. The narrative is organized around these two polarities, seeking a means to bring them within the same frame. Clarissa's act of empathy, when she imagines precisely the moment of death as we have already seen Septimus enact it, and as no one close to him has realized it, both awards Septimus the compensation of recognition of his real being, and justifies her intuitive sympathy as itself crucial in the life of the community. In organizing her narrative around two characters who never meet, Woolf was not only responding to the antagonism between combatant and non-combatant which the war had established, but exploring ways of presenting relationships outside dialogue. In her diary she speaks of human identities as passages which connect at a subterranean level; in those passages Septimus and Clarissa meet (*Diary*, II, p. 263).

In 1925 Woolf wrote eight short stories about guests at Clarissa's party, which she used as a passage to her next novel, *To the Lighthouse* (1927). 'The Introduction', for instance, in which Clarissa ushers a young woman into her social responsibilities, anticipates the relationship between her next mature heroine, Mrs Ramsay, and the novel's atypical ingenue, Lily. In the novel which emerged from this passage of stories, there are two long sections, an Edwardian holiday afternoon culminating in a dinner-party, and a postwar trip by some of the original group to a lighthouse, linked by a short lyric section, 'Time Passes', which describes the dilapidation by weather of the Scottish holiday home. During this both the Edwardian world and the central character disappear. As in *Mrs Dalloway* there is little dialogue, and the narrative moves fluently between the characters' consciousnesses. Woolf worried that her method of 'oratio obliqua' might seem 'hopelessly undramatic' (*Diary*, III, p. 106). She also responded defensively to Fry's comments on the symbolism of the lighthouse, claiming that it was simply a formal device, a line in the narrative; 'I can't manage symbolism except in this vague generalized way' (*Letters*, III, p. 385). Despite her worries about the success of her method, *To the Lighthouse* was received as a modernist masterpiece, and has remained her least controversial achievement. Erich Auerbach's classic account of the novel took its 'multipersonal representation of consciousness, time strata, disintegration of the continuity of exterior events, shifting of the narrative viewpoint' as the seminal example of modern narrative's shift from a comprehensive externality to an ordering of experience by subjective interpretation. The fact that Woolf was both the last writer, and first woman, in his history of Western narrative intensified his account of the novel as an extraordinary departure from tradition.[18]

To the Lighthouse was also Woolf's most autobiographical novel. Near the end of *Mrs Dalloway* the figure of Mrs Hilbery reappears from *Night and Day*, speaking to Clarissa of the beauty of her mother, of whom we do not otherwise hear. In *To the Lighthouse* this brief aunty reminder is expanded into a portrait of Woolf's mother; she describes in 'A Sketch of the Past' her thirty-year obsession by attempts to organize her memories of her mother, until 'in a great, apparently involuntary rush' she developed the idea of the novel.[19] The Ramsays, as portraits of Woolf's parents, are powerfully expressive of the organization of Victorian life around separate spheres for male and female power; the death of the supportive, nurturing Mrs Ramsay in 'Time Passes' coincides with the disintegration of the solid structures of Victorian life, and reduces Mr Ramsay from authority to pathos. Her beauty as observed by others is placed as specifically Victorian; she reminds them of Victorian versions of Greek goddesses, and of Tennysonian ships setting sail. In 'A Sketch of the Past' Woolf attributes her difficulties in ordering her memories of her mother to Julia Stephen's absorption in a wide range of nurturing activities; 'she was living on such an extended surface that she had not time, nor strength, to concentrate, except for a moment, if one were ill, or in some child's crisis, on anyone' (p. 83). This childish awareness of over-extension informs Mrs Ramsay, who appears to others as a flowering tree or glittering fountain, but to herself as 'a wedge-shaped core of darkness'.[20] Her early death is implicitly the inevitable sacrifice exacted by this beneficent expansion to others. In her 1931 talk, 'Professions for Women', Woolf described how the woman writer's first duty was to kill the Victorian 'Angel in the House', and the ideas of self-sacrifice she represented. In *To the Lighthouse* this idea is transformed in Mrs Ramsay's relations with Lily. Lily is unable to complete her painting in the Edwardian age, but in the postwar section it is her intuition of Mrs Ramsay's presence again, in the garden where she once presided, which inspires her understanding of how she can finish it, and of how her relations with Mrs Ramsay have informed her creativity.

Lily is Woolf's first portrait in her novels of a woman as creative artist; she struggles to understand her relations with an especially powerful Angel in the House, she remains single, and her ideas about her painting are unrelated to professional concepts of prestige and reputation. She accepts that this painting, which she created to express her own relations with the world, will be left forgotten in an attic. In her singleness, her detachment from professionalism, her difficult break from the past and from traditional ideas of femininity, she anticipates Woolf's fullest discussion of women writers, *A Room of One's Own* (1929). Woolf's most famous polemic, based on a talk, 'Women and Fiction', given at Newnham and then Girton in 1928, adapts her modernist insistence on a break with the past to a feminist narrative of the past restrictions and present possibilities of women. She begins by contrasting the two Cambridges, the affluent, privileged, male Cambridge and that other Cambridge inhabited by gauche, poverty-stricken, industrious women. It is a comic version of the contrast of glamour and exclusion displayed in such interwar fiction as Lehmann's *Dusty Answer*,

Macaulay's *They Were Defeated* and Sayers's *Gaudy Night*. Woolf's reference to the lack of endowments which has crippled the women's colleges expands into a commentary on the need for economic independence in the wider community which alone will allow women to become powerfully creative. Despite her sympathy for her Cambridge hosts, the shadowy threat of Miss Beale still hangs over her commentary; the purpose of the room is not only to allow independence for creative work, but, in an anticipation of her second great polemic, *Three Guineas*, to protect against the world of committees and competitive professionalism in which women's distinctive qualities might be lost.

Woolf's succeeding history of women's writing is a narrative of suppression of possibilities, in which the only important figures are 'Judith Shakespeare' and Jane Austen. Shakespeare's fictitious sister, already suggested by Schreiner in *From Man to Man*, figures those suppressed possibilities; Austen, accepting the conditions of work within an entirely domestic context, is presented as the only fully achieved woman writer. Woolf's strategy of insisting on the fresh start now available to women requires her to play down past successes, so the work of Charlotte Brontë and George Eliot is said to be deformed respectively by resentment and by the attempt to work within a male tradition, and the extensive achievement of nineteenth-century women writers is marginalized. The same strategy operates for scholarship; Jane Harrison, once noted for her flamboyant lecturing style and colourful dress, appears as a shabby unobtrusive ghost in Newnham gardens, and Woolf invites history students to consider the unexplored field of the under-recorded lives of ordinary women, precisely the area in which some of the most eminent women historians had been working for the previous three decades.

This banishing of powerful ghosts of women's past achievement had the purpose of clearing the field for Woolf to envisage a new women's writing, which would have the characteristics already outlined in her three modernist manifestos, 'Modern Fiction', 'Mr Bennett and Mrs Brown' and 'The Narrow Bridge of Art', but would be distinctively a women's modernism, with the defining theme the hitherto untreated relations of women, the 'Chloe liked Olivia' story. Her perception of the constraints within which previous women's traditions existed also influenced the famous central contradiction of *A Room of One's Own*, her halting between two strategies for women's writing.[21] In Chapter 5 she draws on her reviews of Richardson's *Pilgrimage* to imagine the development of a mode of writing distinctively female in scope and syntax. In Chapter 6 she envisages an escape from gender into a completely fresh start, a comprehensive perspective on life which she terms, borrowing Coleridge's concept, 'androgyny', and represents in the figures of a man and woman entering a taxi together. Woolf's

185

perplexity between these two strategies, though very specific to her own history, relates to the central feminist dilemma of the 1920s, as the women's movement divided between Old Feminism, with its insistence on the achievement of equality between the sexes and the minimizing of sexual difference, and New Feminism, with its programme of distinctive protective legislation for women based on a recognition of inevitable difference. Woolf, mediating this debate through the relations of women writers to the literary tradition, attempts to incorporate the aspirations of both groups. By *Three Guineas* she had moved closer to the positions of New Feminism (see Chapter 1).

When Woolf outlines the centrality to the new fiction of the representation of women's relationships, she alludes to the magistrate who in 1928 presided over the withdrawal of Hall's *The Well of Loneliness* from circulation. *Orlando*, Woolf's own novel of gender ambivalence and tribute to her lover, Vita Sackville-West, had appeared shortly before the hearing, and was Woolf's first popular success, the turning-point in her financial security as a writer.[22] *Orlando* approached the subject of women's relations more obliquely than Hall; where Hall's novel emphasized the fixity of sexual identity, Woolf's fantasy of the fluidity and instability of gender construction was devised with a playfulness which outran any possible attempts at censorship. In *Orlando* gender is a construction of costume and convention easily circumvented, and love is attracted to recognition of likeness, as in the romance of Orlando and Shelmerdine.

Orlando began in the idea of a historical pastiche, 'a Defoe narrative for fun', with a suggestion of Sapphism, to be called 'The Jessamy Brides' (*Diary*, III, p. 131). In developing this concept Woolf turned directly to the suggestive genre of biography, and, taking a subject who lives four centuries and changes sex halfway through, she reveals the utter dependence of conventional biography on two main crutches, gender stereotype and periodization. *Orlando* is also a celebratory biography of Sackville-West, accompanied by photographs of the subject in costume, and drawing on her recent travels in Persia. In Orlando's sex-change Woolf celebrates her lover's likeness and difference, in her longevity Sackville-West's illustrious ancestry which fascinated Woolf, who wrote in 1924 'If I were she, I should merely stride, with eleven elkhounds behind me, through my ancestral woods. She descends from Dorset, Buckingham, Sir Philip Sidney, and the whole of English history' (*Letters*, III, p. 150). She was less fascinated by Sackville-West's writing; Orlando's writing suffers from the historical constraints which have deformed women's production. Her poem, 'The Oak-Tree', written over four centuries, alludes to Sackville-West's prizewinning *The Land* (1926), from which Woolf quotes the passage on fritillaries. The novel has some formal affinities with *The Land*, which also moves, though more randomly, between pastiches of different periods. When Orlando

186

finds herself writing automatically, the general comment on how writing is shaped by context is also personal to Sackville-West, whose 'sleepwalking servant-girl novels' Woolf criticized (*Letters*, V, p. 266).

Woolf began planning both *Orlando* and *The Waves* in the spring of 1927, but put *The Waves* aside to complete *Orlando*, which, as an example of 'writing exteriorly', she found the less taxing project (*Diary*, III, p. 209). *The Waves* (1930) was her most experimental novel, and the one which came closest to fulfilling the ambitions of 'The Narrow Bridge of Art' for a fiction which reached out to other genres, a 'poetry changing easily and naturally into prose, prose into poetry'.[23] In 1927, when the project was still called 'The Moths', Woolf was imagining a 'play-poem', in which a 'continuous stream' of thought and being is centred around a woman and man talking at night (*Diary*, III, p. 139). By 1929 the opening scene was emerging:

> the person who is at the table can call out any one of them at any moment; & build up by that person the mood, tell a story; for instance about dogs or nurses; or some adventure of a childs kind; all to be very Arabian nights; & so on: this shall be Childhood; but it must not be *my* childhood ... The unreal world must be round all this – the phantom waves. (*Diary*, III, p. 236)

At this point Woolf was still envisaging a She narrator, a modernist Scheherazade, endlessly proliferating narratives from the chaotic flow of the world and the variety of human voices. Later in the 1930s she read the letters of Madame de Sévigné, and discovered in her a positive model for the woman writer, encouraging and incorporating the utterances of others; 'the letters of Mme de Sévigné are often shared by other pens ... the voices mingle; they are all talking together in the garden in 1678'.[24] In the final version of *The Waves*, however, the She narrator who was to orchestrate the polyphony of the novel has vanished, except in the residual glimpse in the Elvedon episode of a woman writing, a disappearance which may probably be attributed both to the ideal of androgyny Woolf had formulated, and to her modernist belief that the omniscient author, in whatever form, should remain banished.

The Waves is Woolf's most extreme move towards banishing the materiality she attacked in Edwardian fiction. Six interior monologues alternate irregularly, and exchange images and ideas, without dialogue or the guidance of any Scheherazade/Sévigné narrator. Italicized passages of landscape description, 'the unreal world', frame, and intervene between, each group of monologues. Woolf said of *To the Lighthouse* 'The lyric portions ... are collected in the 10 year lapse, & don't interfere with the text as much as usual' (*Diary*, III, pp. 106–7). She was addressing the same problem as the rural novelists with their notorious 'asterisked passages', how to integrate lyric descriptions of the natural world persuasively with the human narrative. *The Waves* continues this treatment of the lyric passages by marking their separation from the human activity; the compositions, the play of light and shade, the humanizing metaphors, explore the ways in which humans attempt to understand this unreal world, and how it remains apart and unrealized. Within the monologues the humans construct fictions about each other often experienced as painful. Bernard feels his multiplicity of identity contracted in the presence of Neville who requires simply a friend; Susan's love is compared to a bird's impaling beak; Rhoda, unable to endure the torture of contact with the world, commits suicide. For Woolf the novel was 'my first work in my own style' (*Diary*, IV, p. 53), the achievement of a fictional method which finally escaped the redundant materiality of previous fiction.

Her next novel, *Flush* (1933), was another spoof biography, this time of Elizabeth Barrett Browning's spaniel, and a necessary recuperation of the genre's strengths after the poetic vision of *The Waves*. 'It is a good idea I think to write biographies; to make them use my powers of representation reality accuracy; & to use my novels simply to express the general, the poetic' (*Diary*, IV, p. 40). *Flush* satirized two familiar targets, official biography and literary Victorianism, and reorganized the reader's perspective on each, both in Flush's immunity to conventional assumptions about the Victorian era, and in the displacement of Elizabeth's famous romance by her relations with her dog. Woolf, however, rather resented this squib's success; it became a Book Society choice, and her most popular novel apart from *Orlando*. The return to biography led into her next major fiction, an attempt to combine what she saw as her two modes of writing. 'I want to give the whole of the present society – nothing less: facts as well as the vision. And to combine them both. I mean, The Waves going on simultaneously with Night and Day' (*Diary*, IV, pp. 151–2). *The Years* (1937), on which she worked from 1932 to 1936, and which was her only bestseller, developed initially from her 1931 talk, 'Professions for Women', to become the project, 'The Pargiters', which was designed as what Woolf termed an 'essay-novel'. In 'The Pargiters', the story of a late Victorian family, she sought a new relationship between fiction and non-fiction, alternating between essays exploring historical and cultural issues of the period, and fictional chapters exemplifying those issues. In the long process of developing the work Woolf excised the non-fiction sections, though the cultural concerns they expressed still inform the fictional chapters of what then became *The Years*.[25]

The Years shares the concerns of many novels of the 1930s, and might be seen as Woolf's attempt to compose a viable fiction of fact, integrating an insistence on the factual into her innovative method. Woolf had admired Webb's construction of her relations with her age in *My Apprenticeship*, making herself fit in appropriately at each point, but she was seeking less public-spirited forms of representation of how people responded to, and were constructed by, their context. *The Years* takes the popular form of a family saga running from 1880 to the 1930s, but demolishes reader expectations of the genre. Characters whom we expect in 1880 to continue to be central, such as the family rebel Delia, disappear from view until 1930, while the narrative moves off at a tangent after other destinies, refusing the conventional group of the family saga, with some characters consistently central and others peripheral. The dates at which we revisit the family are irregularly spaced, and chosen without obvious reference to major external events. The First World War, which appeared in brackets in *To the Lighthouse*, is this time experienced by a small dinner party in a London cellar, exemplifying Woolf's attempt to register the oblique and personal ways in which external history is experienced.

The Years is Woolf's most comprehensive treatment of the Victorianism from which she recoiled, and the deforming effects of the organization of family and public life around separate spheres. During the narrative the close-knit patriarchal family, apparently so solid in 1880, disintegrates amid general relief. When the family home is sold, the dog is the only casualty; the family scatter into flats, and into lives less constrained by social convention. In this account of the separate spheres it is the men, their public roles prepared for them, who are the main casualties; Edward, divided from his feelings by a distinguished professional career, 'has the look of an insect whose body has been eaten out, leaving only the wings, the shell', while Eleanor, the family spinster, has retained her curiosity about life into old age.[26] The new possibilities of relating to gender identity are suggested, as in *A Room of One's Own*, by a final image of a man and woman entering a taxi.

Woolf's next and last novel began as 'Pointz Hall'; in 1938 she was imagining a fiction which moved further from emphasis on the individual than anything she had written before. She wanted ' "I" rejected: "We" substituted: to whom at the end there shall be an invocation? "We" . . . composed of many different things . . . we all life, all art, all waifs and strays' (*Diary*, V, p. 135; Woolf's ellipses). The novel which developed into *Between the Acts* takes place like *Mrs Dalloway* on a June afternoon, but in a countryside anticipating war, not a city relaxing in its aftermath. The narrative again moves among a group of characters who gather for a celebration, in this case a pageant, but here there is no specific focus on one or two characters. The intrusive 'I' which she attacked as characteristic of men's writing in *A Room of One's Own* becomes a communal polyphony, fostered within the novel by Miss La Trobe, the eccentric lesbian who creates the village pageant, and who is Woolf's latest word on women's writing, the She narrator eliminated from *The Waves*. She is, however, one among many voices, and Woolf's treatment of her work emphasizes the inevitable limits 'and constraints on writing, the dependence on available material, on occasion, the cooperation of others, and natural accident.

The pageant, a form popular at this period, interpreted the history of a community in a series of scenes devised and performed by that community. Traditionally it suggested a story of progress, both to La Trobe's audience who expect a conventional British Empire finale, and to the suffragettes who had organized several differently triumphalist pageants. It was a form which affirmed the community's solidarity, a central topic by 1941 when *Between the Acts* was posthumously published; the hit war film, *Mrs Miniver* (1942), was typical in featuring a village fête to demonstrate British capacity to carry on by means of such annually repeated rituals. La Trobe's treatment, disconcertingly for the audience, avoids structuring the chronological narrative around an idea of progress, presenting a series of scenes which are pastiches of various historical genres, and explore the kinds of possibility and limitation offered by those genres. Many of the words are carried away by the wind, and round the main performers is a chorus, even less frequently audible, of the under-recorded ordinary people. The script does not address the coming war, which is incorporated in the performance only by a chance flight of bombers overhead.

It is the history not included in La Trobe's play which explains the forthcoming conflict. The men of Pointz Hall understand what is about to happen from their newspapers, and in a narrowly militaristic sense, but it is old Mrs Swithin's readings in prehistory which interpret the real significance of the war. Gillian Beer has discussed the fascination of prehistory for Woolf in her first and last novels, especially in that vast area of the past which precedes and resists narrative, and tacitly and enormously contradicts the fantasies of progress which art and historiography construct.[27] While writing *Between the Acts* Woolf was reading another work which undermined the securities of those fantasies, and suggested to her the limits of her capacity to interpret the world. 'Freud is upsetting: reducing one to whirlpool; & I daresay truly. If we're all instinct, the unconscious, whats all this about civilisation, the whole man, freedom &c' (*Diary*, V, p. 250). The struggle to create art is perennial; Miss La Trobe settles down in the pub to plan the next pageant, and Mrs Swithin's reading reaches the construction of Stonehenge. The context of this struggle, however, is humanity's endless war, the product of the enduring, underlying primitive which prehistory and psychology seek to explain. On the last page that war resumes in a scene already imagined by Miss La Trobe. It remains a question whether her art, so dependent on external circumstances, on shifts and accommodations, will survive.

JEAN RHYS

There is a scene in Jean Rhys's first novel, *Quartet* (1928), which seems to allude to the first romantic encounter in Elinor Glyn's *Three Weeks*, where the hero watches the magnolia-faced, scarlet-lipped, black-hatted queen eat her way through a substantial French meal. In Rhys's version the heroine Marya sits in a Paris bar watching another woman perform for a group of male students:

> dazed she watched the lady who was sitting opposite dining slowly and copiously. Soup; a beefsteak; salad; cheese. She was a lady with a pale face, crimson lips, a close-fitting black hat, and eyebrows like half moons. She was indeed exactly like Pierrot and every now and then she would turn and look at herself in the glass approvingly. Eventually, gathering up her belongings, she moved out with stately and provocative undulations of the hips.[28]

Where the stylishness of Glyn's queen is presented as instinctive female dignity, Rhys's woman performs, an exactly calculated performance which is, however, ignored by its targeted audience; the students continue their political discussions, and only Marya watches. This is one example of the recurrent scene in Rhys where one woman watches another perform. For Rhys consciousness of women as objects of the male gaze is always informed by a sense of how much of the romantic repertoire which women carefully learn and perform is expended on inattentive male audiences. The Pierrot reference which links the woman both to the melancholy, lovelorn Pierrot of French poetry, and to the touring Pierrot troupes which were the bottom line in theatrical entertainment in Britain at this period, places the pathos and the drudgery of the performance.

In her stance as alienated exile, in the fragmented narratives in which her heroines pursue identities which remain elusive, in her disruptions of chronology and her concentrated lyricism, Rhys was archetypally modernist, but a modernist whose range of awareness included, unlike Woolf and more knowledgeably than Mansfield, the popular romantic culture of the period. Rhys's writing is always acutely conscious of the repertoire of popular romance on which her women draw, through which they identify their aspirations and organize their performances. Her heroines move in an ambience of romantic fictions. Rebecca West, in 'The Tosh Horse', compared romantic fiction to 'whistles ... sounding certain notes which are clearly audible to dogs'; Rhys can hear those whistles quite clearly.[29] While Woolf's characters in *Mrs Dalloway* and *The Years* hear flower-sellers or children singing popular songs which emerge as weird unintelligible noises, Rhys's heroines identify every song they hear around them in the streets

191

and apply most of them to their own condition. The cinema is another source of romantic fantasy; Anna in *Voyage in the Dark*, as she slips from chorus-girl to prostitute, attends a film about Theodora, the Byzantine dancer and prostitute who became an empress. Sasha in *Good Morning, Midnight* cautions herself against her 'film mind' which is forever conjuring up images of hopeless masochistic love. The range of roles available is limited; Anna is entranced by a dress in a shop-window which would enable her to 'look like a doll or a flower'.[30] While other women, like Marya, observe these performances with empathy and competitiveness and fear, the main audience is often inattentive. *Three Weeks* indulged a fantasy of the absolute centrality of romantic love; Rhys's heroines discover how marginal to the male world is the repertoire to which they have dedicated themselves.

Rhys's perception of her heroines' situation derives from her own origins as a female member of the white colonial population of the Caribbean island of Dominica. Rhys thus produces a redundant woman quite different in construction from the spinster daughters of the clergy which the phrase usually signified in the still largely insular British fiction and journalism of the period. Her Caribbean heroines, Anna, and Antoinette in *Wide Sargasso Sea*, are stranded like Rhys herself between an ideal England known to Dominica through fiction and commercial art, and an ideal Dominica remembered in England for its warmth and colour, and the vitality of the life of its black community. Although her heroines indulge fantasies about both, the reality they experience is determined by their own redundancy. As women they are excluded from the identity and status conferred by the economic power controlled by the white colonial male. As whites they are excluded from the strong sense of communal identity of the majority black population. 'I wanted to be black. I always wanted to be black . . . Being black is warm and gay, being white is cold and sad' (pt. 1, ch. 3) remembers Anna. In the colonial power struggle the white woman has no place except as parasite, the 'white cockroach' identity Antoinette dreads. Woolf writes in *Three Guineas* that 'as a woman I have no country', but for Rhys's heroines experiences of discontinuity and loss of identity are registered in intense physical terms. In her autobiography Rhys titled the chapter describing her journey to England 'It began to grow cold'.

Rhys's sense of the redundancy of the white colonial woman was overdetermined by the jobs she took after she had arrived in England in 1906, as chorus-girl in various touring musicals, and later as mannequin, photographic model, film extra. The title of her unfinished autobiography, *Smile Please* (1979), refers to the obligation on women to perform. Her place in the lowest status, most exploited, most rapidly expendable area of the theatrical profession further determined her analysis of the redundancy of her women. The rest of her career confirmed that analysis; for Rhys the party was always in the next room. At a time when many actresses were supporting the suffrage movement, organizing the Actresses' Suffrage League, putting on feminist dramas, Rhys was touring the English provinces as a chorus-girl, untouched by these activities. When the Left Bank in Paris was a ferment of expatriate modernist and feminist literary activity in the 1920s, Rhys was not part of any network. Her first story was published through her only literary contact, her lover Ford Madox Ford. Ford wrote the preface to her first book, the collection of stories, *The Left Bank* (1926). As Coral Ann Howells points out, where this preface appropriates the Left Bank and its cultural scene by authoritatively mapping its outlines, Rhys's stories dissipate any idea of knowable milieux and networks.[31] As the women writers of the 1930s read and commented on each other's novels, Rhys's were not among them, and, after the lack of response to *Good Morning, Midnight* (1939), she 'disappeared' for nearly thirty years, until her 'resurrection' by *Wide Sargasso Sea* in 1966.

The difficulties of constructing an identity are experienced in the relations Rhys's women have with writing. In the late story, 'The Day They Burned the Books' (1958), the white colonial child complains 'I was tired of learning and reciting poems in praise of daffodils'. For the white colonial literature is something learned and taken on trust, constructed around objects and values which have no connection with her experience.[32] Anna in *Voyage in the Dark* rejects the banal lessons of books, which replicate gossip and codify experience. 'Everybody says the man's bound to get tired, and you read it in all books. But I never read now, so they can't get at me like that anyway' (pt. 1, ch. 7). Sasha's attempts at writing in *Good Morning, Midnight* are compared with the 'real writer' who has just finished a history of Napoleon. Her monosyllabic style communicates no sense of value to her sponsors; 'it gets monotonous, and don't you know any long words, and if you do would you please use them?'.[33] Rhys's persona is constructed out of antagonism to existing forms of writing and in surprised encounter with language.

Her first published work was 'Vienne', three short interior monologues linked by their setting in postwar Vienna, which appeared in Ford's *Transatlantic Review* in 1924 over the monosyllabic pseudonym Jean Rhys (for Ella Gwendolen Williams) and, much expanded, in *The Left Bank*.[34] In the first section, 'The Dancer', the female speaker recalls watching another woman perform. The dance is exquisite, an epiphany for the woman watching; 'for once I'd met sheer loveliness with a flame inside, for there was "it" – the spark, the flame in her dancing' (p. 188). It is the most achieved performance Rhys records in her work, but presented in the same context as are later performances, with the predatory but negligently attentive men, the calculations of the dancer's cost as lover, the reported later wastage of her expertise. The speaker's delight in the performance is qualified by her consciousness of the response of the men she is with, and this double consciousness continues throughout 'Vienne'; this interior monologue is determined by association with male points of view, or an anxiety to guess them. The speaker, who is drifting through central Europe with her suddenly mysteriously wealthy husband, needs to know above all how men value women. Only money can confirm 'the luxury of a soul', can confirm identity when you look in the mirror, and it is men who control money.

'Vienne', a fragmented interior monologue in which an uncertainly located speaker records impressions of an unstable environment, placed Rhys as a modernist. Postwar Vienna, an imperial capital which has suddenly lost its empire and identity, and in the expanded version appears in a collection of stories about another capital, is observed by a female speaker who has suddenly acquired identity through her association with men. In many respects the Rhys persona is a female complement of the authorial persona of Hemingway's *Men without Women* (1927). The laconicism, the evocation of hinterland to the inconsequential dialogue, the sense of gender as performance and as doom, the grace under pressure of these doomed performers, all outline a concept of women attempting to construct a sense of themselves in a disintegrating world. It is a world which effortlessly bridges high modernism and popular culture. Definition of 'it', to which the dancer epiphany alludes, was a widely publicized Hollywood activity of the 1920s, presided over by Hollywood's resident guru on sexuality, Elinor Glyn. The narrator's attempt to isolate the essence of beauty within its commercial context is conducted in awareness of such enquiries. In its longer version 'Vienne' becomes a dark reverse to Anita Loos's comic novel, *Gentlemen Prefer Blondes* (1925), in which two American gold-diggers move eastward through 'the Central of Europe', observing other women perform, assessing the financial possibilities of the men they meet, profiting from the disintegrating cultures around them. The joke in Loos lies in the effortless triumphs of her naively greedy heroines. Rhys's heroines follow similar paths, but to isolation and disintegration.

Rhys produced four novels in the decade after *The Left Bank*, and a number of stories which eventually appeared in the collections *Tigers Are Better-Looking* (1968) and *Sleep It Off, Lady* (1976). The novels record the inner lives of women who have difficulty in perceiving themselves coherently. They observe acutely, but frequently do not have the information to interpret what they see, they experience little sense of control, they attempt and fail to construct an identity for themselves. The Rhys heroine is continually checking the mirror for confirmation that the identity she hopes that she is projecting still exists. Marya, after the disappearance of the Pierrot woman, refers to the mirror only to discover that love has paradoxically made her ugly. *Quartet* was her fictional reconstruction of her relations with Ford and his partner, while her first husband was in jail. (The other three participants all wrote their accounts of the affair.) Ford was both her ex-lover and the patron who had encouraged her to write, and published her first work; the novel argues with Ford, as the fictions of Richardson, von Arnim and West argue with H.G. Wells. Marya attempts to understand a situation which seems controlled by the Ford figure, Heidler, a writer and Left Bank fixer, and to argue for her own point of view against the solidities of male power. These are supported by the solidities of domesticity as exemplified by Heidler's partner Lois, 'the woman who is wondering how she is going to manage about the extra person to dinner' (ch. 14). Marya fails to find a viable position within the quartet, and is significantly absent from both the beginning and end of her story. Indifferently observed by an omniscient narrator on the first page, she disappears before the last, left unconscious, possibly dead, by her enraged husband with whom we leave the house. As an actress Rhys knew what a part lost in status without an onstage death; the scene is final confirmation of Marya's inability to define herself.

Julia, in Rhys's second novel, *After Leaving Mr Mackenzie* (1931), is the most thoroughly displaced of her heroines. Her life has removed most of the formal markers of identity; 'it was not easy to guess at her age, her nationality, or the social background to which she properly belonged'.[35] Bereft even of the status conferred by the economic support of her ex-lover, Mackenzie, she begins not to check her identity; 'she did not look in the glass and made no effort to arrange her hair' (pt. 3, ch. 4). Her performance as Mackenzie's discarded mistress, slapping his face in a café, fails in intended effect, but attracts the attention of another potential lover. Her visit to her dying mother, the only time in Rhys where a character re-establishes contact with her past, fails to provide her with any regained family role. Unlike Rhys's other heroines of the period, she does not have the identity confirmed by a continuous interior monologue; for much of the narrative we observe her through others: Mackenzie, her new lover, her respectable sister, Norah. In the last sentence we are in proximity to someone no longer capable of any definite location of her situation; 'it was the hour between dog and wolf, as they say'.

In *Voyage in the Dark* (1934) Rhys returned to her own experiences as a chorus-girl in Edwardian England. In this novel we are exclusively located with the heroine, Anna, and the discontinuities in the narrative are occasioned by her failure to bring her Dominican past and her English present into relation. Past continually intervenes into Anna's reflections on her immediate situation, until, in the final section where she lies delirious after a backstreet abortion, past and present merge into continuous nightmare. This is the novel which most clearly places the redundancy of the white

195

colonial woman, overdetermined by Anna's move into the disposable profession of chorus-girl. As a child Anna yearned to be black, to find the
identity denied the white colonial woman. As a woman she attempts to
resist the identity thrust upon her by her profession, by the books she reads,
including Zola's *Nana*, the story of the downfall of a prostitute, by the
expectations of those who wish to exploit her, by the doctor's concluding
'you girls are too naive to live, aren't you?'. Anna's attempts to understand
her situation focus on the transition from Dominica to England; as she lies
in bed in her English boarding-house the picture of a dog recalls the disposable commercial art by which England was imagined in Dominica, and
of which she has become part. Again this novel reverses the assumptions
of *Gentlemen Prefer Blondes*. Anna fails to make use of her opportunities,
and, though the other girls talk knowingly of the profits to be made, they
show no more ability. For Loos's fantasy of gold-digging triumph Rhys
substitutes a reality of marginality and expendability as the girls dream of
acquiring some hold on the mysterious economic power possessed by their
stage-door johnnies. The only successful gold-digger is the respectable
woman, Anna's stepmother, Hester, who has turned her early widowhood
into economic security. Hester defines Anna's fall in class; her situation is
presented as uniquely tragic in comparison with that of her working-class
chorus-girl colleagues, Maudie and Laurie, who have not suffered the same
fall from gentility.

The original ending of *Voyage in the Dark* was a long delirium before
dying in which Anna dreams of a carnival in Dominica, in which the white
masks worn in mockery by the black revellers confirm her utter estrangement from her past. It was abridged by Rhys at the suggestion of her
publishers.[36] In the published version Anna survives to resume her cycle,
and perhaps to become in middle-age the heroine of *Good Morning,
Midnight*. That novel begins with another rebirth, of Sasha on holiday in
Paris reliving memories of the streets and cafés she knew twenty years before,
during her marriage and the birth and death of her baby. In Sasha's interior
monologue the coincidence of scene in past and present, along with her
alcoholism, ensure that the penetration of present by past is all-pervasive;
the use of the present tense affords no guide to the reader. Sasha, however,
is the sharpest and most experienced of Rhys's heroines, aware of the undermining and wastage of the romantic roles women play. She remembers
Paulette, who was 'in the romantic tradition', and whom she admired,
but also a carefully prepared encounter sabotaged when Paulette's drawers
collapsed (pt. 3). She is also aware that the romantic performance is more
closely related to the performer's search for identity than to the presumed
target audience. The fur coat which she retains from the past, and the
ash-blonde hairdo, which removes every trace of her original hair colour,

are designed to reconstruct her own sense of identity, not to attract the unwanted gigolo, René.

Good Morning, Midnight seems sometimes to be engaged in undermining the affirmations of earlier modernists. Sasha has a room of her own, but it does not offer the freedom promised by Woolf and help her escape the burden of the past. 'This damned room – it's saturated with the past . . . It's all the rooms I've ever slept in, all the streets I've ever walked in' (pt. 2). When she watches the woman in the window opposite, it is not, like Mrs Dalloway, to be exhilarated by the observation of the difference of another existence, but to reflect 'if I watch her when she is making up she will retaliate by staring at me when I do the same thing' (pt. 1). The remark illustrates the complicity and competition in Rhys's women's awareness of each other. Rhys's 'clean, well-lighted place' in which, as in Hemingway's story of that name, the darkness outside is kept at bay, is likely not to be the café, but the ladies' toilet within the café. Sasha's triple 'Yes' to the sleazy commercial traveller, which concludes the novel, echoes Molly Bloom's affirmation in Joyce's *Ulysses*, but in Sasha's case as an acceptance of further degradation. The colonial who was irritated by poems about daffodils is defining her difference from the great modernist writers. Like her heroines Rhys defines herself in opposition. Sasha, whose wit and bloodymindedness are her only means of control over a derelict and incoherent life, is Rhys's most successfully resistant heroine.

The critical failure of *Good Morning, Midnight* led to Rhys's long silence; if she was already working on the novel which was to become *Wide Sargasso Sea*, as some evidence suggests, that work did not become a matter of record until the late 1950s.[37] *Wide Sargasso Sea*, which was published to critical acclaim in 1966, and finally established Rhys's reputation, seeks to fill a gap in a great Victorian novel, to compensate for the oblivious cruelty with which *Jane Eyre* treats Rochester's mad wife by placing her 'onstage' in her Caribbean context, and explaining the process of her loss of identity. 'Eventually I got back to being a Creole lunatic in the 1840s' wrote Rhys.[38] The central narrative is that of Rochester, which both offers Rhys her major opportunity for quasi-sympathetic exploration of a male consciousness, and displaces her heroine, Antoinette, to the extremities of the novel. She appears first as a child confronting the perplexities of colonialism, and finally as a madwoman who has been deprived of her identity, even of her name. 'Names matter, like when he wouldn't call me Antoinette, and I saw Antoinette drifting out of the window with her scents, her pretty clothes and her looking-glass'.[39] New reader awareness of constructions of gender and race, and the greater accessibility effected by the novel's relation with *Jane Eyre*, ensured Rhys her first success, long after the decade in which most of her distinctive contribution to modernist fiction was made.

ELIZABETH BOWEN

In 1939 Graham Greene described in *The Lawless Roads* his relief in finding a copy of Elizabeth Bowen's first novel, *The Hotel*, in the Mexican hotel where he was staying. Reading Bowen helped him to cope with the dangers of boredom in his rat-infested room; the solid alternative reality provided by the novel kept the menacing darkness of a Chiapas night at bay.[40] Shortly afterwards Bowen herself was similarly engaged in fending off the darkness, writing in wartime London a history of her ancestral home in County Cork. *Bowen's Court* (1942) is a detailed reconstruction of the landscape and history of that solid house across the Irish Sea in a country not at war, complete with maps, family portraits and family tree. In the 'Afterword' Bowen scrutinizes her reasons for this reconstruction:

> I have written (as though it were everlasting) about a home at a time when all homes are being threatened and hundreds and thousands of them are being destroyed. I have taken the attachment of people to places as being generic to human life, at a time when the attachment is to be dreaded, as a possible source of too much pain.[41]

Bowen's awareness of the importance of ceremony and tradition which Bowen's Court embodied, her endless worries about the difficulties and costs of its upkeep, her self-conscious idealization of a home separated from her by war, are further informed by her sense of herself as an anomaly in the history of the house. She is the first female heir and childless; the book, one draft of which she has posted for safety to the United States, is her continuation of the tradition.

Woolf was unimpressed by Bowen's Court when she visited it in 1934, describing it as 'a great stone box, but full of Italian mantelpieces and decayed eighteenth century furniture, and carpets all in holes – however they insisted upon keeping up a ramshackle kind of state, dressing for dinner and so forth' (*Letters*, V, p. 300). Her reaction is suggestive of the difference between the two novelists; the 'great stone box' and its paraphernalia exemplified the area of life which Woolf had eliminated from her fictional perception. *The Hotel*, though modelled on Woolf's *The Voyage Out*, is nonetheless preoccupied with people 'living under the compulsion of their furniture',[42] and all Bowen's succeeding novels share the Edwardian emphasis, rejected by Woolf, on the way material realities shape human lives. In her presentation of herself as professional writer Bowen was also nearer to Bennett than to Woolf; she cultivated the middlebrow audience for media discussion of the arts, reviewing copiously, going on lecture tours to promote her novels, writing a popular history of fiction, *English Novelists*

(1942), and giving radio talks for the BBC, the institution which to Woolf epitomized middlebrow literary values. Although *The Death of the Heart* satirizes the reading habits of the middlebrow public who borrow books from Smoots's circulating library, Bowen's novels, with their romantic titles, and stories of young girls' emotional crises, were more accessible to the borrowers of Smoots than the fiction of Woolf or Rhys.

Among the innovative women writers of the period Bowen was the only one to present herself as cultural authority to the expanding audience for fiction. A 1945 article, 'Notes on Writing a Novel', written for the arts magazine *Orion*, presented that authority in highly prescriptive terms, categorizing the features of the novel, and authoritatively laying down rules and formulae for successful execution. The emphasis is on the modern writer as professional explaining her area of expertise; references to earlier writers (Austen, Flaubert, James, all writers explicitly evoked in Bowen's fiction) coexist with references to detective fiction, the genre with which discussion of formulae was then most associated. The most explicit claim to authority is made through an analogy between novelists and film directors. 'The cinema, cinema-going, has no doubt built up in novelists a great authoritarianism. This seems to me good.'[43] By the analogy with the new medium of cinema, the novelist's rigorous control of every detail to ensure complete realization of her concept is presented as characteristically modern, but the article's recommendations could hardly be further from Woolf's mode of decentred experimental uncertainty. Bowen's specific prescriptions for practice are similarly removed from Woolf's preoccupations; she argues for the 'naive' solution of the omniscient narrator as the most successful narrative mode, and for dialogue as 'the ideal means of showing what is between the characters' (p. 41).

This liking for literary rules and authoritarianism always coexists, however, with a sharp awareness of literature's explosive potential. In a 1947 radio talk she described how, when she was twelve, she read Rider Haggard's *She*. 'After *She*, print was to fill me with apprehension. I was prepared to handle any book like a bomb' (p. 257). In a 1941 review of Compton-Burnett's *Parents and Children* she approvingly describes the dialogue as being like 'the sound of glass being swept up, one of these London mornings after a Blitz' (p. 162). Bowen's own creative response to the war produced *Bowen's Court*, and her best short stories. In the preface to the American edition of her collection of wartime stories, *The Demon Lover*, she explained why wartime experience produced, not a novel, but these 'flying particles of something enormous and inchoate that had been going on'. Bowen thinks of novels in terms of solidity and elaborated structure, and as such inappropriate to the London of the Blitz. 'The violent destruction of solid things, the explosion of the illusion that prestige, power and

199

permanence attach to bulk and weight, left all of us, equally, heady and disembodied' (p. 95). She experimented with short fiction from the beginning of her career, but her most memorable stories are concentrated in the early 1940s, and in her response to wartime London. Their explicit topic is often shattered structures. The title of 'Mysterious Kôr', perhaps her best story, invokes the lost city of *She*, the book which introduced her to fiction's explosive capacity to shatter a world; the story explores the disorientation of three people living in wartime London.

In 'Notes on Writing a Novel' Bowen, an Anglo-Irish woman writer writing in exile in England, insists that novelists should 'write from outside their own nationality, class or sex' (p. 44). This was the orthodox modernist stance, but all Bowen's novels focus on the rival possibilities of living outside or inside traditions, the distinctive confinements of domicile and deracination. The houses which are central in her fictions operate as images of this debate about the desirability and impossibility of living with traditions, and of Bowen's dual attachment to solid structures and to the attractions of disintegrating them. The most ambivalent of the leading women writers of the period, she both assumed the role of custodian of literary continuity and pointed to the inevitable disruptions of tradition. Despite Bowen's claim to write outside gender, the situation of the woman in the house is central to her fiction. More specifically she worked within the genre of domestic realism; Phyllis Lassner has described how Bowen uses the house as metaphor for the genre within which women have achieved pre-eminence, but which has also constrained them.[44]

The Hotel (1927) is set in a British tourist colony in France, and, like *The Voyage Out*, focused on a young girl's uncertainty about her sexual identity, and her preoccupation with a fascinating older woman. This first novel announces Bowen's ambivalent situation of herself between tradition and modernity; the homage to Woolf places the novel in the modern camp, but *The Voyage Out* was written before Woolf's fully modernist phase. Where the novel most distinctively departs from Woolf is in the emphasis on the materiality of the central building, and in the use of the narrative voice. For Woolf expatriation was simply a metaphor for the uncertainties of identity, but for Bowen the characters' decisions to live in hotels rather than houses, the way their conversations revolve around the impossibilities of home life in modern conditions, are as central to the depiction of the uncertainties of identity as the heroine's sexual ambivalence. In a preface to her next novel, *The Last September*, Bowen characteristically explained her use of a central building in her novels as an attempt to master the rules, a solution to the 'mechanical problem' of assembling a range of characters in one place (p. 123). In this novel Bowen also makes her decision to retain the 'naive' solution of the omniscient narrator; what reassured Greene in his Mexican hotel room was the 'acid reality' of the novel, the presence of a sharp, authoritative commentary.

In *The Last September* (1930) the destruction of a house as metaphor for the disruption of a literary tradition is central. In this novel Bowen's imagination sets fire to Bowen's Court, reconstructing the social life of Danielstown, a great house of the Anglo-Irish gentry, in the late summer of 1922 before it burns down in the Troubles. The life of the young heroine, Lois, is shaped and constrained by the traditional ceremonies of gentry life; the depiction of this world of marriageable girls, officers and parties makes frequent reference in episode and character to *Pride and Prejudice*. Lois's encounter with an Irish nationalist in an old mill, derelict industrial potential of an unborn alternative Ireland, briefly reveals to her another narrative of violence and change unfolding outside the social comedy of Danielstown, and threatening its eventual complete disruption. This Gothic episode of the derelict mill operates within the narrative as an interpolated ghost story, disrupting the ordered pattern of a narrative which evokes Austen as a major reference.

Bowen saw *The Last September* as a historical novel; her three other major novels of the 1930s returned to the problematic situation of the young woman in the modern world. In *To the North* (1932) Emmeline's work for a travel agency is an emblem of her crisis of identity. Much of the novel is concerned with journeys, train journeys which reduce the passing countryside to cardboard tourist scenery, car journeys where the English landscape becomes a meaningless sequence of unrelated scenes, plane journeys which leave a miniaturized world below, and indulge in dangerous illusions of clarity and transcendence. Conversations struggle with new conditions, such as the reconstructions of identity required by talking on the telephone. In a crucial discussion of their future relations, conducted on a plane, Emmeline and her lover, defeated by the noise, continue by pencilling comments in the margins of a magazine. In this world of frenetic movement the crucial missing element is the home; Emmeline's eventual suicide is related more to her failure to find one than to her failed love affair. A country cottage weekend, designed to build domesticity into her relationship, fails miserably. The home she shares with a woman friend is lost when the friend marries. 'Timber by timber, Oudenarde Road fell to bits, as small houses are broken up daily to widen the roar of London. She saw the door open on emptiness; blanched walls as though after a fire. Houses shared with women are built on sand.'[45] *To the North* is the most conservative in implication of Bowen's novels, describing the ceaseless whirl of modernity around a yearning for stability.

Bowen's next novel, *The House in Paris* (1935), moves back to a partisanship with modernity, juxtaposing two houses to question the premises of the traditional novel of domestic realism. The architectural oddity of the eponymous house makes it impenetrable to the well-developed social sense of a visiting English child; neither the house nor its residents can be 'placed' within the secure categories she has learned. The Parisian house, setting for the first and third sections, frames the long central section where the source of the anguish the novel records is traced to a London house, where the central characters 'lived like a family in a pre-war novel', and where their 'well-lit explanations of people were like photographs taken when the camera could not lie; they stunned your imagination by *being* exact'.[46] This novel explicitly rejects as inadequate and delusive the Edwardian emphasis on materiality and exactness; insights are seen to lie in the uncertainties and mysteries represented by the Parisian house. Unsurprisingly Woolf found it a great advance in her work (*Letters*, V, p. 429).

Bowen's most famous novel, *The Death of the Heart* (1938), addressed the popular interwar topic of the problematic social role of the teenage girl, and again explicitly invoked Austen as the model of traditional fiction. This time it is *Mansfield Park* which is the specific model, as Portia moves between the orderly upper-class London house, 2 Windsor Terrace, and the noisy disorderly middle-class seaside villa, Waikiki. In this revision of Austen's opposition of Mansfield Park and Portsmouth, however, traditional stability and ceremony exist in the London house only in the antique furniture,. and in the old servant's archaic sense that the place for young girls is the schoolroom, while the villa's *laissez-faire* attracts Portia as Portsmouth did not attract Austen's Fanny. The narrative fails to find a place for Portia in either world, and the demonstrated inappropriateness to modern experience of the secure structures of Austen's fiction reveals a void as attractive and meaningless as Waikiki. The highbrow professional writer in the novel, St Quentin, displays a fashionable cynicism about the possibilities for fiction by referring to Barclay's very lowbrow *The Rosary* as the type for all narrative. Extracts from Portia's diary, strings of events and observations unconnected by any authorial interpretation, exemplify perhaps the only way writing can respond authentically to the modern situation.

Over a decade passed before Bowen's next and most 'difficult' novel, *The Heat of the Day* (1949), a novel set in wartime London which she abandoned writing during the war. In this novel three of the four main characters are professionally engaged in interpretation. The heroine, Stella, is an interpreter, her lover, unknown to her, a spy for Germany pursued by a British agent, while the fourth character, a working-class girl drawn by chance into their orbit, elaborates her own romances about them. In the hectic atmosphere of wartime London with its posted warnings against 'Careless Talk', rival fictions and impossibilities of communication proliferate. Stella lives in a rented flat, an Irish country-house which her son inherits offers a distant promise of stability, but at the book's centre is the monstrous Edwardian suburban mansion which reveals to a reluctant Stella how her lover, brought up amid its grotesque pretences and macho fantasies, might logically have become a spy. Again, as in *The House in Paris*, Edwardian clarity and solidity prove delusive; fiction must respond to a situation where people and relationships have none of the continuity attributed to them by traditional fiction. Stella reflects on the British agent that 'by the rules of fiction, with which life to be credible must comply, he was as a character "impossible" – each time they met, for instance, he showed no shred or trace of having been continuous since they last met'.[47] In this context of interpretation despised popular forms, romances or the spy thriller from which the agent seems to Stella to have wandered, assume as much validity as traditional realist fiction.

During the war Bowen used short stories, her 'flying particles', to reimagine the war experience to which she found the structures of the novel inimical. She was, after Mansfield, the woman writer most committed to the short story, published short stories throughout the interwar period, and shared Mansfield's belief in it as the characteristic literary form of modernity, which permitted an escape from the novel's constricting structures and demand for coherent development of character, into other kinds of perception potentially truer to the fragmented experience of modern life. 'Summer Night' (1941) is one of her stories closest to Mansfield's symbolist methods in 'Prelude', juxtaposing the distinctive imaginative lives of a scattered group of people, while changes in the Irish light and weather effect transitions in location and mood. In *The Demon Lover* the title story is a ghost story, a genre which in its existence outside realist literature, and its threat to realism's apparently solid walls, always attracted Bowen. Ghost stories lurk within her novels as in the mill episode in *The Last September*, or the Paris section of *The House in Paris*. Several stories in *The Demon Lover* play with the uncanny. In 'The Happy Autumn Fields' (1944) a woman immerses herself during a bombing raid in the fancied securities of a Victorian diary; the story refuses ordered framing and transition, involving the reader in violent dislocations in time as it moves between the two periods. 'Ivy Gripped the Steps' (1945) moves between a remembered Edwardian childhood and a house derelict through war to reveal the emotional paralysis of a man stunted in those remote golden boyhood days. In 'Mysterious Kôr' (1944) a woman turns from a London doubly defamiliarized by moonlight and Blitz to imagine an entire perfect ghost city.

Bowen placed 'Mysterious Kôr' last in the volume as the 'keystone' story. It was characteristic of her ambivalence towards fictional form that in the preface to *The Demon Lover* she not only defends her stories as characteristic of the fragmented and hallucinatory experience of the war, but suggests that they build into something larger. Mansfield had argued that Richardson's vast *Pilgrimage* could be disintegrated into nests of short stories; Bowen argues that her 'flying particles' form not a collection, but 'an organic whole', the war novel she had not yet written. As always she wishes to see her work both as supporting a continuous literary tradition, and as engaged in a modernist disintegration of that continuity, and the Second World War offered her her best context for those claims.

SYLVIA TOWNSEND WARNER

In Sylvia Townsend Warner's finest novel, *The Corner that Held Them* (1948), set in a fourteenth-century convent, there is an episode where an ecclesiastical official, journeying through the Fens to investigate some unpaid rents, stops for the night at a leper-house with a musical chaplain, and is introduced to a new music, the Ars Nova, with 'concords so sweet that they seemed to melt the flesh of his bones'.[48] When he next rides that way the leper-house has been burnt down during the Peasants' Revolt, and further experience of this innovative music is lost to him. The novel is permeated with this sense of the precarious survival of artistic products, the uncertainties governing their transmission. The Ars Nova survives outside the Fens, but the manuscript of a poem which might be 'one of the great epic poems of mankind, a poem that would wander from one generation to another' (ch. 13) is thrust into a pocket and lost, and an exquisitely embroidered altar-hanging, designed to restore a convent's fortunes, disappears in a stable. These exceptional products are the visible evidence of a whole community of everyday artistic practice; the international innovation of the Ars Nova is juxtaposed to the local reputation the nuns of the convent of Oby enjoy for their singing of plain-chant, 'vernacular tunes sung and forgotten in the space of a lifetime' (ch. 5). Art is the product of communal working practices and financial exigencies; when Oby loses its only gifted illuminator, other nuns continue to produce the illuminated psalters which are a commercial mainstay for the convent. In place of the singular suppressed genius of Woolf's Judith Shakespeare, Warner constructs a community of artistic practice at many levels, practice which is both gendered (the men encounter and practise the high art of epic poetry or the Ars Nova, the women vernacular tunes and embroidery) and classbased; for the rebels of 1381 the Ars Nova is a symbol of elitism and class oppression.

Warner's understanding of how high art survives within a context of the everyday working practices of anonymous artists predated her conversion to communism in the 1930s. From 1918 to 1930 she worked for a weekly salary of £3 for the Carnegie-funded Tudor Church Music project, which rescued, scored and collated the manuscripts of forgotten Tudor music lying in churches and cathedrals throughout Britain. In the poem 'Tudor Church Music' (1925) Warner describes herself as hesitating between two roles as she transcribes, questioning whether tourists passing through the churches perceive her as wearing 'the mask/Of the scholar deep in his book', or as a ghost of the anonymous scribes.[49] The poem obliterates the distinction, sinking the scholar's prestigious achievements within the anonymous activities which serve to preserve art. Anonymity was Warner's preferred stance; her 1935 collaboration with her partner, Valentine Ackland, *Whether a Dove or Seagull*, aspired to 'the freshness of anonymity', and in 1953, while translating Proust's *Contre Saint-Beuve*, she relished 'the peace and quiet of writing some other person's book'.[50] Her most important discussion of her work, the 1959 lecture 'Women as Writers', associates women with the cultivation of anonymity, describing how 'women as writers seem to be remarkably adept at vanishing out of their writing so that the quality of immediacy replaces them'.[51] Having defined this immediacy as gendered, and attributable to women's entry into art 'through the pantry-window', Warner then qualifies this in class terms by finding it also in those male writers, such as Keats or Clare or Shakespeare, who entered the tradition of high art from a social group not usually associated with its upkeep.

Warner's under-recognition as a writer may be partly attributed to the range of genres – poetry, novels, short stories, biography – she practised. The problems this diversity presents is compounded by her association with non-modernist forms; much of her poetry is pastoral, concerned with the revision and questioning of existing models, while her best novels are in the genre of historical fiction. Her writing of the 1930s, some of her best work, is focused on the Spanish Civil War, a literary terrain often treated as exclusively male. Her assimilation of women into larger groups of the subordinated, as in the 'Women as Writers' lecture, has qualified her reputation as a feminist writer. Beyond this there is an under-insistence in her writing, springing from her self-presentation as a journeywoman among the vast group of anonymous scribes, which has compromised her literary reputation. This self-presentation was gradually evolved. Warner's Harrow childhood, on the margins of the prestigious boys' public-school where her father taught, accustomed her to the 'pantry-window' vantage-point. Her first published work, an article in *Blackwood's Magazine* called 'Behind the Firing-Line by a Lady Worker' (1916), based on her first job, offered a differently anomalous social perspective. Warner later regretted her politically unenlightened war-work as one of the group of genteel blacklegs in munitions factories attacked by Sylvia Pankhurst in *The Home Front*.

In her first published book, the collection of poems *The Espalier* (1925), she associated herself as poet with the anonymous scribes whose work she was currently transcribing. Her pastoralism is identified not only with a nostalgia for rural life but for the artistic forms of that life. Many of the poems are pastiche ballads, grave epitaphs and songs, narratives of betrayed maidens and churchyards, designed as if to vanish into the vast anonymity of the folk tradition. The writers Warner admires and imitates – Crabbe, Clare, Hardy – are those who emerge directly into high art from that anonymity. In 'Wish in Spring' she compares the 'piteous human care' which arranges poems 'on the shelf' (p. 83) with the fluid creativity of the natural world, and she aspires to a poetry which seems nearest to sinking back into that natural world. In her second collection, *Time Importuned* (1928), the ballads are interspersed with poems claiming a more distinct heredity. 'The Load of Fern' recalls Robert Bridges's 'A Passerby', and beyond that Keats's 'To Autumn', to affirm the value of a poetic tradition which continually seeks to renew its means of discussing the continuities of rural life. In 'Allegra' Warner uses another churchyard ballad to embrace both her own birthplace, Harrow, and a favourite but non-pastoral poet, Byron, in the folk tradition; the use as speaker of the ghost of Byron's illegitimate daughter, Allegra, buried at Harrow, allows Warner to claim an oblique descent as Byron's poetic child working in a different tradition. By the end of the 1920s she had adopted a rural life in Dorset; her long poem in heroic couplets, *Opus 7* (1931), pastiches Crabbe to illuminate a countryside devastated by postwar instability and unemployment.

Between her first two volumes of poetry Warner published her first and most commercially successful novel, *Lolly Willowes or the Loving Huntsman* (1926), in which she used witchcraft as a metaphor to reconstruct the secret life of one of the anonymous thousands of redundant women, 'all over England, all over Europe, women living and growing old, as common as blackberries and as unregarded'.[52] She sent a copy to the scholar Margaret Murray, whose *The Witch Cult in Western Europe* (1921) was one of her sources (*Letters*, p. 9). Murray's widely influential thesis was that the witches of early modern Europe were the surviving priestesses of a pre-Christian cult, underground but still powerful. An eminent Egyptologist who bitterly resented her comparative lack of recognition, and made a late career swerve into Renaissance history, her argument that elderly female victims were really figures of occult puissance had an obvious reference to her own situation.[53] Warner's narrative relishes Murray's fantasy of an access of secret power and status for women. Where Mayor's *The Rector's Daughter* had treated the lives of redundant women as tragedy, Warner's comedy discovers the secret sources of power in the spinster's usual appurtenances of jam-making and cats. Lolly is a typical product of the middle-class Victorian family; for her father 'a stuffed ermine which he had known as a boy was still his ideal of the enchanted princess' (ch. 1). Functionless in the post-war world, she settles in a country cottage and rediscovers the secret life of the countryside. Warner's treatment of Murray's thesis, however, remains satirically unconvinced; the meetings of the local coven suffer from the banality of ordinary social events, and the companionable Devil, manifesting himself in Lawrentian guises as huntsman, gamekeeper and gardener, proves a slippery concept, realizable only in death.

The success of *Lolly Willowes* drew on the 1920s interest in spinsters, and on the popularity of fantasy for exploring gender relationships. Lolly's rediscovery of a lost countryside, based on Warner's own decision to root herself in Dorset, also tapped the public enthusiasm for novels of rural life. Warner was established as a known writer, but her 1927 earnings of £1,284 were to be her financial peak.[54] Her second novel, *Mr Fortune's Maggot* (1927), traced the gradual realization of a missionary on a remote Pacific island that his love for a young man, his only convert, is human rather than spiritual. Warner's account of her source, a volume of memoirs by a forgotten woman missionary once read in Paddington Public Library, exemplifies her major theme, the precarious and unexpected ways in which records of human experience survive (*Letters*, p. 10). The novel's poignant emphasis on the secret lives of the unregarded seemed consistent with the preoccupations of *Lolly Willowes*, but her very literary third novel, *The True Heart* (1929), a transposition of the story of Cupid and Psyche into a cross-class romance of the Victorian period, with Persephone, queen of the under-world, figuring as Queen Victoria, dissipated the momentum established by her first novel.

Summer Will Show (1936) was the first of the three mature political and historical novels which were Warner's major achievement. A celebration of the coming out of a genteel Englishwoman to lesbianism and communism, it draws on the partnership with Ackland, membership of the Communist Party (CP) from 1935, and local work as a CP organizer. Where *The Well of Loneliness* laments the social oppression of biological diversity, *Summer Will Show* celebrates a coming out interactive with revolutionary activities in the wider society. The novel is set in Paris during the 1848 Revolution; for Warner the genre of historical fiction is important in enabling the writer to revise the existing perceptions of history which govern political behaviour. As a CP organizer she distributed to local agricultural workers copies of the Hammonds' *The Village Labourer*, the alternative history of the expropriation of the rural population.[55] In her novel she revises influential fictional models of revolutionary encounters, notably Flaubert's *L'Education*

Sentimentale (1869), which traces personal and political disillusion through the 1848 Revolution, and Bennett's *The Old Wives' Tale* (1908), in which an Englishwoman called Sophia pursues her personal and professional interests in politically indifferent juxtaposition to the Paris Commune.

Warner's Sophia makes a very different journey to a Paris of erotic and political enlightenment. The first, English, section is pastiche Victorian novel, familiar and conventional though informed by an active questioning of gender and racial identities. Sophia's successive losses of the husband, property and children which give her social identity are juxtaposed to the startlingly anomalous figure of her bastard mulatto cousin, Caspar, for whom no social identity can be imagined. In the second section, with Sophia's arrival in Paris to reclaim her errant husband from his lover, the Jewish actress, Minna, the narrative escapes purposefully from elegant pastiche of past novels into a different kind of fiction. The passage which carries the weight of this shift is Minna's narrative of her Lithuanian childhood and flight from a pogrom. Minna's dynamic and entrancing narrative, infused with an immediate experience of political realities, exemplifies the power of women to construct their own stories, and achieve personal and political liberation through doing so. Sophia, freed from the frigid conventions which have constrained her speech, responds with a narrative of her own life, and for the rest of the novel the two women's mutual love develops in relation with their political revolutionary activities. The novel's celebration of Sophia's liberation into sexual and political fulfilment is qualified by the failure of the Revolution. Minna is killed by Caspar, for whom finally a role as soldier has been found, and Sophia survives, protected by her rank, to read another liberating narrative, the Communist Manifesto. This conclusion questions the relation of the liberated personal life to political commitment. The death of the artist Minna frees Sophia's capabilities for complete concentration on the Manifesto, the opening lines of which provide the novel's last paragraphs.

In 1936 Warner made her first visit to Spain, to work for an ambulance unit in Barcelona; her second visit was in 1937 as a delegate for the International Congress of Writers in Defence of Culture in Madrid. The two visits inspired the most considerable oeuvre by an English woman writer focused on the Spanish Civil War, most importantly *After the Death of Don Juan* (1938), the most under-rated of her novels. Warner described it as 'a good book . . . swamped by 1938–39 events' (*Letters*, p. 303). Her definition of it as 'an allegory or what you will of the political chemistry of the Spanish War' (*Letters*, p. 51) further explains its failure. This novel is not, like *Summer Will Show*, a narrative of personal bourgeois liberation; the narrative shifts its focus from the upper-class protagonists with whom it opens to revolution as experienced by the people. As in the preceding novel, but with a more explicit emphasis on the need for artistic forms to adapt to circumstance, the narrative switches genre, from upper-class comedy, making elegant satirical play with social conventions, to popular tragedy. The story, set in eighteenth-century Spain, continues that of the Mozart–Da Ponte *Don Giovanni*; those characters who survive the end of the opera travel from Seville through a countryside which entirely fails to conform to the pastoral idyll they expect. Their journey traces the exposure of an insulated high art to the popular world. The intermediate text is Bernard Shaw's Don Juan play, *Man and Superman* (1903); Shaw's comparison of Juan with the Nietzschean superman informs Warner's treatment of him as the embodiment of fascism, reappearing after his supposed death to suppress a peasants' rebellion on the estates of his more liberal father. The novel's great strength is the fluency of its move from comedy to tragedy as the peasants' more pressing concerns crowd out the upper-class intrigues of the beginning.

The final exchange of dialogue is between two peasants. ' "We have lived in a very small place, Diego". "We have lived in Spain." ' Warner's best poems of the Spanish Civil War are short lyrics celebrating places of waiting before the engagement with vital activity; 'Waiting at Cerbere' (1939), 'Journey to Barcelona' and 'Port Bou' (both 1936) describe distinctive locations of this moment of transition from the mundane to the crucial, as in 'Benicasim' (1938):

> Here for a little we pause.
> The air is heavy with sun and salt and colour.
> On palm and lemon-tree, on cactus and oleander
> a dust of dust and salt and pollen lies.
> And the bright villas
> sit in a row like perched macaws
> and rigid and immediate yonder
> the mountains rise. (*Collected Poems*, p. 35)

Warner's Spanish works are infused with a new urgency and conciseness, which is found also in love poems such as 'Drawing you heavy with sleep' (1935) and 'Under the sudden blue' (1939). During this period she wrote many political articles for left-wing journals, and short stories, topical such as those collected in *A Garland of Straw* (1943), or fantasies celebrating the power of narration to liberate as in *The Cats' Cradle-Book* (1940). These works were products of the decade from 1935 to 1945 when her political commitment was at its highest, and evidence of the way that commitment informed her work.

Between 1942 and 1946 Warner wrote *The Corner that Held Them* (1948), a historical novel tracing the fortunes of the Fenland convent of Oby from the Black Death to the Peasants' Revolt. It had roots in her Spanish experience; her 1936 article 'Barcelona', in the *Left Review*, reflects on the relation of Church and people as it describes the gutted churches of Barcelona. The rescue of a valuable altar-hanging, a symbol of the commercial value of works of art, inspires an episode in the novel.[56] Warner's depiction of a religious community, with 'no religion, but a great deal of financial worry and ambition and loneliness' (*Letters*, p. 79), follows the materialist emphasis of Eileen Power's *Medieval English Nunneries*, describing the political intrigues, financial exigencies, pastimes and occasional onset of accidie in a backwater convent. The novel's major source, however, was Warner's experience of the Second World War, and war-work in Dorset. It describes the marginal experience of crisis by a community of women working together, when men are largely absent, at the domestic problems of making ends meet, and the drudgery of bureaucratic routines. Warner originally planned to call it *People Growing Old* (*Letters*, p. 91), a title at odds with the novel's prevalent tone of satirical comedy, but suggestive of the depiction of lives lived under a pressure more mundane but more relentless than that described in her Spanish works. Like Woolf in *Between the Acts*, Warner explores a fiction which moves from the individual to the group; 'it has no plot, and its characters are innumerable and insignificant' she wrote (*Letters*, p. 91). In describing a phase in the history of an institution as it survives through a period of crisis, the novel draws on the political awareness of her 1930s writing, and on her earlier exploration of the lives of redundant women in *Lolly Willowes*, to produce a novel which, like *Between the Acts* or *The Heat of the Day*, responds distinctively to the experience of the Second World War.

REBECCA WEST

At the beginning of her most achieved work, *Black Lamb and Grey Falcon* (1942), Rebecca West distinguishes between idiocy and lunacy:

> Idiocy is the female defect: intent on their private lives, women follow their fate through a darkness deep as that cast by malformed cells in the brain. It is no worse than the male defect which is lunacy: they are so obsessed by public affairs that they see the world as by moonlight, which shows the outline of every object but not the details indicative of their nature.[57]

The occasion of West's definition is the news of the assassination of the King of Yugoslavia in 1934, which she hears in a London hospital. A nurse's response to her distress is to enquire sympathetically if the King had been a personal friend. In identifying the nurse's response as idiocy, West is making one of the dizzying, unreasonable leaps which characterize her writing; there might be many explanations of the nurse's response, such as a heavy work-schedule, republican tendencies, a different grasp of the political realities. Nonetheless the opposition between idiocy, and the lunacy of the assassination, sustains the long following investigation into the role of gender wars in the European situation in the 1930s. Like Woolf's *Three Guineas, Black Lamb* is an attempt, as fascism conquers Europe, to rescue the discussion of gender issues from relegation as a minor topic, by demonstrating its relevance to the European situation. Unlike Woolf she sees this situation as the effect of both sexes following their defining manias, and her account of her journey with her husband around Yugoslavia explores the variety of manifestations of these manias. The book is the culminating product of a career spent exploring postures in the wars of gender.

Cicily Fairfield began her career writing for the feminist *Freewoman* and the socialist *Clarion* between 1911 and 1917, testing out polemical stances and the rhetorical possibilities for a female voice raised in anger and derision. To help her she took the name of the heroine of Ibsen's *Rosmersholm*, a role she had played during her brief acting career. It was an interesting choice, for, though Ibsen's Rebecca begins as an ardent radical, she learns that she cannot dispose cleanly and painlessly of the past. West's second novel, *The Judge* (1922), was to revolve around the opposition between an ardent, naive, young suffragette and an older woman imprisoned by her past suffering. In her early writing West created more successfully than any other woman a flexible polemical voice, which contrived to take advantage both of male swagger and authority, and of a persistent feminine puncturing of male pretension. It was a voice of epigram and digression, and consistently and thoroughly unfair to its targets.[58]

Her first book was *Henry James* (1916), a critical study of the great man published shortly after his death, which placed her as an iconoclast, refusing to take canonical reputations on trust, and exploring the possibilities for a young female critic probing the reputation of an acknowledged master. The long title essay of *The Strange Necessity* (1928) begins in another act of iconoclasm, this time towards one of the great masters of modernism. The essay begins with West's account of buying a volume of Joyce's poetry from Sylvia Beach's Shakespeare Bookshop on the Left Bank in Paris. The self-congratulatory reverence induced in her by the purchase, and by its fashionable context, is punctured when she discovers that the first poem she reads, 'Alone', is bad. The discovery leads to a long reverie on the absolute necessity of art, in which West's 'persistent, nagging preoccupation with *Ulysses*' is explored in the context of a walk around Paris.[59] As in the stream of consciousness fictions of Sinclair and Richardson, the intellectual preoccupations are very firmly embedded in the general context of West's experience. When she continues her meditation on Joyce while trying on a hat or eating strawberries, she suggests that modernism, like its predecessors, has established gender hierarchies. In reordering the relations of the intellectual and the sensuous, in treating male art in the context of female concerns, in outraging the good taste which says you do not pick on the lapses of great men, in comparing the deracinated modern artist with Al Capone, West is challenging the accumulating dignity of male modernism from the continuing playfulness of female modernism. The voice of the essay is similar to that of *A Room of One's Own*, the light, confident tone of a sensible and unpretending woman. West concludes by confirming the greatness of Joyce, but the conclusion's juxtaposition with the next essay, 'Uncle Bennett', on the great relic of Edwardianism, serves as another reminder of the male tendency to create hierarchies.

West's earlier novels are formally diverse, experiments in finding fictional methods to represent the conflicts she discussed in her journalism. Her first, the novella *The Return of the Soldier* (1918), is the story of a war amnesiac's attempt to escape from the world of polarized gender roles, and class divisions. The story plays with the conventional expectations roused by the title. When Chris, a heroic young officer, returns to England, he has forgotten his beautiful country home, his elegant socialite wife, and the past fifteen years, and yearns for the suburban, married Margaret, from whom class divisions estranged him in his student days. The story is told by a third woman, his cousin, whose own suppressed love for him makes her more imaginatively capable than his wife in responding to the relationship. The narrator's efforts to overcome the aesthetic revulsion aroused by her first sight of the suburban Margaret, 'in a black hat with plumes whose sticky straw had but lately been renovated by something out of a little bottle bought at the chemist's',[60] direct the narrative, as we are gradually induced with her to forget that first impression for the Margaret reconstructed by Chris's memories. The novella imagines through Chris's amnesia an ideal world in which love can survive class, time and change, and in which Chris, as his ambivalent name suggests, is not bound by the obligations of a ruling-class male. At the end, however, the three women collude to restore his memories of his class and marriage, and return him to those obligations in the name of 'the truth'. As the narrator recognizes, 'bad as we were, we were yet not the worst circumstance of his return. When we had lifted the yoke of our embraces from his shoulders he would go back to that flooded trench in Flanders' (ch. 6). *The Return of the Soldier* is a fable of gender conflict, but West has deliberately cut herself off from her major strength, the authorial voice she evolved in her early journalism years. The story, told from the limited point of view of the genteel narrator, who lives

212

in a world of exquisite appearances, unarticulated class assumptions and suppressed communications, is too close to pastiche James.

West's long second novel, *The Judge*, rejects the restraint, economy and limited point of view of her first novel. Woolf interpreted the novel's Victorian prolixity as a necessary exorcism of West's love affair with H.G. Wells. 'Poor Rebecca West's novel bursts like an overstuffed sausage. She pours it all in, and one is covered with flying particles . . . But this irreticence does not make me think any the worse of her human qualities' (*Letters*, II, p. 548). In this novel West attempts to understand the relations between her early confident and combative life as a feminist, and her later experiences as unmarried mother. The novel's main experiment, a sudden switching of protagonists halfway through, is part of this attempt. The first half of the novel centres on Ellen, a young suffragette in prewar Edinburgh, whose naive enthusiasm for suffrage demonstrations and martyred leaders is seen in the context of the prurient enjoyment of the spectacle of suffrage by respectable males; 'to discover a woman excited about an intellectual thing was like coming on her bathing; her cast-off femininity affected him as a heap of her clothes on the beach might have done'.[61] The novel's main strength lies in its appreciation here of the currents of sexual excitement running unarticulated below the surface of suffrage activity. Halfway through Ellen meets Marian, her prospective mother-in-law, and the narrative abandons her for the older woman, for whom the meeting triggers painful memories of a life of social ostracism as an unmarried mother. Marian's violent and disordered reveries are used to outline the self-betrayals which prewar feminism failed to address; when the narrative rejoins Ellen in the last pages, she is facing a similar future to Marian's, and the feminist movement's gains are questioned.

With her third novel, the rococo fantasy *Harriet Hume* (1929), West moves back to deliberately imposed restraints, and to the limited point of view of a self-serving politician troubled by vague intimations that women may be less marginal than he has always supposed. The book develops through five scenes in each of which the rising politician, Arnold Condorex, encounters the only other character, his discarded lover, Harriet. Arnold inhabits a fantasy of absolute polarity between the sexes. He is a Great Man in Napoleonic mode and has based his career on creating a new area of political expertise around a non-existent Indian state. He prides himself on his scientific understanding of women, and Harriet, seen entirely through his eyes, is quintessentially feminine, decorative, marginal, associated with muslins and fruit, and so charmingly myopic she is unable to focus properly on the political columns in the daily papers. Although Arnold is partly derived from West's experience of two men of power in her affairs with Wells, and with the press magnate, Beaverbrook, his name may be derived from 'Uncle'

Bennett, whose pride in his female characters West had earlier criticized, describing his Hilda Lessways as 'not so much a study of a woman based upon observation, but a rash deduction from a couple of hairpins'.[62]

Harriet's profession as pianist, as interpreter of great masters, seems appropriately feminine to Arnold, but he is increasingly troubled by her non-professional interpretative powers, her feminine intuition demonstrated by her empathetic knowledge of his political secrets and fears. His reactions to her intuitions are violent and the couple are increasingly estranged. Only the fifth scene imagines a possibility of reconciliation, and that, we gradually realize, is taking place after the death of the antagonists. *Harriet Hume* appeared in the same year as *Orlando*, but, where Woolf's fantasy explores a world of androgyny, West's imagines a world in which the powerful male and the intuitive female, the lunatic and the idiot, are, indeed, as totally polarized as many suppose. It is a fragile world in which neither manages to survive, but its distinct though limited charms are playfully explored. It was West's favourite of her novels, and, although she had again cut herself off from the strengths of her narrative persona, the fantasy allowed a flexibility not present in the two earlier novels.

In 1933 West wrote another iconoclastic attack, a short biography, *St Augustine*, based largely on her reading of the *Confessions*, and influenced by her own confessional experiences in a series of psychoanalytic sessions in 1927. She argues for Augustine's complicity in the collapse of Roman order in North Africa, and the study revolves around his relation with his mother, St Monica, tracing thence the hysterical sexuality and obsession with the duality of guilt and expiation which West saw as the baneful Augustinian legacy. In its fascination with understanding European history in the context of disordered gender relations the book is a preface to *Black Lamb and Grey Falcon*. West's major work emerged from three journeys she made to Yugoslavia in the 1930s for the British Council, and was completed in the context of a Yugoslavia already engulfed in war. In creating a work which moved between personal reminiscence and imaginative reconstruction of the cultural and psychological history of the Yugoslavian lands, West was able to escape the limits of genre which she had observed in her novels, and make full use of the versatile, volatile persona she had developed in her journalism.

In the prologue West traces the roots of her own fascination with Central Europe to hearing in childhood of the assassinations of the Empress Elizabeth of Austria and of Queen Draga of Serbia. Newspaper stories of glamorous, murdered, female royals established Central Europe for West as a region in which the connections of political and sexual antagonisms were evident. In her Yugoslavian journeys she traces the complicity of her 'idiot' preoccupations with royal personalities in the 'lunacy' of high politics. The journey which West narrates, a synthesis of her three journeys, is punctuated by a series of dialogues between her and her two male companions; these replay the race and gender misunderstandings written around them in the conflicts of Yugoslavia. West, who finds the journey a profound emotional experience, seeks to wake a corresponding emotion in her husband, the banker Henry Andrews, who is presented as always intent on analysing and summarizing his experiences. A mine of recondite information, who prefers to plan the day ahead, he frequently rebukes his wife for her tendencies to apocalyptic rhetoric, but his own desire to categorize is shown as a mild form of lunacy. ' "I will sit here and look at the maps" said my husband, who is much given to that masculine form of auto-hypnosis' (p. 203). Across the landscape of Yugoslavia the couple play out in minor comic form the conflicts written tragically around them. The third member of the party is Constantine, their Serbian Jewish guide, a member of the Yugoslav government and personification of the national conflict. In his official capacity he is committed to maintaining that the Yugoslav federal system is working, and to pointing to evidence of this, but as Serb and Jew he is riven by conflicting racial fears. His divided responses are the major link between the Andrews' comic marital argument and the tragic internal tensions of Yugoslavia.

The arguments between the travellers are the continual foreground as they travel south and east into a world of polarized gender identities. 'It is strange, it is heartrending, to stray into a world where men are still men and women still women' (p. 208). *Black Lamb*, like *Harriet Hume*, experiments with a completely polarized world, a fantasy of what it would be like if gender identities were unmixed. In Bosnia the narrative luxuriates in the extreme femininity, drenched in attar of roses, of a woman dubbed 'the Bulbul', and then turns immediately to a peasant woman. Invited to pose, this woman 'arranged herself before the camera with her chin forward, her arms crossed, her weight on her heels, acting a man's pride; I think nothing in her life had ever suggested to her that there is a woman's kind of pride' (p. 403). The journey concludes in the extravagant fantasy of Montenegro, where landladies explain the toilet arrangements in blank verse, and a guide's male sense of honour obliges him to take the party down a lethal precipice when he misses the road.

The journey itself is in the form of a quest to discover the significance of the occult figures of the lamb and the falcon. Like Eliot's *The Waste Land* it travels from the aridity of modern life to discover meaning in the dark lands, and moves away from the West, and back into history, through a series of reconstructions of seminal events. The travellers' arrival in Sarajevo invokes a long, blackly comic narrative of 1914 in which the Archduke Franz Ferdinand's naive and incompetent assassins converge on their quarry for a murder in which the most complicit person is the victim. His troubled marriage and the half million animals he has shot are central to West's account of how 'at last the bullets had been coaxed out of the reluctant revolver to the bodies of the eager victims' (p. 361). Further east Belgrade evokes a story of an earlier assassination, that of King Alexander and Queen Draga in 1903, the story which had fascinated the ten-year-old West. Here the assassins were acting to avenge the country's honour against Draga's alleged sexual improprieties, and the story climaxes in their bungling progress through the palace's tasteless bric-à-brac to the cupboard where the royal couple are hiding. For the adult West the episode is grim farce, an example of a polity which has lost meaning and seeks to recover it in a pantomime of male honour and female depravity. These two grotesque comic narratives are trailers for the third narrative in Old Serbia where the meaning of the lamb and falcon are revealed. West notes a young man incongruously holding a black lamb in a hotel lobby in Belgrade, and at the Sheep's Field in Macedonia she watches the ritual slaughter of black lambs in a fertility rite, of which the Archduke's mass slaughter of animals, to compensate for his inferior status and troubled marriage, was a distant, elaborated echo. In Old Serbia at the Field of Blackbirds she hears the story of the falcon, which every schoolboy is taught to sing, of how in 1389 before the Turkish defeat of the Serbs, King Lazar chose the falcon's gift of a martyr's crown for himself and his people rather than success in battle.

For West this legend and its allure are the final explanation of the pantomime of extravagantly delineated gender identities of honour and sacrifice she has witnessed. These polarized identities, glamorous and charming though they often are, are revealed as the frozen postures of men and women unable to advance beyond the enchanting legends they created long ago. As in *Harriet Hume* death is the cost of this indulgence in extremes of masculinity and femininity. In the epilogue West, writing in wartime, extends the lesson. Women and men must look beyond the reassuring postures of idiocy and lunacy, commemmorated in myths and legends continually recreated, and understand how Europe's conflicts are born in the retreat into such postures.

NOTES

Place of publication is London, unless otherwise stated.

1. Katherine Mansfield, *Notes on Novelists* (Constable, 1930), p. 101.
2. Elizabeth Bowen, 'A Living Writer: Katherine Mansfield', in *The Mulberry Tree: Writings of Elizabeth Bowen*, ed. Hermione Lee (Virago, 1986), p. 76.

3. These stories were collected in *Something Childish and Other Stories* (1924).
4. Bowen, 'A Living Writer', p. 79.
5. Mansfield, *Notes on Novelists*, p. 219.
6. Mansfield, *Notes on Novelists*, pp. 36–8.
7. 'At the Bay' and 'The Voyage' were collected in *The Garden Party and Other Stories* (1922), 'The Doll's House' in *The Doves' Nest and Other Stories* (1923).
8. 'Je Ne Parle Pas Français' was collected in *Bliss and Other Stories* (1920), 'Miss Brill' and 'The Life of Ma Parker' in *The Garden Party*.
9. See S.P. Rosenbaum, *Edwardian Bloomsbury: The Early Literary History of the Bloomsbury Group* (Macmillan, 1994), pp. 339–90.
10. *The Letters of Sylvia Townsend Warner*, ed. William Maxwell (Chatto and Windus, 1982), p. 73. Subsequent quotations are from this volume.
11. Virginia Woolf, *Roger Fry: A Biography* (Hogarth Press, 1940), p. 158.
12. Virginia Woolf, *Jacob's Room* (Harmondsworth: Penguin, 1992), ch. 12.
13. Virginia Woolf, *Moments of Being*, ed. Jeanne Schulkind (Hogarth Press, 1985), p. 210.
14. Virginia Woolf, *The Voyage Out* (Harmondsworth: Penguin, 1992), ch. 16.
15. *Times Literary Supplement*, 6 March 1919, p. 123.
16. Virginia Woolf, *Night and Day* (Harmondsworth: Penguin, 1992), ch. 27.
17. Mansfield, *Notes on Novelists*, pp. 107–11.
18. Erich Auerbach, 'The Brown Stocking', in *Mimesis: The Representation of Reality in Western Literature* (Princeton: Princeton University Press, 1968), pp. 525–53.
19. Woolf, *Moments of Being*, p. 81.
20. Virginia Woolf, *To the Lighthouse* (Harmondsworth: Penguin, 1992), I, ch. 11.
21. See Toril Moi, *Sexual/Textual Politics: Feminist Literary Theory* (Routledge, 1988), pp. 1–18.
22. Leonard Woolf, *Downhill All the Way: An Autobiography of the Years 1919–1939* (Hogarth Press, 1967), p. 143.
23. Virginia Woolf, 'The Narrow Bridge of Art', in *Granite and Rainbow* (Hogarth Press, 1958), p. 21.
24. Virginia Woolf, 'Madame de Sévigné', in *The Death of the Moth and Other Essays* (Hogarth Press, 1942), p. 41.
25. Virginia Woolf, *The Pargiters: The Novel-Essay Portion of the Years*, ed. Mitchell Leaska (Hogarth Press, 1978).
26. Virginia Woolf, *The Years* (Harmondsworth: Penguin, 1992), 'Present Day'.
27. See Gillian Beer, 'Virginia Woolf and Prehistory', in *Arguing with the Past: Essays in Narrative from Woolf to Sidney* (Routledge, 1989), pp. 59–82.
28. Jean Rhys, *Quartet* (Harmondsworth: Penguin, 1987), ch. 16.
29. Rebecca West, 'The Tosh Horse', in *The Strange Necessity* (Cape, 1928), p. 323.
30. Jean Rhys, *Voyage in the Dark* (Harmondsworth: Penguin, 1975), pt. 2, ch. 5.
31. Coral Ann Howells, *Jean Rhys* (Hemel Hempstead: Harvester Wheatsheaf, 1991), pp. 29–41.
32. Jean Rhys, *Tigers Are Better Looking* (Harmondsworth: Penguin, 1972), p. 39.
33. Jean Rhys, *Good Morning, Midnight* (Harmondsworth: Penguin, 1975), pt. 4.
34. The original version of 'Vienne' is reprinted in *The Gender of Modernism: A Critical Anthology*, ed. Bonnie K. Scott (Bloomington: Indiana University Press, 1990), pp. 377–81; the expanded version is in *Tigers Are Better Looking*.
35. Jean Rhys, *After Leaving Mr Mackenzie* (Harmondsworth: Penguin, 1982), pt. 1, ch. 4.

36. The original ending is reprinted in *The Gender of Modernism*, pp. 381–9.
37. See Carole Angier, *Jean Rhys: Life and Work* (Harmondsworth: Penguin, 1992), pp. 370–3.
38. *Jean Rhys: Letters 1931–66*, ed. Francis Wyndham and Diana Melly (Harmondsworth: Penguin, 1984), p. 156.
39. Jean Rhys, *Wide Sargasso Sea* (Harmondsworth: Penguin, 1970), pt. 3.
40. Graham Greene, *The Lawless Roads* (Harmondsworth: Penguin, 1982), pp. 157–8.
41. Elizabeth Bowen, *Bowen's Court* (Longmans, Green, 1942), p. 337.
42. Elizabeth Bowen, *The Hotel* (Cape, 1927), ch. 10.
43. *The Mulberry Tree*, p. 43. All quotations from Bowen articles are from this collection.
44. Phyllis Lassner, *Elizabeth Bowen* (Macmillan, 1990).
45. Elizabeth Bowen, *To the North* (Harmondsworth: Penguin, 1945), ch. 24.
46. Elizabeth Bowen, *The House in Paris* (Cape, 1971), pt. 2, ch. 6.
47. Elizabeth Bowen, *The Heat of the Day* (Cape, 1954), ch. 7.
48. Sylvia Townsend Warner, *The Corner that Held Them* (Virago, 1993), ch. 10.
49. *Collected Poems of Sylvia Townsend Warner*, ed. Claire Harman (Manchester: Carcanet, 1982), p. 82. All quotations are from this.
50. *Letters*, p. 154.
51. *Collected Poems*, p. 269.
52. Sylvia Townsend Warner, *Lolly Willowes* (Leipzig: Tauchnitz, 1930), pt. 3.
53. Margaret Murray, *My First Hundred Years* (Kimber, 1963).
54. See Claire Harman, *Sylvia Townsend Warner: A Biography* (Chatto and Windus, 1982), p. 66.
55. See Wendy Mulford, *This Narrow Place: Sylvia Townsend Warner and Valentine Ackland: Life, Letters and Politics 1930–51* (Pandora, 1987), p. 67.
56. Sylvia Townsend Warner, 'Barcelona', in *The Penguin Book of the Spanish Civil War*, ed. Valentine Cunningham (Harmondsworth: Penguin, 1980), pp. 136–41.
57. Rebecca West, *Black Lamb and Grey Falcon: A Journey Through Yugoslavia* (Edinburgh: Canongate, 1993), p. 3.
58. Much of her early journalism is collected in *The Young Rebecca West: Writings of Rebecca West 1911–17*, ed. Jane Marcus (Macmillan/Virago, 1982).
59. West, *The Strange Necessity*, pp. 13–199.
60. Rebecca West, *The Return of the Soldier* (Nisbet, 1919), ch. 1.
61. Rebecca West, *The Judge* (Hutchinson, 1922), ch. 1.
62. *The Young Rebecca West*, p. 311.

Glossary

Dame: from 1917 women could be awarded the title of Dame of the Order of the British Empire for distinguished achievement, and assume the title 'Dame' before their names. The title is the female equivalent of a knighthood.

Lady writer: a derogatory term much in use in the interwar period and implying that the writer lacked proper professional involvement with her craft.

Land girl: a term used for women who volunteered for agricultural labour in the First World War, or were conscripted to it in the Second World War.

Modernism: a term used to describe and group a number of movements in literature and art in the earlier twentieth century, which emphasized experimentalism, artistic rebirth, and discontinuity with the art of the immediately preceding generations. In literature this emphasis on rebirth included rejection of the continuities, rationality and narrative structures of Victorian writing, in favour of the use of image, myth, disrupted chronology, and the 'stream of consciousness' with its exploration of the fluidity of identity. Modernism's emphases on the unconscious and irrational, and on cultural relativism, were informed by the developing sciences of psychology and anthropology. Modernist writing sought to involve the reader in difficulties of interpretation, and modernists presented themselves as an avant-garde addressing a select readership.

Pastiche: work in the manner of a particular writer or genre, but without the ridiculing intention of parody. The purpose of such work may be homage or a questioning of the work's relation with what it imitates.

219

Redundant women: also surplus women. These terms were both used to describe unmarried middle-class women, and alluded to these women's perceived lack of social function. The imbalance in numbers of women and men of marriageable age, and the supposed problem of the redundant woman, first became a topic for comment after the national census of 1851, and remained a popular topic into the 1920s. The term was not applied to working-class women, who, when unmarried, would be engaged in domestic or industrial labour recognized as necessary.

Separate spheres: the term used to describe Victorian concepts of gender complementarity, where women's activity was seen as properly confined within the private, domestic sphere, with men dominant in the public sphere. Many women in the earlier twentieth century perceived themselves as assaulting this concept.

Chronology

Date	Works by Women	Other Literary Events	Historical/Cultural Events
1900	Corelli, *The Master Christian* Ward, *Eleanor*	Conrad, *Lord Jim* Boots Library launched Net Book Agreement in force	Boer War continues Labour Party founded Boxer Rising in China Planck elaborates quantum theory
1901	Burnett, *The Making of a Marchioness* Nesbit, *The Wouldbegoods*	Hardy, *Poems of Past and Present* Kipling, *Kim* Rowntree, *Poverty* World's Classics launched	Victoria dies; Edward VII accedes First transatlantic wireless transmissions
1902	Ayrton, *The Electric Arc* Meynell, *Later Poems* Nesbit, *Five Children and It* Potter, *The Tale of Peter Rabbit*	Bennett, *Anna of the Five Towns* Conrad, *Heart of Darkness* Doyle, *The Hound of the Baskervilles* James, *The Wings of the Dove* *Times Literary Supplement* launched	Boer War ends Education Act provides for secondary education Australian women win vote

1903	Harrison, *Prolegomena to the Study of
	  Greek Religion*
	Potter, *The Tailor of Gloucester*; *The
	  Tale of Squirrel Nutkin*
		James, *The Ambassadors*
		Moore, *Principia Ethica*
		Yeats, *In the Seven Woods*
			Pankhurst founds WSPU
			Wright brothers make first successful
			  aircraft flight

Date	Works by Women	Other Literary Events	Historical/Cultural Events
1904	Jekyll, *Classic English Gardens* Robins, *The Magnetic North* Sinclair, *The Divine Fire*	Barrie, *Peter Pan* Conrad, *Nostromo* James, *The Golden Bowl*	Russo–Japanese War Rutherford and Soddy outline general theory of radioactivity Workers' Educational Association founded
1905	Burnett, *The Little Princess* Orczy, *The Scarlet Pimpernel*	Forster, *Where Angels Fear to Tread* Wallace, *The Four Just Men*	Abortive revolution in Russia First suffragette jailings Einstein outlines special theory of relativity
1906	Bowen, *The Viper of Milan* Brazil, *The Fortunes of Philippa*	Galsworthy, *The Man of Property* Kipling, *Puck of Pook's Hill* Everyman's Library launched	Liberals win election landslide Dreyfus cleared
1907	Bell, *The Desert and the Sown* Glyn, *Three Weeks* Robins, *The Convert* Queen Victoria, *Letters*	Conrad, *The Secret Agent* Synge, *The Playboy of the Western World* *Cambridge History of English Literature* launched	Boy Scouts founded Norwegian women win vote
1908	Hamilton, *Diana of Dobson's* Leverson, *Love's Shadow* Murray, *Elementary Egyptian Grammar* Richardson, H.H., *Maurice Guest*	Bennett, *The Old Wives Tale* Grahame, *The Wind in the Willows* *English Review* launched	Suffragette activity intensifies Austria annexes Bosnia
1909	Barclay, *The Rosary* Hamilton, *Marriage as a Trade*	Wells, *Ann Veronica; Tono-Bungay*	Old age pensions for over-seventies Suffragette hunger strikes begin Girl Guides founded Bleriot flies Channel

1910	Richardson, H.H., *The Getting of Wisdom* Sinclair, *The Creators*	Edward VII dies; George V accedes First Labour Exchanges open Post-Impressionist Exhibition Miners' strike
	Bennett, *Clayhanger* Forster, *Howards End* Russell and Whitehead, *Principia Mathematica*	
1911	Burnett, *The Secret Garden* Mansfield, *In a German Pension* Schreiner, *Woman and Labour*	Parliament Act reduces powers of House of Lords First Official Secrets Act Copyright Act Agadir Crisis
	Conrad, *Under Western Eyes* Lawrence, *The White Peacock* *Freewoman* launched	
1912	Dell, *The Way of an Eagle* Harrison, *Themis* Potter, *The Tale of Mr Tod*	Miners', dockers' and general transport strikes National Health Insurance Act First Balkan War *Titanic* sinks X-ray crystallography begins
	Marsh, ed., *Georgian Poetry* *Poetry Review* launched	
1913	Belloc-Lowndes, *The Lodger* Reeves, *Round About a Pound a Week*	Cat and Mouse Act Second Balkan War Bohr models atom
	Lawrence, *Sons and Lovers* *New Statesman* launched	
1914	von Arnim, *The Pastor's Wife* Holme, *The Lonely Plough*	First World War begins (Aug.) Battles of Mons, Marne, Ypres Irish Home Rule Bill suspended
	Joyce, *Dubliners* Tressell, *The Ragged Trousered Philanthropists* Yeats, *Responsibilities*	
1915	Cornford, *Spring Morning* Hutchins, *Women in Modern Industry* Richardson, D., *Pointed Roofs* Wickham, *The Contemplative Quarry* Woolf, *The Voyage Out*	Defence of the Realm Act Dardanelles campaign *Lusitania* sunk Women's Institutes founded Einstein outlines general theory of relativity
	Buchan, *The Thirty-Nine Steps* Ford, *The Good Soldier* Lawrence, *The Rainbow* Maugham, *Of Human Bondage*	

Date	Works by Women	Other Literary Events	Historical/Cultural Events
1916	Garnett's Chekhov translations begin Kaye-Smith, *Sussex Gorse* Mew, *The Farmer's Bride*	Joyce, *A Portrait of the Artist as a Young Man* Shaw, *Pygmalion* *Wheels* launched by Sitwells *Vogue* launched	Conscription introduced Battles of Verdun, Jutland, Somme Dublin Easter Rising
1917	Meynell, *The Father of Women* Richardson, H.H., *Australia Felix* Webb, *Gone to Earth* Woolf, 'The Mark on the Wall'	Eliot, *Prufrock* *History* launched	US enters war (Apr.) Battle of Passchendaele (Jul.–Nov.) Russian Revolution (Oct.) Balfour Declaration on Jewish state
1918	Mansfield, 'Prelude' Stopes, *Married Love* West, *The Return of the Soldier*	Hopkins (posth.), *Poems* Strachey, *Eminent Victorians*	First World War ends (Nov.) Women over thirty win vote Influenza pandemic
1919	Clark, *Working Life of Women in the Seventeenth Century* Hull, *The Sheik* Richardson, D., *The Tunnel* Sinclair, Mary Olivier Woolf, *Night and Day*; 'Modern Fiction'	Keynes, *Economic Consequences of the Peace* Shaw, *Heartbreak House* Whitehead, *Principles of Natural Knowledge* *Children's Newspaper*, *Homes and Gardens*, *Peg's Paper* and *Schoolfriend* launched	Versailles Peace Conference Communist risings in Germany and Hungary Sex Disqualification (Removal) Act Nancy Astor becomes first woman MP First transatlantic flight
1920	von Arnim, *Vera* Christie, *The Mysterious Affair at Styles* Macaulay, *Potterism*	Eliot, *The Sacred Wood* Fry, *Vision and Design* Wells, *Outline of History* *Time and Tide* launched	League of Nations founded First public broadcasting stations opened American women win vote

1921	Dane, *A Bill of Divorcement*	Lawrence, *Women in Love* Russell, *The Analysis of Mind*	Separate Irish Parliaments established Stopes opens first family planning clinic
1922	Crompton, *Just-William* Mansfield, *The Garden Party* Power, *Medieval English Nunneries* Sitwell, *Facade* Woolf, *Jacob's Room*	Eliot, *The Waste Land* Joyce, *Ulysses* *Criterion* launched by Eliot *Good Housekeeping* launched	Irish Troubles: Free State established Italian Fascists take power BBC founded Insulin discovered Tutenkhamun's tomb opened
1923	Macaulay, *Told by an Idiot* Sayers, *Whose Body?* Woolf, 'Mr Bennett and Mrs Brown'	Lawrence, *Kangaroo* Wodehouse, *The Inimitable Jeeves*	USSR established Matrimonial Causes Act gives wives equality in divorce
1924	Kennedy, *The Constant Nymph* Mayor, *The Rector's Daughter* Rathbone, *The Disinherited Family* Webb, M., *Precious Bane*	Ford, *Parade's End* (–1928) Forster, *A Passage to India* Richards, *Principles of Literary Criticism* Shaw, *St Joan*	First Labour Government (Jan.–Oct.) Zinoviev Letter crisis British Empire Exhibition
1925	Brent-Dyer, *The School at the Chalet* Compton-Burnett, *Pastors and Masters* Russell, *Hypatia* Woolf, *Mrs Dalloway*; *The Common Reader* Young, *William*	Dearmer, ed., *Songs of Praise* Eliot, 'The Hollow Men' Whitehead, *Science and the Modern World*	Return to gold standard Unemployment Insurance Act
1926	Christie, *The Murder of Roger Ackroyd* Sackville-West, *The Land* Schreiner, *From Man to Man* Warner, *Lolly Willowes* Webb, B., *My Apprenticeship*	Lawrence, T.E., *Seven Pillars of Wisdom* Lawrence, D.H., *The Plumed Serpent* Milne, *Winnie the Pooh* Tawney, *Religion and the Rise of Capitalism*	General Strike (May) Miners' strike (May–Nov.) Adoption first legalized Council for Preservation of Rural England founded

225

Date	Works by Women	Other Literary Events	Historical/Cultural Events
1927	Bowen, *The Hotel* Lehmann, *Dusty Answer* Rhys, *The Left Bank* Waddell, *The Wandering Scholars* Woolf, *To the Lighthouse*	Dunne, *Experiment with Time* Powys, *Mr Weston's Good Wine* *Close Up* launched	German economy collapses Heisenberg outlines uncertainty principle Lindbergh flies Atlantic
1928	Hall, *The Well of Loneliness* Rhys, *Quartet* Strachey, *The Cause* West, *The Strange Necessity* Woolf, *Orlando*	Lawrence, *Lady Chatterley's Lover* (private printing) Sassoon, *Memoirs of a Foxhunting Man* Waugh, *Decline and Fall* Yeats, *The Tower* Completion of O.E.D. (1884–)	Women aged twenty-one to thirty win vote Fleming discovers penicillin Baird demonstrates colour TV and transatlantic TV transmission
1929	Allingham, *The Crime at Black Dudley* Bowen, *The Last September* West, *Harriet Hume* Woolf, *A Room of One's Own*	Graves, *Goodbye to All That* Priestley, *The Good Companions* Yeats, *The Winding Stair* Book Society founded	Wall Street Crash (Oct.) World economic crisis begins Second Labour Government takes office
1930	Cam, *The Hundred and the Hundred Rolls* Delafield, *The Provincial Lady* Pinchbeck, *Women Workers and the Industrial Revolution* Stephenson, *Bacterial Metabolism*	Auden, *Poems* Eliot, 'Ash Wednesday' Waugh, *Vile Bodies*	Gandhi begins Indian civil disobedience campaign CFCs, tampons and latex condoms first made
1931	Benson, *Tobit Transplanted* Cooperative Women's Guild, *Life as We Have Known It* Mitchison, *The Corn King and the Spring Queen*	Coward, *Cavalcade* Owen (posth.), *Poems*	National Government formed Labour Party expels PM Macdonald and other ministers Means test for dole introduced

	Pankhurst, *The Suffragette Movement* Rhys, *After Leaving Mr Mackenzie* Woolf, *The Waves*		Spanish Republic established Japan invades Manchuria
1932	Gibbons, *Cold Comfort Farm* Holtby, *Virginia Woolf* Leavis, *Fiction and the Reading Public*	Gibbon, *Sunset Song* Huxley, *Brave New World* Leavis, *New Bearings in English Poetry* *Scrutiny* launched *Oxford Companion to English Literature*	Nazis largest party after German elections Democrats win landslide in US elections British Union of Fascists founded Chadwick discovers neutron
1933	Brittain, *Testament of Youth* Robinson, *The Economics of Imperfect Competition* White, *Frost in May* Woolf, *Flush*	Greenwood, *Love on the Dole* Orwell, *Down and Out in Paris and London*	Unemployment peaks at 15 per cent Hitler becomes German Chancellor New Deal launched in US
1934	Bodkin, *Archetypal Patterns in Poetry* Holtby, *Women in a Changing Civilization* Jameson, *Company Parade* Jesse, *A Pin to See the Peepshow* Rhys, *Voyage in the Dark* Stark, *The Valleys of the Assassins*	Graves, *I Claudius* Toynbee, *Study of History* (–1954) Waugh, *A Handful of Dust*	Hitler becomes Führer Unemployment Act creates Assistance Boards Peace Pledge Union founded Vitamin C synthesized
1935	Bowen, *The House in Paris* Cooper, *We Have Come to a Country* Heyer, *Regency Buck*	Eliot, *Murder in the Cathedral* Left Book Club launched Penguin Books launched	Italy invades Abyssinia German Jews lose civil rights Radar developed by Watson-Watt DC3 first mass-produced commercial aircraft British Council founded

227

Date	Works by Women	Other Literary Events	Historical/Cultural Events
1936	Holtby, *South Riding* Lehmann, *The Weather in the Streets* Smith, *Novel on Yellow Paper* Warner, *Summer Will Show*	Auden, *Look Stranger* Keynes, *General Theory of Employment, Interest and Money* *New Writing* launched by Lehmanns	George V dies; Edward VIII accedes (Jan.) Abdication Crisis; George VI accedes (Dec.) Germany occupies Rhineland (Mar.) Spanish Civil War begins (Jul.) Jarrow March (Oct.) Sino-Japanese War begins (Dec.)
1937	Bottome, *The Mortal Storm* Jameson, 'New Documents' Richardson, D., *Pilgrimage* Smith, *A Good Time Was Had By All* Woolf, *The Years*	Auden and MacNeice, *Letters from Iceland* Caudwell, *Illusion and Reality* Orwell, *The Road to Wigan Pier* Tolkien, *The Hobbit* *Woman* launched	Guernica air raid (Apr.) Irish Free State becomes Eire Matrimonial Causes Act allows divorce for desertion and insanity Mass Observation launched Whittle develops first jet engine
1938	Bowen, *The Death of the Heart* du Maurier, *Rebecca* Warner, *After the Death of Don Juan* Woolf, *Three Guineas*	Greene, *Brighton Rock* Waugh, *Scoop* *Picture Post* launched	Germany annexes Austria (Mar.) Munich Crisis (Sept.) Germany occupies Czech Sudetenland (Oct.) Cristallnacht (Nov.)
1939	Godden, *Black Narcissus* Lascelles, *Jane Austen: Her Mind and Art* Rhys, *Good Morning, Midnight* Thompson, *Lark Rise*	Isherwood, *Goodbye to Berlin* Orwell, *Homage to Catalonia* Yeats, *Last Poems*	Fascists win Spanish Civil War (Mar.) Germany occupies Czechoslovakia (Mar.), signs non-aggression pact with USSR (Aug.), invades Poland (Sept.) Second World War begins (Sept.) Nuclear fission discovered by Hahn and Meitner

1940	Britain, *Testament of Friendship* Stark, *A Winter in Arabia*	Graves and Hodge, *The Long Weekend* Greene, *The Power and the Glory* Orwell, *Inside the Whale*	Germany occupies Norway, Denmark, Benelux, and (May) France Battle of Britain and Blitz Penicillin developed as antibiotic Krebs outlines citric acid cycle
1941	Bowen, *Look at All Those Roses* Woolf, *Between the Acts*	*c*.20m. books destroyed in London raids	Germany invades USSR (June) Pearl Harbor bombed; US enters war (Dec.)
1942	Blyton, *Five on a Treasure Island* Cable and French, *The Gobi Desert* West, *Black Lamb and Grey Falcon*	Beveridge, *Report on Social Security* Lewis, *The Screwtape Letters*	Singapore falls (Feb.) Allies advance in North Africa Fermi initiates first nuclear chain reaction Oxfam founded
1943	Jameson, *Cloudless May* Raine, *Stone and Flower* Ridler, *Nine Bright Shiners*	Eliot, *Four Quartets*	Germans surrender at Stalingrad (Jan.) and in North Africa (May) Mussolini falls (Jul.) Allies invade Italy (Sept.)
1944	Irwin, *Young Bess* Lehmann, *The Ballad and the Source*	Maugham, *The Razor's Edge*	Normandy landings (June) Battle of the Bulge (Dec.) Bretton Woods monetary conference Education Act introduces universal selective secondary education
1945	Bowen, *The Demon Lover*	Orwell, *Animal Farm* Waugh, *Brideshead Revisited*	Yalta Conference (Feb.) Allies win war in Europe (May) Hiroshima and Nagasaki (Aug.); Allies win war with Japan Labour landslide in elections (Jul.) Family allowances introduced

General Bibliographies

Note: Place of publication is London, unless otherwise stated.

SOCIAL AND CULTURAL HISTORY OF WOMEN

ALEXANDER, Sally, *Becoming a Woman and Other Essays in Nineteenth Century and Twentieth Century Feminist History* (Virago, 1994). (Especially for important title essay.)

BLAND, Lucy, *Banishing the Beast: English Feminism and Sexual Morality* (Harmondsworth: Penguin, 1995). (Detailed account of difficult relationship.)

BOLT, Christine, *The Women's Movements in the United States and Britain from the 1790s to 1920s* (Hemel Hempstead: Harvester Wheatsheaf, 1993). (A comprehensive history.)

BRANSON, Noreen and HEINEMANN, Margot, *Britain in the 1930s* (Weidenfeld and Nicholson, 1971). (Useful social history.)

DAVIN, Anna, 'Imperialism and Motherhood', *History Workshop*, 5 (1978), pp. 9–65. (Important essay.)

DYHOUSE, Carol, *Feminism and the Family in England, 1880–1939* (Oxford: Blackwell, 1989).

—— *No Distinction of Sex? Women in British Universities 1870–1939* (UCL Press, 1995).

GRAVES, Robert and HODGE, Alan, *The Long Weekend: A Social History of Great, Britain 1918–39* (Faber and Faber, 1940). (Lively contemporary overview.)

230

JEFFREYS, Sheila, *The Spinster and Her Enemies: Feminism and Sexuality 1880–1930* (Pandora, 1985).

LEWIS, Jane, *The Politics of Motherhood: Child and Maternal Welfare in England 1900–39* (Croom Helm, 1980).

—— *Women in England 1870–1950: Sexual Divisions and Social Change* (Hemel Hempstead: Harvester Wheatsheaf, 1984). (Valuable concise summary.)

LIDDINGTON, Jill and NORRIS, Jill, *One Hand Tied Behind Them: The Rise of the Women's Suffrage Movement* (Virago, 1978). (Good study of working-class feminism.)

MELMAN, Billie, *Women and the Popular Imagination in the 1920s: Flappers and Nymphs* (Macmillan, 1988). (Studies reactions to female popular culture.)

REEVES, Maud Pember, *Round About a Pound a Week* (Bell, 1913). (Classic study of London working-class domestic life.)

STEEDMAN, Carolyn, *Childhood, Culture and Class in Britain: Margaret McMillan 1860–1931* (Virago, 1990). (Suggestive cultural analysis.)

TILLY, Louise A. and SCOTT, Joan, *Women, Work and Family* (Methuen, 1987). (Concise analysis.)

VICINUS, Martha, *Independent Women: Work and Community for Single Women: 1850–1920* (Chicago: University of Chicago Press, 1985).

WEEKS, Jeffrey, *Sexuality, Politics and Society: The Regulation of Sexuality Since 1800* (Longman, rev. edn 1989). (Important study.)

REFERENCE GUIDES AND BIBLIOGRAPHIES

BANKS, Olive, *A Biographical Dictionary of British Feminists*, 2 vols (Harvester, 1985–89). (Concise outlines of politically active women, including writers.)

BLAIN, Virginia, CLEMENTS, Patricia and GRUNDY, Isobel, *A Feminist Companion to Literature in English: Women Writers from the Middle Ages to the Present* (Batsford, 1990).

CHEVALIER, Tracy, ed., *Twentieth Century Children's Writers*, 3rd edn (Chicago: St James's Press, 1989).

CLINE, Cheryl, *Women's Diaries, Journals and Letters: An Annotated Bibliography* (New York: Garland, 1989).

DAIMS, Diva and GRIMES, Janet, *Towards a Feminist Tradition: An Annotated Bibliography of Novels in England by Women 1891–1920* (New York: Garland, 1982).

REILLY, John, ed., *Twentieth Century Crime and Mystery Writers* (Macmillan, 1980).

SHATTOCK, Joanne, *The Oxford Guide to British Women Writers* (Oxford: Oxford University Press, 1993). (Valuable source: concise outlines and bibliographies.)

TODD, Janet, ed., *Dictionary of British Women Writers* (Routledge, 1989). (Valuable source: covers some non-fiction writers not in Shattock.)

UGLOW, Jenny and HINTON, Frances, *Macmillan's Dictionary of Women's Biography* (Macmillan, 1982).

WILLISON, I.R., ed., *New Cambridge Bibliography of English Literature*, IV (Cambridge: Cambridge University Press, 1972.)

READERSHIP, AUTHORSHIP AND PUBLICATION

BEAUMANN, Nicola, *A Very Great Profession: The Women's Novel 1914–39* (Virago, 1983). (Explores middlebrow women's reading.)

CAREY, John, *The Intellectuals and the Masses: Pride and Prejudice Among the Literary Intelligentsia* (Faber, 1992). (Forceful attack on avant-garde anti-populism.)

COCKBURN, Claud, *Bestseller: The Books Everyone Read 1900–39* (Sidgwick and Jackson, 1972). (Lively, biased to male bestsellers.)

ELIOT, Simon, *Some Patterns and Trends in British Publishing 1880–1919* (Bibliographical Society, 1994).

FLINT, Kate, *The Woman Reader 1827–1911* (Oxford: Clarendon Press, 1993). (Detailed account of women's reading practices.)

JOSEPH, Michael, *The Commercial Side of Literature* (Hutchinson, 1925). (Informative overview of 1920s literary market.)

KEATING, Peter, *The Haunted Study: A Social History of the English Novel 1875–1914* (Secker and Warburg, 1989). (Detailed study of writing profession.)

KELLY, Thomas, *Books for the People: An Illustrated History of the British Public Library* (Deutsch, 1977).

KINGSFORD, R.J.L., *The Publishers' Association 1896–1946* (Cambridge: Cambridge University Press, 1970).

LEAVIS, Q.D., *Fiction and the Reading Public* (Chatto and Windus, 1932). (Classic pioneer analysis.)

LEE, A.J., *The Origins of the Popular Press 1855–1914* (Croom Helm, 1976).

LOVELL, Terry, *Consuming Fiction* (Verso, 1987). (Concise study of women as readers and writers.)

MCALEER, Joseph, *Popular Reading and Publishing in Britain 1914–50* (Oxford: Clarendon Press, 1992). (Includes chapters on popular women's fiction and journalism.)

SPENDER, Dale, *Time and Tide Wait for No Man* (Pandora, 1984). (Anthology of extracts from the feminist weekly with useful critical introductions.)

WHITE, Cynthia, *Women's Magazines 1693–1968* (Michael Joseph, 1971). (Pioneer study.)

LITERARY HISTORIES

General histories

BRADBURY, Malcolm and MACFARLANE, James, eds, *Modernism 1880–1930* (Brighton: Harvester, 1978).

CUNNINGHAM, Valentine, *British Writers of the Thirties* (Oxford: Oxford University Press, 1988). (Wide-ranging, thematic approach, mostly male writing.)

FOX, Pamela, *Class Fictions: Shame and Resistance in the British Working-Class Novel 1890–1945* (Durham, N.C.: Duke University Press, 1994). (Valuable on scattered working-class women's material.)

HYNES, Samuel, *The Auden Generation: Literature and Politics in Britain in the 1930s* (Faber, 1976). (Important account of the 1930s: thin on women's writing.)

PYKETT, Lyn, *Engendering Fictions: The English Novel in the Early Twentieth Century* (Edward Arnold, 1995). (Traces roots of modernism in gender debates.)

STEVENSON, Randall, *Modernist Fiction: An Introduction* (Hemel Hempstead: Harvester, 1992).

TROTTER, David, *The English Novel in History 1895–1920* (Routledge, 1993). (Thematic approach addresses relations of highbrow and popular writing.)

Histories of women's writing

CROSLAND, Margaret, *Beyond the Lighthouse: English Women Novelists in the Twentieth Century* (Constable, 1981). (Wide range in middlebrow writing, anecdotal.)

DOWSON, Jane, ed., *Women's Poetry of the 1930s* (Routledge, 1996). (Useful critical introductions and bibliographies.)

DUPLESSIS, Rachel Blau, *Writing Beyond the Ending: Narrative Strategies and Twentieth-Century Women Writers* (Bloomington: Indiana University Press, 1985). (Important study of formal developments.)

GILBERT, Sandra and GUBAR, Susan, *No Man's Land: The Place of the Woman Writer in the Twentieth Century*, 3 vols (New Haven: Yale University Press, 1987–94). (Ambitious, provocative study, mainly modernist and American in focus.)

HANSCOMBE, Gillian and SMYERS, Virginia, *Writing for Their Lives: The Modernist Women 1920–40* (Women's Press, 1987). (Modernist activity outside Bloomsbury, anecdotal.)

LIGHT, Alison, *Forever England: Femininity, Literature and Conservatism Between the Wars* (Routledge, 1991). (Valuable analysis of popular and conservative women's writing.)

MILLER, Jane Eldridge, *Rebel Women: Feminism, Radicalism and the Edwardian Novel* (Virago, 1994). (Valuable study of pioneer Edwardian feminist writing.)

MOI, Toril, *Sexual/Textual Politics: Feminist Literary Theory* (Methuen, 1985). (Important study of feminist theory from Woolf on.)

MONTEFIORE, Jan, *Feminism and Poetry: Language, Experience, Identity, in Women's Writing* (Pandora, 1987). (Useful analysis of theoretical issues).

SCOTT, Bonnie K., ed., *The Gender of Modernism: A Critical Anthology* (Bloomington: Indiana University Press, 1990). (Useful critical introductions and bibliographies in anthology which explores relations of modernism and gender debates.)

—— *Refiguring Modernism*, 2 vols (Bloomington: Indiana University Press, 1995). (Modernism and gender, focus on West and Woolf.)

SHOWALTER, Elaine, *A Literature of Their Own: British Women Novelists from Brontë to Lessing* (Princeton: Princeton University Press, 1977). (Classic history of women's writing.)

TYLEE, Claire, *The Great War and Women's Consciousness: Images of Militarism and Womanhood in Women's Writing 1914–64* (Basingstoke: Macmillan, 1990). (Detailed survey of women's war writing.)

Studies of genres

Autobiography

ANDERSON, Linda, *Women and Autobiography in the Twentieth Century: Remembered Futures* (Hemel Hempstead: Harvester Wheatsheaf, 1997). (Good chapters on Woolf and Brittain.)

BENSTOCK, Shari, ed., *The Private Self: The Theory and Practice of Women's Autobiographical Writing* (Chapel Hill: University of North Carolina Press, 1988). (Useful collection of feminist approaches.)

HEILBRUN, Carolyn, *Writing a Woman's Life* (Women's Press, 1988).

SMITH, Sidonie, *A Poetics of Women's Autobiography* (Bloomington: Indiana University Press, 1987).

STANLEY, Liz, *The Autobiographic I: The Theory and Practice of Feminist Autobiography* (Manchester: Manchester University Press, 1992).

Children's writing

CADOGAN, Mary and CRAIG, Patricia, *You're a Brick, Angela: A New Look at Girls' Fiction 1839–1975* (Gollancz, 1976). (Wide-ranging, entertaining.)

CARPENTER, Humphrey, *Secret Gardens: A Study of the Golden Age of Children's Literature* (Allen and Unwin, 1985). (For Potter, Burnett, Nesbit.)

DUSINBERRE, Juliet, *Alice to the Lighthouse: Children's Books and Radical Experiments in Art* (Macmillan, 1987). (Argues for importance of innovations in children's writing to later modernist experiment.)

HUNT, Peter, *An Introduction to Children's Literature* (Oxford: Oxford University Press, 1994).

WALL, Barbara, *The Narrator's Voice: The Dilemma of Children's Fiction* (Macmillan, 1991).

Popular fiction

ANDERSON, Rachel, *The Purple Heart Throbs: The Sub-literature of Love* (Hodder and Stoughton, 1974). (Unreferenced early survey of field.)

CAWELTI, John, *Adventure, Mystery and Romance: Formula Stories as Art and Popular Culture* (Chicago: University of Chicago Press, 1976). (Influential genre analysis, primarily American, but includes Christie and Sayers.)

KNIGHT, Stephen, *Form and Ideology in Crime Fiction* (Macmillan, 1980). (For Christie.)

MODLESKI, Tanya, *Loving with a Vengeance: Mass Produced Fantasies for Women* (Routledge, 1982). (Influential analysis, emphasis on Gothic).

RADFORD, Jean, ed., *The Progress of Romance: The Politics of Popular Fiction* (Routledge and Kegan Paul, 1986). (Good collection, emphasizes adaptability of form.)

RADWAY, Janice A., *Reading the Romance: Women, Patriarchy and Popular Literature* (Chapel Hill: University of North Carolina Press, 1984). (Study of contemporary romance, but relevant analysis of reading practices.)

The short story

ALLEN, Walter, *The Short Story in English* (Oxford: Clarendon Press, 1981). (Sections on Mansfield, Bowen and Warner.)

BAYLEY, John, *The Short Story: Henry James to Elizabeth Bowen* (Brighton: Harvester, 1986).

HANSON, Clare, *Short Stories and Short Fiction 1880–1980* (Macmillan, 1985). (Sections on Mansfield and Bowen.)

HEAD, Dominic, *The Modernist Short Story* (Cambridge: Cambridge University Press, 1992). (Sections on Woolf and Mansfield.)

NOTE ON WOMEN'S MAGAZINES

This period saw a great increase and diversification in periodicals addressed to women readers. In 1900 the most popular women's magazine was *The Girl's Own Paper*, which was addressed to a mixed juvenile and mature readership; launched in 1880 it ran until 1948, and under the new title, *The Heiress*, until 1965. Its competitors in the juvenile market included *The Girls' Realm* (1898–1915) and *The Girls' Friend* (1899–1931), and in the adult market, *Home Chat* (1895–1959), the first *Woman* (1890–1910) and two continuing titles, *The People's Friend* (1869) and *The Lady* (1885). The suffrage movement produced political journals representing the various groups within the movement; most influential were the WSPU *Votes for Women* (1907–18), the NUWSS *The Common Cause* (1909–14) and the East End group's *The Women's Dreadnought* (1914–17), continued as *The Workers' Dreadnought* until 1924. The short-lived but very influential *The Freewoman* (1911–12), retitled *The New Freewoman* (1912–13), addressed a wider feminist cultural agenda; retitled again as the modernist *The Egoist* (1913–20), it dropped feminist issues. The most influential feminist journal between the wars, *Time and Tide* (1920–63), also dropped its feminist agenda after the 1930s to become an arts journal. Many continuing titles were launched in this period including *Vogue* (1916), *Homes and Gardens* (1919), *Good Housekeeping* (1922), *Women's Own* (1932) and *Woman* (1937). Popular and influential magazines which did not survive the period included *Peg's Paper* (1919–40), which pioneered the magazine specifically addressing young working-class women, and the flurry of magazines targeting schoolgirl readers, *Schoolfriend* (1919–29), retitled *Schoolgirl* (1929–40), *Schoolgirls' Own* (1921–36) and *Schoolgirls' Weekly* (1922–39).

Individual Authors: Notes on Biography, Major Works and Criticism

Each entry consists of:

1. An outline of the author's life
2. Selected autobiographies, letters, and biographies
3. Selected critical works

The place of publication is London, unless otherwise stated. Many of the innovative, and the popular, writings are still in print; a number of the less accessible, 'middlebrow' writers have been reprinted recently, often by Virago. Where short works have been reissued recently in collections this is indicated in the outline.

ARNIM, Elizabeth von (1866–1941), born Mary Annette Beauchamp in Sydney into a shipping magnate's family, cousin of Katherine Mansfield. Lived in Britain from 1869, married Count Henning von Arnim in 1891, and lived on his Pomeranian estate with their five children until his death in 1910. She returned to Britain in 1914 after a period in Switzerland. Her first book, *Elizabeth and her German Garden* (1898), published anonymously, a feminist gardening memoir, was a bestseller. Most later books were published as by 'Elizabeth'. Her two best novels, powerful, feminist studies of marital discord, were *The Pastor's Wife* (1914), written during her love affair with H.G. Wells 1910–13, and *Vera* (1921), the plot of which resembles du Maurier's *Rebecca*, based on her second, disastrous marriage to Earl Russell, 1916–19. Her last success was the idyllic *The Enchanted April* (1923).

Arnim, Elizabeth von, *All the Dogs of My Life* (Heinemann, 1936).

Usborne, Karen, *Elizabeth* (Bodley Head, 1986).

See: Miller, Jane Eldridge, *Rebel Women: Feminism, Modernism and the Edwardian Novel* (Virago, 1994).

237

ALLINGHAM, Margery (1904–66), born in London to parents who were both prolific writers of serial fiction for magazines; she began writing magazine fiction in her teens. Her first book was a blood and thunder romance, *Blackkerchief Dick* (1923). *The Crime at Black Dudley* (1929) began her series of crime novels, centred on the detective Albert Campion. In the 1930s she became recognized as a leading crime story writer with such novels as *Police at the Funeral* (1931), *Flowers for the Judge* (1936), *Dancers in Mourning* (1937) and *The Fashion in Shrouds* (1938). She continued to publish Campion novels after the Second World War, notably *A Tiger in the Smoke* (1952). In 1927 she married the writer and illustrator, Philip Youngman Carter, and settled in Essex; Carter finished her last novel, *A Cargo of Eagles* (1968).

> Thorogood, Julia, *Margery Allingham: A Biography* (Heinemann, 1991).

See: Mann, Jessica, *Deadlier than the Male: An Investigation into Female Crime Writing* (David and Charles, 1981).

BARCLAY, Florence (1862–1921), born F. Charlesworth in Surrey into a rector's family, spent her later childhood in her father's East London slum parish, and married his curate, Charles Barclay, in 1881. After honeymooning in the Holy Land, they settled in the parish of Hertford Heath; they had eight children. During an illness in 1905 she began the romantic novel, *The Rosary* (1909), a massive bestseller. Other bestselling novels combining romance and religion followed, including *The Mistress of Shenstone* (1911), *The Following of the Star* (1911) and *The White Ladies of Worcester* (1917). Barclay's lecture tours and attention to her fan clubs were characteristic of the new bestseller writer.

> *The Life of Florence Barclay: A Study in Personality by One of her Daughters* (Putnam, 1921).

See: Anderson, Rachel, *The Purple Heart Throbs: The Sub-Literature of Love* (Hodder and Stoughton, 1974).

BELL, Gertrude (1868–1926), born into a Durham ironmaster's family. In 1888 she was the first woman to take a First in Modern History at Oxford, and then travelled widely in the Middle East, and studied Persian and Arabic. Her first publications were the travel sketches, *Persian Pictures* (1894), and the poetry translations, *Poems from the Divan of Hafiz* (1897). Her major travel books are *The Desert and the Sown* (1907), based on a 1905 journey from Jerusalem to Antioch, and *Amurath to Amurath* (1911), based on her archaeological work at the palace of Ukhaidir near Baghdad, on which she also wrote *Palace and Mosque at Ukhaidir* (1914). Her status as an orientalist launched her on her later, political career, first as a key member of the Arab Intelligence Bureau during the First World War, and then as an adviser during the founding of the modern state of Iraq. She was Director of Antiquities 1923–26 in Baghdad, where she died of a barbiturates overdose.

The Letters of Gertrude Bell, 2 vols, ed. Florence Bell (Benn, 1927).

Gertrude Bell: From Her Personal Papers 1889–1914, ed. Elizabeth Burgoyne (Benn, 1958).

Wallach, Janet, *Desert Queen: The Extraordinary Life of Gertrude Bell* (Weidenfeld, 1996).

Winstone, H.V.F., *Gertrude Bell* (Cape, 1978).

See: Melman, Billie, *Women Orientalists: Englishwomen and the Middle East 1718–1918* (Macmillan, 1992).

Said, Edward, *Orientalism* (New York: Pantheon, 1978).

BENSON, Stella (1892–1933), born in Easthope, Shropshire, into a landowning family, worked in London from 1912 for the women's suffrage movement, and then during the war as a clerk in East London, and later as a land girl. In 1918 on medical advice she went to California, where she tutored parttime in English composition at Berkeley, and then in 1919 to Hong Kong, where she taught language classes. In 1921 she married James O'Gorman Anderson, an Irish customs official in China; they lived at various postings in China with annual visits to England. Her novels, all critically wellreceived, use fantasy to explore isolation and alienation. *I Pose* (1916) was based on her suffragette experience, *Living Alone* (1919) on her war-work, *The Poor Man* (1922) on her time in California, and her major work, *Tobit Transplanted* (1931), on her experience of southern Manchuria. The last won the Femina/Vie Heureuse Prize. She also wrote short stories, notably the collection *The Man who Missed the Bus* (1928), and articles on her travels and on Chinese life, some collected in *The Little World* (1925). From 1931 she was heavily engaged in campaigning against child prostitution. She died of pneumonia in China.

Roberts, Richard E., *Portrait of Stella Benson* (Macmillan, 1938).

Grant, Joy, *Stella Benson: A Biography* (Macmillan, 1987).

BOWEN, Elizabeth (1899–1973), born in Dublin into an Anglo-Irish family settled at Bowen's Court, County Cork, since 1775. Her childhood was disrupted by her father's nervous breakdown in 1906, a move to Kent, and her mother's death in 1912. She attended boarding-school and art school in England, and in 1923 married Alan Cameron, an education officer who later worked for the BBC Schools Service. Her first book was the short story collection, *Encounters* (1923), her first novel, *The Hotel* (1927). In the 1930s she became a prominent figure on the London literary scene, and recognized as a leading novelist of the generation succeeding Woolf. Her novels placed themselves in a tradition descending from Austen, as social comedies centred on the romances of young girls, but were informed by awareness of modernism, and by Bowen's sense of herself as 'colonial'. They included *The Last September* (1929), set in Ireland in the Troubles, *Friends and Relations* (1931), *To the North* (1932), *The House in Paris* (1935), *The Death of the Heart* (1938) and *The Heat of the Day* (1949), based on Bowen's experiences of wartime London and work for the Ministry of Information. She was also a major exponent of the short story, Mansfield's main successor. Collections included *The Cat Jumps* (1934), *Look at All Those Roses* (1941) and *The Demon Lover* (1946), and her *Collected Stories*, ed. Angus Wilson, appeared in 1981. She undertook much reviewing, and lecture tours and radio talks, partly to maintain Bowen's Court, which she inherited in 1940 and lived in from 1946 until forced to sell it in 1959. After the war she continued to publish novels, notably *The Little Girls* (1964).

Bowen, Elizabeth, *Bowen's Court* (Longmans, Green, 1942), and *Pictures and Conversations* (Cape, 1975).

The Mulberry Tree: Writings of Elizabeth Bowen, ed. Hermione Lee (Virago, 1986). (Includes several short memoirs.)

Glendinning, Victoria, *Elizabeth Bowen: Portrait of a Writer* (Weidenfeld and Nicholson, 1977).

See: Bennett, Andrew and Royle, Nicholas, *Elizabeth Bowen and the Dissolution of the Novel* (Basingstoke: Macmillan, 1995). (Argues for Bowen as radical and innovative.)

Bloom, Harold, ed., *Elizabeth Bowen* (New York: Chelsea House, 1987).

Heath, William, *Elizabeth Bowen: An Introduction to her Novels* (Madison: University of Wisconsin Press, 1961).

Lassner, Phyllis, *Elizabeth Bowen* (Macmillan, 1990). (Good brief study, placing Bowen's relation to domestic realism.)

Lee, Hermione, *Elizabeth Bowen: An Estimation* (Vision, 1981).

BRAZIL, Angela (1869–1947), born in Preston, father a cotton-mill manager, mother Anglo-Brazilian, attended various, mostly day, schools in Liverpool and Manchester, and art school in London. Her first published works, the play series *A Mischievous Brownie* (1899), the story *A Terrible Tomboy* (1904), and stories for the magazine *Little Folks*, were for very small children, but she found her niche in the school story with *The Fortunes of Philippa* (1906), based on her mother's schooldays. Its successors, including *The Nicest Girl in the School* (1909), *The Manor School* (1910) and *A Fourth Form Friendship* (1911), made Brazil's name synonymous with the school story, and established the formula which governed the genre during its immense popularity in the interwar period. From 1911 she lived with her siblings in Coventry, continuing to publish popular school stories up to *The School on the Loch* (1946).

Brazil, Angela, *My Own Schooldays* (Blackie, 1925).

Freeman, Gillian, *The Schoolgirl Ethic: The Life and Work of Angela Brazil* (Allen Lane, 1976).

See: Cadogan, Mary and Craig, Patricia, *You're a Brick, Angela: A New Look at Girls' Fiction 1839–1975* (Gollancz, 1976).

Frith, Gill, ' "The Time of Your Life": The Meaning of the School Story', in Carolyn Steedman, Cathy Urwin and Valerie Walkerdine, eds, *Language, Gender and Childhood* (Routledge, 1980).

BRITTAIN, Vera (1893–1970), born in Newcastle-under-Lyme into a paper manufacturer's family. Entered Oxford in 1914, but left in 1915 to become a Voluntary Aid Detachment (VAD) nurse in Malta and France, losing her fiancé Roland Leighton, her brother Edward, and several male friends during the war. In 1919 she returned to Oxford to complete her history degree, and then settled in London with fellow-graduate Winifred Holtby to pursue a journalistic career. In 1925 she married George Catlin, a politics professor at Cornell; they had two children. She soon returned to London to continue her career as a successful and prolific journalist, writing for the *Manchester Guardian, Yorkshire Post, Nation* and *Time and Tide* among others; some of her journalism is collected in *Testament of a Generation*, ed. Paul Berry and Alan Bishop (1985). Her five novels, including *Dark Tide* (1923) and *Honourable Estate* (1936), were less successful. Her major success was her war memoir, *Testament of Youth* (1933), the most famous woman's book about the First World War. Lecture tours in Europe and America established her as a popular speaker, though her campaigning from 1936 for the Peace Pledge Union, and her outspoken pacifism during the Second World War, dented that popularity. She remained politically active until her death, campaigning for the Campaign for Nuclear Disarmament (CND) during the 1950s. Her later works included her biography of Holtby, *Testament of Friendship* (1940). Her daughter, Shirley Williams, became a leading politician.

Brittain, Vera, *Testament of Youth* (1933) and *Testament of Experience* (1957) (both Gollancz).

Chronicle of Youth: War Diary 1913–17, ed. Alan Bishop (Gollancz, 1981).

Chronicle of Friendship: Diary of the 1930s, ed. Alan Bishop (Gollancz, 1986).

Selected Letters of Winifred Holtby and Vera Brittain, ed. with Geoffrey Handley-Taylor (Hull: Brown, 1960).

Berry, Paul and Bostridge, Alan, *Vera Brittain: A Life* (Chatto, 1995).

See: Anderson, Linda, *Women and Autobiography in the Twentieth Century: Remembered Futures* (Hemel Hempstead: Harvester Wheatsheaf, 1997).

Kennard, Jean, *Vera Brittain and Winifred Holtby: A Working Partnership* (Hanover: University of New Hampshire Press, 1989).

BURNETT, Frances Hodgson (1849–1924), born F. Hodgson in Preston into a hardware merchant's family, moved to Tennessee in 1865, and in 1868 began writing stories for American magazines. She married Dr Swan Burnett, an eye specialist, in 1873; they had two sons. She divorced him in 1898, and was briefly married to another doctor, Stephen Townsend, 1900–01. Her first novel, *That Lass of Lowries* (1877), was about women pithead workers in Lancashire. She continued to write for adult as well as child audiences; her bestseller, *Little Lord Fauntleroy* (1883), was addressed to both. From 1898 to 1907 she lived in Maytham Hall, Kent, which inspired *The Secret Garden* (1911), written after returning to New York. Her Edwardian works include *The Making of a Marchioness* (1901), a satirical comedy of high society, the 1903 play and 1905 novel, both titled *The Little Princess*, and based on her 1887 story, *Sara Crewe*, and her most enduring success, *The Secret Garden*, which first appeared as the serial, 'Mistress Mary', in the adult *American Magazine*, but became established as a children's classic.

Burnett, Frances Hodgson, *The One I Knew Best of All* (Warne, 1893).

Thwaite, Ann, *Waiting for the Party: The Life of Frances Hodgson Burnett 1849–1924* (Secker and Warburg, 1974).

See: Carpenter, Humphrey, *Secret Gardens: A Study of the Golden Age of Children's Literature* (Allen and Unwin, 1985).

Dusinberre, Juliet, *Alice to the Lighthouse: Children's Books and Radical Experiments in Art* (Macmillan, 1987).

CABLE, (Alice) Mildred (1878–1952), born in Guildford into a master-draper's family, studied medicine at London University, and in 1900 travelled to China for the China Inland Mission. She worked in a Mission school in Hwochow with the sisters Evangeline (1869–1960) and Francesca (1871–1960) French until 1923, when they were instructed to take the

Mission's teaching into the Gobi Desert. They travelled in the Gobi 1923–38, lecturing at universities and scientific societies on their leaves in Britain. Their books included *Through Jade Gate and Central Asia* (1927), *A Desert Journal: Letters from Central Asia* (1934), and their major work, *The Gobi Desert* (1942), written after war had enforced their return to Britain in 1938. This work of spiritual discovery also won the Royal Central Asian Society's Award for its contribution to geography. The trio continued to live together in Dorset, working for the Bible Society for which Cable was a noted speaker, and regarding their work as indivisible.

Platt, W.J., *Three Women: Mildred Cable, Francesca French, Evangeline French* (Hodder and Stoughton, 1964).

CHRISTIE, Agatha (Mary Clarissa) (1890–1976), born A. Miller in Torquay into a wealthy leisured Anglo-American family. In 1914 she married Archibald Christie of the Royal Flying Corps; they had one daughter. During the war she worked as a VAD nurse and in a dispensary. After a much publicized divorce in 1928, she married the archaeologist Max Mallowan in 1930; much of her 1930s writing was done on excavations in Iraq. Her first novel, *The Mysterious Affair at Styles* (1920), introduced the Belgian detective, Hercule Poirot. Her second, *The Secret Adversary* (1922), was a spy thriller, but the great success of *The Murder of Roger Ackroyd* (1926) established her as the leading writer of 'puzzle plot' crime stories. A succession of Poirot stories maintained her vast and continuing popularity; they included *Murder on the Orient Express* (1934), *The ABC Murders* (1936), *Murder in Mesopotamia* (1936) and *Death on the Nile* (1937). She also experimented with a historical whodunit, *Death Comes As the End* (1945), introduced an elderly female detective, Miss Marple, in *The Murder at the Vicarage* (1930), and wrote several domestic novels under the name Mary Westmacott, notably *Absent in the Spring* (1944). In the postwar period she continued to publish Poirot and Marple novels of an increasingly nostalgic kind, and wrote several successful plays including the long-running *The Mousetrap* (1952) and *The Witness for the Prosecution* (1953). Her works have been much filmed. She became a Dame in 1971.

Christie, Agatha, *An Autobiography* (Collins, 1977).

Morgan, Janet, *Agatha Christie: A Biography* (Collins, 1984).

See: Knight, Stephen, *Form and Ideology in Crime Fiction* (Macmillan, 1980).

Light, Alison, *Forever England: Femininity, Literature and Conservatism Between the Wars* (Routledge, 1991).

Shaw, Marion and Vanacker, Sabine, *Reflecting on Miss Marple* (Routledge, 1991).

COMPTON-BURNETT, Ivy (1884–1969), born in Middlesex, the eldest of seven children in a homoeopathic doctor's family. Her childhood was disrupted by her mother's death in 1892, and family tensions following her father's remarriage. She studied classics at London University 1902–06, then lived turbulently with her family until 1915. Her first novel, *Dolores*, was published in 1911. In 1916–17 two sisters killed themselves, and a brother died in the war. In 1918 she survived the influenza pandemic, and began a quieter life with Margaret Jourdain, the furniture historian. In 1925 she published *Pastors and Masters*, the first in the series of dialogue novels about family conflict, which established her as one of the most distinctive voices of the period. These included *Men and Wives* (1931), *More Women than Men* (1933), *A House and its Head* (1935), *A Family and its Fortune* (1939) and *Parents and Children* (1941). She continued writing novels until her death, and became a distinguished, eccentric figure on the London literary scene. She became a Dame in 1967.

Spurling, Hilary, *Ivy When Young: The Early Life of Ivy Compton-Burnett 1884–1919* (Gollancz, 1974), and *Secrets of a Woman's Heart: The Later Life of Ivy Compton-Burnett 1920–62* (Hodder and Stoughton, 1984).

Dick, Kay, ed., *Ivy and Stevie: Ivy Compton-Burnett and Stevie Smith: Conversations and Reflections* (Duckworth, 1971).

See: Burkhart, Charles, *The Art of Ivy Compton-Burnett: A Collection of Critical Essays* (Gollancz, 1972).

Light, Alison, *Forever England: Femininity, Literature and Conservatism Between the Wars* (Routledge, 1991).

Liddell, Robert, *The Novels of Ivy Compton-Burnett* (Gollancz, 1955).

COOPER, Lettice (1897–), born L. Eccles into an engineer's family, read classics at Oxford 1916–18, worked at her father's engineering firm in Leeds, and joined the Labour Party. During the Second World War she worked for the Ministry of Food. Her first novel, *The Lighted Room*, was historical, and in the postwar period she wrote children's stories and biographies. Her major achievements were her three 1930s novels about class and family tensions, *We Have Come to a Country* (1935), *The New House* (1936) and *National Provincial* (1938). Her most notable postwar novel was *Fenny* (1953).

See: Beaumann, Nicola, *A Very Great Profession: The Woman's Novel 1914–39* (Virago, 1983).

CORNFORD, Frances (1886–1960), born F. Crofts Darwin in Cambridge, where she lived most of her life. Her mother, Ellen Crofts, was a lecturer in English at Newnham, and Wordsworth's great-niece, her father Francis was Charles Darwin's son. Her mother's death in 1903 triggered the first of a series of nervous breakdowns. In 1909 she married the classicist Francis Cornford; they had five children. She published her first book, *Poems*, in 1910. She had strong links with the Georgian movement, especially through her friendship with Rupert Brooke, who, however, disliked her distinctively direct and sometimes childlike poems. Later collections included *A Spring Morning* (1915), *Different Days* (1928) and *Mountains and Molehills* (1934). From 1936 to 1940 she had a severe nervous breakdown; her eldest son, the poet John Cornford, was killed in the Spanish Civil War, and her husband died in 1943. She continued to publish poetry in the postwar period, and her *Collected Poems* was published in 1954.

> Fowler, Helen, 'Frances Cornford', in Edward Shils and Carmen Blacker, eds, *Cambridge Women: Twelve Portraits* (Cambridge: Cambridge University Press, 1996).

See: Dowson, Jane, 'The Importance of Frances Cornford', *Charleston Magazine*, Spring 1994, pp. 10–14.

CROMPTON, Richmal (1890–1969), born R.C. Lamburn in Bury into a curate's family, studied classics at London University 1911–14, and became a classics teacher. In 1919 she published her first William story, 'The Outlaws', in the *Home Magazine*, and subsequent stories there, and in the *Happy Mag*. The first William books, *Just-William* and *More William*, appeared in 1922, and, when crippled by polio in 1923, she retired from teaching to pursue a full-time writing career. For the rest of her life she wrote an adult novel in tandem with each William book, but it was the latter by which she was recognized. Notable later volumes include *William the Conqueror* (1926) and *William the Outlaw* (1927); the series, stretching eventually to thirty-eight volumes, continued into the postwar period and retains its popularity.

> Cadogan, Mary, *Richmal Crompton: The Woman Behind William* (London: Unwin, 1987).

See: Cadogan, Mary and Craig, Patricia, *You're A Brick, Angela: A New Look at Girls' Fiction 1839 to 1975* (Gollancz, 1976).

DARYUSH, Elizabeth (1887–1977), born E. Bridges in London, daughter of Robert Bridges, Poet Laureate 1913–30. She lived in Oxford 1907–23, studied Persian in the early 1920s, and married Ali Akbar Daryush, a Persian government official, in 1923. They lived in Persia 1923–27, and then in Oxford. Her first collection of poems, *Charitessi*, was published in 1911; her second, *Verses* (1916), began a series of seven, including *Third Book Verses* (1933) and *Fourth Book Verses* (1934), which, like *The Last Man and Other*

Verses (1936), were strongly informed by a sense of social injustice. Daryush later reacted against this phase in her poetry, and in her *Collected Poems* (1976) emphasized her experiments with syllabic metre as her distinctive achievement. Her poetry was better known in the United States, largely through the championship of the critic, Yvor Winters.

See: Davie, Donald, 'Introduction', in Elizabeth Daryush, *Collected Poems* (Manchester: Carcanet, 1976).

Winters, Yvor, 'Robert Bridges and Elizabeth Daryush', in his *Uncollected Essays and Reviews*, ed. Francis Murphy (Allen Lane, 1974).

DELL, Ethel M(ary) (1881–1939), born in London into an insurance agent's family, began writing early and published some stories in magazines. After several rejections her first novel, *The Way of an Eagle*, a turbulent romance set in the Raj, was published in 1912, and became a massive bestseller. A series of romances repeating the formula, including *Knave of Diamonds* (1913), *The Keeper of the Door* (1915) and *The Lamp in the Desert* (1919), made her name synonymous with romantic fiction between the wars. In 1922 she married Lieutenant-Colonel Gerald Savage. Unlike her rivals she shunned publicity and lived reclusively; this had no apparent effect on her enormous sales.

See: Anderson, Rachel, *The Purple Heart Throbs: The Sub-Literature of Love* (Hodder and Stoughton, 1974).

DU MAURIER, Daphne (1907–89), born in London to actors Muriel Beaumont and Gerald du Maurier, the original Captain Hook; her grandfather was George du Maurier, author of *Trilby*. She began writing early, mainly short stories inspired by Mansfield. In 1932 she married Major, later General Sir, Frederick Browning. She had several love affairs, including in the late 1920s with the film director Carol Reed, and in the late 1940s with the actress Gertrude Lawrence. Her first novel, the seafaring romance *The Loving Spirit*, was published in 1931; bestsellerdom came with her fourth, the smuggling yarn *Jamaica Inn* (1936). Her biggest success was the contemporary Gothic romance, *Rebecca* (1938), an enormous and enduring bestseller, and the model for the Gothic romance revival of the 1960s. Later successes included *Frenchman's Creek* (1941), and in the postwar period *My Cousin Rachel* (1951) and *The Scapegoat* (1957). She also wrote a biography of her father, *Gerald* (1934), and a family history, *The Du Mauriers* (1937). From 1943 she lived in Cornwall, the setting for many of her novels. Many of her fictions were filmed. She became a Dame in 1969. Although her books were admired for their mastery of romantic formulae, she always aspired to be recognized for a more serious, psychological fiction.

du Maurier, Daphne, *Growing Pains: The Shaping of a Writer* (1977) and *The Rebecca Notebook and Other Memories* (1981) (both Gollancz).

Forster, Margaret, *Daphne du Maurier* (Chatto and Windus, 1993).

See: Light, Alison, *Forever England: Femininity, Literature and Conservatism Between the Wars* (Routledge, 1991).

GIBBONS, Stella (Dorothea) (1902–89), born in London into a doctor's family, studied journalism at London University, and worked as a journalist and reviewer in the 1920s. She married the actor Allan Webb in 1933; they had one child. Her first book, *The Mountain Beast and Other Poems*, was published in 1930, but, although she went on to publish much poetry and fiction, she is known almost entirely for *Cold Comfort Farm* (1932), her parody of rural fiction, which won the Femina/Vie Heureuse Prize, and has long outlasted most of its targets.

GLYN, Elinor (1864–1943), born E. Sutherland in Jersey into a family with aristocratic connections, and brought up there and in Canada. After a successful London debut as a society beauty, she married Clayton Glyn, a rich landowner, in 1892; they had three children. Her first book, *The Visits of Elizabeth* (1900), was a country-house comedy. In 1907, as her husband neared bankruptcy, she published *Three Weeks*, which became a massive bestseller, scandalous in its pioneering of sexually explicit scenes. Other romances, including *His Hour* (1910), *The Sequence* (1913) and *The Great Moment* (1923), maintained her success as a romantic novelist. Her strong publicity flair was assisted by several high-profile liaisons, including with Lord Curzon. In the 1920s she became well-known in Hollywood as an adviser on courtship etiquette, and wrote screenplays and courtship manuals. She returned to Britain in 1929.

Glyn, Elinor, *Romantic Adventure* (Nicholson and Watson, 1936).

Glyn, Anthony, *Elinor Glyn* (Hutchinson, 1955).

Hardwick, Joan, *Addicted to Romance: The Life and Adventures of Elinor Glyn* (Deutsch, 1994).

See: Anderson, Rachel *The Purple Heart Throbs: The Sub-Literature of Love* (Hodder and Stoughton, 1974).

Kermode, Frank, 'The English Novel *c.*1907', in *Essays on Fiction 1971–83* (Routledge and Kegan Paul, 1983).

Trotter, David, *The English Novel in History 1895–1920* (Routledge, 1993).

247

HALL, Radclyffe (1880–1943), born Marguerite Radclyffe-Hall in Bournemouth, and brought up there and in London by her divorced mother. In 1901 she inherited her father's fortune. From 1908 to 1915 she lived in London with Mabel Batten, converting to Roman Catholicism. From 1915 until her death she lived with Una Troubridge, mostly in Paris. Her first published work was a collection of poems, *Twixt Faith and Stars* (1906). Her earlier novels, including *The Unlit Lamp* (1924) and *Adam's Breed* (1926), were well received, the latter winning the Femina/Vie Heureuse Prize. She is largely known, however, for *The Well of Loneliness* (1928), which employed the formulae of romantic fiction to popularize Havelock Ellis's scientific explanation of sexual deviance. The novel was found an obscene libel and withdrawn from circulation, making Hall's name synonymous with the lesbian cause.

> Brittain, Vera, *Radclyffe Hall: A Case of Obscenity* (Femina Books, 1968).

> Troubridge, Una, *The Life and Death of Radclyffe Hall* (Hammond Hammond, 1961).

See: Franks, Claudia Stillman, *Beyond the Well of Loneliness: The Fiction of Radclyffe Hall* (Amersham: Avebury, 1982).

> Radford, Jean, 'An Inverted Romance: *The Well of Loneliness* and Sexual Ideology', in Jean Radford, ed., *The Progress of Romance: The Politics of Popular Fiction* (Routledge and Kegan Paul, 1986).

HAMILTON, Cicely (1872–1952), born C. Mary Hamill in London into an army captain's family, attended boarding-schools in Britain and Germany, was briefly a teacher, and in the 1890s an actress in touring productions. She augmented her earnings with sensation fiction for magazines, and experimented with one-act plays. In 1908 she had a West End hit with the four-act comedy, *Diana of Dobson's*, produced by the company managed by Lena Ashwell; it is collected in *The Years Between*, ed. Fidelis Morgan (1994). She became active in the suffrage movement, was a popular speaker, wrote several plays for performance at rallies, including *How the Vote Was Won* (1909) and *A Pageant of Great Women* (1910), and founded the Women Writers' Suffrage League. She also wrote the lively polemic, *Marriage as a Trade* (1909). From 1914 she nursed in France for the Scottish Women's Hospitals, and in 1917 joined Ashwell's acting company touring the Western Front. In 1919 her war novel, *William, an Englishman*, was first winner of the Femina/Vie Heureuse Prize. Her other five novels included, most notably, *Theodore Savage* (1922). She continued to be prominent in the women's movement, and was an editor of *Time and Tide* in the 1920s.

Hamilton, Cicely, *Life Errant* (Dent, 1935).

Whitelaw, Lis, *The Life and Rebellious Times of Cicely Hamilton: Actress, Writer, Suffragist* (Women's Press, 1990).

See: Holledge, Julie, *Innocent Flowers: Women in Edwardian Theatre* (Virago, 1981).

Spender, Dale, *Women of Ideas and What Men Have Done to Them* (Ark Books, 1982).

Tylee, Clare, *The Great War and Women's Consciousness: Images of Militarism and Womanhood in Women's Writing 1914–64* (Macmillan, 1990).

HARRISON, Jane Ellen (1850–1928), born in Cottingham near Hull into a timber-merchant's family, educated at Cheltenham Ladies' College and among the first generation of women students at Cambridge. She continued her classical studies in London at the British Museum and became a popular visiting lecturer at schools. A visit to Greece in 1880 expanded her research interest in the rituals which underlay Greek art and religion. In 1898, after several failed attempts at academic appointments, she became a Research Fellow at Newnham, and one of the Cambridge Ritualist group, which included Francis Cornford and Gilbert Murray. Her first major book was *Prolegomena to the Study of Greek Religion* (1903), a study of early Greek ritual. Other works included *Themis* (1912), *Ancient Art and Ritual* (1913) and *Epilegomena to the Study of Greek Religion* (1921), the last influenced by her reading in Freud and Jung. From 1914 she was a keen student of Russian language and culture. In her last years she lived with Hope Mirrlees, her ex-student and 'ghostly daughter', in Paris and London.

Harrison, Jane, *Reminiscences of a Student's Life* (Hogarth Press, 1925).

Peacock, Sandra J., *Jane Harrison: The Mask and the Self* (New Haven: Yale University Press, 1988).

Stewart, Jessie, *Jane Ellen Harrison: A Portrait from Letters* (Merlin, 1959).

See: Ackerman, Robert, 'Jane Ellen Harrison: The Early Work', *Greek, Roman and Byzantine Studies*, 13 (1972), pp. 209–30.

Lloyd-Jones, Hugh, 'Jane Harrison 1850–1928', in Edward Shils and Carmen Blacker, eds, *Cambridge Women: Twelve Portraits* (Cambridge: Cambridge University Press, 1996).

HEYER, Georgette (1902–74), born in London into a teacher's family, attended schools in London and Paris, and history lectures at Westminster College. In 1925 she married George Rougier, a mining engineer and later a barrister; they had one child. She published her first book, *The Black*

Moth, in 1921; her first big success was *These Old Shades* (1925). In subsequent novels she refined on the 'Regency' formula of romantic comedies in a Georgian setting, which claimed Austen as their model. Later works included *The Masqueraders* (1928), *A Convenient Marriage* (1934) and *Regency Buck* (1935). Two novels about the Peninsular campaign, *An Infamous Army* (1937) and *The Spanish Bride* (1940), were more closely based on historical research, and she sometimes used other historical periods, as in *The Conqueror* (1930). She continued to publish new Regency novels until her death; they remained immensely popular, and were models for the Regency romance revival of the 1970s.

Hodge, Jane Aikin, *The Private World of Georgette Heyer* (Bodley Head, 1984).

See: Robinson, Lilian, *Sex, Class and Culture* (Methuen, 1978).

HOLME, Constance (1880–1955), born in Milnthorpe, Westmoreland, into a family which had been land-agents there for generations, and claimed descent from a Spanish survivor of the Armada, the subject of her third novel, *The Old Road from Spain* (1915). In 1916 she married Frederick Punchard, a land-agent at Kirkby Lonsdale. Her first novel, *Crump Folk Going Home* (1913), began a series of novels about working life in Westmoreland, most notably *The Lonely Plough* (1914). Her later novels were influenced by modernist fictional techniques; they include *The Splendid Fairing* (1919), which won the Femina/Vie Heureuse Prize, and *The Things which Belong* (1925). World's Classics reissued all her works in the 1930s, and some of her prefaces are informative.

See: Cavaliero, Glen, *The Rural Tradition in the English Novel 1900–39* (Macmillan, 1977).

HOLTBY, Winifred (1898–1935), born in Rudstone in the East Riding of Yorkshire; her father was a farmer, her mother became the Riding's first woman alderman. She attended school in Scarborough, and studied history at Oxford 1917–21, serving in the Women's Army Corps in 1918. Thereafter she lived in London with Vera Brittain, after Brittain's marriage remaining a member of the household. She was a prolific journalist, writing for the *Manchester Guardian*, the *Yorkshire Post* and *Time and Tide*, of which she became an editor in 1926; some of her articles are collected in *Testament of a Generation*, ed. Paul Berry and Alan Bishop (1985). She was very active in the women's movement, and, after a visit to South Africa in 1926, in support for African labour movements. Her 1933 novel, *Mandoa Mandoa*, was based on her African experiences. Her regional novels included her first novel, *Anderby Wold* (1923), *The Land of Green Ginger* (1927) and the bestselling *South Riding* (1936), published after her early death from kidney failure. She also wrote *Virginia Woolf* (1932), the first critical study in English of Woolf, and *Women in a Changing Civilization* (1934).

Letters to a Friend, ed. Alice Holtby and Jean McWilliam (Collins, 1937).

Brittain, Vera, *Testament of Friendship* (Gollancz, 1940).

See: Kennard, Jean, *Vera Brittain and Winifred Holtby: A Working Partnership* (Hanover: University of New Hampshire Press, 1989).

Leonardi, Susan, *Dangerous by Degrees: Women at Oxford and the Somerville College Novelists* (New Brunswick: Rutgers University Press, 1989).

Shaw, Marion, 'Feminism and Fiction Between the Wars: Winifred Holtby and Virginia Woolf', in *Women's Writing: A Challenge to Theory* (Hemel Hempstead: Harvester Wheatsheaf, 1986).

IRWIN, Margaret (Emma Faith) (?–1967), a popular novelist who successfully evaded publicity. She published her first novel, the time-travel romance, *Still She Wished for Company*, in 1924. In 1929 she married John Monsell, an artist. *Royal Flush* (1932) was the first of a series of historical romances centred on the House of Stuart, and presented as fictionalized biography. Others were *The Stranger Prince* (1937) and *The Gay Galliard* (1940). Her biggest success, however, was with a Tudor in *Young Bess* (1944), a romance of Elizabeth I's girlhood; there were two postwar sequels. She also wrote several one-act historical plays.

See: Crosland, Margaret, *Beyond the Lighthouse: English Women Novelists in the Twentieth Century* (Constable, 1981).

Light, Alison, '*Young Bess*: Historical Novels and Growing Up', *Feminist Review*, 33 (1989), pp. 57–71.

JAMESON, (Margaret) Storm (1891–1986), born in Whitby into a family whose long association with seafaring and shipbuilding provided the material for her historical trilogy, *The Triumph of Time* (1927–31). She attended school in Scarborough, and studied English at Leeds University 1909–12, winning a research scholarship for graduate study in London. Her MA thesis was published as *Modern Drama in Europe* (1920). In 1913 she married Charles Clarke; they had one child, and as a housebound mother she wrote her first novel, *The Pot Boils* (1919). In 1925 she divorced Clarke, and in 1926 married the historian, Guy Chapman. She worked in an advertising agency, edited the magazine *New Commonwealth*, and became English agent for the American publisher Knopf. In the 1930s she was very active in organizing political activity among writers to promote awareness of the European situation. She also assiduously promoted the importance of documentarist fiction, notably in her 1937 article, 'New Documents', collected in *A Civil Journey* (1939). Her major documentarist novels are the condition-of-England trilogy, *The Mirror in Darkness* (*Company Parade*, 1934, *Love in Winter*, 1935, and *None Turn Back*, 1936) and her panoramic novel about the fall of France, *Cloudless May* (1943). She was English President of PEN 1938–45, and heavily engaged in refugee relief; after the war she travelled and lectured widely in Europe.

Jameson, Storm, *No Time Like the Present* (Cassell, 1933) and *Journey from the North*, 2 vols (Collins/Harvill, 1969–70).

JESSE, F(ryniwyd Marsh) Tennyson (1888–1958), born in Kent into a clergyman's family, a great-niece of Tennyson. She studied art in Newlyn, Cornwall, and then became a journalist; she was one of the few women war reporters in the First World War. In 1918 she married the dramatist H.M. Harwood; they collaborated on several plays. She is best known, however, for her novels, which include *Moonraker* (1927), a feminist pirate romance, *The Lacquer Lady* (1929), a historical novel set in Burma, and her most famous, *A Pin to See the Peep-Show* (1934), based on the 1922 Bywaters–Thompson murder trial. The last deployed her keen interest in crime; she also wrote an analysis of murderers, *Murder and its Motives* (1924), and edited several volumes in the series, *Notable British Trials*, beginning with *Madeleine Smith* (1927).

Colenbrander, Joanna, *A Portrait of Fryn: A Biography of F. Tennyson Jesse* (Deutsch, 1984).

KAYE-SMITH, Sheila (1887–1956), born in Sussex into a surgeon's family. Her first novel, *The Tramping Methodist*, was published in 1908, but her first major success came with *Sussex Gorse* (1916), which began a series known as the 'Sussex novels', modelled on Hardy's Wessex novels. Later novels include *Little England* (1918), *Green Apple Harvest* (1919) and *Joanna Godden* (1921). In 1924 she married Theodore Penrose Fry, a Sussex vicar and later a baronet. In 1925 they both converted to Roman Catholicism. The favourable critical reception of her novels did not survive Gibbons's onslaught in *Cold Comfort Farm*, but she continued to publish novels. She also wrote *Talking of Jane Austen* (1943) with G.B. Stern.

Kaye-Smith, Sheila, *Three Ways Home* (Cassell, 1937).

See: Cavaleiro, Glen, *The Rural Tradition in the English Novel 1900–39* (Macmillan, 1977).

Drew, Elizabeth A., *The Modern Novel: Some Aspects of Contemporary Fiction* (Cape, 1926).

LEAVIS, Q(ueenie) D(orothy) (1906–81), born Q.D. Roth in London into a draper's family. She attended school in London, and studied English at Cambridge 1925–28. In 1929 she became a Research Fellow at Girton, the only academic appointment she was to hold, and also married Frank Raymond Leavis, severing relations with her family, who disapproved of a Gentile husband. They had three children. Her doctoral thesis was published as *Fiction and the Reading Public* (1932); the book's sociological approach and focus on popular literature was distinctive and influential, anticipating the methods and concerns of the journal *Scrutiny*, which began appearing later that year. She was heavily engaged in editorial and secretarial work for *Scrutiny*, and was its liveliest polemicist. She continued to publish literary criticism and supervise undergraduate work after the war. Her reputation remains overshadowed by that of her husband.

Kinch, M.B., Q.D. *Leavis, 1906–81: An Appreciation* (Retford: Brynmill Press, 1981).

See: Mulhern, Francis, *The Moment of Scrutiny* (New Left Books, 1979).

Robertson, P.J.M., *The Leavises on Fiction: An Historic Partnership* (Macmillan, 1981).

Thompson, Denys, *The Leavises: Recollections and Impressions* (Cambridge: Cambridge University Press, 1984).

LEHMANN, Rosamond (Nina), (1901–90), born in Buckinghamshire into a barrister's family. Her brother John became a leading editor, her sister Beatrix a leading actress. She studied modern languages at Cambridge 1919–22. She was married and divorced twice, to Leslie Runciman 1922–27, and to the sculptor Wogan Phillips 1928–42. She had two children; her daughter's death is the focus of her autobiography, *The Swan in the Evening* (1967). Her first novel, *Dusty Answer* (1927), was a scandalous success; later novels, which established her as a leading novelist especially concerned with the representation of women's consciousness and sexuality, included *A Note in Music* (1930), *Invitation to the Waltz* (1932), *The Weather in the Streets* (1936) and *The Ballad and the Source* (1944). She continued to publish novels after the war, notably *The Echoing Grove* (1953).

Lehmann, Rosamond, *The Swan in the Evening: Fragments of an Inner Life* (Collins, 1967).

See: Kaplan, Sydney Janet, *Feminist Consciousness in the Modern British Novel* (Urbana: University of Illinois Press, 1975).

Simons, Judy, *Rosamond Lehmann* (Macmillan, 1992).

Tindall, Gillian, *Rosamond Lehmann: An Appreciation* (Chatto and Windus, 1985).

MACAULAY, (Emilie) Rose (1881–1958), born in Rugby, where her father was a master at Rugby School, distantly related to the historian Macaulay. She spent most of her childhood in Italy, and studied history at Oxford 1900–03. Her first novel, *Abbots Verney*, appeared in 1906, and several well-received novels and volumes of poetry followed. In 1912 an uncle's legacy enabled her to leave home and rent a flat in London. During the war she worked for the Ministry of Information. She converted to Roman Catholicism, but a long secret affair, begun in 1918, with a married colleague and fellow-Catholic, Gerald O'Donovan, estranged her from the Church. Her first major success, *Potterism* (1920), began a series of satirical topical novels, including *Dangerous Ages* (1921), which won the Femina/Vie Heureuse Prize, *Told By an Idiot* (1923), *Orphan Island* (1924) and *Crewe Train* (1926). Her own favourite was the historical novel, *They Were Defeated* (1933). She was also a prolific journalist. During the Second World War she drove ambulances, and suffered O'Donovan's death in 1942, and the loss of all her books and papers in the Blitz in 1941. After the war she continued to be a prominent figure on the London literary scene, wrote travel books and more novels, notably *The Towers of Trebizond* (1956), and was made a Dame in 1957.

Macaulay, Rose, *Letters to a Friend* (1961), *Last Letters to a Friend* (1962) and *Letters to a Sister* (1964), all ed. Constance Babington-Smith (Collins).

Babington-Smith, Constance, *Rose Macaulay* (Collins, 1972).

Emery, Jane, *Rose Macaulay: A Writer's Life* (Murray, 1991).

MANSFIELD, Katherine (1888–1923), born Kathleen Mansfield Beauchamp in Wellington, New Zealand, into a banker's family. She attended schools in New Zealand, studied in London 1903–06, and returned to London in 1908 to begin writing short stories, influenced by Chekhov and by Symbolist writing. After an affair with Garnet Trowell, a violinist, she married George Bowden in 1909, and left him immediately for Germany, where she miscarried her child by Trowell. Her first collection of stories, *In a German Pension* (1911), was based on this episode. From 1912 she lived with the critic John Middleton Murry, whom she married in 1918, after divorcing Bowden; they became close friends with D.H. and Frieda Lawrence. In response to her brother's death in 1915 she turned to her New Zealand memories for material, and 'Prelude' (1918), developed from a longer version, 'The Aloe' (1930), was a landmark in the development of the short story. From 1916 she was friendly with Woolf, and they developed their modernist techniques in competition. Her later collections of stories were *Bliss and Other Stories* (1920), *The Garden Party and Other Stories* (1922) and posthumously *The Dove's Nest and Other Stories* (1923) and *Something Childish and Other Stories* (1924), both edited by Murry, who also published her *Poems* (1923), her reviews, *Novels and Novelists* (1930), and selections from her letters and journals. More of her criticism appears in *Critical Writing of Katherine Mansfield*, ed. Clare Hanson (1987). In her last years she travelled widely in Europe with Murry, or her close friend Ida Baker, seeking relief from the tuberculosis which caused her early death.

> *The Journal of Katherine Mansfield* (1927), *The Letters of Katherine Mansfield*, 2 vols (1928) and *Katherine Mansfield's Letters to John Middleton Murry* (1937), all ed. John Middleton Murry (Constable).

> *The Collected Letters of Katherine Mansfield*, ed. Vincent O'Sullivan and Margaret Scott, 3 vols to date (Oxford: Clarendon Press, 1984–).

> Alpers, Anthony, *The Life of Katherine Mansfield* (Cape, 1980). (Detailed study of relation of life and works.)

> Tomalin, Claire, *Katherine Mansfield: A Secret Life* (Viking, 1987). (Focuses especially on illness.)

See: Bowen, Elizabeth, 'A Living Writer: Katherine Mansfield', in *The Mulberry Tree: Writings of Elizabeth Bowen*, ed. Hermione Lee (Virago, 1986).

> Fulbrook, Kate, *Katherine Mansfield* (Brighton: Harvester Wheatsheaf, 1986). (Good introductory study.)

> Hankin, Cherry, *Katherine Mansfield and her Confessional Stories* (Macmillan, 1983).

> *Modern Fiction Studies*, special Mansfield issue, 24, 3 (1978).

MARSH, (Edith) Ngaio (1899–1982), born in Christchurch, New Zealand, into a bank clerk's family, studied painting, and then became an actress in a company touring Australasia. In 1928 she journeyed to London, and worked in interior decorating. In 1934 she published her first crime novel, *A Man Lay Dead*, which, like its successors, featured the detective, Inspector Alleyn. Later Alleyn novels often drew on her theatrical experience, as in *Enter a Murderer* (1935), or on artistic milieux, as in *Artists in Crime* (1938), or were set in New Zealand, as in *Vintage Murder* (1937). Her 1930s novels established her as a leading crime writer; after the war she continued to publish Alleyn novels, and was heavily involved in establishing a theatre company in New Zealand.

> Marsh, Ngaio, *Black Beech and Honeydew* (Collins, 1966).

> Lewis, Margaret, *Ngaio Marsh: A Life* (Chatto and Windus, 1991).

See: McDorman, Kathryne, *Ngaio Marsh* (Boston: Twayne, 1992).

MAYOR, F(lora) M(acdonald) (1872–1933), born in Surrey; her mother, Jessie Grote, was a linguist and translator, her father, James Mayor, a professor of classics and moral philosophy at London University. She studied history at Cambridge, but neglected study for the theatre, and was an actress 1896–1903. Her first novel, *Mrs Hammond's Children* (1901), was published under her stage name, Mary Stafford. In 1904, after the death of her architect fiancé, Richard Shepherd, she became an invalid, living with her parents and later with her twin, Alice. Her major novels, *The Third Miss Symons* (1913) and the very successful *The Rector's Daughter* (1924), are harrowing studies of redundant women. She also wrote *The Squire's Daughter* (1929).

Oldfield, Sybil, *Spinsters of this Parish: The Life and Times of F.M. Mayor and Mary Sheepshank* (Virago, 1984).

See: Williams, Merryn, *Six Women Novelists* (Basingstoke: Macmillan, 1987).

MEW, Charlotte (1869–1928), born into an architect's family in Bloomsbury, where she lived throughout her life. Three of her siblings died young, and two were confined in mental hospitals. She attended school in London, and lectures at the University. Her first publications were stories for the magazines *Temple Bar* and the *Yellow Book* in the 1890s, and she continued to publish stories and essays, but her major work is her collection of poems, *The Farmer's Bride* (1916). It was admired for its innovative use of free verse and its passionate lyricism; admirers included Hardy, who helped secure her a civil list pension in 1922, and Sinclair, for whom she had an unrequited passion. She lived with her remaining sibling, Anne, and in 1928 poisoned herself after Anne's death. A second collection of poems, *The Rambling Sailor*, appeared in 1929, and her *Collected Poems and Prose*, ed. Val Warner, in 1981.

Fitzgerald, Penelope, *Charlotte Mew and her Friends* (Collins, 1984).

See: Day, Gary and Wisker, Gina, 'Recuperating and Revaluing: Edith Sitwell and Charlotte Mew', in Gary Day and Brian Docherty, eds, *British Poetry 1900–50* (Macmillan, 1995).

Leighton, Angela, *Victorian Women Poets: Writing Against the Heart* (Hemel Hempstead: Harvester Wheatsheaf, 1992).

Warner, Val, 'Introduction', *Collected Poems and Prose of Charlotte Mew*, ed. Warner (Carcanet/Virago, 1981).

MITCHISON, Naomi (Margaret) (1897–), born N.M. Haldane in Edinburgh into a physiologist's family; her brother John became a leading scientist. She attended school in Oxford, and studied science at the University 1913–15.

During the war she was a VAD nurse, and in 1916 married Richard Mitchison, a barrister and later a Labour MP 1945–64; they had eight children. She was active in left-wing politics, visited the USSR in the 1930s, and also campaigned for birth-control clinics. Her first book, *The Conquered* (1923), began a series of historical fictions, set in the ancient world, which drew parallels with contemporary European politics. Others were *When the Bough Breaks and Other Stories* (1924), *Cloud-Cuckoo-Land* (1925), *Black Sparta: Greek Stories* (1927), her most famous novel *The Corn King and the Spring Queen* (1931), and *The Blood of the Martyrs* (1939). She also wrote *We Have Been Warned* (1935), based on her USSR visit. In 1937 the Mitchisons moved from London to Argyll, and she was thereafter active in Scottish politics. She continued to publish fiction after the war, and her political activities included becoming a tribal mother in Botswana.

Mitchison, Naomi, *Small Talk: Memoirs of an Edwardian Childhood* (1973), *All Change Here: Girlhood and Marriage* (1975) (both Bodley Head), and *You May Well Ask; A Memoir 1920–40*, (Gollancz, 1979).

Benton, Jill, *Naomi Mitchison: A Century of Experiment in Life and Letters* (Pandora, 1990).

NESBIT, E(dith) (1858–1924), born in London; her father ran an agricultural college, run by her mother after his death in 1862. She attended several schools in England and France, and began publishing verse in magazines in her teens. In 1880 she married Hubert Bland, a brush-manufacturer and later journalist; they had four children, and his rapid business failure made her writing essential to the family income. She also brought up Bland's two illegitimate children as her own; the family's other unconventionalities included her own love affairs, for example with Shaw. In 1883 the Blands became founder members of the Fabian Society, and were thereafter heavily involved in its activities. Her first book was a socialist romance, co-written with Bland under the name 'Fabian Bland', *The Prophet's Mantle* (1885). She wrote adult fiction, verse and political pamphlets, until the success of *The Story of the Treasure-Seekers* (1899), the first of her innovative and influential family adventure stories for children. Its first sequel, *The Wouldbegoods* (1901), was her biggest financial success; *The Railway Children* (1906) was another success in the genre. In 1902 *Five Children and It* began the series of fantasies which were her most distinctive work, and which were all serialized in the *Strand Magazine*. They included its two sequels, *The Phoenix and the Carpet* (1904) and *The Story of the Amulet* (1906), *The Enchanted Castle* (1907), and her own favourite, *Harding's Luck* (1909). After Bland's death in 1914 she married Thomas Tucker, a marine engineer, in 1917.

Nesbit, E., *Long Ago When I Was Young* (Whiting and Wheaton, 1966).

Briggs, Julia, *A Woman of Passion: The Life of E. Nesbit 1858–1924* (Hutchinson, 1987).

Moore, Doris Langley, *E. Nesbit: A Biography* (Benn, 1933).

See: Dusinberre, Juliet, *Alice to the Lighthouse: Children's Books and Radical Experiments in Art* (Macmillan, 1987).

ORCZY, Baroness (Emma Magdalena Rosalia Maria Josepha Barbara) (1865–1947), born in Tarna Oss, Hungary, into an aristocratic landowning family. After peasant riots against mechanization wrecked the family estate, they moved to Budapest, and then to Brussels and Paris, where she attended convent-school. She studied art in London, and married fellow-artist Montague Barstow; they had one child. Her first book, with Barstow, was a translation, *Old Hungarian Fairy Tales* (1895), and she wrote several more children's stories and historical romances, before finding success with a French Revolutionary play, *The Scarlet Pimpernel* (1903), and its bestselling novel version of 1905. A string of sequels to the novel maintained her success as a leading historical romancer; they included *I Will Repay* (1906), *The Elusive Pimpernel* (1908), *El Dorado* (1913), *Lord Tony's Wife* (1917), and continued until *Mam'zelle Guillotine* (1940). She also created two fictional detectives in *The Old Man in the Corner* (1909), which had several sequels, and *Lady Molly of the Yard* (1910). From 1918 she lived in Monte Carlo, returning to Britain in 1945.

Orczy, Baroness, *Links in the Chain of Life* (Hutchinson, 1947).

PANKHURST, (Estelle) Sylvia (1882–1960), born in Manchester into a doctor's family. Her mother Emmeline became leader of the militant suffragette movement, the WSPU; her father Richard, to whom she was close, campaigned for radical causes, and stood as Independent Labour Party candidate. She won successive scholarships to study art in Manchester, Venice and London, but in London became responsible for organizing WSPU activity in the East End. She was first imprisoned in 1906, and several times thereafter. Her socialist views, and friendship with the Labour leader Keir Hardie, increasingly estranged her from the Tory feminism of her mother and elder sister Christabel, and in 1913 she led the East End branch out of the WSPU. She launched a paper, the *Women's Dreadnought*, which continued to appear through the war, during which she campaigned for the rights of East End women and children. She lived with the Italian socialist Silvio Corio; they had one child. She wrote two memoirs, *The Suffragette Movement* (1931) and *The Home Front* (1932), and a biography, *The Life of Emmeline Pankhurst* (1935). She later campaigned for Ethiopian independence.

Pankhurst, Sylvia, *The Suffragette Movement: An Intimate Account of Persons and Ideals* (Longmans, Green, 1931); *The Home Front: A Mirror of Life in England During the World War* (Hutchinson, 1932); 'Sylvia Pankhurst', in *Myself When Young by Famous Women of Today*, ed. Margot Oxford and Asquith (Muller, 1938).

Pankhurst, Richard Keir, *Sylvia Pankhurst, Artist and Crusader: An Intimate Portrait* (New York: Paddington Press, 1979). (Her son's memoir, emphasizing her artistic interests.)

Romero, Patricia, E. *Sylvia Pankhurst: Portrait of a Radical* (New Haven: Yale University Press, 1987). (The most comprehensive biography.)

POTTER, (Helen) Beatrix (1866–1943), born in London into a wealthy leisured family. During a secluded childhood she surrounded herself with small animals, whom she practised drawing. Her first project, an illustrated history of fungi, was rejected for publication, but in 1901 she published privately *The Tale of Peter Rabbit*, based on an illustrated letter to a child. Its success encouraged the publishers Frederick Warne to publish it with colour illustrations in 1902, followed in 1903 by *The Tailor of Gloucester*, also first published privately, and *The Tale of Squirrel Nutkin*. Their success was immediate, and sixteen more of her distinctive illustrated books followed in 1904–13, establishing her as the leading figure in books for small children. They included *The Tale of Two Bad Mice* (1904), *The Tale of Mrs Tiggywinkle* (1905), *The Tale of Jemima Puddleduck* (1908) and *The Tale of Mr Tod* (1912). In 1905, after the death of her fiancé, the publisher Norman Warne, she bought Hill Top Farm in the Lake District, the setting for several later books. She wrote little after 1913, though an uncharacteristic fantasy, *The Fairy Caravan* (1927), was published in America only. She married a local solicitor, William Heelis, in 1913, became a well-known farmer of Herdwick sheep, and an active early supporter of the National Trust to which she left her property. Her works are widely translated and remain a focus of publicity and tourism.

The Journal of Beatrix Potter from 1881–97, ed. Leslie Linder (Warne, 1966).

The Letters of Beatrix Potter, ed. Judy Taylor (Warne, 1989).

Lane, Margaret, *The Tale of Beatrix Potter: A Biography* (Warne, 1946).

Taylor, Judy, *Beatrix Potter: Artist, Storyteller and Countrywoman* (Warne, 1986).

See: Greene, Graham, 'Beatrix Potter', in *The Lost Childhood and Other Essays* (Eyre and Spottiswode, 1951).

Linder, Leslie, *A History of the Writings of Beatrix Potter, Including the Unpublished* (Warne, 1971).

POWER, Eileen (1889–1940), born in Altrincham into a stockbroker's family, attended schools in Bournemouth and Oxford, and studied history at Cambridge 1907–10. She then studied at the Ecole des Chartres in Paris 1910–11, was Research Fellow at LSE 1911–13, and Director of Studies at Girton 1913–20. In 1920 she won a travelling scholarship to China, and in 1921 became a lecturer, and from 1931 Professor, at LSE. She worked closely with the historians G.C. Coulton at Cambridge, and R.S. Tawney at LSE, where she ran the Economic History Society from 1926. In 1937 she married the historian Michael Postan, who had been her research assistant. She was an active supporter of the women's movement and peace organizations. Her publications in social and economic history included her expanded MA thesis, *Medieval English Nunneries c.1275–1535* (1922), the popular history, *Medieval People* (1924), the article 'Peasant Life and Rural Conditions (*c.*1100 to *c.*1500)' in *Cambridge Medieval History*, VII (1932), and the lectures *The Wool Trade in English Medieval History* (1941), edited by Postan after her death from a heart attack. She also collaborated on history books for children with her sister Rhoda. Her lectures on women's history were published im *Medieval Women*, ed. Postan (1975).

> Berg, Maxine, 'Eileen Power', in Edward Shils and Carmen Blacker, eds, *Cambridge Women: Twelve Portraits* (Cambridge: Cambridge University Press, 1996), and *A Woman in History: Eileen Power 1889–1940* (Cambridge: Cambridge University Press, 1996).

See: Davis, Natalie Zemon, 'History's Two Bodies', *American Historical Review*, 93 (1988), pp. 1–30.

RHYS, Jean (1890–1979), born Ella Gwendoline Rees Williams in Roseau, Dominica, to a Creole mother and immigrant Welsh doctor father. She attended convent school in Roseau, journeyed to Britain in 1907 for school in Cambridge, and studied at RADA 1908–09. She worked as a chorus-girl in touring musicals, and also as model and film extra. After a love affair with a stockbroker, Lancelot Smith, she married Jean Lenglet, a Dutch journalist, in 1919; they had two children, but one died in infancy. They travelled in Europe; in 1923, during Lenglet's imprisonment in France for currency offences, she became the lover of the writer Ford Madox Ford, who encouraged her writing. Her first book was *The Left Bank and Other Stories* (1927); her first novel, *Quartet* (1928), was based on her affair with Ford. Three further novels, all closely based on her experiences, followed in the 1930s, *After Leaving Mr Mackenzie* (1930), *Voyage in the Dark* (1934) and *Good Morning, Midnight* (1939). She returned to Britain in 1928, and after divorce from Lenglet in 1933, married Leslie Tilden-Smith, a literary agent, in 1934; after his death in 1944 she married Max Hamer, a solicitor, imprisoned for embezzlement 1950–52. She then lived in obscurity and alcoholism in London, Cornwall and Devon, and published little; in 1949 she was briefly imprisoned in Holloway for assault. *Wide Sargasso Sea* (1966), a Caribbean prequel to *Jane Eyre*, established her reputation, and she was belatedly recognized as perhaps the greatest British woman writer of the period after Woolf. Her novels were all reissued, and two collections of her stories appeared, *Tigers Are Better Looking* (1968) and *Sleep It Off, Lady* (1976).

Rhys, Jean, *Smile Please* (Deutsch, 1979).

The Letters of Jean Rhys 1931–66, ed. Francis Wyndham and Diana Melly (Deutsch, 1984).

Angier, Carole, *Jean Rhys: Life and Work* (Deutsch, 1990).

See: Bowlby, Rachel, *Still Crazy After All Those Years: Women's Writing and Psycho-Analysis* (Routledge, 1992). (Good chapter on *Good Morning, Midnight*.)

Harrison, Nancy, *Jean Rhys and the Novel as Women's Text* (Chapel Hill: University of North Carolina Press, 1988).

Howells, Coral Ann, *Jean Rhys* (Hemel Hempstead: Harvester Wheatsheaf, 1991). (Perceptive analysis and good place to start.)

James, Louis, *Jean Rhys* (Longman, 1978). (The first important critical study.)

Mellown, Elgin W., *Jean Rhys: A Descriptive and Annotated Bibliography of Works and Criticism* (New York and London: Gale, 1984).

O'Connor, Teresa, *Jean Rhys's West Indian Novels* (New York: New York University Press, 1986).

Roe, Sue, 'The Shadow of Light: The Symbolic Underworld of Jean Rhys', in Sue Roe, ed., *Women Reading Women's Writing* (Brighton: Harvester, 1987). (Perceptive essay.)

Spivak, Gayatri Chakravorty, 'Three Women's Texts and a Critique of Imperialism', *Critical Inquiry*, 12 (1985), pp. 243–61. (Seminal essay on *Wide Sargasso Sea*.)

Staley, Thomas, *Jean Rhys: A Critical Study* (Macmillan, 1979).

RICHARDSON, Dorothy (1873–1957), born in Abingdon into a wealthy leisured family, attended various schools, and, after her father's bankruptcy in 1891, worked as pupil-teacher in Hanover, as teacher and governess in England, and cared for her mother, who killed herself in 1895. She worked as dental receptionist in London 1896–1906, was politically active in left-wing and women's movements, and became a journalist, encouraged by H.G. Wells, with whom she had a love affair ending in a miscarriage. In

1917 she married the artist Alan Odle: they lived in London and Cornwall. Her first novel, *Pointed Roofs* (1915), inaugurated the sequence of thirteen novels, *Pilgrimage*, closely based on her experiences, and a major development in stream of consciousness technique. The next ten novels, *Backwater* (1916), *Honeycomb* (1917), *The Tunnel* (1919), *Interim* (1919), *Deadlock* (1921), *Revolving Lights* (1923), *The Trap* (1925), *Oberland* (1927), *Dawn's Left Hand* (1931) and *Clear Horizon* (1935), appeared with the twelfth, *Dimple Hill*, in the first collected *Pilgrimage* (1938). The thirteenth, *March Moonlight*, appeared posthumously in the 1967 edition of *Pilgrimage*. Her journalism included a regular column in the film magazine *Close Up* (1927–33). Her place as an important innovator in modernist fiction is undisputed.

Fromm, Gloria, *Dorothy Richardson: A Biography* (Urbana: University of Illinois Press, 1977).

See: Hanscombe, Gillian, *The Art of Life: Dorothy Richardson and the Development of Feminist Consciousness* (Peter Owen, 1982).

Heath, Stephen, 'Writing for Silence: Dorothy Richardson and the Novel', in Suzanne Kappeler and Norman Bryson, eds, *Teaching the Text* (Routledge and Kegan Paul, 1983). (An important article.)

Kaplan, Sydney, *Feminist Consciousness in the Modern British Novel* (Urbana: University of Illinois Press, 1975).

Pykett, Lyn, *Engendering Fictions: The English Novel in the Early Twentieth Century* (Edward Arnold, 1995). (Places work in relation to precursors and Woolf.)

Radford, Jean, *Dorothy Richardson* (Hemel Hempstead: Harvester Wheatsheaf, 1991). (Good introductory study.)

Sinclair, May, 'The novels of Dorothy Richardson', *The Egoist*, 5 (1918), pp. 57–9. (Seminal modernist article.)

RICHARDSON, Henry Handel (1870–1946), born Ethel Florence Lindesay Richardson in Melbourne, Australia; her English mother and Irish doctor father emigrated during the 1850s gold-rush. Her mother's work as postmistress paid for her Melbourne schooling. She studied music in Leipzig 1892–95, then married George Robertson, a professor of philology first at Strasbourg, and then from 1904 at London University. She lived in Britain from 1904. Her first novel, *Maurice Guest* (1908), was based on her Leipzig experiences, the second, *The Getting of Wisdom* (1910), on her school-days. Her major work, the trilogy *The Fortunes of Richard Mahoney* (*Australia Felix*, 1917, *The Way Home*, 1925, *Ultima Thule*, 1929) was based on her parents' experiences as immigrants as recorded in letters and journals. It was very well-received, and she was a Nobel nominee in 1932.

Richardson, Henry Handel, *Myself When Young* (Heinemann, 1948).

See: Buckley, Vincent, *Henry Handel Richardson* (Melbourne: Landsdowne Press, 1973).

McLeod, Karen, *Henry Handel Richardson: A Critical Study* (Cambridge: Cambridge University Press, 1985). (The most comprehensive study.)

Palmer, Nettie, *Henry Handel Richardson: A Study* (Sydney: Angus and Robertson, 1950). (The first critical study.)

ROBINS, Elizabeth (1862–1952), born Louisville, Kentucky, into a banker's family; in 1878 left her Ohio school to join a touring actors' company. In 1887 she married fellow-actor George Parks. After his suicide she journeyed to Britain in 1888, where she became famous for her performances in Ibsen. In 1900 she retired from the stage, after a journey in Alaska during the gold-rush, to concentrate on writing and work for the suffrage movement. She founded the Actresses' Franchise League, was President of the Women Writers' Suffrage League, and an editor of *Time and Tide* in the 1920s. Of her earlier works the most successful were the novels *George Mandeville's Husband* (1894), under the pseudonym C.E. Raimond, and *The Magnetic North* (1904), based on her Alaskan journey. Her successful play, *Votes for Women* (1907), became the novel, *The Convert* (also 1907). Some of her suffrage articles were published in *Way Stations* (1913); her major postwar work was the polemic *Ancilla's Share: An Indictment of Sex Antagonism* (1924). She published Henry James's letters to her in *Theatre and Friendship* (1932).

Robins, Elizabeth, *Both Sides of the Curtain* (Heinemann, 1940).

See: Mulford, Wendy, 'Socialist-feminist Criticism: A Case Study, Women's Suffrage and Literature 1906–14', in Peter Widdowson, ed., *Re-Reading English* (Methuen, 1982).

RUCK, Berta (1878–1978), born Amy Roberta Ruck in India into an army officer's family, lived in Merioneth with her grandmother from 1880 until her parents' return in 1888, when her father became Chief Constable of Caernarvonshire. She attended school in Bangor, and studied art in London and Paris. In 1909 she married the novelist Oliver Onions; they had two children. She worked as an illustrator, but turned to writing romantic fiction for magazines, especially *Home Chat*, a serial which became her first novel, *His Official Fiancée* (1914). A series of topical romantic novels during the First World War, including *The Lad with Wings* (1916), *The Girls at His Billet*, and *The Bridge of Kisses* (both 1917), established her as a leading romantic novelist. Postwar novels, such as *Sweethearts Unmet* (1918), addressed themselves to the romantic problems of demob. She was an enthusiastic publicist on lecture tours in Britain and America, and continued publishing until 1972.

Ruck, Berta, *A Storyteller Tells the Truth: Reminiscences and Notes* (Hutchinson, 1935).

SAYERS, Dorothy L(eigh) (1893–1957), born in Oxford into a headmaster's family, educated by governess and at school in Salisbury, and studied modern languages at Oxford. After teaching, and work in publishing, she worked as copywriter for an advertising agency 1921–31. In 1924 she had an illegitimate son, who was brought up by a cousin, and in 1926 she married the journalist Oswald Fleming. Her first novel, *Whose Body?* (1923), introduced the detective Lord Peter Wimsey, and subsequent Wimsey novels established her as a leading crime novelist. They included *Unnatural Death* (1927), *Murder Must Advertise* (1933), based on her advertising experiences, *The Nine Tailors* (1934), her major critical success, and *Gaudy Night* (1935), set in Oxford. The last Wimsey novel, *Busman's Honeymoon* (1937), began as a play, co-written with Muriel St Clare Byrne. She attempted to raise the status of the genre, co-founding the Detection Club in 1930, and working on a never-finished study of Wilkie Collins. After 1937 she turned to other genres, including religious drama, notably in her controversial radio series, *The Man Born To Be King* (1941–42), and later translation of Dante's *Inferno* (1949) and *Purgatorio* (1955).

The Letters of Dorothy L. Sayers 1899–1936, ed. Barbara Reynolds (Hodder and Stoughton, 1995).

Hitchman, Janet, *Such a Strange Lady: An Introduction to Dorothy L. Sayers* (New English Library, 1975).

Reynolds, Barbara, *Dorothy L. Sayers: Her Life and Soul* (Hodder and Stoughton, 1995). (The fullest and most sympathetic biography.)

See: Hannay, Margaret P., ed., *As Her Whimsy Took Her: Critical Works on the Work of Dorothy L. Sayers* (Kent, Ohio: Kent State University Press, 1979).

Harman, R.B. and Burger, M.A., *An Annotated Guide to the Works of Dorothy L. Sayers* (New York: Garland, 1977).

Youngberd, Ruth, *Dorothy L. Sayers: A Reference Guide* (Boston: G.K. Hall, 1982).

SCHREINER, Olive (Emilie Albertina) (1855–1920), born in Basutoland to an English mother and German father, both Methodist missionaries. She worked as a governess with various farming families 1870–80, spent part of 1873 at Kimberley during the diamond-rush, and began writing. She lived in London 1881–89, and in 1883 her novel, *The Story of an African Farm*, under the pseudonym Ralph Iron, was published to great acclaim. She participated in the political debates of the period: close friends included Eleanor Marx, Karl Pearson, Havelock Ellis and Edward Carpenter. In 1889 she returned to South Africa, and in 1894 married Samuel Cronwright, a farmer; they had one child who died the same day. She lived in England again 1913–20, and in South Africa from 1920. In the 1890s she published two collections of short allegories, *Dreams* (1891) and *Dream Life and Real Life* (1893). Her major works after 1900 were the feminist polemic, *Woman and Labour* (1911), which became the handbook of the women's movement, and the unfinished novel, *From Man to Man* (1924), on which she had been working since 1875. The novel *Undine* (1929) also dated from the 1870s.

Letters of Olive Schreiner 1876–1920 and *The Life of Olive Schreiner,* both ed. Samuel Cronwright-Schreiner (Fisher Unwin, 1924).

Letters of Olive Schreiner 1871–99, ed. R. Rive (Oxford: Oxford University Press, 1988).

Furst, Ruth and Scott, Ann, *Olive Schreiner* (Deutsch, 1980).

SINCLAIR, May (1863–1946), born Mary Amelia St Clair Sinclair in Cheshire into a Liverpool shipowner's family. Her parents separated after her father's bankruptcy in 1870, and until her mother's death in 1901 she lived at home, caring for her four brothers, who all died of heart disease. She spent one year at Cheltenham Ladies' College, where the headmistress, Dorothea Beale, encouraged her to read philosophy and psychology. Her first book was *Nakiketas and Other Poems* (1887), her first novel *Audrey Craven* (1897), and her first success was the novel *The Divine Fire* (1904), which established her reputation as a leading novelist in Britain and America. Her major themes were women's situation and the dilemmas of modern writers, most successfully treated in *The Creators* (1910) and *The Three Sisters* (1914), the latter developed from her critical study, *The Three Brontës* (1912). She was a committed progressive, whose causes included the suffrage movement, the development of psychoanalysis as a founding member of the London Medico-Psychological Clinic, and the promotion of modernism, in her essays on Pound, Eliot and especially Richardson. In a 1919 review of *Pilgrimage* she launched the phrase 'stream of consciousness'. During the war she drove an ambulance at the front, and wrote the war novel, *The Tree of Heaven* (1917). Her postwar fiction evolved in response to her interest in modernism and psychoanalysis, notably in *Mary Olivier: A Life* (1919) and *The Life and Death of Harriett Frean* (1922). Her reputation did not survive the 1920s, but she was an important figure in the transition to modernism.

See: Boll, T.E.M., *Miss May Sinclair, Novelist: A Biographical and Critical Introduction* (Rutherford, N.J.; Fairleigh Dickinson University Press, 1973).

Kaplan, Sydney Janet, *Feminine Consciousness in the Modern British Novel* (Urbana: University of Illinois Press, 1975).

Robb, Kenneth, 'May Sinclair: An Annotated Bibliography of Writings About Her', *English Literature in Transition*, 16, 3 (1973), pp. 177–231.

Zegger, Hrisey, *May Sinclair* (Boston: Twayne, 1976).

SITWELL, Edith (Louisa) (1887–1964), born in Scarborough into an aristocratic family: her brothers Osbert and Sacheverell also became writers, all three reacting against the parental milieu. She was educated by governesses, including Helen Rootham, with whom she lived in London from 1914. She published her first volume of poems, *The Mother*, in 1915; *Clowns' Houses* (1916) established her as a leading innovative poet. The Sitwells published an annual anthology, *Wheels* (1916–21), in opposition to the Georgian school of poetry. Her most famous work, *Facade* (1922), a collaboration with the composer William Walton, confirmed her reputation as a controversial figure; its first performance in 1923 was a major 1920s avant-garde event. *Gold Coast Customs* (1929) juxtaposed Ashanti and Mayfair rituals. In the 1930s she worked in the more profitable form of biography, including *Victoria of England* (1936), and wrote one novel, *I Live Under a Black Sun* (1937), about Swift. In the Second World War her poetic reputation was revived, notably by *Street Songs* (1942), but later, though she continued to publish and lecture, she was best known as a colourful eccentric.

Sitwell, Edith, *Taken Care Of* (Hutchinson, 1965).

Edith Sitwell: Selected Letters, ed. John Lehmann and Derek Parker (Macmillan, 1970).

Glendinning, Victoria, *Edith Sitwell: A Unicorn Among Lions* (Weidenfeld and Nicholson, 1981).

See: Day, Gary and Wisker, Gina, 'Recuperating and Revaluing: Edith Sitwell and Charlotte Mew', in *British Poetry 1900–50: Aspects of Tradition* (Macmillan, 1995).

Yeats, W.B., 'Modern Poetry', in *Essays and Introductions* (Macmillan, 1969).

SMITH, Stevie (1902–71), born Florence Margaret Smith in Hull into a shipping agent's family, brought up in Palmers Green, London, by her aunt with whom she lived throughout her life, attended school in London and, after a secretarial course, became secretary to the publishers Newnes and Pearson 1922–52. Her first book was *Novel on Yellow Paper* (1936), written after Cape rejected her poems, and advised fiction. Her first volume of poetry, *A Good Time Was Had By All* (1937), was followed by *Tender Only to One* (1938) and *Mother, What Is Man?* (1942), and five postwar volumes. By the 1960s she was recognized as an important poet, and her poetry readings were very popular. Her *Collected Poems* appeared in 1975.

Dick, Kay, ed., *Ivy and Stevie: Ivy Compton-Burnett and Stevie Smith: Conversations and Reflections* (Duckworth, 1971).

Barbera, Jack and McBrien, William, *Stevie: A Biography of Stevie Smith* (Heinemann, 1985).

Spalding, Frances, *Stevie Smith: A Critical Biography* (Faber, 1988).

See: Heaney, Seamus, 'A Memorable Voice', in *Preoccupations: Selected Prose 1968–78* (Faber, 1980).

Montefiore, Jan, *Feminism and Poetry: Language, Experience, Identity, in Women's Writing* (Pandora, 1987).

Pumphrey, Martin, 'Play, Fantasy and Strange Laughter: Stevie Smith's Uncomfortable Poetry', *Critical Quarterly*, 28, 3 (1986), pp. 85–96.

STARK, Freya (Madeline) (1893–1993), born in Paris to parents who were both painters, brought up in Devon and Asolo, Italy, where her mother ran a carpet factory, studied English and then history at London University from 1912, but left to nurse in Italy during the war. In the 1920s she learned Arabic, and in 1927 began travelling in the Middle East. Her first book was *Baghdad Sketches* (1932). *The Valleys of the Assassins* (1934), which established her as a leading travel writer, was based on her Persian journeys 1930–31, and, like its successors, illustrated by her photographs. It won geographic medals, as did *The Southern Gates of Arabia* (1936) and *A Winter in Arabia* (1940). During the war she worked for the Ministry of Information as an Arabist. In 1947 she married Stuart Perowne, a diplomat, but they soon separated. She continued to travel well into old age, with Asolo as her base, and to publish travel books and autobiographies. She became a Dame in 1972.

Stark, Freya, *Traveller's Prelude* (1950), *Beyond Euphrates* (1951), *Coast of Incense* (1953) and *Dust in the Lion's Paw* (1961) (all Murray).

The Letters of Freya Stark 1914–80, ed. Lucy Moorehead, 8 vols (Salisbury: Compton Russell/Michael Russell, 1974–82).

STRACHEY, Ray (1887–1940), born Rachel Costelloe in London into a wealthy leisured family. After her parents' separation in 1891 she lived with her Roman Catholic father, but was brought up by her Quaker grandmother, the preacher Hannah Whitall-Smith. She studied maths at Cambridge, and while there wrote a novel, *The World at Eighteen* (1907), and worked for the women's suffragist movement, the NUWSS. In 1911 she married Oliver Strachey of the well-known family. She was an adviser to Nancy Astor from 1918, and stood as an Independent in three elections 1918–23. She became an expert in women's employment, and from 1919 ran the London Women's Service Bureau, which became the Women's Employment Federation in 1934. Her major work was *The Cause: A Short History of the Women's Movement in Britain* (1928). She also wrote two biographies, *A Quaker Grandmother: Hannah Whitall-Smith* (1914) and *Millicent Garrett Fawcett* (1931), the handbook, *Careers and Openings for Women* (1935), and edited an important collection of feminist essays, *Our Freedom and its Results* (1936).

Harrison, Brian, *Prudent Revolutionaries: Portraits of British Feminists Between the Wars* (Oxford: Clarendon Press, 1987).

THOMPSON, Flora (1877–1947), born F. Timms at Juniper Hill, Oxon. into a stonemason's family, in 1890 became assistant to the postmistress in Fringford, and then from 1897 post office assistant at Grayford, Hants. In 1900 married post office clerk John Thompson; they lived in Bournemouth and Liphook, and had three children. Encouraged by winning a magazine competition, she wrote stories, poems and essays for magazines, a nature column for *Catholic Fireside* (1920–27), and ran a correspondence society for would-be writers, the Peverel Society. Her first book, a poetry volume, *Bog Myrtle* (1921), went unnoticed, but a 1937 article in the *Lady*, 'Old Queenie', expanded to become her fictionalized childhood memoir, *Lark Rise* (1939). From 1945 it appeared with its sequels, *Over to Candleford* (1941) and *Candleford Green* (1943), as the trilogy, *Lark Rise to Candleford*. It achieved instant classic status. A final memoir, *Still Glides the Stream*, appeared in 1948.

Lane, Margaret, *Flora Thompson* (Murray, 1976).

See: Dusinberre, Juliet, 'The Child's Eye and the Adult's Voice: Flora Thompson's *Lark Rise to Candleford*', *Review of English Studies*, 35, 137 (1984), pp. 61–70.

English, Barbara, 'Lark Rise and Juniper Hill: A Victorian Community in Literature and History', *Victorian Studies*, 29 (1985), pp. 7–34.

WADDELL, Helen (1889–1965), born in Tokyo into a Presbyterian missionary family, and spent early life in Japan. She studied to MA level at Queen's University, Belfast, 1909–12. After caring for her stepmother 1912–20, she lectured in Oxford and London 1920–23, and studied medieval Latin poetry in Paris 1923–25. Her major work, *The Wandering Scholars* (1927), was a surprising popular success. The free translation, *Medieval Latin Lyrics* (1929), and the novel, *Peter Abelard* (1933), followed; later works included *Poetry in the Dark Ages* (1948). She published several more translations, and was a popular visiting lecturer.

Blackett, Monica, *The Mark of the Maker: A Portrait of Helen Waddell* (Constable, 1973).

Corrigan, Felicitas, *Helen Waddell: A Biography* (Gollancz, 1986).

WARNER, Sylvia Townsend (1893–1978), born in Harrow, and educated at home by her father, a Harrow School master. From 1913 she had a long-term secret love affair with the musicologist, Percy Buck. She worked in a munitions factory in the First World War, and from 1918 lived in London, working as editor and transcriber on the ten-volume *Tudor Church Music* project, 1918–30. Her first book was the volume of poetry, *The Espalier* (1925), her first novel the bestselling *Lolly Willowes or the Loving Huntsman* (1926). From 1930 she lived in the country, mainly in Dorset, with her partner, the poet Valentine Ackland. She became a friend and supporter of the Dorset novelist, T.F. Powys. In 1935 she joined the Communist Party, was active in local organizing, and travelled twice to the Spanish Civil War. She continued to publish poetry, including *Time Importuned* (1982) and *Opus 3* (1931), but is best known for her novels, *Mr Fortune's Maggot* (1927), *The True Heart* (1929), *Summer Will Show* (1936) and *After the Death of Don Juan* (1938). She also published several collections of stories, including *The Cats' Cradle-Book* (1940) in America only, and *A Garland of Straw* (1943). During the war she worked on her major novel, *The Corner that Held Them* (1948). Her postwar work was mainly in stories, including the *New Yorker* stories which appeared as *Kingdoms of Elfin* (1977), and in poetry; her *Collected Poems*, ed. Clare Harman, appeared in 1982.

Diaries of Sylvia Townsend Warner, ed. Clare Harman (Chatto and Windus, 1994),

The Letters of Sylvia Townsend Warner, ed. William Maxwell (Chatto and Windus, 1982).

Sylvia and David: The Townsend Warner/Garnett Letters, ed. Richard Garnett (Sinclair Stevenson, 1994).

Harman, Clare, *Sylvia Townsend Warner: A Biography* (Chatto and Windus, 1989).

Mulford, Wendy, *This Narrow Place: Sylvia Townsend Warner and Valentine Ackland: Life, Letters and Politics 1930–51* (Pandora, 1989).

See: Brothers, Barbara, 'Writing Against the Grain: Sylvia Townsend Warner and the Spanish Civil War', in Mary Broe and Angela Ingram, eds, *Women's Writing in Exile* (Chapel Hill: University of North Carolina Press, 1989).

Castle, Terry, *The Apparitional Lesbian: Female Homosexuality and Modern Culture* (New York: Columbia University Press, 1993). (Chapter on *Summer Will Show*.)

Davie, Donald, *Under Briggflats: A History of Poetry in Great Britain 1960–88* (Manchester: Carcanet, 1987). (Two brief essays on Warner.)

Marcus, Jane, 'A Wilderness of One's Own: Feminist Fantasy Novels of the Twenties – Sylvia Townsend Warner and Rebecca West', in Susan Squier, ed., *Women Writers and the City* (Knoxville: University of Tennessee Press, 1984).

Poetry Nation Review 23, 8, 3 (1981), special Warner issue, ed. Clare Harman.

WEBB, Beatrice (1858–1943), born B. Potter in Standish, Glos. into a railway magnate's family, and educated at home. The philosopher Herbert Spencer, a family friend, was an early influence. She ran the household from her mother's death in 1888. Through philanthropic work in London she became friendly with Mary and Charles Booth, and began working as social investigator for Booth's *Life and Labour of the People of London* (1891–1902); research included incognito work as a sempstress in the East End. Her first book was *The Co-operative Movement in Great Britain* (1891). In 1892, after a long, unrequited passion for Joseph Chamberlain, she married Sidney Webb; they became a famous partnership in the Fabian Society and Labour Party, collaborating on several books, beginning with *A History of Trade Unionism* (1894), and launching LSE in 1895 and the *New Statesman* in 1913. Her own works included the *Minority Report on the Poor Law Commission* (1909), and most notably the memoir, *My Apprenticeship* (1926), based on her diaries of the 1880s. *Our Partnership* was posthumously published in 1948.

Webb, Beatrice, *My Apprenticeship* (1926) and *Our Partnership* (1948) (both Longmans, Green).

The Diary of Beatrice Webb, ed. Norman and Jeanne Mackenzie, 4 vols (Virago/LSE, 1982).

The Letters of Sidney and Beatrice Webb, ed. Norman Mackenzie (Cambridge: Cambridge University Press, 1978).

Cole, Margaret, *Beatrice Webb* (Longmans, Green, 1945). (Memoir by close associate.)

Mackenzie, Norman and Jeanne, *The First Fabians* (London: Weidenfeld and Nicholson, 1977).

Seymour-Jones, Carolyn, *Beatrice Webb: Woman of Conflict* (Allison and Busby, 1992).

See: Caine, Barbara, 'Beatrice Webb and her Diary', *Victorian Studies* 27 (1983), pp. 81–9.

Nord, Deborah, *The Apprenticeship of Beatrice Webb* (Macmillan, 1985). (Good study and place to start.)

WEBB, (Gladys) Mary (1881–1927), born G.M. Meredith in Leighton, Shropshire, into family of a headmaster, later farmer. She was educated at home, and from 1895 ran the house for her invalid mother. In 1912 she married Henry Webb, a teacher; they lived first in Weston-super-Mare, and then in Shropshire again, market gardening for additional income. Her first novel, *The Golden Arrow* (1916), was followed by the more successful *Gone to Earth* (1917). The remaining novels were *The House in Dormer Forest* (1920), *Seven for a Secret* (1922), *Precious Bane* (1924), which won the Femina/Vie Heureuse Prize, and the unfinished *The Armour Wherein He Trusted* (1928). Her earlier poems and essays were collected in *The Spring of Joy* (1917). From 1920 she lived in London, but failed to find much reviewing work. Her premature death was followed by a massive boom in her sales when the Prime Minister praised her work.

Barale, Michele, *Daughters and Lovers: The Life and Writing of Mary Webb* (Middletown: Wesleyan University Press, 1986).

Coles, Gladys Mary, *Flowers of Light: The Biography of Mary Webb* (Duckworth, 1978).

See: Cavaliero, Glen, *The Rural Tradition in the English Novel 1900–39* (Macmillan, 1977).

Cockburn, Claud, *Bestseller: The Books Everyone Read 1900–39* (Sidgwick and Jackson, 1972). (Essay on reception of *Precious Bane*.)

WEST, Rebecca (1892–1983), born Cicily Isabel Fairfield in London to Scottish mother and Irish father. After her parents' separation in 1901 she lived with her mother in Edinburgh where she attended school. From 1907 she campaigned for the suffrage, in 1910–11 she studied at RADA, and from 1911 wrote for the feminist magazine, the *Freewoman*. She and H.G. Wells were lovers 1913–22; their son Anthony was born in 1914. She later had an affair with the press magnate Lord Beaverbrook, before marrying the banker Henry Andrews in 1930. Her first book was the critical study, *Henry James* (1916), her first novel *The Return of the Soldier* (1918). She was best known as a prolific and controversial journalist; her early journalism is collected in *The Young Rebecca: Writings of Rebecca West 1911–17*, ed. Jane Marcus (1982). Her books included the novels, *The Judge* (1922), *Harriet Hume* (1929) and *The Thinking Reed* (1936), the critical collection,

The Strange Necessity and Other Essays (1928), the psycho-biography, *St Augustine* (1933), and her major work, the political commentary, *Black Lamb and Grey Falcon: A Journey through Yugoslavia* (1942). Postwar works included the controversial political study, *The Meaning of Treason* (1947), and several novels, notably *The Fountain Overflows* (1956). She became a Dame in 1959.

Glendinning, Victoria, *Rebecca West: A Life* (Weidenfeld and Nicholson, 1987). (Authorized biography.)

Ray, Gordon, N., *H.G. Wells and Rebecca West* (Macmillan, 1974). (Written with West's involvement.)

Rollyson, Carl, *Rebecca West: A Saga of the Century* (Hodder and Stoughton, 1995).

See: Hynes, Samuel, 'In Communion with Reality', in *The Essential Rebecca West*, ed. Hynes (Harmondsworth: Penguin, 1983).

Orel, Harold, *The Achievement of Rebecca West* (Macmillan, 1986).

Packer, Joan Garrett, *Rebecca West: An Annotated Bibliography* (New York: Garland, 1994).

Scott, Bonnie K., *Refiguring Modernism: Vol. 2: Postmodern Feminist Readings of Woolf, West and Barnes* (Bloomington: Indiana University Press, 1995). (Argues for West's importance as feminist and modernist.)

Weldon, Fay, *Rebecca West* (Harmondsworth: Penguin, 1985). (Feminist introduction, focused on Wells affair.)

WHITE, Antonia (1899–1980), born Eirene Adeline Botting in London into a classics master's family, and in 1908 sent to Convent of Sacred Heart, Roehampton, after her father's conversion to Roman Catholicism. She studied at RADA in 1919, and acted briefly. She was married three times, to Reggie Greene-Wilkinson 1921–23, to Eric Earnshaw Smith, a civil servant, 1925–29, and to the journalist Tom Hopkinson 1930–38: the first two marriages were annulled, the third ended in divorce. She spent the year 1923–24 in a mental hospital after the failure of her first marriage, and left the Church in 1925. She had two daughters, one from a love affair with the mining engineer Silas Glossop in 1928, and one in her third marriage. During the 1920s she worked for an advertising agency and for Harrods. Her first novel, *Frost in May*, based on her convent experiences, appeared in 1933: its critical and popular success was followed by another breakdown. She recovered with the help of psychoanalysis, worked as a fashion editor, had numerous love affairs, and during the war worked for the intelligence services. She returned to the Church in 1948. Her postwar books included three more autobiographical fictions, *The Lost Traveller* (1950), *The Sugar House* (1952) and *Breaking the Glass* (1954), and many translations.

White, Antonia, *The Hound and the Falcon* (Collins, 1969), (memoir of her reconversion), and *As Once in May*, ed. Susan Chitty (Virago, 1983). (Childhood memoir.)

The Diaries of Antonia White, ed. Susan Chitty, 2 vols (Constable, 1991).

Chitty, Susan, *Now to My Mother: A Very Personal Memoir of Antonia White* (Weidenfeld and Nicholson, 1985).

Hopkinson, Lyndall, *Nothing to Forgive* (Chatto and Windus, 1988). (Memoir by her other daughter.)

See: Williams, Merryn, *Six Women Novelists* (Basingstoke: Macmillan, 1987).

WICKHAM, Anna (1884–1947), born Edith Mary Alice Harper in London into a piano-tuner's family, which emigrated to Australia in 1890. She attended schools in Brisbane and Sydney, studied singing in Paris 1904–05, and in 1905 married Patrick Hepburn, a lawyer; they had four children, and a stormy relationship until his death mountaineering in 1929. In 1911, after her first poetry volume, *Songs of John Oland*, was published, she spent six weeks in a mental hospital. Later volumes included *The Contemplative Quarry* (1915), *Man with a Hammer* (1916), *The Little Old House* (1921) and *Thirty-Six New Poems* (1936). She became a well-known figure on the London and Paris literary scenes. Many of her papers were destroyed during a bombing raid in 1943. She hanged herself in 1947.

Wickham, Anna, 'Fragment of an Autobiography: Prelude to a Spring Clean' (1935) in *The Writings of Anna Wickham, Free Woman and Poet*, ed. R.D. Smith (Virago, 1984).

Smith, R.D., 'Anna Wickham: A Memoir' in above.

See: Enright, D.J., 'Pride of Ink', *Listener*, 17 May 1984.

WOOLF, (Adeline) Virginia (1882–1941), born A.V. Stephen in London. Her philanthropist mother Julia wrote *Notes from Sick-rooms*; her philosopher father Leslie edited the *Dictionary of National Biography*. She was educated at home. An unhappy period between her mother's death, 1895, and her father's, 1904, was followed by a severe breakdown. In 1904 she settled in Bloomsbury, began writing reviews and stories, and became part of the Bloomsbury group of artists and thinkers, which included her sister, the painter Vanessa Bell, the art critics Clive Bell and Roger Fry, and also E.M. Forster, Lytton Strachey and John Maynard Keynes. In 1912 she married the writer Leonard Woolf. From 1908 she worked on her first novel, *Melymbrosia*, which became *The Voyage Out* (1915); its completion triggered another breakdown in 1913. In 1917 the Woolfs launched the

Hogarth Press; the first publication was *Two Stories*, and her story, 'The Mark on the Wall', developed her modernist techniques. In 1919 she published her second novel, *Night and Day*, and the modernist manifesto, 'Modern Fiction'. *Jacob's Room* (1922), partly inspired by her brother Thoby's death in 1906, was her first fully modernist novel; it was followed by *Mrs Dalloway* (1925) and *To the Lighthouse* (1927), which established her as a leading modernist. Two important modernist essays were 'Mr Bennett and Mrs Brown' (1923) and 'The Narrow Bridge of Art' (1929). A Cambridge lecture, 'Women and Fiction', developed into the feminist polemic, *A Room of One's Own* (1929). Her remaining novels were the gender fantasy, *Orlando* (1928), her most experimental novel, *The Waves* (1931), her bestselling family saga, *The Years* (1937), and *Between the Acts* (1941), developed from *Pointz Hall*, and published unrevised after her drowning. Her second feminist polemic, *Three Guineas*, appeared in 1938, and the biography, *Roger Fry*, in 1940. Her essays were collected in *The Common Reader* (1925), *The Common Reader: Second Series* (1932), and in several posthumous collections, *The Death of the Moth and Other Essays* (1924), *The Moment and Other Essays* (1947), *The Captain's Deathbed and Other Essays* (1950) and *Granite and Rainbow* (1958). Her *Collected Essays*, ed. Leonard Woolf, 4 vols, appeared in 1966–67, and *Essays*, ed. Andrew McNeillie, 4 vols to date, from 1986. Other publications include *Collected Shorter Fiction*, ed. Susan Dick (1985), several early drafts of works including *Melymbrosia*, ed. Louise de Salvo (1982), *Women and Fiction*, ed. S.P. Rosenbaum (1992), *The Pargiters: The Novel-Essay Portion of The Years*, ed. Mitchell Leaska (1978), *Pointz Hall*, ed. Mitchell Leaska (1982), and holograph drafts of *To the Lighthouse*, ed. Susan Dick (1982), *Orlando*, ed. S.N. Clarke (1993) and *The Waves*, ed. J.W. Graham (1976).

Woolf, Virginia, *Moments of Being*, ed. Jeanne Schulkind, rev. 2nd edn (Hogarth Press, 1985). (Autobiographical writings, including 'A Sketch of the Past'.)

The Letters of Virginia Woolf, ed. Nigel Nicholson and Joanne Trautmann, 6 vols (Hogarth Press, 1975–80).

The Diary of Virginia Woolf, ed. Anne Olivier Bell and Andrew McNeillie, 5 vols (Hogarth Press, 1975–80).

A Writer's Diary, ed. Leonard Woolf (Hogarth Press, 1953). (Selection focused on Woolf's comments on writing.)

A Passionate Apprentice: The Early Journals of Virginia Woolf, ed. Mitchell A. Leaska (Hogarth Press, 1990).

Virginia Woolf's Reading Notebooks, ed. Brenda Silver (Princeton: Princeton University Press, 1983).

Bell, Quentin, *Virginia Woolf: A Biography*, 2 vols (Hogarth Press, 1972). (The family biography by her nephew.)

Gordon, Lyndall, *Virginia Woolf: A Writer's Life* (Oxford: Oxford University Press, 1984). (Perceptive study, drawing especially on unpublished writing and early drafts of novels.)

Lee, Hermione, *Virginia Woolf* (Chatto and Windus, 1996). (The most comprehensive and detailed life, very illuminating.)

Mepham, John, *Virginia Woolf: A Literary Life* (Basingstoke: Macmillan, 1991). (Useful focus on her life as professional writer.)

Rose, Phyllis, *Woman of Letters: A Life of Virginia Woolf* (Routledge and Kegan Paul, 1978). (Feminist, provocative, emphasizes Woolf's self-narration.)

See: Abel, Elizabeth, *Virginia Woolf and the Fictions of Psychoanalysis* (Chicago: Chicago University Press, 1989). (Places work in context of Bloomsbury interest in psychology.)

Auerbach, Erich, 'The Brown Stocking', in *Mimesis: The Representation of Reality in Western Culture*, trans. Willard Trask (Princeton: Princeton University Press, 1953). (Seminal essay on *To the Lighthouse*.)

Barrett, Michele, 'Introduction', to Barrett, ed., *Virginia Woolf: Women and Writing* (Women's Press, 1979).

Batchelor, John, *Virginia Woolf: The Major Novels* (Cambridge: Cambridge University Press, 1991).

Beer, Gillian, *Arguing with the Past: Essays in Narrative from Woolf to Sidney* (Routledge, 1989). (Contains four important essays on Woolf.)

Bowlby, Rachel, *Virginia Woolf: Feminist Destinations* (Oxford: Blackwell, 1988).

—— ed., *Virginia Woolf* (Longman, 1992). (Useful collection of critical essays.)

Caughie, Pamela, *Virginia Woolf and Postmodernism: Literature in Quest and Question of Itself* (Chicago: University of Illinois Press, 1991).

De Salvo, Louise, *Virginia Woolf's First Voyage: A Novel in the Making* (Macmillan, 1980).

—— *Virginia Woolf: The Impact of Childhood Sexual Abuse on Her Life and Work* (Women's Press, 1989).

Dick, Susan, *Virginia Woolf* (Edward Arnold, 1989). (Brief analysis of Woolf's fictional innovations.)

Hanson, Clare, *Virginia Woolf* (Basingstoke: Macmillan, 1994). (Psychoanalytical approach.)

Hawthorn, Jeremy, *Virginia Woolf's Mrs Dalloway: A Study in Alienation* (Sussex University Press, 1975).

Holtby, Winifred, *Virginia Woolf* (Wishart, 1932). (Earliest critical study; valuable on Woolf's significance to 1930s feminists.)

Kirkpatrick, Brownlee Jean, *A Bibliography of Virginia Woolf*, 3rd edn (Oxford: Clarendon Press, 1984).

Laurence, Patricia, *The Reading of Silence: Virginia Woolf in the English Tradition* (Stanford: Stanford University Press, 1991).

Leaska, Mitchell, *The Novels of Virginia Woolf: From Beginning to End* (Weidenfeld and Nicholson, 1977).

Lee, Hermione, *The Novels of Virginia Woolf* (Methuen, 1977). (Good introductory study.)

Marcus, Jane, *Virginia Woolf and the Languages of Patriarchy* (Bloomington: Indiana University Press, 1987).

Miller, Joseph Hillis, *Fiction and Repetition: Seven English Novels* (Cambridge: Harvard University Press, 1982). (Important essays on *Mrs Dalloway* and *Between the Acts*.)

Minow-Pinkney, Makiko, *Virginia Woolf and the Problem of the Subject* (Brighton: Harvester, 1987). (Feminist approach via Kristeva.)

Moi, Toril, *Sexual/Textual Politics* (Methuen, 1985). (Important analysis of *A Room of One's Own* in context of French feminist criticism.)

Naremore, William, *The World Without a Self: Virginia Woolf and the Novel* (New Haven: Yale University Press, 1973).

Poole, Roger, *The Unknown Virginia Woolf* (Cambridge: Cambridge University Press, 1978). (The works related to her medical history.)

Roe, Sue, *Writing and Gender: Virginia Woolf's Writing Practice* (Hemel Hempstead: Harvester Wheatsheaf, 1990). (Perceptive analysis.)

Rosenbaum, S.P., *Edwardian Bloomsbury* (Basingstoke: Macmillan, 1994). (Detailed survey of early writing.)

Warner, Eric, ed., *Virginia Woolf: A Centenary Perspective* (Macmillan, 1984). (Useful collection.)

Zwerdling, Alex, *Virginia Woolf and the Real World* (Berkeley: University of California Press, 1986). (Argues strongly for her engagement with contemporary political issues.)

Index